Overexploitation or Sustainable Management:
Action Patterns of the Tropical Timber Industry
The Case of Pará (Brazil) 1960–1997

Overexploitation or Sustainable Management:
Action Patterns of the Tropical Timber Industry
The Case of Pará (Brazil)
1960–1997

Imme Scholz

FRANK CASS
LONDON • PORTLAND, OR
Published in association with the
German Development Institute, Bonn

First published in 2001 in Great Britain by
FRANK CASS PUBLISHERS
Crown House, 47 Chase Side
London N14 5BP, England

and in the United States of America by
FRANK CASS PUBLISHERS
c/o ISBS
5824 N.E. Hassalo Street
Portland, Oregon 97213–3644

Website: www.frankcass.com

British Library Cataloguing in Publication Data

Scholz, Imme
    Overexploitation or sustainable management: action
    patterns of the tropical timber industry: the case of Para
    (Brazil), 1960–1997. – (GDI book series; no. 15)
    1. Lumber trade – Environmental aspects – Brazil – Para
    (State) 2. Logging – Environmental aspects – Brazil –Para
    (State) 3. Forest management – Brazil –Para (State)
    I. Title II. Deutsches Institut fur Entwicklungspolitik
    333.7'5'098115

    ISBN 0714651540 (cloth)

    Library of Congress Cataloging-in-Publication Data

Scholz, Imme, 1964
    Overexploitation or sustainable management: action
patterns of the tropical timber industry: the case of Para
(Brazil), 1960–1997 / Imme Scholz
        p.m. – (GDI book series, ISSN 1460-4175; no.15
    "Published in association with the German Development Institute,
    Bonn."
    Includes bibliographical references.
    ISBN 0-7146-5154-0 (cloth)
    1. Lumber trade –Environmental aspects –Brazil – Para (State) 2.
    Logging – Environmental aspects –Brazil – Para (State) 3. Forest
    management –Brazil – Para (State) I. Title. II. Series.
    HD9764.B73 P297 2000
    333.75'0981'15–dc21   00 -0660100

Printed in Great Britain by
Antony Rowe Ltd, Chippenham, Wilts

Contents

Tables in the Appendix

Abbreviations

ABIMCI	Associação Brasileira da Indústria de Madeira Compensada e Industrializada (Brazilian Association of the Plywood and Timber Industry)
AdT	Amigos da Terra (Friends of the Earth)
AIMEX	Associação das Indústrias Exportadoras de Madeira do Estado do Pará e Amapá (Association of Timber Exporters of Pará and Amapá)
BASA	Banco da Amazônia (Bank of Amazonia)
BMELF	Bundesministerium für Ernährung, Landwirtschaft und Forsten (Federal Ministry of Food, Agriculture and Forests)
BUND	Bund für Umwelt und Naturschutz Deutschland (German Federation for the Environment and Protection of Nature)
CITES	Convention on International Trade with Endangered Species of Wild Flora and Fauna
CNPq	Conselho Nacional do Desenvolvimento Científico e Tecnológico (National Council for Scientific and Technological Development)
CNS	Conselho Nacional dos Seringueiros (National Association of Rubber Tappers)
COIAB	Conselho dos Povos Indígenas da Amazônia Brasileira (Association of Indigenous Peoples of the Brazilian Amazon Region)
CONTAG	Confederação Nacional dos Trabalhadores na Agricultura (National Farm Workers' Union)
CVRD	Companhia Vale do Rio Doce (Brazilian Mining Company)
DBH	Diameter at Breast Height
DC	Development Cooperation
EE	Extraction Economy
EIA	Environmental Impact Assessment

EMBRAPA- CPATU	Empresa Brasileira de Pesquisa Agrária – Centro de Pesquisas Agroflorestais nos Trópicos Úmidos (Brazilian Agrarian Research Institute – Center for Agro-forestry Studies in the Humid Tropics)
FAO	Food and Agriculture Organization
FCAP	Faculdade de Ciências Agrárias do Pará (Faculty of Agrarian Sciences in Pará)
FFT	Fundação Floresta Tropical (Tropical Forest Foundation)
FIEPA	Federação das Indústrias do Estado do Pará (Industry Association of Pará)
FoE	Friends of the Earth
FSC	Forest Stewardship Council
FUNAI	Fundação Nacional do Indio (National Indian Foundation)
GDP	Gross Domestic Product
GPP	Gross Primary Production
GPV	Gross Production Value
GNP	Gross National Product
GTA	Grupo de Trabalho Amazônico (Working Group of NGOs in the Amazon Region)
GTZ	Deutsche Gesellschaft für Technische Zusammenarbeit (German Society for Technical Cooperation)
HDI	Human Development Index
HWWA	Hamburger Weltwirtschafts-Archiv – Institut für Wirtschaftsforschung (Institute for Economic Research, Hamburg)
IAG	International Advisory Group of the PPG-7
IBAMA	Instituto Brasileiro do Meio Ambiente (Brazilian Environmental Institute)
IBDF	Instituto Brasileiro de Desenvolvimento Florestal (Brazilian Institute for the Development of Forests)

IBGE	Instituto Brasileiro de Geografia e Estatística (Brazilian Institute for Geography and Statistics)
ILO	International Labour Organization
IMAZON	Instituto do Homem e Meio Ambiente na Amazônia (Institute of Man and the Environment in the Amazon Region)
IMF	International Monetary Fund
INCRA	Instituto da Reforma Agrária (Institute for Agrarian Reform)
INPA	Instituto Nacional de Pesquisas da Amazônia (National Research Institute for the Amazon Region)
INPE	Instituto Nacional de Pesquisas Espaciais (National Institute for Space Research)
IPAAM	Instituto de Proteção Ambiental do Estado de Amazonas (Institute for Environmental Protection of the Federal State of Amazonas)
IPAM	Instituto de Pesquisa Ambiental da Amazônia (Institute for Environmental Research in the Amazon Region)
IPEA	Instituto de Pesquisa Econômica Aplicada (Institute for Applied Economic Research)
ISI	Import-Substituting Industrialization
ISO	International Standards Organization
ITTO	International Tropical Timber Organization
KfW	Kreditanstalt für Wiederaufbau
MDF	Middle-dense Fiberboard
NGO	Nongovernmental Organization
Npp	Net Primary Production
NRPP	Natural Resources Policy Program
NVA	Net Value Added
NZZ	Neue Zürcher Zeitung
OECD	Organization for Economic Cooperation and Development

OSB	Oriented-strand Board
PDA	Plano de Desenvolvimento da Amazônia (Development Plan for the Amazon Region)
PE	Production Economy
PGAI	Programa de Gestão Ambiental Integrada (Program for Integrated Environmental Management)
PIN	Plano de Integração Nacional (National Integration Plan)
PND	Plano Nacional de Desenvolvimento (National Development Plan)
PPG-7	G-7 Pilot Program to Conserve the Brazilian Rainforest
R&D	Research and Development
SBS	Sociedade Brasileira de Silvicultura (Brazilian Forestry Society)
SEBRAE	Serviço Brasileiro de Apoio à Pequena e Média Empresa (Brazilian Promotion Service for Small and Medium-sized Enterprises)
SECTAM	Secretaria de Ciência e Tecnologia e do Meio Ambiente do Pará (Pará Ministry of Science, Technology and the Environment)
SHIFT	Studies on Human Impact on Forests and Floodplains in the Humid Tropics
SIVAM	Sistema de Vigilância da Amazônia (Surveillance System for the Amazon Region)
SMEs	Small and Medium-sized Enterprises
SPVEA	Superintendência do Plano de Valorização Econômica da Amazônia (Superintendency for the Economic Exploitation of Amazonia)
SUDAM	Superintendência do Desenvolvimento da Amazônia (Development Superintendency of Amazonia)
UN	United Nations
UNCTAD	United Nations Conference on Trade and Development
UNDP	United Nations Development Program

UNEP	United Nations Environment Program
URV	Unidade Real de Valor (Real Unit of Value)
VDH	Verein der deutschen Holzhandelshäuser (Association of German Timber Traders)
WHO	World Health Organization
WTO	World Trade Organization
WWF	World Wide Fund for Nature

Brazil: Structure according to Federal States

Source: U. Holtz (ed.) (1981): Brasilien. Eine historisch-politische Landeskun-
de, Quellen und Anmerkungen, Paderborn

Summary

This study deals with the relations between economic development, use of natural resources, and innovation processes in the case of the timber industry in the federal state of Pará in the eastern Amazon region of Brazil. The study uses a historical reconstruction of the economic and technological development paths of the timber industry since the 1950s to establish how the dominant use pattern of the tropical forest came about and what role the given ecological conditions, the Brazilian government's Amazon development policy, and the world timber market play in this process. The study focuses on action patterns and routines of the timber companies, and does so with an eye to determining both their role in the expansion of the industry and their innovative capacities.

The timber industry has attracted little interest in socioeconomic research on the Amazon region because the focus of such studies has as a rule been on processes of deforestation and their causes. Since deforestation was above all a consequence of the expansion of farming and cattle-ranching up to the 1980s, and this expansion was promoted by the public programs aimed at economic integration of the region, the development of the timber industry and its linkages with other industries has often fallen through the grid defined for the field under research.

As a rule studies dealing with the timber industry have the following shortcomings:

– they proceed on the assumption of rational action patterns on the part of the economic agents, but without deriving these patterns empirically. The premise guiding the research is that there is an abundance of homogeneous timber resources and therefore no economic incentive for improving the efficiency of logging and timber processing;

– they neglect to view the development of the Amazon timber industry in the context of the Brazilian timber industry and the world market for timber, in this way failing to account for the effects of technical change on the competitiveness of tropical timber.

The theoretical and empirical deficits may cause misinterpretations of data, erroneous assessments of the development dynamics of the timber industry and produce misguided policies concerning legal and economic incentives.

Methodological Approach

To close the gap, this study uses a methodological approach which takes into account the interrelation between economic decisions and actions on the one hand and the economic, institutional, and ecological frameworks on the other. This approach combines elements of the sociological theory of structuration (Giddens), evolutionary economics, which deals with the economic causes and effects of technical change (Nelson and Winter), and ecological economics (Daly, Barbier).

Giddens sees economic action, like any other form of social action, as day-to-day behavior in the form of routines. In the course of a routine the valid social rules are applied and confirmed; the actors reelaborate them again and again in adapting them to altered conditions. The scope open to actors in given situations is restricted by constraints such as material conditions, the sanctioning power of others, or by the given action context, i.e. the routines of competitors in the market. These constraints have been constituted by society; they would not exist unless they were confirmed again and again by social action.

Nelson and Winter define routines as the sum of existing operational knowledge, which is useful and applicable only in the specific social and techno-organizational context of an enterprise or a branch of industry; routines make its regular use possible.

Routines also help to analyze the innovative behavior of firms. Routines are the base for technological trajectories or paths which firms and branches of industry follow while using and improving technologies and organizational patterns within the scope of their specific restrictions. Entrepreneurial learning processes are, in the view embraced by this approach, subject to the (perceived) economic chances offered by innovations, the incentives in the corporate environment, the skills of the companies concerned, and the organizational arrangements and mechanisms that favor (or discourage) the takeover of innovations. The approach also explains how conservative attitudes inimical or skeptical to innovation come about: changes in entrepreneurial routines entail costs, so that improvements will tend more to follow incremental innovations along the path defined by the technology in use than radical innovations.

The problem of given ecological conditions is considered neither by the theory of structuration nor by evolutionary economics. Since both approaches define economic action not in abstract terms but in a given context, the ecological factors can be integrated into the approach as additional contextual factor.

With regard to the timber industry in Pará the following questions arise:

– What are the techno-organizational elements and patterns to which the routines of entrepreneurial action in Pará's timber industry can be traced back?

– How have these elements and patterns changed in the course of the past 35 years? What economic and institutional incentives (e.g. subsidies, environmental legislation and monitoring) have been influential here?

– What have been the roles of the ecological conditions in the Amazon region and the world market trends for timber?

– What specific restrictions result from these routines for entrepreneurial learning processes? How do the economic actors themselves explain their day-to-day activities? Are they in a position to grasp changes in their context, anticipate potential crises, and find new solutions to problems? Can Pará's timber entrepreneurs be described generally as conservative and inimical or skeptical to innovation?

In the Amazon region the ecological conditions as well as the world market are externally determined constraints in that the Amazon actors have hardly any chance to influence them in their favor. First, there is too little knowledge of how the tropical forest ecosystem functions, so that the high energy throughput in tropical forests cannot be used for the mass production of timber without putting the forest at risk. Second, the share of the Amazon region in the world timber market is too low to have an impact on price levels and trade flows. So these two external contraints are described before Pará's timber industry is analyzed.

The Ecological Conditions of Tropical Forest Management

There is as yet no agreement on principles to which any sustained use of tropical forests would have to be oriented, which is not surprising in view of the limited scope of our present knowledge of tropical forest ecosystems. Forestry tests in the Amazon region have shown that a sustainable timber production can be guaranteed, if at all, only when natural regeneration of the tropical forest is stimulated and damage to forest and soil is kept as low as possible during logging and transportation. Monocultural plantations growing native or exotic species (eucalyptus, pine) cannot be recommended since they involve high costs and pest risks and burden the natural ecosystems.

Nature-oriented forest management demands of a logging firm felling and production scheduling that is geared strongly to a forest's natural sustainable timber supply and not – as usual – primarily to demand. The marketing of timber with an eye to safeguarding returns and profits is faced with the problem of having to sell far greater numbers of species in smaller quantities than is usual. These species are often known only in local markets, where they command low prices. In addition, only very few species of tropical sawnwood find acceptance in the industrialized countries, and it takes several years to introduce new species. Moreover, the industrialized countries demand certain wood lengths, which leads to very large quantities of waste in cutting timber to length. The yield per cubic meter of stemwood in the export-oriented companies is for this reason only 35 %, i.e. 65 % of stemwood is lost.

If we take these additional costs into account in calculating the costs of sustainable forest management and compare them with local timber prices, we find that sustainable forest management is, at present price levels, not affordable. Nature-oriented tropical forest management has prospects only if the efficiency of logging, transportation, and processing is increased and if markets are enlarged and diversified.

The World Market for Tropical Timber

In 1996 the world trade in timber had a volume of US$ 133.2 billion; the share of the developing countries in this trade was US$ 23.7 billion. The dominance of the industrialized countries is above all linked with the importance of pulp and paper exports, which together account for 60 % of the value of the world trade. The shares of the developing countries in these segments is merely 13.1 and 9.2 %, respectively. The value of sawnwood exports was somewhat more than US$ 25 billion, and the developing countries' share of this was 17 %. The developing countries had a 46 % share of board exports (plywood, veneer, fiber- and particle boards), which in 1996 amounted to some US$ 16 billion.

The shares of tropical timber in the world market continue to fall. This is due to a lesser degree to changing preferences of customers who prefer light wood or reject tropical timber because they do not want to contribute to the destruction of tropical forests. To a higher degree, the decrease is due to the substitution pressure on tropical timber: on the one hand, other materials such as PVC and aluminum are increasingly used, above all for windows, on the other technical change has brought new wood products whose technical properties are equal to or even better than tropical timber. These new reconstituted wood panels are made from homogeneous fibers and particles on the basis of sawmill wastes or wood chips. The wood is increasingly produced on plantations in new locations in Europe (Spain, Portugal) or the southern hemisphere (New Zealand, South Africa, Chile, south and southeast Brazil) where growth conditions are most favorable. Planning and increase of wood production in such plantations is possible within a relatively short time, with costs per cubic meter of eucalyptus or pine decreasing. The costs per cubic meter eucalyptus or pine wood are thus below those of tropical timber.

The future of the world timber market will be characterized by growing demand for wood fibers that are produced in plantations and processed to manufacture technology-intensive reconstituted wood panels. This implies a shift in the crucial comparative advantages of timber-producing countries from an inherited endowment with stands of native timber to a man-made resource base in the form of plantations with high productivity and low production costs.

The Amazon timber industry will have a chance only if it gives up the idea of competing with mass products on the world market and instead develops wood products for high-quality niche markets that demand wood with specific properties, for example for furniture, musical instruments and artists' materials. In the long run, the physical volume of tropical timber in the world market will decrease, while the monetary value may increase.

The Timber Industry in Pará: Results of the Empirical Research

The routines pursued by the entrepreneurs in Pará's timber industry are homogeneous and have been quite stable since the 1960s. This homogeneity and stability can be explained by the fact that the companies have always been able to adapt to the changing structural constraints (economic incentives and chances) that they have been exposed to with the help of smaller, incremental innovations along the technological path once embarked upon. There have been formal sanctions and regulations, above all the forest code, yet these have had hardly any relevance in practice, mainly because of considerable institutional weaknesses. The day-to-day consciousness and the knowledge of the actors in the timber industry has thus hardly developed. The entrepreneurs are not able to grasp fully the new quality of the difficulties they have encountered in the 1990s, and strategies to overcome problems usually follow the traditional routines. The willingness and the ability of Pará's timber industry to resort to problem-solving innovations are low. Entrepreneurs who break away from the old routines – by introducing methods of nature-oriented forest management or specializing in a market segment in order to increase product quality or company productivity – are still the exception to the rule.

The industry was characterized by an extensive growth pattern that showed hardly any signs of intensification. Between 1960 and 1985 incremental innovations, above all mechanized logging and the use of a broader spectrum of species, enabled the industry to increase its physical production volume, yet the productivity level of the southern Brazilian timber industry was not matched. The productivity of Pará's companies has been stagnating ever since. Moreover, the focus has been on sawnwood since the 1970s. The growth of the industry thus rested mainly on expansion instead of productivity growth and diversified production. Scarcity profits were made in the 1980s with the logging of expensive precious wood, especially mahogany and cedro. An analysis of the economic performance of the municipalities where the timber industry is concentrated confirms the thesis of an expansion pattern that has had no dynamic effect on local or regional economic development.

The dominant pattern of natural resource use – the routine of Pará's timber industry – consists of the following elements:

–   the "typical sawmill" is a small family-owned operation with up to 16 workers that uses a band saw to produce some 4200 m^3 of sawnwood per annum; the machinery in use is as a rule old (and may even have been taken over from predecessors) and in a poor state of maintenance; the workers have no formal training, being trained instead on the job;

–   the productivity of these sawmills has hardly changed throughout the years; since the 1970s the band saws used can output between 17 m^3 and 22 m^3 of sawnwood per day;

–   logging operations are conducted using power saws, tractors, bulldozers, and trucks; at the same time the predominant method is still conventional selective cutting, a practice restricted to a limited number of species and carried out in an unplanned fashion in company-owned, non-company-owned, or publicly accessible forest areas; logging is geared to the marketability of species and not to safeguarding a sustainable supply of timber;

–   there are no fundamental differences within the industry as regards productivity, technological capability, and adherence to the law.

–   the number of marketable species remained roughly the same from 1970 to 1994; due to the depletion of virola and mahogany the priorities have changed in favor of tauarí, curupixá, and jatobá;

- management focuses on purchasing stemwood (if the sawmill does not itself log) and marketing the sawnwood produced, which as a rule is sold in the domestic Brazilian market; there is for the most part no regular bookkeeping aimed at cost control; the overriding company goal is to accumulate profits and not to consolidate and grow in one branch of the industry;

- logging and processing are seen as temporary activities – until the timber supplies surrounding the sawmill have been depleted; since the forest is regarded as a free good that will in any case have to make way to farming or cattle-ranching, investments are at best geared to increasing the productivity of logging operations by means of mechanization or to finding highly valuable stands of precious timber, mainly mahogany.

The environment of the sawmills – the constraints to which they are subject – has changed again and again in the course of the past three decades, but without compelling any drastic change in entrepreneurial routines, since the new structures have tended more to be enabling than restrictive:

- the factors triggering the growth in the timber industry since the 1960s have been on the one hand the depletion of the primary forests in the south of Brazil and the opening up of the Amazon region, which eliminated the critical obstacles to expanding production into this region: road construction provided access to the forests of the *terra firme* and the sales markets of the richer south and southeast, the official settlement policy made sufficient manpower available in rural regions;

- on the other hand demand was marked by powerful dynamics: producers always found buyers for their wares; the domestic market was not particularly demanding in terms of quality, requiring instead only large supplies, which could be delivered thanks to the mechanization of logging;

- the export ban on logs imposed in 1974 drastically reduced the Amazon industry's external orientation, in Pará exports fell from a share of over 60 % of output to some 10 %; since the sawnwood produced did not as a rule meet the quality standards of the world market, producers switched to the large and growing domestic market;

- instead of leading to a contraction of the timber industry, the recession in the 1980s led to growth in a subsegment, that of export-oriented firms; these firms on the one hand benefited from export subsidies by at least in part using the low-interest loans they obtained for speculation and on the other hand profited from the high external demand for mahogany, which persisted until the beginning of the 1990s.

Since the 1980s, however, new constraints have emerged, and they have exposed firms to more far-reaching pressure to adjust:

- The high ecological and social costs of the settlement programs in the Amazon region have become visible; this circumstance was instrumental in awakening the interest of Brazilian environmental groups and the international public in preserving the Amazon forests; subsequently the Brazilian government had to take practical measures designed to protect these forests;

- in 1992 the G7 pilot program on the protection of the Brazilian tropical forests was agreed on by Brazil, the World Bank, and the G7 states; this encouraged demarcation of indigenous peoples' areas, establishment of nature-conservation areas, and the development of environmental administrations in the Amazon states;

- in the 1990s the instrument of voluntary ecological certification of firms began to gain ground; in the international trade in tropical timber it was the industrialized countries that first recognized the chance offered by this instrument to constructively counter the boycott campaigns of environmentalist groups; certification of forest management now came in for increasing discussion in Pará as well;

- in the 1990s timber scarcity also for the first time made itself felt in the centers of Pará's sawnwood production; the impairment of forest regeneration capacity by selective logging and massive land conversion in some areas began to force firms in the timber industry either to close, to relocate, or to look into reforestation;

–   finally, in mid-1994, the *Plano Real* brought the country a new currency that has since then been a successful tool in fighting inflation; at the same time this plan brought Brazil a higher exchange rate and high interest rates; these changes highlighted the productivity gap in the timber industry, subsequently leading to a good number of company closures.

Most entrepreneurs responded defensively to the timber scarcity and the new environmental and economic challenges by calling for subsidies and changes to the forest statute. Although the insight is growing that exports to the European countries and the US are increasingly going to be linked to environmental stipulations, hardly any changes in practical action have made themselves felt that would indicate that entrepreneurs are committed to coming up with any realistic solutions that would offer the industry long-term perspectives.

In particular the severe consequences of traditional logging practices for continued timber production (to say nothing of the protection of forest ecosystems) have not become part of the general practical knowledge of the actors: in view of the limited number of marketable species, selective logging is seen as the only economically rational harvesting method. Seen in this way, the conservatism of the tropical-timber markets has become an incontrovertible fact to which the sawmill owners feel forced to adapt. This means that they do not recognize the natural conditions of timber production as a natural boundary set to the industry. Another consequence of this view is that the creation of plantations appears more plausible as a solution than management of forest stands that are in the end regarded as unproductive.

The Results Seen in their Theoretical Context

Routine and technological development path are concepts that can be used to explain why the entrepreneurial action pattern current in Pará's timber industry has, despite its turbulent setting, remained stable for nearly four decades and why Pará's share in the world market for tropical timber has, despite the region's huge timber stands, not developed as rapidly as the shares held by Malaysia and Indonesia.

Stability: The entrepreneurial routine in Pará consists in constant over-exploitation of the forest, persistent low levels of company productivity, and a low degree of value added. This pattern of resource utilization emerged in Brazil in the context of a mercantilist colonial economy geared to the needs of the colonial power; the Portuguese colonial economy strengthened this use pattern by failing largely to develop any industrialization strategy for motherland and colony alike. The development policy pursued by the Brazilian central government for the Amazon region since the beginning of the 1970s saw the region above all in the role of resource supplier and foreign-exchange earner and accordingly fostered economic activities based on the pattern of destructive exploitation because environmental regulations were either nonexistent or not enforced.

No changes in the routine emerged in the period covered by the present study, because there was no reason for them:
- The natural abundance of timber lasted until the 1990s in Pará's production sites.
- The high demand in an unexacting domestic market made it unnecessary to introduce cost-reducing and/or quality-raising measures.
- The external market demanded only certain species and qualities as well as quantities that were not subject to dynamic growth.

These specific marketing conditions reinforced the original routine as well as the view that the timber industry was an industry not particularly demanding in technological terms and one marked by a low level of dynamics, one in which it was easy to make high profits in the short term with a minimum of expense and effort. On the other hand they increased the potential of forest damage; growing demand seemingly made mechanization of logging and transportation attractive, but without awakening any interest in preserving a sustainable supply of timber.

By working out industry-specific patterns of technical change, evolutionary economics provides an additional explanation for the stability of routines. Pará's timber industry belongs to the category of supplier-dominated industries which neither induce nor engender technical change on their own, benefiting instead from innovations introduced by their suppliers. The dynamics between users and producers of technology is marked by mutual influences. The relationship between timber industry and the construction of specialized machinery can be called a stable supplier-customer relation without external pressure for innovation: thanks to persistent high demand and low wage costs, the timber industry saw no reason to increase its productivity, conversion efficiency, and product quality, which would have required regular machine innovation or replacement. In this situation the simplest and safest approach for machine-builders was to continue to offer the time-tested machines. Technical innovations did not prevail because there was no demand for them.

World-market share: in 1974 the ban on log exports for Amazon timber was imposed; this is a measure that was used in Indonesia and Malaysia to encourage the export of processed wood products. But in Pará the consequences were different: the timber industry converted to production of sawnwood, but it sold this wood mainly in the domestic market, which placed far lower demands on quality than the industrialized countries, which until then had purchased roundwood from Pará. The problem was thus not the change involved in sawing the timber, it was meeting the higher standards placed on the quality of processing, which would have required investment in technical equipment and manpower qualification. The consequence was a drastic decrease in export content.

The strategy of inward-looking industrialization that brought Brazil high growth rates up to the beginning of the 1980s formed the framework for the expansion strategy of Pará's timber industry and made it possible to retain traditional routines. Retention of a world-market orientation might even then have opened up for the Amazon timber industry the path taken by the Malaysian and Indonesian industries; the price for technological learning would have been increasing deforestation rates.

The development of Brazil's share in the world timber market is in line with the explanation given by the evolutionary theory of technical change for different world-market shares: it is differences in technological skills and innovative capacities, embodied in variously efficient company routines, and the cumulative effects of technological learning processes, and not natural (or given) factor endowments, that explain the different performance of industries and economies in international terms. In this view the dynamic change of world-markets shares is closely linked with the diffusion processes of new technologies and products that contribute to the erosion of innovation rents, in this way keeping the motor of technical change running. A high level of technological competence (skills plus innovativeness) thus constitutes a source of absolute advantages in the world market. What is crucial to securing world-market shares is the technical knowledge that permits firms to produce innovative products and to utilize process innovations more efficiently and quickly than others as a means of reducing input coefficients and increasing labor productivity.

Against this background the current situation in Brazil's timber and pulp industry may be characterized as follows: While the south, thanks to direct investments from Chile and Portugal, is able to produce new, technology-intensive wood panels, the north is left behind. Only Asian plywood corporations that continue to bank on the path marked out by traditional methods of processing tropical timber are interested in investing in the Amazon region as a means of safeguarding the continuation of their own production in the face of the depletion of Asia's stands of tropical forest. The Brazilian pulp industry, on the other hand, at a very early point of time started looking to an externally oriented strategy in line with the international best practice.

The **characteristics and functional cycles of the Amazon region's ecosystems** place limits on the utilization of renewable natural resources, and these are not recognized by the day-to-day knowledge that finds expression in the dominant entrepreneurial routines encountered there. The failure to take cognizance of the ecological specifics of the Amazon region has a number of different causes: first, it is associated with a low level of diffusion of existing knowledge concerning local ecosystems: this is due to the low level of formal education among the greater part of the population, the low regard in which the traditional knowledge of forest dwellers is held, and a lack of professionalism on the part of forest and sawmill owners, who regard it as unnecessary to have any reasonable measure of knowledge of forestry. Second, the blindness for nature of existing routines has to do with the premise that processing timber from the primary forest is a temporary affair that will sooner or later have to make way for more productive forms of land use. The third complex of causes is connected with this last reason; it is the weakness of institutions in enforcing legal restrictions on forest utilization: if conservation is viewed merely as a cost factor with uncertain benefits, and managing the primary forest is seen as an unprofitable activity, there is no justification for investing in strengthening the institutions entrusted with these tasks. This is why not even the introduction of safe property rights will work as an instrument to be used in introducing sustainable systems of forest use.

The structural characteristics of tropical forest ecosystems require the development of adapted management patterns, since the reproduction behavior of tropical tree species does not permit the creation of the homogeneous industrial forests with predictable maturation periods familiar from the temperate zones. The processing and marketing patterns of sawmills and other timber-processing companies will also have to take account of the structural characteristics of the tropical forests: due to the factor of biodiversity timber quantities of certain magnitudes can be obtained in the tropics only on the basis of greater qualitative heterogeneity. This heterogeneity could be turned to account by developing market niches that have need for the special aesthetic and physical features of tropical woods. Increasing labor productivity, product quality, and the depth of processing would make it possible to achieve higher yields and thus offer companies a permanent perspective.

The case of the tropical-timber industry in Pará does not indicate a general incompatibility between **economic development, an external orientation, and the preservation of life-support systems**. It has instead become clear that practical consideration of the conditions to which the reproduction of the natural life-support systems is tied is dependent on the routines and constraints that determine entrepreneurial or, in general, social action. These routines and constraints bear the marks of society and history; and it is to this extent possible to recognize systematic links between economic constraints and more or less consideration of natural life-support systems, though these links do not obey any universal, that is, abstract and ahistorical, logic.

A stronger focus on exports – in view of the high demand in the world market – might have increased the deforestation rate even more in the Amazon region in the 1970s and 1980s. Now, in contrast, a focus on certain ecologically sensitive markets in Europe and the United States could promote the introduction of nature-oriented forest management and the efficient processing of tropical timber in the region and thus produce positive effects. The maintenance of the export ban on logs is a precondition because otherwise the Amazon region might become an attractive place for Asian companies whose raw material sources are more or less exhausted.

Action Options to Promote a Sustainable Forest Management and Timber Industry

The analysis points to a number of options that can promote a sustainable forest management and timber industry. Development cooperation can make its contributions to all options, in particular in the framework of the G7 pilot program to conserve Brazil's tropical forests (PPG-7).

The concern in forestry must be to gain general acceptance for the model of nature-oriented forest management, which aims at supporting the natural regeneration of forests as a means of ensuring sustainable timber production. Clear-felling and substitution of the primary forest by plantations or stepping up timber production by means of various methods of enrichment-planting have proven to be inappropriate approaches. Degraded areas should be used to experiment with plantations, while methods stemming from nature-oriented forest management should be employed to exploit the timber resources of the primary forest.

The task of putting these models into practice calls for an invigoration and qualification of environmental policy and environmental authorities in the Brazilian states of the Amazon region; this would place the disputes in this policy field on a less emotional footing and gradually contribute to devising solutions to impending problems. A coherent tropical-forest policy combining ecological and socioeconomic goals would not only entail positive local and regional effects (and cause relatively low short-term economic costs), it would also enormously improve Brazil's international repute and widen the political options open to it.

At the sectoral level new tropics-specific ecological factors and new technological trends emerging in the world market are giving rise to a new model for the tropical-timber industry. The perspective open to the tropical-timber industry must be sought in the attempt to reconcile the reproduction-related ecological needs of the tropical forest with its economic interests in utilizing the latter; the means to this end must be sought in a strategy of flexible specialization in niche markets: supply of small quantities of diversified and high-quality products with complete information on their technical properties and potential uses would be an interesting and wholly new development perspective for the tropical-timber industry, which might in this way develop an interest in sustainable forest management.

The task of transforming this model into reality in the timber industry of Pará (and the Amazon region) can be promoted by retaining the export ban on tropical logs, more intensively monitoring the logging of and trade in mahogany, and encouraging certification of tropical forestry. The goals of these measures would have to be to intensify the innovation pressure to which Pará's timber industry is presently, for the first time for decades, exposed due to the depletion of local forest stands and substitution by new, technology-intensive wood panels.

The export ban on tropical logs may at first glance appear to constitute an obstacle to the funding of sustainable forestry, since as a rule log prices are higher in the world market than they are domestically. But this measure is for the time being the most important dam against the encroachment of the financially highly powerful investors presently active in the market: Asian timber corporations out to obtain logging concessions in the tropical-forest regions of Africa and Latin America with an eye to supplying their plywood factories with huge quantities of unprocessed timber. In Brazil the export ban forces these corporations to take over or develop local processing capacities, thus preserving or creating jobs; the restrictive practices of environmental authorities in granting licenses and the economic crisis in Asia have thus far prevented any large-scale logging activities here. It must, however, be anticipated that Asia's demand for tropical logs will soon increase again. But even if the export ban is retained, it would be a grave strategic error to bank on Asian investors: they represent the ecologically unadapted and technologically outmoded development path of a tropical-timber industry specialized in the production of cheap and simple mass goods, which neither contributes to sustainable patterns of resource utilization nor increases regional welfare.

The objective of stronger controls on the logging of and trade in mahogany would be to close off the sawmill owners' option of continuing to specialize in this valuable timber, in this way making quick, high profits. It is only when this option has been shut off for good that the economic interest in sustainable forest management can gain ground. At present there are contingents only on exports of mahogany; due to the high domestic demand for this timber it would make sense to extend this measure to the domestic trade as well.

Voluntary certification of ecological forestry methods draws on the market mechanism: in Europe certified timber can on the one hand command higher prices than noncertified timber and on the other hand this makes it possible to secure sales markets over the long term, since a growing demand here runs up against a slowly increasing supply. Certification also relies on the information and participation of civil society; this means that local residents, environmental groups, and consumer organizations check whether certified products rightly bear their certificates and whether the practice of certified firms is in accord with the standards. They can always count on media interest in uncovering abuses and improper behavior. Certification is in this way also an instrument that can be used by civil society to strengthen (and control) environmental authorities.

A campaign aimed at certification of forestry practices should start out with the export markets, in order later to focus on the domestic market as well. Certified timber can presently be sold in all European markets; a growing supply from Brazil could contribute to weakening the conservatism of the importers in the industrialized countries as a means of forcing them to meet their duty – of looking to new, ecologically oriented consumer preferences and altering their consumption accordingly. In view of the strength of the environmental movement in the south and southeast of Brazil, which has been fighting for the preservation of the tropical forests for over 20 years now, an attempt could be made to develop a domestic market segment for certified tropical timber. The better part of Amazon timber is used domestically in the building and furniture industries; the process of its replacement by plantation timber has already begun in the south and southeast. It is, in other words, necessary to develop new market segments for tropical timber in the domestic market.

Conversion to sustainable forest management and further processing of timber products will call for demanding learning processes in the companies concerned: management must learn to make use of specialized know-how and to use forest inventories as the basis of the logging and forest-tending that can stimulate the growth of species which can be marketed profitably. At the same time this type of forest use will oblige the processing companies to broaden the spectrum of marketable species by introducing new species to the markets at home and abroad and raising the productivity and quality of timber-processing. To achieve this, the companies involved will have to learn to develop horizontal cooperative relationships that can be instrumental in dealing more efficiently with the tasks facing them as well as to maintain intensive and constant relations with their customers as a means of familiarizing themselves with the latter's needs.

1 Introduction: Statement of the Problem and Structure of the Study

The Amazon and the tropical rainforest – as late as in the postwar era these keywords were used to evoke images of a luxuriant, green landscape, images understood either as a reference to fertile soils and big chances for resolute pioneers or as a source of noxious vapors, poisonous vermin, and mythological animals like the Anaconda, which drew all of life under its spell and could break even the drive of the pioneer. In either case the jungle was the symbol of a powerful, extravagant nature that could lead men to wealth or doom (Hurtienne 1993). Today when we hear the word Amazon we see wholly different images: tracts of scorched earth in which burnt stumps reach toward a gray sky out of swampy or ash-covered, smoldering ground. The life of indigenous peoples and rare animal and plant species is threatened by the advance of big cattle ranches, logging operations, and smallholders, all of whom, driven by the prospects of big profits or determined to secure their naked survival, have, for some thirty years now, been gradually destroying the earth's last closed rainforest area. This, however, has not only meant the irrevocable destruction of the local habitat for rare forms of life, it at the same time also poses, on a global level, a threat to the natural foundations of life itself: the loss of species is diminishing the natural reservoir of nutritional and medicinal plants on which biotechnology must draw its resources. Burning the forests contributes to the greenhouse effect, and it in turn is leading to unforeseeable climatic changes with potentially disastrous consequences – rises in sea levels, changes of temperatures and precipitation patterns with their effects on food production.

The Amazon rainforest, once a symbol of unfettered life itself, has become a sign pointing to the man-made threat to life on earth. For ordinary consciousness the jungle, often portrayed as a powerful force of nature capable, if need be, of turning its superior vital force against human intruders, has, thanks to popular science, taken on the character of an ancient albeit fragile ecosystem vulnerable to utter destruction at the hand of man within a number of decades.

As a consequence of this transformation of the symbolic role of the Amazon rainforest the latter has come to stand for the change in the relation between society and nature that has gained ascendancy in the 20th century. If the efforts of the last 200 years toward technical and social progress entailed subjugating and harnessing the forces of nature toward the end of exploiting them for the production of food, energy, and other goods, we are today experiencing the growth of an awareness that the natural reservoir has limits and can be exhausted. Technical progress and social change (to the extent that this can be consciously controlled) must from now on follow a more economical use of natural resources.

In 1990, at the G-7 summit in Houston, the world's seven economic powerhouses, acting on a German initiative, offered Brazil their participation in a pilot program designed to protect Brazil's rainforests. The aim of this program (PPG-7) is to encourage learning processes, in the Amazon region and the international community alike, geared to determining how the goals of environmental and resource protection might be brought into line with the goals of economic development and poverty alleviation at the local, regional, and global levels. Having overcome some initial problems, PPG-7 has, since 1996, met with a number of successes, in particular as regards the creation of protected areas for indigenous peoples and support for local initiatives aimed at a sustainable use of natural resources. The German government is funding roughly half of the US$ 320 million earmarked for the program, which, aside from forest protection, also provides for an institutional invigoration of the environmental authorities in the Amazon region and support for sustainable forest management.

The present study sees itself in the context of the agenda addressed by the goals of PPG-7: Its subject is the relationship between economic development, resource use, and innovation processes; the topic is developed with reference to the timber-processing industry in the Brazilian state of Pará in the eastern region of the Amazon. The study uses a historical reconstruction of the economic and technological development paths of the timber industry since the 1950s to establish how the dominant use pattern of the tropical forest came about and what role the given ecological facts, the Brazilian government's Amazon development policy, and the world timber market play in this process. The study focuses on action patterns and routines of the companies actively involved, and does so with an eye to determining both their role in the expansion of the industry and their innovative capacities.

The timber industry has attracted little interest in socioeconomic research on the Amazon region because the focus of such studies has as a rule been on processes of deforestation and their causes. Since deforestation is above all a consequence of the expansion of farming and cattle-ranching, and this expansion has been promoted by the public programs aimed at economic integration of the region, the development of the timber industry and its intertwinement with other industries has often fallen through the grid defined for the field under research. The present study aims to close that gap.

The reason why the timber industry was chosen as the subject of the present study is that an analysis of entrepreneurial action strategies can help us to understand what factors are instrumental in the ruthless exploitation of the tropical forest. As a rule studies dealing with the timber industry have the following shortcomings:

–   they proceed on the assumption of instrumentally rational action patterns on the part of the economic agents, but without looking into the matter empirically. The premise guiding the research is that there is an abundance of homogeneous timber resources; what the research strategies center on under these conditions is not efficient exploitation and processing but reduction of transportation costs, which account for the better part of production costs;

–   and then they neglect to view the development of the Amazon timber industry in the context of the Brazilian timber industry and the world market for timber, in this way failing to account for the effects of technical change on the competitiveness of tropical timber.

The aim of the present study is therefore to answer the following questions:

–   How and under the impact of what economic incentives and institutional conditions has the timber industry in Pará developed since the Amazon region was first opened up in infrastructural terms in the 1960s?

– What are the techno-organizational elements to which the entrepreneurial action patterns encountered in the Pará timber industry can be traced back? How have these elements and patterns changed in the past 35 years? What economic and institutional incentives have played a role here (e.g. subsidies, environmental legislation and monitoring)?

– What influence does the ecology of the tropical forest have on the timber supply and utilization chances of the timber industry?

– What role will technological innovation play for the future competitiveness of tropical timber from the Amazon region both in the domestic Brazilian timber market and in the world timber market?

– What specific restraints do these action patterns entail for entrepreneurial learning processes and innovation? Can Pará's timber entrepreneurs generally be described as conservative and inimical or skeptical toward innovation?

Once these questions have been answered, we will be able to explain the expansion of the small and medium-scale saw mills and plywood factories in Pará and in the Amazon region as a continuation of the traditional development path of the Brazilian timber industry, which is based on overexploitation. At the same time, the south and southeast of the country have experienced the rise of a capital-intensive, competitive, outward-looking pulp industry based on eucalyptus plantations, which have attracted the lion's share of the investments made in the timber industry.

In the 1990s the economic and ecological framework conditions changed radically for the state of Pará: monetary stability and declining economic growth in Brazil compelled the companies of the industry, for the first time for decades, to cut costs systematically; the declining world demand for tropical timber sent prices downward; at the same time the procurement costs for stemwood rose because the forest stands surrounding the timber industry in the Amazon region had been depleted and the control of the environmental authorities had been stepped up under the pressure of world public opinion. The industry is now faced with the challenge of radically altering its action pattern, marked as it is by overexploitation of the tropical forests and an insufficient depth of processing, if it is to survive.

The following sections present the study's empirical and theoretical points of departure (1.1), make some preliminary remarks on the choice of the field of inquiry (1.2), and describe the way in which the study is structured (1.3).

1.1   Empirical and Theoretical Points of Departure

The **empirical** point of departure for the study was the question as to the extent to which foreign-trade relations promote or hinder the emergence of environmentally sustainable patterns of resource utilization in developing countries. This question posed itself in connection with previous work on the complex of trade and environment, in particular as regards the responses of exporters in developing countries to standards imposed in their OECD sales markets concerning the ecological quality of their products and production processes (Scholz 1993, 1996a; Scholz et al. 1994).

A number of NICs have begun to pursue a competition- and trade-oriented development strategy geared to building dynamic exporting industries as motors of economic growth; the existing factor endowments of these countries are the reason why, at least for an initial phase, the competitiveness of their exporting industries is based on an extensive exploitation of (renewable) natural resources as well as on low wage costs. Successful integration into the world economy by building new exporting industries and by pursuing a development path that is economically and ecologically sustainable in the long run – these objectives would appear to be mutually exclusive, at least in view of the newspaper articles and scientific reports available on the ruthless exploitation of natural forests and fishery resources, the depletion of soils, and the impending exhaustion of water resources in the interest of the exporting industries of developing countries. The perspective in these articles is often dominated by a justifiable concern over possible irreversible damage to the ecosystems in these countries; but they tend to occlude the environmental changes that have taken place there in recent years as well as to bias any more precise analysis of the agents responsible for these changes, their motives, and their objectives. A further factor is that it is precisely in the countries that are pursuing a world-market-oriented growth strategy that we have seen the emergence of a debate on environmental policy, indeed one that engages the various domestic actors no less than the purchasers of their products in the industrialized countries. This debate is concerned among other things with the question as to what features an environmentally compatible product must display, whether more environmentally sound management and manufacturing methods are possible, who is to bear the costs of developing and introducing them, and what role should be played by the state and social groups in elaborating and monitoring environmental policy.

The foregoing is based on two observable developments:

First, export-oriented companies in developing countries more and more frequently see themselves confronted in their European sales markets with ecological standards covering their products and the processes used to produce them (Scholz 1993; Bennett and Verhoeve 1994). These new standards compel these companies to engage in complex learning processes that comprise environmental, technological, and organizational dimensions and can require both simple and highly complex adjustments of products, production sequencing, and production processes. As is shown by the experience of the OECD countries, successful learning processes of this sort require – apart from innovative businesses – economic, political, legal, and administrative framework conditions that create incentives to improve the environmental soundness of production and product alike as well as institutions in the business environment (training and advanced training, research and technology, finance, and trade and environmental policies) which offer support in searching for adapted solutions.

Second, empirical research on ecological adjustment processes at the level of firms and sectoral institutions conducted in recent years emphasizes the growing importance of environmental product quality.[1]

The Chilean case study, for instance, has shown that outward-looking and competition-oriented policies have entailed ambivalent effects: on the one hand they have encouraged the commercial exploitation of natural resources, and done so at the expense of losses sometimes high in absolute terms. On the other hand the orientation in terms of the quality and efficiency standards of the OECD countries has increased the willingness to undertake ecologically grounded adjustment measures. Companies and R&D institutions have started to build up the technological and organizational knowledge base needed to work out adjustment measures and put them into practice (Scholz et al. 1994).

Ecological learning processes induced externally (via trade relations) run up against limits where they encounter solidified constellations of economic power and interests and the organizational and articulation capacities of potential agents of environmental reform processes are, due to the historical particularities of political structures, weakly developed (labor unions, consumers, social movements, smallholders, indigenous population groups). Learning processes can be inhibited when the executive branch is unable to adequately exercise its supervisory and support functions in the field of environmental protection because it lacks the manpower resources and structures at the regional and local levels are weakly developed[2] or when environmental and resource protection is accorded a priority too low compared with other issues on the social-policy agenda.

In more general terms, the following questions arise: What factors and conditions have given rise to the empirically observed ecological awareness and the actual propensity to act in an environmentally responsible fashion in certain areas of the export sector? Is there any promotion or support of social learning processes that go above and beyond this? Are environmental reforms encouraged in this way?

The **theoretical** perspective of the debate on sustainable development does not necessarily appear to support the proposition that integration into the world economy can under certain conditions promote the introduction of more environmentally sound production patterns. This proposition is accepted by the greater part of the theoretical and/or practice-oriented studies on possibilities, limits, and regulatory needs of strategies of sustainable development which are markedly influenced by tenets of neoclassical environmental economics. This perspective would indicate that the fundamental problem consists in increasing the allocative efficiency of (renewable and nonrenewable) natural resources. This goal – according to the general hypothesis – can be reached by harnessing the market mechanisms for the consumption of environmental goods and at the same time using political regulations to ensure and legitimate the effectiveness of market-oriented instruments (Endres and Querner 1993; Pearce and Turner 1990).

Approaches such as ecological economics are more critical with regard to the issue of free trade. Their analysis is marked by a fundamental critique of industrial society (high energy and material intensity of industrial patterns of production and consumption), and they accord the highest priority to environmental and resources protection as a means of putting a stop to the destruction of global life-support systems. They call for an orientation of economic activities in terms of equilibrium models that take the limited carrying capacity of ecosystems into account (steady-state economy) (Daly 1992b; Costanza 1991).

What role is played by trade relations in these approaches? In the classical line of argument external trade contributes to welfare gains in that the countries involved specialize in different fields according to their comparative advantages, gradually come to engage in complementary economic activities, and can in this way achieve increases in overall economic efficiency. In ecological regards, too, these countries are in competition with one another: they have different natural-resource endowments, different levels of pollution, and different systems of legal and economic regulation. If all countries have comparable environmental-protection goals, and compliance with them is in fact monitored, it is possible to neutralize the negative environmental impacts of external trade. More recent approaches to analyzing the dynamic determinants of competitiveness (man-made competitive advantages) (Nelson and Winter 1982; Hurtienne and Messner 1994; Esser et al. 1994) also see external trade as exercising functions that increase efficiency, and with it welfare, in that competition compels economic agents, who are interlinked via global markets and production structures, to engage in constant processes of learning and innovation. An optimization of production patterns in ecological terms would, in this view, constitute a welcome side-effect, which would materialize when technological development in the leading countries proceeds in this direction.

Ecological economics has a more negative view of external trade, and there are three reasons for this. First, external trade allows an economy to expand its throughput of energy and material beyond the "natural" (ecosystem-related) boundaries of its geographic territory, in this way dumping the ecological costs of its patterns of production and consumption on other economies. Second, external trade relations serve as a transmission belt for proliferating the production and consumption patterns of an industrialized society, in this way supplanting traditional economic modes. The assumption is that traditional forms of utilization of natural resources are more sustainable than modern ones; this is not always borne out by the empirical evidence. Third, the integration of many developing countries into the world economy displays a structural pattern on which these countries, for lack of any alternative efficient industries, are compelled to overexploit their natural resources in order to earn the foreign exchange they need to service their debts abroad and finance their imports (Ekins 1993a and b; Daly and Cobb 1989).

So when the issue is the relationship between external trade and the introduction of sustainable modes of economic activity, the question we should focus on is under what economic, ecological, political, and social conditions the hypothesis that external trade interlinkages lead to increases in efficiency can be applied to the task of coping with ecological problems in developing countries.

Seen from a sociological angle, the economic view of the problem is insufficient in that it, in three respects, proceeds from presuppositions that are not accessible to analysis:

–   the historical development and change of the specific relation of society to nature are omitted from the analysis;

–   rational action is frequently reduced to economic cost-benefit rationales, without taking account of its sociohistorical and spatial embeddedness. The assumption made here by the author – with reference to Giddens' theory of structuration – is that the action patterns or routines of the agents reflect historical and present experiences that ensure a successful process of societal reproduction. Accordingly, even action patterns known to be destructive over the medium and long term must first of all be investigated with an eye to this dimension if signs of change are to be perceived;

– the conditions under which ecological preferences emerge (ecological awareness) are not investigated in (neoclassical) economics; yet on the other hand patterns of explication are taken over unquestioningly – like that put forward by Inglehart (1977, 1990), who sees the increased significance of ecological priorities, as opposed to economic priorities, largely as a reflex of the satisfaction of material needs (postmaterialism). This approach is unable to explain the specific characteristics of environmental movements in developing countries (threat to the immediate material life-support systems).[3] An analysis of the relation of society to nature has first to distinguish between industrialized countries and developing countries and second to take account of the different forms in which they are integrated into the world market.[4]

But a purely sociological view of the relation between nature and society would likewise prove insufficient in that it would tend to give too little consideration to the autonomy and inherent dynamics of nature and its manifold influences on social action.[5] Sociology itself generates no knowledge about nature, it at best gives rise to thoughts on society's dealings with the latter. The theoretical approaches that predominate in sociology are either positions that, with reference to Luhmann, concern themselves with social observation of the natural environment or, with reference to Beck, look into the inequitable distribution of ecological risks and the social conflicts that arise in view of ecological problems. The discipline furthermore documents and investigates, in its discussion of the reductionist views of natural-resource economics, traditional rules that are used, for instance in agrarian societies, to regulate the collective use of natural resources (land, forests, stocks of fish) in such a way as to avoid any overexploitation of them. There are, however, also sociological studies that take over the premise of economics which states that the relation between society and nature is marked primarily by the relationship between social ends and various scarce resources (natural resources, human labor) (Berger 1994).

With an eye to eluding the pitfalls of restricted economic and sociological views, while at the same time making use of their good points, the present study pursues an interdisciplinary approach:

- Structuration theory (Giddens) and evolutionary economics (Nelson and Winter) are here used to investigate the development of the relation between society and nature, with specific reference to the Pará timber industry, as a dynamic process in which the changing demands of the world market, the given ecological facts, and the demands imposed by the need to reproduce internal social relations become operative. This dynamic process is constituted by the action of conscious agents. The goal is to reconstruct how the structure of integration into the world market and patterns of resource use (and changes of it) find expression in the action patterns of the agents and under what conditions these action patterns change.

- In order to accord adequate attention to the tendencies in the world timber market as well as to the given ecological facts in which a sustainable exploitation of tropical forests must look for orientation, the study presents findings from these fields.

1.2   Preliminary Remarks on the Choice of the Field of Study

The pronounced sociostructural and economic differentiation between developing countries as well as their differing ecological conditions make it necessary to delimit the topic of the study in a manner that does justice both to theoretical considerations and empirical factors.

One of the findings of the investigation conducted in Chile is that external trade with countries with a high level of environmental protection can, under certain conditions, lead to an improvement of the environmental compatibility of products and production processes in the exporting country. The following conditions have a conducive impact on the exporting country: Trade partners are informed of environmental standards in time; these standards are clearly justified; and they do not give rise to suspicion of protectionist intentions. Higher production costs incurred in connection with the higher environmental compatibility of the product under consideration can be made up for, or more than made up for, by increased sales prices. The latter thus constitute an incentive. Furthermore, open markets, support for technology transfer and environmental cooperation projects boost the credibility of ecologically grounded trade-related measures.

The exporting country can use, among others, the following conditions to encourage industry's willingness to make environmentally motivated adjustments: There is little possibility of switching to other export markets with lower or nonexistent environmental standards, or this option is not viable on account of the lower prices that can be commanded there. The export dependency in the sectors affected by such environmental standards is so great that there is no possibility of using the domestic market as an alternative and there is no way around adjusting to the quality standards of customers. An economic policy geared to competition and the world market is used to promote orientation toward international efficiency standards, and in fact encourages the companies involved to take account of long-term trends in the industrialized countries in shaping their own entrepreneurial strategies.

The case of Chile, however, displays a number of structural characteristics that make it difficult to draw any general conclusions on the connection between environmental standards and external trade beyond this specific case. These special characteristics include:

– the relatively great shares of exports that go to the EU and the US (the countries with the highest environmental standards);

– the great significance of the export sector for the overall economy; and

– the – seen in regional terms – greater experience of Chilean economic agents with world-market orientation, a factor which has increased their capacity to learn and their willingness to adjust.

Company-level learning processes that encourage adjustment to environmental standards in Europe go back more than 20 years in Chile.

In other countries of the region these conditions do not exist, and thus it is not possible simply to assume that the results and policy recommendations of this study can be transferred to them. Of particular importance is the question as to the positive correlation between external trade and environmental and resource protection among larger NICs that have already reached a more or less high level of industrialization, i.e. countries in which the domestic market has a relatively large weight of its own and industrialization is reflected in the makeup of exports. Under what conditions can in such economies external environmental standards set in motion positive processes of learning and adjustment?

Brazil is a country for which, *inter alia*, the above-named structural characteristics apply. Furthermore, an important difference to Chile is that the process of trade liberalization has not yet been completed here. This has been changing since the monetary reform of July 1994, which led to stable, though overvalued, exchange rates and dramatically reduced inflation. In 1997 the share of external trade (imports and exports) in Brazil's GDP was roughly 15 %. The relatively high level of diversification of the Brazilian export sector as well as the great number of Brazilian companies producing exclusively for the domestic market have thus far diminished the pressure to adjust stemming from European environmental standards to which Brazilian exporters are exposed. But at present clear-cut changes are in sight that seem to confirm the results from the Chile study: world-market-oriented corporations are investing in company-level environmental protection, having their in-house environmental management programs certified as per ISO 14000, and developing, under the pressure of shareholders and national environmental legislation, company-level environmental guidelines and targets (Ernst and Young 1996; Maimon 1995). The pulp/paper and mining industries are particularly active in this respect.

In the private sector of the federal state of Pará, the biggest exporter in the Brazilian Amazon region, there are, with the exception of some major corporations in the fields of mining and crude oil, few such signs that something is in the making, although the state has some structural characteristics that resemble the features peculiar to Chile:

– Pará exports above all primary processed raw materials from mining, agriculture, fishery, and the timber trade, i.e. ecologically sensitive and simple products with a low level of processing;

– a relatively large share of these exports go to the EU and the US, the countries with the highest environmental standards;

–   though the export sector is of great significance for Pará's economy, it is underdiversified.

There are differences to be observed above all in the structure of the export sector: Pará's export sector resembles Chile's during the period of import-substitution industrialization, in which over 70 % of foreign-exchange revenues stemmed from copper exports, which were in the hand of the Chilean state enterprise Codelco. A position analogous to that of Codelco is held in Pará by the Companhia Vale do Rio Doce (CVRD). The company, privatized in 1997, exploits Pará's mineral resources either on its own or in cooperation with Japanese and other international corporations, accounting for some 60 % of the state's export revenues.

The structure of the timber industry is entirely different. This sector is dominated by small and medium-size companies in both production and exports. There is only one major corporation in each branch of the industry, one of which produces pulp, another plywood, while a third one manufactures kitchen items and simple furniture of wood. Some 68 % of the stemwood cut in the Amazon region is processed in Pará; Pará's timber exports account for roughly 67 % of those of the Amazon region and 27 % of Brazil's total timber exports.

The Pará timber industry has had to deal with the environmental-quality standards of its European and North American customers since the beginning of the 1990s. Being the world's largest closed tropical rainforest area, Brazil has come under strong international pressure to do more than it has done to protect these forests.

For the actors in Pará and Brazil, whose understanding of nature is more or less in line with the above-sketched picture of a powerful force that is abundant in resources and needs only to be subjugated and made accessible to exploitation in order to increase general welfare, this is an unprecedented experience. Pará's history has been marked by the ups and downs brought by different economic cycles based on the exploitation of specific natural resources; the first were the *drogas do sertão* (spices, resins and other forest produce); this was followed at the end of the 19th century by the rubber boom; when it collapsed in 1912, it was replaced by extraction of Brazil nuts, plant fibers, resins, latex, and timber, the backbone of a contracted economy now restricted to the domestic market (Hurtienne 1988). Since the 1970s exports of mineral resources and, to a lesser extent, timber as well as agriculture and financial transfers from the federal government have constituted the base of Pará's economy.

Owing to these features – an economy marked by colonial structures and integration into the world market, regional economic significance of the timber industry, a pronounced export orientation by Brazilian standards, adjustment pressure stemming from altered economic and environmental framework conditions – the state of Pará and Pará's timber industry proved to be an exemplary case that seemed suited to look into the question of the significance of the state's given ecological conditions and interlinkages with the world market for the development of patterns of resource use.

In dealing with the Amazon region it is important to bear in mind how the region is defined: Brazil's Amazon region is intersected by two delimited regional entities, the geographically defined northern region, consisting of the states of Acre, Amapá, Amazonas, Pará, Rondônia, Roraima, and Tocantins, and the ecologically defined *Amazônia Legal*, which includes the northern-region states already named as well as the state of Mato Grosso (mid-western region) and parts of the states of Goiás (mid-west) and Maranhão (north east) and accounts for roughly 50 % of Brazil's territory. The ecosystems of *Amazônia Legal* consist of the various forest formations of the Amazon region (according to the classification usual in Brazil: the *campinarana* – sandy wooded areas, the closed and the open tropical rainforests, the deciduous tropical forest, and secondary forest formations), woody savannas (*cerradão*) and unforested savannas (*cerrado*), transition areas between two forest types, and deforested areas.

When the present study speaks of the Amazon region, what is meant are the states of Acre, Amapá, Amazonas, Pará, Rondônia, and Roraima. It was only in the 1980s that the state of Tocantins was carved out of the northern part of the state of Goiás. The state is located on the fringe of the Amazon region and has no significance in terms of the timber industry. Whenever the state of Mato Grosso – whose territory is marked

Figure 1:   Annual Growth of Deforested Areas, 1978-96

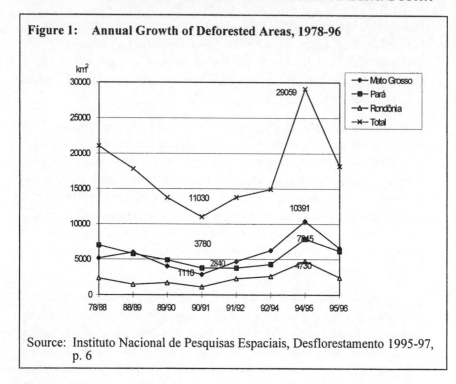

Source: Instituto Nacional de Pesquisas Espaciais, Desflorestamento 1995-97,
             p. 6

above all by *cerradão* and, to a lesser extent, constitutes the transition area to the open rainforest – is taken into consideration, special note is made of the fact.

Finally, a brief overview of the deforestation rates in the Amazon region and their contribution to global carbon-dioxide emissions. The deforestation process in the different regions of Brazil has been monitored by satellite by INPE (Brazilian Institute for Space Research) since the end of the 1970s. The most recent published data indicate that the overall deforested area in Amazônia Legal has risen from 25,000 km^2 in 1974 to 517,000 km^2 in 1996. In the same period the percentage of deforested area in Amazônia Legal has risen from 0.5 to 8 % of the total surface area.

It was the period between 1978 and 1988 that saw the greatest increase in deforestation; the percentage of the area of Amazônia Legal deforested in this decade grew from 2 to 6 %. After 1988 the intensity of

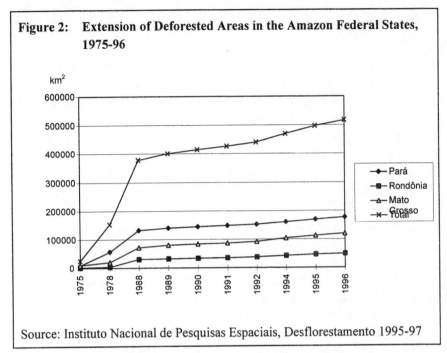

Figure 2:   Extension of Deforested Areas in the Amazon Federal States,
            1975-96

Source: Instituto Nacional de Pesquisas Espaciais, Desflorestamento 1995-97

deforestation declined and again showed a sharp rise between 1994 and 1995. Between 1990 and 1991 11,200 km² had been deforested, in 1994/95 the figure was 29,792 km². The rate of increase subsequently declined to roughly 20,000 km².

The relative percentage of deforested areas in the individual states differs greatly, the highest shares for 1996 being observed in Maranhão (30 % of the state's total area), Rondônia (20 %), Pará (14 %), Mato Grosso (13 %); while the center of the spectrum is made up by Acre and Tocantins (9 % each), with Amazonas and Roraima (2 %) and Amapá (1 %) closing the scale.

Referred to Amazônia Legal's surface area (without the shares of Maranhão and Goiás), we find the following distribution of deforestation: Pará has always had the largest relative share, though, compared with Mato Grosso, the state with the second largest – and growing – share, it shows a declining tendency. Rondônia ranges third. Both the agricultural production capacity and the timber industry of the Amazon region are concentrated in these three states.

Deforestation in the Amazon region is for the most part associated with the fire clearance of forested areas, which entails carbon dioxide emissions that contribute to the greenhouse effect and thus to global warming.[6] The significance of these emissions can be assessed from two perspectives: from the perspective of their share of worldwide CO_2 emissions or from the perspective of their emission potential if deforestation goes on. The burning of forested areas in Brazil's Amazon region accounts for some 0.3 gigatons of carbon emissions per year;[7] this amounts to 3 - 5 % of the world's C-emissions. The greater part of global C-emissions stem from the combustion of fossil energies (Loske 1996, p. 43). In contrast to their relatively low present contribution, the emission potential of the Amazon forests is immense in that the latter store some 80 - 90 billion tons of carbon in the form of above-ground biomass (Salati and dos Santos 1999, p. 17). However, it is important to bear in mind that the development of emissions cannot be projected in a linear form in keeping with deforestation, since second-growth vegetation in turn absorbs carbon; net emissions would thus be below the absolute values.

Brazil has had a very low share both in current global CO_2 emissions and in the rise of CO_2 concentrations in the earth's atmosphere since 1800 (Loske 1996, pp. 41 - 60). Brazil's per capita emissions amount to no more than 1.4 t CO_2 annually (by way of comparison: the figure for Germany is 11 t); the reason for this is above all that a large part of Brazil's energy output stems from hydroelectric power plants and not from the combustion of fossil energies. And so despite its relatively high energy intensity as far as output is concerned (26.8 gigajoules / US$ 1000 of GDP), the country's carbon intensity is quite low (6.9 kg C / gigajoules and 0.18 t C / US$ 1000 of GDP).[8] Brazil's percentage of the world's CO_2 increase since 1800 is roughly 0.6 %; the share of the developing countries in general is 16.3 %; while that of the industrialized countries is 83.7 %.

1.3   Structure of the Study

The study's second and third chapters are concerned with the state of the research and development of a theoretical-methodological approach for the empirical investigation. To this end various areas of theory are looked into for their usefulness for the topic of the study; these include in particular the concepts of sustainable development, ecological economics, natural-resource economics, sociological approaches to economic action (in particular the theory of structuration), and evolutionary economic theory. The red thread through this discussion is the question as to how a given type of social action, specifically the economic utilization of natural resources, is conceived in each theoretical approach. The choice of approaches was determined by the shortcomings of the present state of the research on deforestation processes as well as by the role played in these processes by the timber industry and the world market.

Chapter 4 is concerned with the ecological conditions in the Amazon forest, the natural base of forestry. The chapter starts out with a brief overview of the present state of knowledge of tropical-ecological research in the eastern Amazon region; this is followed by a presentation of the principles of nature-oriented sustainable forestry and a discussion of how these principles could be put into practice in Pará. The points of reference here are on the one hand the results of experiments that have been conducted in different forest-research stations since the 1960s and on the other hand the criteria for certification of sustainable forest management in Pará.

Chapter 5 presents quantitative and qualitative trends in the world timber market and analyzes their significance for the tropical-timber trade. The chapter first sets out the dimensions, structure, and development of the world market for tropical timber against the background of the general development of the world timber market. The chapter also presents the development of German tropical-timber imports and Brazilian and Pará timber exports. The chapter concludes with a discussion of the changes in the technology and organization of wood-processing and their probable impacts on market shares for tropical timber.

Chapters 6 and 7, in which the results of the empirical investigation are summarized, make up the centerpiece of the study: Chapter 6 discusses the structure and the situation of Pará's timber industry in the 1990s, presenting the results of in-detail empirical studies conducted by other institutes and the evaluation of the author's own qualitative interviews. Chapter 7 deals with the historical development process of the timber industry since the 1950s, in order to explain the origins and the different phases in the development of the patterns of action that mark the exploitation of the tropical forest in Pará. This historical reconstruction makes use of contemporary empirical studies and an analysis of statistical time series compiled from economic censuses and annual statistical reports of IBGE and FAO. As a reference, the chapter also presents the corresponding statistical data on the timber industry in the country as a whole and in Paraná, the center of the Brazilian timber industry.

Chapter 8 summarizes and places in a theoretical framework the findings from the previous four chapters on the ecological conditions required for tropical forestry and agriculture, the world market for timber, the advance of the plantation system, and the development patterns of the tropical-timber industry in Pará.

Finally, Chapter 9 presents the conclusions for development cooperation that can be drawn at the sectoral level concerned with promoting an ecologically and economically sustainable tropical-timber industry as well as at the higher level concerned with a sustainable development strategy for the state of Pará, to which the sectoral strategy would have to be adapted.

2   Determinants of Natural Resource Use: Theoretical Approaches from the Field of Economics and the State of Research

The guiding question of the present study is as to what factors determine the forest exploitation of the Pará timber industry and what role its external-trade orientation plays here. What are the theoretical approaches that are available to answer these questions? The following two chapters discuss the strong and weak points of economic and sociological approaches that can be used to address the guiding question referred to above, in order then, building on these approaches, to develop the theoretical-methodological approach pursued in this study. The red thread leading through this discussion is the question as to how social and economic action and the relation between society and nature are conceived in each approach.

The point of departure for the theoretical-methodological considerations developed here is on the one hand the concept of sustainable development and on the other the studies that sum up the present state of the research in the social sciences on the exploitation of the tropical forests in the Amazon region. The concept of sustainable development provides the normative frame of reference for research studies that analyze the socioeconomic development processes under consideration of the given ecological conditions and aim to develop recommendations for viable development paths sustainable in both socioeconomic and ecological terms. This normative concept has not yet been realized in research and policy; environmental and resource economics as well as ecological economics offer in part competing, in part complementary answers. The empirically founded state of our knowledge on the economic dimension of the exploitation of the tropical forests in the Amazon region is based largely on neoclassical instruments of inquiry. The models used as a rule proceed from gross simplifications as regards the action rationality of the agents involved and the production factors that must be considered, and in doing so they miss some important structural characteristics, details, and trends (Chapter 2).

It was therefore necessary to look for alternative approaches to economic and social action and the relation between society and nature that widen the spectrum of the factors to be considered, but without impairing its transparency. What proved helpful were sociological approaches that do not reduce economic action to instrumentally rational decisions on the allocation of scarce resources and evolutionary economic theory, which understands entrepreneurial action patterns as the result of historically embedded social processes and emphasizes the dynamic, unpredictable change of these action patterns effected by technological innovation. The New Institutional Economics was not discussed at any length in this connection in that it, at the level of the model of action on which it is based, offers no alternative, in the sense mentioned above, to the neoclassical approach. It does admit that economic decisions may be seen as rational only under restricted conditions, since there are always difficulties involved in acquiring and processing information, and opportunistic behavior (deceit, cunning) can never be ruled out, and it derives from these circumstances the need for institutions that diminish uncertainty and increase the likelihood of rule-governed behavior. Yet it, unlike evolutionary economic theory (Chapter 3), fails to see any necessity to change the definition of *homo oeconomicus* as a utility-maximizer.

The present study's methodological approach proceeds along interdisciplinary lines with an eye to supplementing and/or correcting economic analyses of entrepreneurial action by making use of analyses stemming from other perspectives. This means systematically including findings from these disciplines in the inquiry with a view to identifying mutual relations and intersecting fields. According to this understanding of interdisciplinarity it is not fruitful to search for a new queen of the sciences, superior to all other disciplines and methodologically universal; the concern is instead to acknowledge the epistemological autonomy of individual disciplines and, building on them, to arrive at an overall view, which can never be more than a tentative one. Referred to the topic of the present inquiry, interdisciplinarity means analyzing entrepreneurial action patterns in their historical context and identifying their techno-organizational dynamics. This also entails consideration of external factors such as ecological conditions and trends in the world market.

2.1   State of the Research: an Initial Overview

In the last twenty years the number of publications in the social sciences on the subject of the exploitation of tropical forests has increased steadily; the aim of most of the studies is to use an analysis of the causes of deforestation to make well-founded proposals on environmental- and economic-policy measures as a means of counteracting the continuing trend toward further deforestation.[1] These studies, and some more specialized publications on the trade with tropical timber and the tropical-timber industry, came about in the context of the initiatives on a boycott of tropical timber that emerged in the 1980s and were intended by their initiators, environmental groups, to diminish the economic incentives for logging operations.[2]

A standard work on the causes of the destruction of tropical forests, commissioned by Greenpeace, was published by Amelung / Diehl (1992). Jepma (1995) developed a model that can be used to calculate the effects of economic and trade-related measures on patterns of land use and future deforestation rates in tropical forests. Amelung (1997) and Thiele (1996) analyze the costs and benefits of the exploitation and destruction of tropical forests from the perspective of allocation theory and develop proposals for coming to grips with market and policy failure.

The studies by social scientists on the Amazon region differ in terms of their focal points: a number of early studies by Brazilian and US authors are concerned with the dynamics and the political economy of opening up the Amazon region with the aid of large-scale development programs sponsored by the Brazilian federal government (Cardoso and Müller 1977; Moran 1981; Bunker 1985; Hecht and Coburn 1989). These studies pointed in particular to the ecological limits faced by any development of the Amazon region along conventional lines. Usually, when discussing the Amazon timber industry two unpublished dissertations dealing with the timber industry in Rondônia and Pará are cited;[3] a general overview of the subject can be found in a dissertation on the timber industry in the west of Pará that was completed in 1990 and published in 1993 (Ros-Tonen 1993). Some more recent empirical studies on the Amazon timber industry, restricted to Pará, were published in the 1990s, both in Brazil and in highly reputed international journals, by a research group at IMAZON, an independent research institute in Pará.[4]

Independently of these works, a good number of ethnological studies have appeared since the 1940s that deal with indigenous traditions of resources utilization and derive from them proposals on sustainable systems of forest and land use (Browder 1989; Balée and Posey 1989).

The majority of the studies in the field of social sciences dealing with the utilization of the tropical forests proceed from theoretical approaches of a neoclassical hue: The German Kiel *Institut für Weltwirtschaft* looks into the problematic from the angle of allocation theory, the Anglo-Saxon authors assume a perspective defined by natural-resource economics. The former derive the necessity of protecting tropical forests above all from the efficiency advantages offered by a forestry-related use of forests as opposed to converting them for use for agriculture or cattle-ranching as well as from the costs associated with the forest-clearance-related loss of biodiversity. Anglo-Saxon authors often take over the premise of ecological economics stating that we live in a world marked – in the long run – by limited physical and energy resources and fragile natural life-support systems and further pointing out that man-made technologies and other forms of capital will not be able to replace this natural capital.

It was particularly important to consider the state of the research on tropical forest ecosystems in order to be able to recognize the significance of collective environmental services provided by the tropical forest (including biodiversity, CO_2 sink function, hydrological cycle, aesthetic values) and the dangers posed by traditional selective logging practices and conversion of forest areas to the reproduction of the tropical forest. The complexity of the ecosystem tropical forest, the great number of endemic plant, animal, and insect species encountered there, and the growth rates of many tree species render the system vulnerable to sustained outside interventions, which, in the extreme, can lead to an irreversible collapse of the ecosystem. This is also true of conversion: complete removal of the plant cover of large areas can diminish soil fertility and lead to erosion and aridity; rehabilitation of such areas requires great investments that make them unprofitable compared with areas in other regions. In economic terms this means that short-term profits from timber harvests or conversion are countered in the long term by high costs, which are exacerbated by the risk of irreversible consequences.

Both groups of authors assume at the microeconomic level that economic agents display rational behavior when they seek to increase their gains over the short or medium term, and in doing so seek their orientation in the given system of economic incentives. These incentives are as a rule organized in such a way as to favor private utility vis-à-vis public utility: profits made in the timber trade are based on extremely low concession fees or land prices, so that the costs of stemwood production reflect only the costs of logging operations and transportation, but not the (opportunity) costs that accrue in replenishing timber stands. A balance between private and public utility would call for changes in the intertemporal allocation (postponement of present utility stemming from overexploitation in favor of future utility stemming from adapting logging operations to the rhythm of natural regeneration) and sectoral allocation (restriction of the conversion of forests to agricultural areas). These changes, the argument goes, can be achieved by initiating regulatory measures in the areas of economic, fiscal, and environmental policy as well as through international compensation payments from the industrialized countries to the tropical countries (for lost or unrealized present utility).

The specialized studies on the timber trade and the timber industry broaden the analysis by pointing to the inefficiency of extracting and processing tropical timber, a state of affairs that is explained with reference to the allegedly inexhaustible timber reserves in natural forests and the – as it were – cost-free provision of logs. The squandering of tropical timber was intensified by the export bans on logs which were used in the 1970s by many tropical countries (except Sarawak and Sabah in Malaysia) to promote local processing. The export bans led to a drastic jump in the domestic supply of stemwood, which lowered log prices in domestic markets. The consequence of this was that domestic producers were not compelled to introduce efficient processing methods.

The studies explicitly concerned with the Brazilian part of the Amazon emphasize that it was not the timber industry that drove the deforestation process but a Brazilian development policy that was geared to bringing this huge region closer to Brazil's economic centers with an eye to an economic exploitation of the natural resources present there. Brazil's development policy centered on an agricultural development of the region, first through large-scale cattle ranches, which were initially supported with lavish subsidies, and then by means of settlement programs for smallholders along the Transamazônica and in Rondônia. The timber industry arrived in the region as a free-rider along with the road-building and colonization programs. Its share in primary deforestation was small; but it did profit directly from the timber supply accruing in connection with the forest clearance undertaken to win arable land and indirectly from infrastructure development, the growth in the labor supply, and tax breaks (e.g. complete exemption from income taxes for 10 years) that were granted to them along with most other new businesses operating in the Amazon region. Compliance with forest legislation, which had been in force since the 1930s and was tightened up in 1965 to include restrictive provisions on native forest exploitation, was as a rule not monitored by the environmental authorities.

In reviewing the literature on forest utilization in the tropics and in particular in the Amazon region the following points can be observed:

– Methodological: as a rule the authors analyze the incentive system, in order then to draw direct conclusions on the behavior of the economic agents, instead of starting out by investigating social action apart from the incentives and the observable results, in order then to arrive at propositions on causal relations;

– sectoral: as a rule the authors view the field of inquiry defined as "tropical-forest utilization" in multisectoral terms in that they deal with all economic sectors active in the tropical forest (including agriculture, forestry, mining, and the timber industry), but they just as often neglect to place the development of the market for tropical timber in the general context of the world market for wood products, which leads them to make flawed assessments of future demand (and thus also of the present and future economic value of tropical-timber resources); in the case of Brazil the Amazon timber industry is investigated without taking account of the economics of timber plantations and the dynamic pulp and paper industry in the south of Brazil.

The consequence of these shortcomings is that a number of studies involve implicit assumptions that are not empirically verified, though they can have a pronounced influence on the results. Recent studies on the Amazon region are based on the notion that since the Amazon tropical forests are huge in area and abundantly endowed with timber resources, the timber industry must be gigantic in size. This notion has contributed to the formation of "modern myths" about the economic potential of the timber industry. The figures on the timber felled, the number of sawmills in operation, the profits realized, the extent of deforestation, and the international demand for tropical timber can never be big enough; as a rule there is no discussion on the official data, although the poor quality of the statistical data, at least in the field of natural resources, is generally well known. The following evidence is as a rule adduced to demonstrate the hugeness of the Amazon timber industry:

–   according to statistics of the Brazilian Geographic Institute IBGE that are cited by all of the relevant studies, some 82 % of the roundwood industrially processed in Brazil (without the consumption of the pulp industry) stems from the Amazon region, over 70 % of it from the state of Pará alone. The register of the environmental protection agency IBAMA lists over 2,400 wood-processing companies for Pará alone and some 3,200 for the Amazon region as a whole. For 1990 the IMAZON institute calculated for a typical sawmill in Pará an average net profit rate of roughly 20 %; for sawmills specialized in mahogany it estimated annual profits of up to US$ one million.

–   The purchase of bankrupt sawmills, plywood factories, and large areas of forest in Pará and the Amazon region by Asian timber corporations in 1997 is, for many authors, proof of the growing international interest in the Amazon tropical forest. Entrepreneurs hope (and environmentalists fear) that the investments made by these corporations will – in the end – lead to a massive increase in exports of Amazon timber, ushering in a Golden Age for the industry.

A sober analysis of the situation, however, reveals a somewhat different reality:

–   in calculating roundwood production the contribution of eucalyptus and pine plantations is normally neglected, although, according to IBGE data, 60 % of the timber industrially processed in Brazil is eucalyptus and pine. If this figure is included in the calculation, Pará's share of the roundwood output in Brazil drops from 82 % to just over 40 %. According to empirical investigations conducted by IMAZON, Pará's share of Brazil's timber output amounts to no more than some 29 %.[5]

– The number of sawmills in operation in the Amazon region is also far lower than what is indicated by IBAMA: IMAZON counted no more than 780 mills in Pará and roughly 1451 for the Amazon region as a whole.[6]

– In contrast to the great expectations fanned again and again since the 1960s by the Amazon region's opulent timber resources (Pandolfo 1994 and SUDAM 1973a), the Amazon timber industry has not succeeded in developing into a dynamic sector, boosting the region's industrialization process and providing a broadly effective improvement of incomes there. The Amazon region's share in the gross value added of Brazil's timber, furniture, and pulp/paper industries increased between 1960 and 1985 from 0.8 to 5.6 %. The timber industry's growth was based above all on an increase of the number of sawmills and plywood factories; in the furniture and pulp/paper industries (the most dynamic sector) the Amazon region's share was negligible.

– Finally, the interest of Asian corporations in the Amazon region's natural-forest resources in no way mirrors an increased international demand for tropical timber. On the contrary, the share of tropical timber in the world market is on the decline, while timber products from planted forests in the industrialized countries continue to enjoy a dominant position. At the same time, the world market share of wood panels and pulp won from the eucalyptus and pine plantations in the new production sites of the southern hemisphere (Chile, New Zealand, the south of Brazil) as well as in Spain and Portugal is on the increase. These plantations are monocultures; their operation entails risks for the stability of ecosystems (decrease of biodiversity, impairment of the hydrological cycle and soil fertility) and often leads to a displacement of the traditional rural population. Thanks to the great number of industrial uses to which homogeneous wood fibers can be put, plantations can offer greater profitability than would be possible with the use of timber from primary forests (Mather 1997; Dudley, Jeanrenaud and Sullivan (1995).

But myth formation is not merely an empirical problem. The researcher's interest in his/her subject of inquiry, and thus also in his/her choice of the segment he/she investigates and his/her decision on which empirical data are important and unimportant, is determined above all by the theoretical approach he/she has selected. A critique of the above-named results would miss its mark if it sought its orientation only in an empirically underpinned counterargument. A more precise analysis of the dynamics of the Amazon timber industry calls for theoretical-methodological instruments that have proven their mettle in dealings with the premises and propositions of the dominant approaches encountered in natural-resource economics and ecological economics.

But before we embark on the task, a brief word on the debate over sustainable development, which today constitutes both the normative and the systematic frame of reference for nearly all investigations concerned with the utilization of natural resources.

2.2   Sustainable Development

The debate over sustainable development, which got underway in the 1960s at the latest, documents the break with the notion that improvements of living standards achieved in the present will automatically – in the sense of a linear or cumulative increase in welfare – contribute to creating better life chances for future generations. Entire economic and development policies, strategies, and programs had rested on this notion; the general goal of many programs of the postwar era had been to propagate throughout the world the model of society and the standard of living perceived as typical of the USA.[7]

The break with this notion is mirrored in the definition given in 1987 by the Brundtland Commission: *"Sustainable development is development that meets the needs of the present without compromising the ability of future generations to meet their own needs."* (WCED 1987, p. 43) This definition makes it clear that the satisfaction of present needs may, in the same or even in larger measure, inhibit, or indeed even prevent, the satisfaction of the needs of a future generation. The normative task of economic and development policy, to improve the people's living conditions at the national and international level, thus now also includes the responsibility to do so in such a way that future life chances are not impaired.

The Brundtland Report popularized the concept of sustainable development, outlining a new conception of development that interlinked the environmental current, with its growth critique, with the current that linked the development of the South with a reorganization of the world economic order and an orientation toward the satisfaction of basic needs. The phase of the critique expressed by the Brundtland Commission coincides with the emergence of ecological economics, whose main point of criticism was the incompatibility of continuously high growth with the aims of environmental and natural-resource protection.

The Brundtland Commission's definition sees as the goal of sustainable development the satisfaction of the needs of present and future generations; the Commission indicates eight means of reaching this goal: reinvigorated growth; qualitative modification of growth; satisfaction of basic needs in the areas of employment, nutrition, energy, water, and health; reduction of population growth; protection and improvement of the resource base; technological reorientation and risk management; consideration of the environmental and economic dimension in all decisions; reorganization of international economic relations (WCED 1987, p. 49).

The UN Conference on Environment and Development in 1992 in Rio de Janeiro took over and refined the definition of means; the following statements in the Rio declaration are of central significance:

–   It is acknowledged that the developing countries have a right to development as a precondition for the satisfaction of the economic, social, and environmental needs of present and future generations (Principle 3);

–   all states are called upon to cooperate for the protection and restitution of the global environment and to share the resulting costs on the basis of the principle of "common but differentiated responsibilities" (Principle 7); which is to say that the industrialized countries, in view of their great share both in the degradation of the environment and the technical and financial problem-solving resources largely in their possession, will have to make advance concessions and/or take on higher costs;

– all signatories are obliged to introduce effective environmental legislation and to establish protection goals adapted to their specific development level (Principle 11);

– finally, all states are called upon to promote free trade and open economic systems that accelerate economic growth, in this way helping to make sustainable development possible and to prevent environmental degradation (Principle 12).

The Rio compromise consists in linking the growth orientation of the economic system to effective environmental-protection measures. Without the commitment of all signatories, including in particular the dynamically growing developing countries in Asia and Latin America, to an effective environmental protection, the commitment to free trade would certainly not have been made. That is to say that the global economic efficiency gains that result from free trade and can at least theoretically be translated into broadly effective welfare gains are not to be achieved at the expense of the environment. This is to be ensured by means of effective environmental regulations at the national and international level. This was intended to encounter two fundamental reservations as regards the compatibility of a growth-oriented economic system and the conservation of natural life-support systems:[8]

– The first reservation concerns the biophysical limits of growth defined by the finite character of nonrenewable resources, the danger of overexploitation of renewable resources (which could lead to a collapse of their regeneration capacity), and an overstrain of the assimilation capacity of the environment for the by- and waste products of production and consumption (e.g. toxic wastes, CO_2 emissions). What is behind this reservation is the premise that "natural capital" can in the end not be replaced by man-made capital; the accumulation of monetary values or technology (in the form of knowledge, machines, and plant) is no replacement for the fundamental biogeochemical processes that make life on earth possible.[9] The premise concerning the biophysical limits of growth fundamentally challenges the view of development economics that investment of the returns stemming from the exploitation of natural resources in the development of other industries constitutes an accumulation process involving growing net returns.

–   The second reservation concerns the possibility that an economy might use external trade to expand its consumption of energy and material beyond the "natural" (ecosystem-related) limits on the carrying capacity of its geographic territory, thus burdening other economies with the costs of its patterns of production and consumption.

These reservations were encountered on the one hand through the definition of rules for dealings with natural resources and on the other hand with the familiar economic argument that genuine free trade would trigger development surges in the countries of the South that could be used to initiate a process of structural change, to develop efficient modern enterprises, and to achieve broad-based income improvements.

The rules for the use of natural resources entailed the establishment of operational targets which are intended to be used as orientation points for environmental instruments to control production and consumption with a view to ensuring sustainability in the sense of the continuous provision of a supply of resources and the protection of natural life-support systems as well as to curbing the dynamics of growth:[10]

–   The rate at which renewable natural resources are used must not exceed their natural rate of regeneration.

–   The level of emissions into the natural environment must not over-burden the assimilation capacity of ecosystems, i.e. the effective functioning of ecosystems must not be impaired.

–   The use of nonrenewable resources must go hand in hand with the parallel development of a supply of renewable resources of comparable utility.

–   The temporal dimension of human interventions in the environment (e.g. reduction rate of emissions) must be in a reasonable relation to the temporal dimension of the natural processes that are decisive for the assimilative capacity of the ecosystems.

–   Risks and dangers to human beings and the effective functioning of
    ecosystems which are caused by human activity must be avoided.

There are quite different views on what environmental- and economic-
policy instruments can best be used to put these rules into practice.
Various theoretical views on the significance of the environment within
the process of economic development have considerable influence both
on the detailed definition of development goals and on the choice of the
instruments to be used. They represent different paradigms of the relation between nature and society which have developed inside the discipline of economics and elsewhere (Pearce and Turner 1990; Colby
1991).

Each of the paradigms contains aspects relevant for the analysis of the
use patterns of natural resources. For each paradigm as well as for
mixed forms of them we can find examples in the literature on the utilization of tropical forests in general and the Amazon region in particular. The dominant approaches stem from natural-resource economics;
depending on their theoretical orientation, they advocate either the introduction or enforcement of property rights or the creation of markets
for the use of environmental resources. The biophysical limits for the
economic exploitation of resources are as a rule underlined in the studies in question, indeed these limits are often even the point of departure
of the analysis, and to this extent we can note a broad diffusion and
acceptance of this central premise of ecological economics. The social
dimension of the (sustainable) exploitation of tropical-forest resources
is as a rule neglected: Persons who are actively engaged in resource
exploitation and whose activities are to be changed appear in the analyses only in the abstract. The reasons for the dominant destructive exploitation patterns are derived from interest-driven agent responses to
given incentive systems; the need to change this exploitation pattern is
grounded with reference to the paramount logic of global environmental protection. This construct necessarily gives rise to a practically
unbridgeable gulf between local and global interests, which makes it
increasingly more difficult to envision enforceable measures in the area
of environmental and economic policy.

Table 1:   Economic Paradigms of the Relation between Nature and Society in Development

Paradigm	Frontier Economics	Environmental and Natural Resource Economics		Ecological Economics	Deep Ecology
		Environmental Protection	Natural Resource Management		
Model	"progress" as infinite growth of economy and welfare	"tradeoff" between economic growth and environmental protection	"sustainability" as precondition for "green growth"	"sustainability" sets absolute natural limits to the growth of the economic subsystem	"ecotopia", against growth, in favor of harmony with nature
Relation between nature and society	very markedly anthropocentric	anthropocentric	moderately anthropocentric	moderately anthropocentric	ecocentric
Major threats	famine, poverty, disease, "natural disasters"	disease due to pollution, threats to flora and fauna	natural-resource degradation, poverty, population growth	uncertainty, irreversible changes of the functions of the global ecosystem	breakdown of global ecosystem, natural disasters caused by man
Main issues	free goods, exploitation of infinite natural resources	environmental protection ("end-of-pipe" clean-up, legalization as economic externality)	global efficiency, internalization of environmental costs	ecologize the economy, co-evolution of society and nature	back to nature, equality of all species
Who pays?	property owners (individuals or state)	polluter, taxpayer	polluter, producers and consumers	pollution prevention pays, ecological tax reform	avoid costs by avoiding development
Shortcomings of the paradigm	creative but mechanistic; no awareness of significance of natural life-support systems	concessions of frontier economics to environmental movement	fails to adequately consider social factors and uncertainty	transition from growth economy to steady-state economy remains unclear	how to reduce world population and the level of economic growth and welfare

Table 1 (continued)

Economic and environmental strategies	technical progress, growth, substitution of natural capital by man-made capital, free self-regulating markets	technical progress, growth, substitution of natural capital by man-made capital, end-of-pipe technologies, command-and-control regulations	technical progress, "green" growth, risk management, reduction of population growth	qualitative growth, sufficiency in the North, management of uncertainty, prevention of dangers and pollution, technical progress is no absolute solution, reduction of population growth	stability as a goal, reduction of size of market economy and world trade, reduction of world population
Instruments	energy and input-intensive production systems, high R&D expenditure (conquest of space)	property rights, creation of markets for environmental goods, get the prices right, some prohibitions and limits, market-based compensation payments from Northern to Southern countries		creation of markets for environmental goods, limits for the use of environmental goods, cooperation between public and private actors, between North and South (compensation payments)	low technical level, traditional knowledge
Analytical approach and planning methods	neoclassical or Marxist, closed economic system, reversible equilibria, maximization of net present value	neoclassical plus environmental impact assessment, optimal pollution level, willingness to pay, compensation payments	neoclassical plus natural capital, ecological GNP, environmental and social monitoring	economy as an open system embedded in biogeochemical processes; cost-benefit analysis and calculation of optimal depletion rate	bioregional planning from below, conservation of cultural and biological diversity, economic autonomy instead of linkages / globalization

Source: adapted from Colby (1991)

Environmental and resource economics takes over from allocation theory the reduction of economic decisions to instrumental rationales and then applies them to the exploitation of natural resources. The premises and the scope of this approach are the subject of the following section.

2.3   Environmental and Resource Economics[11]

Environmental economics is concerned with general issues from the interface between economic and natural systems, while resource economics deals with more specific issues bound up with the utilization of renewable and nonrenewable natural resources.

Both disciplines emerged in the 1960s as it was becoming clear that in modern industrial societies growth rates entail high levels of environmental and health burdens which large segments of the population were no longer willing to accept and which it would be very expensive to remedy.[12] Environmental economics is concerned with the microeconomic, static analysis of economic externalities that arise in connection with the use of environmental goods as consumer goods. The causes of environmental problems must be sought in the fact that, for instance, a firm derives benefits from the cost-free use of an environmental good, while nonparticipating third parties (as a rule the general public) are forced to bear the detriments of this exploitation of the environment. This is the case, for instance, for production-related emissions into air and water, and the environmental regulations obliging the polluters to avoid such emissions have been in effect for not more than a few decades. Natural resource economics, on the other hand, focuses on the problem of the intertemporal allocation of natural resources and for this reason provides dynamic analyses of optimal economical dealings with renewable and nonrenewable resources, which nature provides in limited quantities.[13]

The following premises are some of the basic elements of economic modeling that, geared to analyzing defined issues, are now being expanded to cover the natural environment:

–   The market is the most efficient mechanism for allocating scarce resources; under the conditions of competition among individual agents in the marketplace, the egoistic, rational behavior of individuals leads to an optimal satisfaction of both individual and aggregate social needs.

- The economic exploitation of natural resources is institutionalized, through private property rights, collective use rights, or other legal forms.

- The functioning of the market mechanism is explained with reference to the Pareto-optimum: every individual decides freely what supply best meets his demand, no one is forced into a decision. Under these conditions no one takes a decision that does not fully satisfy him under the given constraints. What goes for the individual (once an exchange has taken place, no one is worse off than beforehand) holds true for the aggregate as well.

- The precondition for any complete freedom of decision is, apart from the absence of power, perfect information on the part of all market participants on present and future supply and demand.

- Under these conditions a good's market price comes about via the balance of demand and supply, i.e. price (and its fluctuations) is an expression of scarcity and nonscarcity.

- Demand results from the preferences of individuals, which must be viewed as given.

Proceeding on these premises, environmental problems, their costs, and their redressal or avoidance can be formulated as follows: under the condition of an efficient price system there is no reason to doubt the feasibility and desirability of economic growth, what is meant by efficiency here is that the prices will include the costs required to reestablish or preserve the quality of the environment under the condition of economic activity at high and rising levels. As a response to rising prices, technical progress (e.g. by more efficient utilization or discovering possibilities of substitution) will counter any further scarcity of natural resources. Technical progress in any case constantly increases the productivity of labor and capital; this trend could be expanded to cover natural resources as well, if it were possible to integrate them into the market mechanism.

The economization of the environment is conceived in two forms: the first form states that the environment is appropriated by private owners who, as rational economic agents, will seek to maximize their individual utility by means of a utilization as efficient as possible, thus at the same time safeguarding the collective interest. This approach goes back to Coase (1960) and states that market failure (= environmental pollution, overexploitation of resources) comes about when property rights are either not clearly defined or when they are not assigned to those agents who will profit most by the most efficient use of the environment. For this approach the public sector as a surrogate owner is no alternative to the private owner in that the public owner will also show a propensity to maximize its individual utility, e.g. by giving in to the short-term use interests of pressure groups. Advocates of the property-rights approach would thus concede that there is market failure, though this would not lead them to assume any superiority on the part of collective institutions.

One example from tropical forestry, discussed in Chapters 6 and 7 of the present study, is the controversy surrounding the superiority of concessions (and the adequate shape given to them) as opposed to private ownership of forests. In Asia and Africa the rule is that the state owns the forests and grants private use rights in the form of concessions. The destructive exploitation observed in most cases of concessions is described in the literature as a consequence of the short duration of the concession agreements and the falsely conceived royalty system (payment estimated on the basis of the quantity of timber felled and not the supply of timber available) (Repetto and Gillis 1988). In Brazil no exploitation of forests is possible without a land title, and the dominant form of exploitation is all the same destructive: this form of exploitation is typical for public land or areas earmarked for conversion to arable or grazing land; in the latter case the forests on private land are kept in reserve. The advocates of sustainable forest management in the Amazon region argue either with reference to the private-property approach (the Asian and African experiences with concessions are claimed to show what that model leads to) or with reference to the concession model (it is only here that the environmental authorities have the say and can exercise real influence on logging operations). Both groups know that the decisive factor is the restriction on free access to public land.

In the view of the second form, the state, as the protector of higher-level interests, uses taxes and fees to ensure that the exploitation of natural resources has its price, and thus figures in the economic rationale of private agents. Pollution or overexploitation is, it is true, viewed as market failure, but solutions based on the introduction of property rights are seen as inadequate. The activities of private owners should find their orientation in the optimal level of exploitation, according to which marginal utility would correspond to the marginal costs of regeneration. This, however, thanks to the general problem of imperfect information and the not entirely predictable consequences of the degradation / overexploitation of environmental goods, does not translate out into practicable policy. So environmental-protection standards must be set politically; the job of economics is to determine the most cost-effective packages of policy measures. The definition of standards and instruments is not a neutral process that can be geared to objective economic and ecological data; it is instead a search process determined by trial and error and keyed to coming up with results that are "satisficing" instead of "optimal."[14]

The most important arguments of the critique advanced against environmental economics, with its neoclassical hue – arguments not always intended to justify a radical alternative but often, in the absence of them, keyed to pointing out weaknesses – are the following:[15]

–   The **value concept** of economics cannot be used to evaluate environmental goods;

–   the trust placed in the **market mechanism** is untenable;

–   ditto the trust placed in the **price mechanism**, which is supposed to indicate changes in scarcities even for environmental factors and natural resources;

–   the trust placed in **technical progress** and the unlimited substitutability of natural capital by man-made capital is unwarranted;

–   finally, it cannot be assumed that **ecosystems** will inevitably recover from human interventions.

In mainstream economics the **value** of a good is viewed as equivalent to its monetary value as expressed in the individual preferences of consumers, i.e. demand. Here value is the outcome of the interaction between the demander and the object of his demand; this interaction is made up primarily of the demander's goals, which are to be reached by acquiring the object. Value accordingly has a pronouncedly subjective dimension inasmuch as it is posited as a function of the specific evaluative context of the demander (his ends). It is thus relatively independent of the overall spectrum of qualities inherent in the object.

If a price is to be assigned to the exploitation of the environment as a means of tying the latter into economic decision-making, environmental goods must be evaluated. This is normally done by determining rehabilitation costs (e.g. the costs resulting from water purification would be included in the water prices) or the willingness to pay on the part of those concerned. To calculate willingness to pay, we can take either individual preferences – e.g. if we are considering tourists who are willing to pay to visit a protected natural park – or collective preferences when the issue is to preserve a collective good like clean air. Collective preferences also rest on this form of individual valuation, i.e. on the extent to which the taxpayer is prepared to bear the costs required to safeguard the collective good.

It is precisely in dealing with the economic valuation of environmental goods that the subjective concept of value poses problems, since as a rule these goods are collective goods. The case is often such that conservation values are not perceivable from the individual perspective, or the costs of conservation are distributed unevenly across individuals. Owing to its objectivity, the concept of natural life-support systems goes beyond the scope of the value concept held by neoclassical economics.

The trust placed in the **market mechanism** (whose effectiveness is said to be safeguarded by the activities of rational environment-owners or by means of efficiency-related prices) is bound up with heroic assumptions that pose considerable difficulties for their defenders when the issue involved is no more than economic decisions; the matter is more difficult still when the concern is to take account of the environmental dimension. The critique of this position has various dimensions:

– A more exact (empirical and historical) observation of markets shows that they do not function as an aggregation of individuals acting on a voluntary basis but form social institutions whose functioning is in turn dependent on other social (historically contingent) institutions (like, for instance, legal certainty, realization of a monetary economy). These social institutions shape individual and collective behavior.

– Individual preferences, which are seen by neoclassical economics as exogenously determined and thus as given, are molded in cultural-historical terms and change over the course of time. Individuals have both private preferences and general preferences referred to the collective; the relations of the preferences to each other are marked by different historical balances. The neoclassical concept of rationality, however, ahistorically assumes unchanging, homogenous preferences on the part of economic agents that are geared exclusively to individual utility.

– Agents active in the market never have perfect information; nor do they ever act in power-free spaces.[16]

The trust placed in the **price mechanism** has likewise proven problematical: How are natural life-support systems to be priced, since they are used collectively and cannot be split up into individually utilizable units (e.g. air, biodiversity)? Price approximations can be derived from calculation of the costs of purification technologies and determination of user willingness to pay; but these are no more than approximations, and they provide no guarantee that the "ecological value" for present and future generations will be fully internalized. With natural raw materials we have the problem that in the long and short term price changes seem hardly to be affected by scarcity; on the contrary: we can note empirically that prices for raw materials are falling in relation to the prices for industrial goods.[17] This is above all bound up with the fact that both the information on the scope of resources available and the calculation of the period of time for which these stocks will suffice are necessarily marked by a large measure of uncertainty. For nonrenewable raw materials, the information on the size of stocks has been corrected again and again by new prospecting successes; calculating the time-frame for the stocks available is made difficult by changes in demand, i.e. by the breadth and significance of the economically relevant technical usability of a given raw material. The consequence is that current raw-material prices are unable to mirror future scarcities.

Box 1:   Rubber Boom

The classical product example in the context of the Amazon region for the extensive impacts of technical progress is rubber: As early as in the 18th century scientific attention had been attracted to latex, a waterproof material used by the indigenous peoples of the Amazon region to make shoes. Once the process of vulcanization had been invented, the way was open for an industrial utilization of natural rubber, for which great demand had arisen in connection with the growth of the bicycle and automobile industries as well as other branches of industry. Natural rubber was obtained from a tree species (*Hevea brasiliensis*) which – like most other species – occurred only sporadically in the forest; so rubber tappers had to walk relatively long distances between the individual tapping points.

The trading establishments that supplied the world market with rubber from the towns of Manaus and Belém sought to increase yields by organizing expeditions far into the forests and to step up profits by exploiting labor by means of peonage (Santos 1980). In parallel to this, experiments were being conducted with the aim of considerably reducing the costs of rubber production: as early as the middle of the 19th century – when the rubber boom was just beginning to take shape – British greenhouses were already experimenting with cultivating rubber trees in plantations. 1910 saw the first deliveries to the world market from Malaysia, and within two years Brazilian rubber exports had collapsed. The Malaysian rubber plantations were not only able to increase production according to plan, they were also – thanks to the concentration of trees in a smaller area – far more cost-effective in production.

It was only then that the first experiments with setting up rubber plantations were begun in the Amazon region; but the most spectacular attempt, made by Henry Ford in the west of Pará, failed as a result of the ecological conditions (monocultures of native plants are extremely vulnerable to pests) (Dean 1987; Costa 1993). Only in the south of Brazil, in the state of São Paulo, for instance, were rubber plantations more or less productive. But these plantations, too, were more expensive in production than their Malaysian counterparts.

The great variety of dynamic effects of **technical progress** plays a major role here:

– improved extraction/production technologies are increasing the exploitable stocks of raw materials, and thus their supply,[18]

– the development of surrogate materials or wholly new technologies lowers the demand for the original raw material concerned.[19]

What is important for economic dynamics is above all the second level of effect: in the last hundred years growing demand for natural raw materials has often led to their substitution by synthetic materials, in this way influencing the quantitative supply and the costs of production and extraction. This as a rule guided demand away from the natural raw material and toward the raw material that was synthesized or reproduced in artificial production systems.

At a fundamental level ecological economics has been concerned with the limited scope of technical progress – i.e. the substitutability of natural capital by man-made capital – as well as with the function of ecosystems for the economy, and, proceeding from these positions, has developed a very extensive critique of mainstream economics.

2.4   Ecological Economics

Unlike neoclassical environmental economics, ecological economics does not proceed by transferring its efficiency concepts to nonmarket goods like environmental goods, seeking instead to re-embed economic processes in the context of the utilization of nature. Bearing this common feature in mind, we can identify different currents of this approach which set different theoretical-methodological priorities. These currents include as approaches the coevolution of ecological and economic systems (Norgaard), an attempt to broaden neoclassical environmental economics (Pearce), and approaches that borrow on Geogescu-Roegen's analysis of the consequences of the laws of thermodynamics for the field of economics, seeking to further develop this approach (Daly, Costanza).

The basic idea of ecological economics is to view the earth as an eco-system whose finite nature sets limits on growth and the maximum dimensions of subsystems. This entails a shift of the perspective on ecology: thinking no longer centers on economic valuation (the prob-lem of neoclassical environmental and natural-resource economics) but on the question how it is possible to limit the expansion of the eco-nomic subsystem. This view, new to economics, which radically alters the object domain of economic analysis and the parameters for efficient allocative decisions, has developed on the basis of the influence of two noneconomic disciplines, ecology (biology) and thermodynamics (physics). Impressed by the environmental movement, several econo-mists in the 1960s began to look for new impulses in these disciplines with a view to coming up with a better understanding of processes at the interface between economics and nature.[20] The work of Georgescu-Roegen on the significance of the law of entropy for the economic pro-cess paved the way for this new approach.

Ecology is a subdiscipline of biology, one that investigates the relations between organisms and their environment; in so doing it breaks nature down into different ecosystems with specific characteristics.[21] What is important for the analysis of the interface between environment and economy is the propositions made by ecology on the composition and the development dynamics of ecosystems. This information can be used to understand the impacts of human interventions in ecosystems and to better assess their economic scope.

Composition: Ecosystems are made up of abiotic (nonliving) and biotic (living) elements; the former are subdivided into anorganic and organic elements, the latter into producers, consumers, and decomposers. The producers are the green plants that take up solar energy and convert it into chemical energy (photosynthesis), in this way making it accessible to other organisms; they constitute the basis for any assimilation of energy by consumers and decomposers. Consumers are animals that find their nourishment in plants or other (herbi- or carnivorous) ani-mals. Decomposers are microorganisms, bacteria and fungi, that break down plant and animal material into simpler components, resupplying the producers with nutrients in the process. Decomposers are instru-mental in recycling matter and/or nutrients within an ecosystem.

Modern ecology discerns two levels of ecosystem integration: the first level is that of populations; ecologists here study how in a given habitat the population of organisms of one species changes in terms of its size, density, growth potential, and the type of natural selection process in which it finds itself. The second level is that of the community of different species that stand in direct and indirect interrelation to one another in a given area, a factor that controls their continued existence. The third level is the ecosystem itself, which consists of several communities that interact with their physical environment.

Development dynamics: Ecosystems develop in a long-term succession process in which in the course of time different states of equilibrium are succeeded by one another (thus succession). This is an ordered, unidirectional process. At each stage the complexity and the biomass of the ecosystem increases, while its characteristic features change. The dynamics of succession results from changes of the physical environment that are caused by the plant and animal communities; succession is controlled by the communities that make up the ecosystem. The physical environment (the abiotic elements, the climate, etc.) determines the patterns, the rate of change, and the scope of succession. The succession process culminates in a stable state of equilibrium (climax), in which a maximum of biomass and symbiotic functions can be sustained.

Natural succession permits ecosystems to develop complex limiting feedback mechanisms that safeguard their stability in two respects:

- by expanding the ecosystem's control over the physical environment and protecting the former from external disorders, and

- by regulating the density and size of the populations and communities.[22]

How does ecology define the relation between man and his natural environment? On the one hand man, as a consumer of plant and animal biomass, moves for the most part at the end of complex food chains; even if it were possible to imitate the processes of photosynthesis, thus putting an end to dependence on natural biomass production, artificial nutrient production would be forced to make use of cells that have come about by natural means. On the other hand man is the only species that has developed the ability to manage its physical environment in the interest of its survival; here it has only rarely been possible to find a balance between the roles of inhabitant and manipulator of ecosystems.

A disturbed balance between man and the environment impairs the stability and the resilience of the ecosystem. Stability is the ability to maintain relatively constant values in species composition, biomass, and productivity and to restore this relative equilibrium rapidly following short-term external impacts (steady state, stable oscillation). Resilience is the ability of the ecosystem to retain its structure and extension by means of long-term adaptive processes. One example for the purpose of illustration: A forest ecosystem can maintain its equilibrium in the face of rates of precipitation declining for seasonal reasons by using deep roots to supply itself from groundwater. The composition of the species is adapted to these seasonally limited moisture shortfalls. A resilient ecosystem responds to longer-term climatic change by altering its species composition and giving preference to trees and other plants with lower moisture needs (and smaller evaporation areas).

Human interventions can trigger changes that impair the structure of ecosystems, thus endangering their stability-guaranteeing mechanisms. These include changes of biodiversity and population levels which hamper the process of succession. If, on the other hand, human management methods seek their orientation in the natural paths of succession and use the natural control and stabilization mechanisms, human utilization presents no obstacle to ecological stability and resilience.

Damage to ecosystems can cause a collapse of natural limiting feedback mechanisms, which are replaced by positive feedback mechanisms: the latter intensify the initial disorder through new, successive ecological interactions instead of alleviating and isolating it, in this way finally leading to the termination of the original succession and the buildup of a new ecosystem. An example would be the formation of savannas on forest land that was cleared in response to demand for timber or farmland, eroded by precipitation and wind, and whose natural plant cover cannot be restored by natural means – i.e. without external energy inputs in the form of fertilizers, saplings, etc.

Thermodynamics is a branch of physics concerned with the transformation of energy into work (mechanically usable energy) and waste heat (unusable energy).[23] What is important here for the economic-ecological analysis is the first and second laws of thermodynamics and the concept of entropy.

The First Law of Thermodynamics states that the quantity of energy and matter is constant (can neither be created nor destroyed) and therefore remains constant, though in an altered form, even when it has been transformed.

The Second Law of Thermodynamics refers to the flow of energy in a system, distinguishing between free (accessible) and bound (inaccessible) energy. Free energy is unevenly distributed and occurs only in high-order forms, e.g. the kinetic energy of a waterfall or in fossil fuels. These qualitative characteristics make it possible for it to be transformed into mechanical work. Bound energy comes about as a byproduct of the transformation of energy and matter, takes the form of waste energy, is distributed uniformly (dissipation), and cannot be used for mechanical work. An example: in the combustion of anthracite, a fossil fuel with a comparatively high energy concentration, part of the resulting heat can be used, e.g. for heating water, while another part is dissipated in space, its potential direct use being "lost." The Second Law of Thermodynamics states on the one hand that the transformation of energy into work is always accompanied by a loss of energy in the form of waste heat and that the energy transformed into work can later also be transformed into bound energy. It on the other hand states that heat can pass spontaneously only from a hotter to a colder body, never the other way around. This means that the flow of energy is a directional process with a predictable end.

The Second Law of Thermodynamics defines the concept of entropy: the measure for the qualitative state of energy in a system (according to the Second Law the quantity of energy of course remains constant). Entropy increases when the energy in a system passes from an accessible to an inaccessible state. Entropy is thus a negative measure referring to the utility of energy. An increase of entropy entails a decrease of utility.

On the Compatibility of Evolution / Ecological Succession and the Second Law of Thermodynamics[24]

Evolution is normally described as a process in which the complexity of organisms or systems grows in the direction of increasingly organized systems. This description appears at first glance to contradict the Second Law of Thermodynamics, which in its classical form assumes that in isolated systems entropy rises, tending toward a maximum of disorder. How can this contradiction be resolved?

To measure entropy exactly it is usual to proceed on the assumption of isolated systems; to be able to describe the process according to the rules of mechanical physics, we proceed on the assumption of very slow processes that can be reversed without causing permanent damage to the system environment. These conditions are as a rule not given in reality: neither is it possible to exactly measure entropy nor are the environmental changes caused by macroscopic thermodynamic changes reversible.

Thermodynamics distinguishes between three system types: closed systems that exchange with their environment only energy but not matter; open systems that exchange with their environment both energy and matter; and isolated systems that exchange with their environment neither matter nor energy. Based on this definition the earth is defined as a closed system that absorbs solar energy, giving off waste heat, but not matter.

Living systems are open systems that exchange energy and matter with their environment. That means that the process of their evolutionary development into higher states of complexity cannot be explained by theories based on quantifiable events in isolated systems. One way out of this aporia is the theory of dissipative structures which the physicist Prigogine developed by applying the entropy concept of classical thermodynamics to open systems in disequilibrium, and hence also to irreversible processes such as biological change and evolution. He defines entropy by using an interpretation of the Second Law of Thermodynamics grounded in probability theory which conceives entropy not as a state of equilibrium but as the measure for a state between two possible micro- or macroscopic states. The Second Law then states for this case:

"Systems do not tend to pass into states that are less probable than the state in which they are." This makes it possible to study systems outside a state of equilibrium.

Prigogine (Prigogine 1973; Prigogine and Stengers 1980) distinguishes two types of entropy change: increase of entropy within a system due to irreversible processes and the flow of entropy out of a system due to exchange processes between system and environment (dissipation). It is possible for open systems to dissipate an increase of entropy, in this way keeping the entropy level in the system low, thus moving away from the state of thermodynamic equilibrium.

> *„All evolutionary changes of open systems towards higher complexity can be explained by this relation that shows how evolution comes to terms with the Second Law of Thermodynamics. Systems far from thermodynamic equilibrium can only develop and maintain their low entropy states by constant dissipation of energy and matter from their environment."* (Binswanger 1993, p. 215)

New structures arise when the assimilation of energy and matter from the system's environment and the ensuing entropy emissions into the system's environment are so high that certain transition phases are exceeded and the system is unable to return to its original state. This new state is even further removed from thermodynamic equilibrium than the old state, but to maintain its stability it continues to need a high input of free entropy and the corresponding possibilities of dissipation.

The most important proposition of the theory of dissipative structures is that evolution and the maintenance of open systems in a state of disequilibrium is possible only on the basis of irreversible thermodynamic processes that dissipate energy and matter from the environment, in this way increasing entropy in the environment. The growth of entropy in the environment increases to the extent that the system's internal state moves away from thermodynamic equilibrium, i.e. as order and complexity increase (Binswanger 1993, p. 216).

So the theory of dissipative structures can be used to describe life cycles of ecosystems and their evolution from the point of view of ther-

modynamics. The efficiency of the organization of the internal processes of ecosystems and organisms has increased in the course of evolution.[25] The direction of the evolution of living systems is defined in
terms of the goal of reaching a steady state safeguarded against external
disorders by internal feedback mechanisms. This steady state is the
result of two principles of ecological evolution (or the succession of the
stages of development of an ecosystem) (Odum 1980):

- the *maximum-power principle* according to which natural selection
  continues to increase organic-system mass and system-energy
  throughput as long as it finds unused residues of matter and accessible energy;

- the decrease of specific entropy production, i.e. per unit of biomass, while total entropy production increases. The reason for this
  is that in the early phases of succession there is little biomass and
  thus little competition for nutrients, while increasing growth is accompanied by increasing competition, a process from which more
  efficient utilizers of nutrients and sunlight benefit.

Theoretical Inferences to be Drawn from Ecology and Thermodynamics

What consequences result from the findings of ecology and thermodynamics for the analysis of the processes encountered at the interface
between economics and ecology? Both disciplines indicate different but
complementary reasons why human life cannot exist independently of
its natural environment and why technical progress cannot abrogate our
dependence on the resources provided by nature. The conclusion is that
human utilization of the environment must adapt to the laws of nature;
this does not diminish the significance of technical progress, it simply
indicates that it must take a direction different from the one on which it
has embarked.

Ecology's explanation of human dependence on nature is that human
nutrition depends on plant biomass production and that man is not able
to govern the preservation of natural or artificial (i.e. influenced by
human intervention) ecosystems, because their complexity is beyond
today's state of knowledge and our technical capabilities.[26]

The ecological arguments based on the dependence of economic activity on nature can be supplemented with the information borrowed from thermodynamics that any transformation of energy and matter requires energy, but that the availability of energy is limited. Recycling of materials cannot solve the scarcity problem either, since the latter is always dependent on inputs of external energy. Artificial – as opposed to natural – production of biomass or ecosystem regulation also requires huge additional energy inputs, even for the production and operation of the control instruments needed for the purpose – a senseless waste in view of the high level of efficiency of natural ecosystems.

> Stated in thermodynamic terms, this means: *"Economic activity is not the controlled transformation of matter, using energy and maintaining the mass of matter. Economic activities instead create a continuous flow of entropy by transforming low-entropy states into states with high entropy. These entail grave interventions in our natural environment and can be sustained only as long as potentials of low entropy are available whose free energy can be utilized."* (Stephan and Ahlheim 1996, pp. 34 f.)

Potentials of low entropy result above all from supplies of fossil fuels; harnessing solar energy offers many possibilities, but it is faced with the problem that the energy concentration of solar rays is lower than that of fossil fuels.

Establishing efficiency and sufficiency as the guiding principles of our dealings with natural resources is a demand justifiable in terms of both ecology and thermodynamics. Here the concept of efficiency is altered in comparison with its use in conventional environmental economics. In applying the notion of economic efficiency to the environment, conceived as a nonmarket good, the latter made the environment accessible to economic analysis, though in doing so it neglected the problem of uncertainty (Which ecosystems are essential for survival? Is their stability and resilience ensured?) and the methodological question whether an analysis geared to individual preferences is suited to investigating environmental problems in the first place (collective good; rights of other species). Seen from the widened standpoint of ecological economics, efficiency in the utilization of nature means that these aspects have to be taken into consideration.

A second dimension of the dependence of nature emphasized by both disciplines results from the significance of the time axis for the analysis of economic utilization of the environment. Ecology stresses that the high velocity of human interventions often overstrains the response mechanism of the natural ecosystems, endangering their stability and resilience. Thermodynamics points to the directionality and irreversibility of flows of matter and energy; while recycling implies a partial reversal of a flow of matter, it at the same time increases the flow of energy. In conclusion, the foregoing points to the problem of the duration and velocity of natural and economic processes and the problem of their irreversibility.

The time-frame of human activities is as a rule very small; the rate of reproduction of natural resources or the rate of succession of ecosystems very frequently exceeds this frame. This can be illustrated with reference to the extreme example of natural oil resources: They came about in the course of millions of years; in principle this process can be repeated in the course of geohistory, though it is wholly incompatible with the time-frame of human utilization. Even the regeneration of resources such as forests, which are renewed in imaginable periods of time, and are therefore seen as renewable resources, often takes decades and is thus incompatible with the usual calculations of the profitability of economic activities.

> This is made clear by the concentration of German forestry on pure timber production, neglecting the other, indispensable environmental services provided by the forest. The soil rent theory advanced by one of the classic 19th century writers on forestry, M.R. Pressler, dictated: "*The main point of forestry is: to use timber production on a given area of land to achieve the highest possible net profit. (...) True, your beech timber forest operations are fine and good, in the narrow forestry sense, artful and valuable; but in the sense of financial output? What use have I as a landowner, indeed what use has the state, for an economic art that brings in not even the most*

modest return on capital? An art that goes begging?" The result of this financial analysis was the pine or fir plantation for
which, in the words of F.W. Pfeil, another classic, *"the slightest resources and the smallest sacrifices are all that is needed
to reach our end, the satisfaction of all our timber needs in the
quickest and surest manner."* (Both quoted after Sperber
(1996), pp. 42 - 43)

If energy and matter are dissipated by the process of economic utilization more rapidly than ecosystems can regenerate and (by absorbing
solar energy) replenish energy resources, the increasing disorder (entropy) in the natural environment due to the throughput of energy and
matter will cause irreparable damage. This means not only that the supply of scarce resources but also the capacity we have to dispose of by-
products and wastes in the natural environment are limited. The so-
called global environmental problems that have become apparent at the
end of the 20th century illustrate the present level of disorder in the
natural environment: global warming due to CO_2 emissions, the perfo-
ration of the ozone shield, the growing levels of soil degradation and
desertification, and diminishing biodiversity are interpreted by ecological economics as unintended consequences of the uncontrolled expansion of the economic subsystem. These inferences prove, in the view of
ecological economics, that the resilience of natural ecosystems has
reached its limits under the growing pressure of economic exploitation
and that it is time for a radical change of course (Goodland 1992; Daly
1992a and c).

How, in theoretical terms, does ecological economics now introduce
these noneconomic findings into the discipline of economics? Daly
(1992) defines the economic production process as an irreversible
throughput of flows of energy and matter through the economic system,
a process which results in an increase of entropy.[27] Increasing degradation of the environment is seen as an increase of entropy, as an immediate consequence of the appropriation of natural resources by the economic system. Put bluntly, the connection between consumption of the
environment and development can be formulated as follows: The complexity of the socioeconomic order as well as the levels of consumption

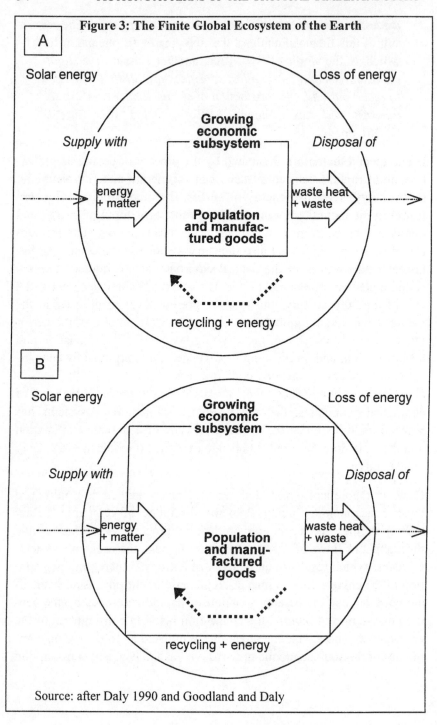

Figure 3: The Finite Global Ecosystem of the Earth

Source: after Daly 1990 and Goodland and Daly

and the technological level of industrial society are necessarily based on a high level of consumption of the environment.

From the viewpoint of ecological economics the subdivision of the discipline into environmental and natural-resource economics along the lines of static and dynamic considerations is unsuitable: the external effects that accrue when the environment is exploited also have a dynamic component in that any calculation of the costs and benefits of avoiding or eliminating them would have to take account of the assimilation capacity of natural ecosystems with an eye to stability aspects. For this reason Odum (1980) broadens the concept of natural resources to include all natural life-support systems. As a multifunctional storehouse of natural capital, the natural environment provides flows of multipurpose services that are essential for human life and hence at the same time for economic activities (welfare). The essential services are:

–   Supply of the natural resources used as energy and material inputs in the economic process;

–   assimilation and degradation of waste products from the economic process of production and consumption;

–   provision of a flow of environmental services for individuals and production systems (here it is not a matter of directly physical exchange processes but of the maintenance of stable ecosystems and the general environmental quality needed for life).

From an economic viewpoint a problem of **relative scarcity** arises when, in utilizing the environment, one of these three functions is overstressed at the expense of the others. This is true above all of the third function, since the physical dependence of economic activities does not enter into market-mediated processes.

> „Resource-dependent economic growth will tend to bias natural-resource allocation towards meeting the physical needs of the expanding economic process – in terms of the provision of raw materials and the assimilation of waste. This would be to the detriment of the provision of environmental services, unless economic policy explicitly corrects this allocation process

by taking into account the growing relative scarcity of these natural services. " (Barbier 1989, p. 97)

Technological progress can alleviate this relative scarcity to the extent that it is possible to lower consumption by raising efficiency.

A problem of **absolute scarcity** is caused by the cumulative effects of protracted overutilization and degradation of the environment. The optimism of conventional approaches (see the paradigms of frontier economics, environmental protection, and resource management in the diagram) that assume a capacity for self-correction on the part of the economic system (technical innovations are sufficiently stimulated by price signals; physical capital replaces natural capital) is not shared for three reasons:

1. Environmental degradation that may culminate in the collapse of ecosystems can be observed above all for nontradable environmental "goods," the scarcity of which is not accompanied by any corresponding price signals.

2. The form taken on by environmental degradation is not that of a predictable and gradual decrease in environmental quality, it instead takes place in sudden, discontinuous, and relatively unpredictable surges triggered by cumulative environmental degradations and chain reactions.

3. Technical progress can in the best case only help to avoid unnecessary environmental destruction; it is, however, unable to recycle all matter or energy in general. A constantly growing throughput of energy and matter leads irrevocably to an increase in entropy.

These three arguments stress the inappropriateness of the market mechanism in safeguarding all economically relevant environmental functions (1), the significance of nonlinear, erratic processes that increase uncertainty and make risks difficult to predict (2), and the strong hypothesis that in the long term a collapse of the ecological foundations needed to sustain human life is probably inevitable (3).[28]

While the first argument still holds out hope that political governance could compensate for the problems posed by market failure, the second and third arguments evince a fundamental skepticism vis-à-vis human governance and problem-solving capacities. What we therefore find at the heart of ecological economics is a more skeptical view of the potentials of technical progress.

> *„Given the complexity of ecological relationships, ... the uncertainty over the future and even current preferences for environmental functions and resources, and the physical limits to resource-saving techniques, the effectiveness of innovations in ameliorating environmental deterioration may be constrained. If this is the case, then the trade-off between consumption and environmental improvement services, and between more growth and increased environmental preservation may be unavoidable."* (Barbier 1989)

This skepticism is based on the proposition that man-made capital (physical capital and labor) is restricted in its ability to replace natural capital and, above all, increase its productivity. There are three possibilities for the latter case (Daly 1992c):

1. Increase of the flow of natural capital, i.e. of the net growth of renewable natural resources; the limit set to this possibility is defined by biological growth rates;

2. increase of efficiency, i.e. of product output per unit of resource input; the limit here is defined by the constancy of the matter/energy balance;

3. increase of end-consumer efficiency; here the limit is not defined physically but is flexible due to new technological possibilities, changes in socioeconomic organization, and a qualitative change of needs going beyond basic needs.

Since the first two possibilities run up against absolute limits, efforts should be concentrated on the third. Changes due to technical progress fundamentally entail the following options: to replace individual, especially scarce (above all nonrenewable) resources, with others; to replace physical capital with human labor,[29] thus lowering consumption of energy and material; and to increase the efficiency of resource use. Each of these three alternatives illustrates the complementarity (as opposed to the substitutability) of man-made and natural capital.

Methodological Approaches in Ecological Economics

How are these demanding theoretical principles and guidelines now realized in methodological terms? As was noted above, ecological economics is marked by methodological diversity, which is not surprising when we consider that the findings of ecology and thermodynamics on the finite nature of natural resources do not lead to any cogent conclusions on methodological approaches. Many studies, however, make use of a methodological arsenal that – critical as the former may be – comes closest to that known from environmental and natural resource economics. The reason is that some economists expressly wish to link up with the neoclassical mainstream for lack of any alternative paradigm that is at the same time methodologically highly developed and practical; and thus it is that, to name the few as representative of the many, Pearce, Turner, Markandya, and also Barbier argue in this vein, though the last-named author rightly seeks to gain critical distance to the material-balance approach of Pearce and others.

Pearce / Turner (1990) developed the concept of the circular economy, which they use to broaden, in three steps, neoclassical economics to include the environmental dimension: the point of departure is an input-output matrix used to describe economic processes. Its components are goods, firms, primary inputs (capital and labor), and the aggregate demand of firms and private households. This matrix is in need of a common unit of measure to be able to calculate costs and benefits and the effects of price increases on demand; all of the elements are therefore represented as monetary variables. In a second step this matrix is expanded to include "environmental goods" on the input side and the "environment as a sink for waste products" on the output side. The unit of measure for these additional elements is tons. When interactions between economy and environment are to be calculated, the environment values must be monetized. Thus, in a third step, the authors step back from the matrix and develop a circular model that depicts three essential processes: the generation of a utility stemming from the processing of resources into commodities, the resource cycle (resource removal and recycling), and the feedback effects of environment use (overstraining the assimilative capacity of ecosystems limits their productivity).

Since this model depicts material and energy flows and utility functions of goods and resources, it can be used as a basis for material balances that can in turn be used to calculate the economic functions of the environment (as resource supplier, waste decomposer, and life-support system). The goal of material balances is to guide the utilization of natural resources and the use of the environment as a sink in terms of keeping the natural capital stock constant over time. The above-named rules for the utilization of natural resources and the environment are derived from this goal.

Since natural capital cannot be fully replaced by man-made capital, a constant stock of natural capital must be conceived as an unchanging physical volume or in the form of constant prices per unit (in that increasing scarcity is reflected by rising prices) or in the form of a constant value (because prices, and with them monetary value, would rise if the physical volume decreased). This creates a number of methodological problems: how is the optimal stock of natural capital or the correct initial level determined? How is it possible to set approximately correct shadow prices for environmental goods? How is it possible to solve the problem that changes in the prices of natural resources do not indicate scarcities?

Instruments like cost-benefit analyses, calculations of the net present value of a natural resource with competing utility functions (entailing the basic problem of defining a discount rate), and determination of willingness to pay and shadow prices all have the disadvantage of being marked by an "economic lopside": aggregated individual economic preferences necessarily carry more weight than intertemporal justice (preservation of stocks for future generations). The outcome of a dynamic cost-benefit analysis of the utilization of a hypothetical natural resource for example is thus that growing stocks of natural capital entail cost increases in the form of lost utility (because the stock has been protected and not used). It is certainly also possible to use the cost-benefit curve and the stock-development curve to calculate an optimal stock; but here too, due to the above-mentioned difficulties in monetizing the life-support system, we are not told whether this economic optimum also corresponds to the ecological optimum.

So economic analyses have to be supplemented and/or corrected by analyses from other perspectives. Ecological economics has the merit of having delved at some length into noneconomic disciplines;[30] this gives it an edge over other disciplines, e.g. sociology. But it has not succeeded in complementing the broad outline of the problem suggested by ecology and thermodynamics by including new methodological instruments equally comprehensive in scope. It is indeed even questionable whether this is possible at all: economic analyses must deal with cost-benefit relations; they are expected to make the short- and medium-term rationales behind economic decision processes accessible to reflection and provide help in selecting policy instruments.

This means that an interdisciplinary approach is better suited to looking into the various facets of the interface between economics and ecology. Interdisciplinarity would imply defining the areas of competence of the individual disciplines and their interfaces with an eye to the object of inquiry. It would also imply that the representatives of the individual disciplines will have to open up to the logic of the problem and the methodology of data collection used by the other disciplines if they are systematically to include the findings of the latter in their own inquiry. According to this understanding of interdisciplinarity there is little point in searching for the queen science that is superior to all other disciplines and methodologically universal; the concern is rather to acknowledge the methodological and epistemological autonomy of individual disciplines and, building on it, to arrive at an overall view that is never anything more than preliminary.[31]

2.5   Economic Analyses of the Exploitation of Tropical Forests

The following look at economic analyses of the exploitation of tropical forests points to the advantages and weaknesses of the methodological approaches used. Only some of the authors discussed would see themselves as belonging to the field of ecological economics; but all of the analyses proceed on the assumption of a need for global environmental protection, and in particular of a need to prevent any further deforestation of tropical forests, for reasons of species protection and protection of the climate. The different perceptions of the interface between ecology and economics become evident in the analytical focus chosen to investigate the reasons for deforestation and the overexploitation of the tropical forest as well as to identify political solutions.

2.5.1   Utilization of the Amazon Forest from the View of Ecological Economics: Edward Barbier

Barbier's study (1989, Chapter 6) may be seen as an attempt to broaden neoclassical natural-resource economics to make room for ecological aspects. For Barbier the Amazon forest is an example for the revised concept of scarcity: in the short term the degradation of the tropical forest through selective logging and conversion to farmland, especially for cattle-ranching, jeopardizes the hydrological cycle as well as biodiversity and soil fertility in the regions affected; it also destroys the life-support systems of traditional forest dwellers and their cultures. Since these losses and risks are beyond monetization, they are not taken into account when programs and projects are planned: *"Allocation of the region's scarce natural resources is thus automatically biased towards economic development that is less rather than more environmentally sustainable."* (Barbier 1989, p. 126)

In the long term large-scale deforestation can lead to climate change in the Amazon region and neighboring areas. Deforestation severely impairs the capacity of the rainforest to itself generate some 50 % of regional precipitation through evaporation; less rainfall impairs the nutrient cycles in the forest and the neighboring regions, which are intensively used for agricultural purposes (Chaco Paraguayo, the mid-west of Brazil). Furthermore, deforestation entails combustion of large quantities of biomass and thus very high CO_2 emissions, which accelerate the greenhouse effect.

The deforestation process is encouraged by Brazil's misdirected development and integration policy for the Amazon region: *"Most of the extensive deforestation of the Amazon – over 15 million ha by 1987 – can be directly related to government-financed programmes and subsidies, particularly for ranching and colonization. In addition, certain general macro-economic policies – such as the income tax, the land tax, and land titling regulations – are providing economic incentives for deforestation."* (Barbier 1989, p. 131)

Some of these tax arrangements are still in effect; thus farming and cattle-ranching are still subject to lower taxes than other economic activities. Land-ownership legislation has remained largely unchanged inasmuch as deforestation is still seen as a proof of land use and in this way constitutes a prerequisite for a land title – and is thus stimulated. The law on land taxation was, however, altered in 1996. Land clearance as a first step toward putting it to a "productive use" is in itself no longer enough to gain a tax reduction of up to 90 %; instead, fallow, unforested land is today subject to the maximum tax rate. The rules governing the subsidies for the creation of cattle ranges have also been changed; cattle ranges are permissible only in natural savanna areas.

As a basic solution, one that would not only be restricted to the Amazon region, Barbier proposes explicitly according sustainable development a target function in the planning and implementation of economic-policy measures. He entertains no illusions as to the inadequacy of the instruments available for the purpose – including cost-benefit analyses, introduction of an ecological gross national product, correction of the incentive system, analysis of the sustainability of production systems – and sees these instruments as an approach to giving increased consideration to limiting ecological factors in economic decisions, since it is not possible to fundamentally harmonize the ecological logic with the economic logic: *"The pursuit of sustainable economic development will require reconciling crucial trade-offs – not the least being the trade-off between resource-using economic growth and appropriate resource-management objectives."* (Barbier 1989, p. 205)

2.5.2   Natural-resource Extraction as an Economic Dead End: The Model of Alfredo Homma

Alfredo Homma analyzes the economic dynamics of extractivism. He restricts his model's validity to plant extraction, explaining in this way why the extraction of forest products is necessarily replaced by the planned cultivation of these products and why extractivism cannot constitute a paradigm for the sustainable development of the Amazon region (Homma 1992).[32]

Up to the 1950s the Amazon economy was dominated by *extrativismo vegetal*, the extraction of vegetable forest products, including rubber, Brazil nuts, resins, oils, fruit, fibers, and timber.[33] These activities accounted for over half the value of the primary sector's output and constituted the most important source of income of the rural population. Since the end of the 1950s some of the most important products of this sort have been cultivated systematically or replaced by synthetic products, a problem exacerbated by the emerging exhaustion of natural stocks: rubber was first supplanted by the rubber plantations in Malaysia, later by synthetic rubber; the plant poison *timbó* and rosewood oil were displaced by synthetic substances. *Guaraná*, a bean containing caffein, is now grown on plantations in the state of Amazonas. As far as timber, nowadays one of the most important products extracted in the Amazon region, is concerned, scarcities are already becoming evident in certain regions of the Amazon and for certain species (mahogany, virola).

For timber production Homma provides an explanation of why overexploitation of the primary forest could expand in the Amazon region while at the same time plantation areas were increasing in the south of Brazil. His model indicates some factors that influence the long-term profitability of timber production and processing in the Amazon region.

According to Homma, the economic cycle constituted by the extraction of vegetable forest products consists of four phases:

- first phase: expansion of extraction thanks to sizable stocks and monopolistic positions in the raw-materials market (the latter factor can be used to explain the rubber boom in the Amazon region);

- second phase: stabilization of extraction at a high level at which supply and demand are in equilibrium, a state close to the maximum extraction capacity (defined by the biological growth rate); extraction costs and sales prices rise, since, in the face of constant (biological) growth rates, the supply can be increased only by exploiting very remote locations; the high demand for these products stimulates experiments with domestication of the plants and their systematic cultivation on plantations;

- third phase: decline of extraction because of diminishing stocks (disturbed natural regeneration) and rising extraction costs; accompanied, usually, at the same time by declining product quality;

- fourth phase: extraction substituted by systematic cultivation of formerly wild plants on plantations or synthetic production of their active substances.

The fourth phase does not materialize if cultivation fails or substitution proves impossible; this is the case, for example, for the Brazil nut.

If the extraction of vegetable forest produce is to be sustainable, it must be profitable, raise the standard of living of the gatherers, and not impair the regenerative capacity of the plants and the ecosystem of which they are part. That these parameters are as a rule not realized is explained by the model with reference to the economics of extraction:

- The supply curve remains constantly high, since it is defined by the natural biological growth rate.

- The demand curve shifts in keeping with market growth and rising prices until it intersects the supply curve.

The end of the extraction cycle can thus be interpreted as a consequence of resource exhaustion (due to overexploitation, i.e. the supply curve shifts to the left) or as a consequence of supply rigidity despite high prices. According to Homma, extractivism as a rule bears the seeds of its demise in itself: the product's success is expressed in growing demand and the use of the product in industrial production processes; the industrial use, however, presupposes at least a constant minimum availability, and for the most part a growing supply, of the product. Extraction of forest produce is unable to cope with this demand pressure. The high demand (with correspondingly high prices) stimulates substitution of forest products through cultivation on plantations or chemical substitution. These forms of production have the benefits of lower production costs, the possibility of returns to scale, as well as higher yields per unit of land and homogeneous product properties. This means that the rigidity of the natural supply and the rising production costs of extraction can be overcome.

These economic advantages of plantations and/or chemical substitutes result in the decline of the competitiveness of forest-produce extraction: the advantage of cost-free provision by nature is eroded by extraction costs that necessarily rise when demand grows. In addition, the cultivated or chemically manufactured product is of consistently high quality; and it is also possible to increase output quantity when this is indicated by planning and when costs decline.

Extractivism can continue to exist in competition with cultivated vegetable produce only when it is based on the self-exploitation of gatherers without any economic alternative, or when it is subsidized. Pointing to the ecological services provided by rubber tappers who protect the tropical forest, it being the source of their income, the Brazilian federation of rubber gatherers in 1997 succeeded in obtaining price supports for natural rubber as a means of ensuring that the latter will continue to have a chance against the far cheaper plantation rubber from Malaysia.

In looking at timber extraction, we must ask which phase of the cycle it is presently in: the first phase (expansion), the second phase already (stabilization), or indeed the third phase (decline). According to Homma, it is in the first phase: since there is no perfect substitute for tropical timber, there is no question of substitution through plantation cultivation as long as the stands of primary forest are very large, since cultivation costs are far higher than the level at which the demand curve intersects the supply curve of extraction. *"The introduction and dissemination* (of plantation cultivation, I.S.) *always depend on the existing capital stock of extraction."* (Homma 1992, p. 180)

Looking at the situation from the angle of the dynamics of demand and, above all, substitution, however, as Homma suggests doing, we find that this assessment necessarily shifts (see Chapter 5). Growing demand from industry for a raw material that offers a homogeneous processing quality and is available in great quantities at low prices has led to technological innovations which are increasingly displacing solid sawnwood and plywood (areas in which tropical timber is strong) and replacing them with technology-intensive reconstituted wood panels. Manufacturing these wood panels requires large quantities of homogeneous wood fiber, which is produced on pine and eucalyptus plantations. In addition, changes in consumer preferences in the industrialized countries (light-colored woods, rejection of the destruction of tropical forests) have been observed that are leading to a displacement of tropical hardwood by species from the temperate zones, above all oak from North America.

The substitution pressure that Amazon timber extraction should be experiencing due to strong industrial demand has thus already begun. To this extent we should assume, contrary to Homma's assessment, that timber extraction is already in the third or fourth phase of the cycle.

2.5.3   Nutrient Mining on the Agrarian Frontier and Destruction of Tropical Forests: Studies by the World Bank and IMAZON

The common methodological denominator of the studies presented here[34] is their description of deforestation processes in the Amazon region with the aid of a model in which the advance of agriculture into forest areas (agrarian frontiers) constitutes the decisive dynamic factor. The model used by the authors is based on a combination consisting of the property-rights approach (North) with the approach used to explain the distribution of economic activities in space and time due to the maximization of the net present value of land use (Thünen).

The central concept used in the World Bank studies is nutrient mining. This term, defined as the unsustainable extraction of nutrients from the soil, is used by the World Bank to characterize farming, cattle-ranching, and timber extraction as destructive forms of soil and forest utilization aimed at short-term profit maximization. Since, in the World Bank's view, this goal function inevitably leads to a rapid loss of soil fertility and to deforestation, the tropical forest is treated as a nonrenewable resource that is destroyed by the unsustainable mining of nutrients (World Bank 1992, p. 84).

The IMAZON studies dealing chiefly with forestry do not always use the concept of nutrient mining; but they do assign central significance to the advance of the agrarian frontier. Almeida / Uhl (1995) and Stone (1997 and 1998) make explicit theoretical reference to the studies of the World Bank authors mentioned above.

Though reduction of the analysis to property rights and the dynamics of nutrient mining results in an elegant analysis, its explanatory power all the same proves extremely limited and even misleading.

Nutrient Mining in the Amazon Region

In principle the World Bank proceeds on the assumption that the introduction of secure, durable property rights is sufficient to attain a sustainable utilization of resources. *"If all goods and services provided by forests, including environmental services, could be bought and sold, and land were owned with secure title, the tradeoff among forest functions, and between forest and non-forest uses of land would be determined by the public's willingness to buy the different services: if the public preferred the services of the intact forest over timber and agricultural products, the landowner would be paid more to preserve the forest than to convert it to agricultural use."* (World Bank 1992, p. 84) But because there are neither secure property rights nor a market for these environmental services, the forest owner can profit only by felling the forest or by converting it into farm- or rangeland.

The dominance of nutrient mining (*"unsustainable extraction of nutrients from the forest soil through logging, annual cropping and ranching"*) (World Bank 1992, p. 27; Schneider 1995, p. 15) is explained by the World Bank as a rational response of the economic agents in a region characterized by insecure property rights and a surplus of cheap land. This land is made accessible through public road-building. Following a few years of exploitation, yields begin to decline; the economic logic of nutrient mining now states that it is at this point, thanks to lower land prices, more worthwhile to deforest new areas than to invest in improvement of soil fertility and intensification of the use of the areas already developed. Although, according to Thünen, the criterion of market proximity influences use decisions, in the case of agriculture the World Bank regards high fertilizer prices and land rights on the agrarian frontier as more crucial factors that influence farmers to migrate in view of declining yields. This process of leaching out and opening up forest land varies in the Amazon region as a function of soil quality, access to undeveloped areas, the availability of manpower and credit, and property rights on land. The inevitable consequence of the economic logic of nutrient mining is, however, that the different user groups (farmers, cattle ranchers, and loggers) continue to exert constant pressure on forested areas.

The classical course of this land-development process goes on for roughly 10 - 20 years, beginning with road-building, which is then followed by logging. This in turn is followed by smallholders who grow annual crops and sell their land to ranchers as soon as the yields have begun to decline. The latter now use the ranges for a few years until their nutrient value has been so depleted by proliferation of low-nutrient grasses and weeds that cattle-ranching is no longer profitable there. The areas are now abandoned, and their original plant cover fails to regenerate. The cycle begins anew:

> *"With accessible land sufficiently cheap, it is more profitable to move the farm to the nutrient-rich, pest-free environment, than to import the fertilizers and pesticides to the farm. Similarly, in the timber industry, what are commonly viewed by northern forestry experts as wasteful logging practices are actually a rational response to a situation where land is cheap relative to labor. Whether a given farmer, rancher, or forester intends to remain (geographically) stable or not, economic forces will probably force him to adapt to a land-surplus economic environment."* (World Bank 1992, p. ix)

The selective, extremely loss-intensive logging practiced by the Amazon timber industry is explained by the World Bank with reference to the large supply of timber there. Afforestation and plantations are not profitable as long as there are large areas of primary forest which – thanks to a lack of environmental controls – can be logged at very low costs. In the view of the World Bank, logging these primary forests would be sustainable if this gave rise to new industries in the Amazon region or elsewhere whose aggregate production value exceeded that of the forests (World Bank 1992, p. 22).

Since the nutrient-mining cycle takes 10 - 20 years, decisions on breaking through this logic and the benefits afforded by it go beyond the temporal horizon of local actors, e.g. local environmental or economic policymakers. From an overall Brazilian viewpoint, on the other hand, the economic utility of the deforestation dynamics in the Amazon region is, in view of its low productivity, far below the costs caused by the ecological damage. These costs include lost future utility from the exploitation of genetic resources, damage due to sedimentation of rivers, climate-changing CO_2 emissions, and the effects of deforestation on the microclimate of the Amazon region (droughts, forest-fire danger).

This analysis leads the World Bank to pronounce the following policy recommendations:

–   Access to forested land must be regulated through restriction of road-building; in addition, conservation areas must be created. The aim is to make land scarce, thus driving up land prices.

–   The price distortions that have promoted agricultural investments in the Amazon region (above all subsidized credit) should be reduced. (The World Bank failed to take into consideration that subsidized loans for cattle ranches in primary-forest areas had already been done away with.)

–   Introduction of market-based instruments should be used to change the behavioral patterns of Amazon actors; since the introduction of a tax on slash-and-burn clearance practices or tradable fire-clearance rights is unrealistic, it should be made possible to lease the land to foreign actors interested in forest protection in order in this way to organize financial transfers into the region. Indigenous persons and gatherers of forest produce should have a free hand to exercise their sustainable forms of utilization.

- Since the political decision-makers in local communities have a short-term decision horizon and also have little resistance to local pressure groups, environmentally relevant decisions should be taken at higher administrative levels.

Objections

The World Bank's analysis is full of contradictions and inconsistencies, and these led the Brazilian government to voice harsh criticism, which had to be included in the report. The main points of this criticism were the lack of differentiation between smallholders and big landowners, subsistence production and production for the market; the failure to define the elements of a sustainable development strategy for the Amazon region that include the interests of the local population; and the lack of consideration of the fact that sustainable forms of life in the forest, e.g. based on the gathering of forest produce, have until now meant a large measure of economic and social exclusion for these population groups.

Further objections generally concern the completely insufficient consideration given to differentiated forms of land use that have developed in some regions on the basis of long-term utilization interests: It can, for instance, thus be precisely the experience of insecure land rights that heightens the interest of farmers in stabilizing their place of abode; and of what use are low production costs when products cannot be sold due to long distances to markets and poor roads? In addition, contrary to the World Bank's argument, family farms are in a position to increase their per hectare yields and at least to stabilize their incomes. This applies for farms in the older settlement areas in the northeast of Pará and the more recent settlements along the Transamazônica and even in Rondônia. These successes are based on diversified production systems that include, beside fallow-cropping, cultivation of permanent cultures and animal husbandry.

One widespread error consists in equating small farming in the Amazon region with shifting cultivation. This amounts to confusing the features of nomadic land use by indigenous peoples with migration processes of new settlers who, due to lack of ecological knowledge and agricultural extension services, have introduced unadapted production systems and failed in the attempt. These settlers then often sell their land to cattle ranchers who then move in to take it over. At least in the northeast and southeast of Pará and along the Transamazônica, however, we find agrarian production systems that are marked by permanent cultures and animal husbandry on top of the traditional fallow-cropping. These production systems are relatively stable for two reasons: because of their degree of diversification and because of the crop-rotation principle on which a parcel is farmed. Two to three years of cropping are succeeded in the ideal case by a seven- to ten-year fallow. This makes it possible to preserve soil fertility over the long term.

The soil itself is not a collection of nutrients that are extracted in a linear fashion and thus exhausted, as the World Bank asserts with its concept of nutrient mining. It is instead a living system in which the interaction between soil and (secondary) vegetation gives rise to a process of nutrient-recycling. This applies in particular for extensive forms of land use, which make it possible for secondary vegetation to grow back rapidly, thus, in principle, encouraging a restoration of the original vegetation, albeit in a modified form. Only in the case of intensive land use (mechanized tillage and chemical inputs) is the soil-regeneration capacity of the land drastically diminished (Nepstad et al. 1995). The World Bank, however, sees precisely in intensification the only way to a sustainable utilization of land.

A further problem is that the World Bank operates without any definition of the concept of sustainable development as a frame of reference for its analysis, introducing in its place – because of its fixation on the resource land – the concept of geographic stability (as a counternotion to the forest-destroying dynamics of migration). The economic activities associated with this category, with its positive overtones, include, apart from the gathering of forest produce (which is actually one of the traditional activities of nomadic indigenous groups), large-scale mining (as opposed to illegal gold-prospecting) and the construction of dams and hydroelectric power plants. It might be objected here that extractivism is stable only as long as small quantities are sold and large areas are available; once interest in commercial utilization grows, overexploitation and substitution by cultivated or synthetic products are inevitable. In addition, it is precisely large-scale projects like the iron mine in Carajás, the construction of the railroad line needed to transport out the iron ore and the dam in Tucuruí needed to supply the mine with power, and the aluminium-smelting works in Pará that have engendered markedly destabilizing socioeconomic and ecological effects. The large-scale projects in Carajás and Tucuruí set in motion major waves of migration on the part of those who were left without work when construction was finished. They sometimes joined the army of gold prospectors, or settled as smallholders, exacerbating the process of deforestation. The dam inundated large areas of forest and displaced local smallholders and fishermen.

The World Bank's assessment of the timber industry is also problematical. It not only defines – in contrast to the definition of nutrient mining – logging as sustainable when the returns are invested in other industries; this is a crude application of the untenable thesis of the substitutability of natural capital by man-made capital. In addition, changes in the timber industry, associated with the stabilization of sawmills on old agrarian frontiers (intensification of logging by broadening the spectrum of commercial species, investments in the expansion of processing or in the sale of land), were not included in the World Bank's analysis; this would cast doubt on the assumptions of the model of nutrient mining and the constantly advancing agrarian frontier.

Forestry and the Timber Industry

The IMAZON studies have more to say about the explanatory power of the property-rights/agrarian-frontier approach for the dynamics involved in forestry and the timber industry (Barros and Veríssimo 1966; Almeida and Uhl 1995; Stone 1997, 1998).

In its analyses of sustainable land use IMAZON always distinguishes between farmers, cattle ranchers, and sawmill owners, who, under the conditions of abundant land and insufficient capital and know-how, attempt to maximize the net present value of land use. As the age of a settlement increases (i.e. as the agrarian frontier nears) the intensity of the forms of utilization also slowly increases, since property rights have in the meantime been consolidated. Using a comparative model for calculating the net present value (per hectare yields) of the three forms of land use over a cycle of 90 years, we find that the per hectare returns on forestry and timber-processing are lower than those on intensified cattle-ranching (2nd place) and intensified agriculture (1st place) (Almeida and Uhl 1995).

The outcome of this analysis speaks in favor of the strategy of most landowners (including sawmill owners) of banking in the long term on conversion of forests for agricultural use. Two aspects, however, are problematical: first, the assumption of a 90-year cycle, which in fact overstrains the decision-making horizons of most actors and could also not be used to justify sustainable forestry, since the latter probably requires a cycle of not more than 30 - 35 years; second, the assumption of a clearly functional separation between farmers, cattle ranchers, and timber processors. Observation of the investment behavior of sawmill owners shows that many of them invest their returns in land purchases and when the forest stands have been depleted decide on the basis of the market situation (and the subsidies available) whether to invest in cattle-ranching or farming. Sawmills often serve to accumulate the capital needed to purchase land, cattle, and farm machinery. And so the assumption of a functional differentiation and corresponding professionalization of the actors is unrealistic.[35]

Not even under the assumption of consolidated property rights do rational economic decision-making processes in the Amazon region obey the logic of profit maximization over a protracted period of time; what they do obey is the logic of adjustment to macroeconomic and market conditions, which may change rapidly. What finds expression in this decision-making behavior is the experience gathered over decades with numerous, for the most part short-term, stabilization and adjustment programs with changeful interest-rate, monetary, and exchange-rate policies which – when short-term adjustment works – can offer very high speculative returns. This investment opportunity is open to all large farms and timber-processing firms that have access to credit or produce for markets in the south or abroad.

An example: The first half of the 1980s saw the expansion of the timber industry in the Amazon region; there was at the same time growth in timber exports. To what extent these were motivated by the then high foreign mahogany demand or by export subsidies is unclear. Many timber exporters invested the subsidies in the capital market, cashing in on the high rates of interest available there; that is, the involvement in this export business may have been a means of obtaining loans and profitably investing them (Browder 1987).

IMAZON's analyses of the possibilities of intensifying forest use (in the sense of the permanent cultivation of an area of land) assume owners committed in the long term to forestry and/or the timber industry, and thus prove to be unrealistic. It is one thing to assume that economic agents plan to remain in a branch of industry for a long period of time and that rational decision-making motives can be derived from this fact; it is quite another to investigate empirically whether this is really the case. IMAZON's empirical studies at any rate confirm the earlier findings of other authors who had noted a high level of volatility and a brief temporal existence of timber-processing firms (Pandolfo 1969; Bruce 1976; and Mercado 1980).

The analysis conducted by Stone (1997 and 1998) has a different focus; it applies the World Bank's property-rights/agrarian-frontier model to the timber industry in Pará. Under the conditions of insecure property rights, high transportation costs (remote markets), abundant land, and low log prices, we find highly mobile, relatively inefficient sawmill operations that are highly selective in their logging. Their remoteness from their sales markets lowers the net value of their economic activity (gross returns minus transportation costs), while the costs of enforcing property rights rise.

As the agrarian frontier grows in age, land markets develop and the companies start investing in logging, transportation, and processing. This implies that the center is brought closer by better roads (thus making it possible to lower transportation costs) and by the presence of government institutions (which secure the public monopoly on the use of force). Strengthened property rights lead to investment in plant and equipment; the processing capacities grow and the demand for logs rises. The result is local supply bottlenecks, which raise log prices and make logging in more remote forest areas profitable.

Higher log prices force the sawmills to introduce new, cost-reducing technologies (larger trucks), invest in further processing (plywood production), and even enter the export trade in order to increase revenues. This expands the operating radius of these companies to more remote forest areas, which in turn increases transportation costs: The sawmills must, at a given point of time, decide whether to close, migrate to a more abundantly forested location, or whether to invest in forest management or the creation of plantations (unrestricted timber production at a fixed site). At this juncture the agrarian frontier at this site can be regarded as closed.

Stone's model is based on a comparison of logging, transportation, and processing costs and of revenues and profits between 1990 (IMAZON survey) and 1995 (Stone's survey). In the author's opinion these five years saw the decisive aging process of the agrarian frontier in that his survey found increasing investment and rising costs for local logging rights for this period. But a closer look (see Chapters 6 and 7 of this study) gives rise to a number of empirical objections to the model's prognostic power, all of which are linked to the model's simplicity: the investments made in 1995 were made in the tradition of selective logging, there are no indications of an intensification and diversification of forest management, timber-processing, and markets. The venture into the export trade will prove to be of short duration: it is based on marketing two or three species, 90 % of which are exported to France; the local stands will be exhausted in a few years. After 1995 a great number of sawmills closed, and there is no indication of a growing number of plywood factories. On the contrary, even the successful sawmill owners are now looking to alternative sources of income, such as the mechanized cultivation of maize and soybeans on their large-scale farms (for which the state of Pará has announced massive subsidies).

What this means is that property rights and log prices are not enough to depict the decision rationales of sawmill owners and that other factors will have to be included in the analysis of the instability of timber-processing companies. Stone's model provides no answer to the question why the preferences of sawmill owners, including those in older settlement areas, remain so doggedly against any kind of sustained forestry or forest management.

2.5.4   Tropical-timber Trade and Tropical-forest Protection: The Analysis Conducted by Edward Barbier's Working Group

Since the end of the 1980s a working group around Edward Barbier, in cooperation with the London International Institute for Environment and Development, has been looking to the interdependencies between tropical-timber trade and tropical-forest protection (Barbier, Burgess, Bishop and Aylward 1992, 1994; Barbier 1994). These studies are concerned with determining the share of the tropical-timber industry in deforestation, analyzing the economic incentives for exploiting tropical forests, and, finally, assessing the impacts of economic- and trade-policy interventions on the protection of the tropical forests.

The definition of sustainable forest management used by these authors is based on that of the International Tropical Timber Organization (ITTO):

> *"Sustainable forest management is the process of managing permanent forest land to achieve one or more clearly specified objectives of management with regard to the production of a continuous flow of desired forest products and services without undue reduction in its inherent values and future productivity and without undue undesirable effects on the physical and social environment."*[36]

No objections to the definition, though one might object to the way in which the authors, in view of the fact that their overriding concern is to analyze the dynamics of deforestation, restrict themselves to a sustainability definition for the forestry-related utilization of the tropical forest. This means omitting any assessment of the economic, social, and ecological benefits and costs of deforestation for agrarian purposes and various other conceivable agricultural uses. These, however, could influence an assessment of the timber industry's exploitation of the tropical forest in terms of sustainability aspects, as is shown by the findings of Almeida and Uhl (1995). In leaving any such comparative intersectoral view out of consideration, the authors suggest that sustainable forest management involves the greatest ecological, social, and economic benefits. This position is justified by defining the tropical forest as a *"form of natural capital"* which *"has the potential to contribute to the long run economic productivity and welfare of tropical forest countries."* (p. 21) The authors do not explain in what form this could materialize, though they do point to and assess the negative environmental impacts of logging.

The authors assume in principle that sustainable forest management must be more profitable than competing forms of land use if it is to prevail. This can be achieved when timber is exported to high-price markets where the ecological quality of the timber is checked through voluntary instruments such as the ecological certification of forest management.

But what, in the authors' view, is more important is to reduce market and policy failure in the tropical-forest countries with an eye to harmonizing as far as possible the private and the social efficiency of logging. By private efficiency the authors mean efficient production of timber involving maximization of future yields through sustainable forest management. Social efficiency means for the authors safeguarding the production of nontimber products as well as the ecological services provided by forests. This division is in line with the distinction between forest utility functions that can be privately appropriated and forest utility functions that benefit the general public or future generations. This distinction fails to note that timber production – precisely in complex tropical forest ecosystems – is dependent on the stability of the ecosystem, and that it is therefore impossible to clearly distinguish the so-called social functions of the forest from its economic function.[37] In addition, the authors neglect the fact that extraction of nontimber products is for the gatherers themselves primarily an economic function, and thus one that represents a private interest.

In general, to address the problem of market and policy failure the authors favor the introduction of market-based instruments instead of administrative regulations geared to invigorating market mechanisms that can indicate scarcity. The authors' proposals on introducing better concession management, cutting subsidies that favor the conversion of forested areas, and correcting market distortions reflect the state of the art. It focuses on instruments important above all in Asia and Africa, e.g. concession conditions and the establishment of royalties and stumpage fees on harvested logs.

It is highly regrettable that the authors scarcely take notice of the case of Brazil: it invariably appears in this study, as in a number of others, as evidence for the negative effects of subsidies for the conversion of forests for use as rangeland and for public settlement programs. The authors fail to note that forest policy in the Amazon region is based on property rights (logging permits are conditioned on private ownership of land and on forest-management plans) and that log prices are set by the market. This means that in the Amazon region two conditions are in force that are called for for other countries, even though this has not meant that any more sustainable logging practices are to be observed there.

What is positive about the authors' analysis of the tropical-timber industry and trade is that it places the dynamics of these sectors in the context of general trends in the world timber market and in world timber production. Thus their analysis shows that:

- the share of tropical timber in the value of the world timber market is only 11.4 %;
- the supply capacity of the tropical-forest countries is declining, though this scarcity of tropical timber is not leading to rising prices because the growing supply of hardwood logs from the temperate zones is holding prices stable;
- compared with timber plantations, the significance of the tropical forests in meeting world timber demand is declining;
- the demand for tropical-timber products is declining in the industrialized countries because of substitution tendencies due to new wood panels and other materials such as plastic and metal, while the demand from developing countries will rise.

Although the proportion of tropical timber in the timber traded throughout the world is small, the tropical-timber industry has great economic significance for a number of producer countries, contributing between 3 and 6 % to the GNP of Malaysia and Indonesia, the countries with the most pronounced export orientation, and between 2 and 3 % in Ivory Coast, Gabon, Ghana, and Brazil. In all of these countries it is an important employer and foreign-exchange earner.

In addition, the tropical-timber industry is said to be an important provider of *"rural infrastructure in development,"* as the authors put it (p. 16). What they mean here is that it is timber firms that build roads and open up rural, well-forested areas with low population densities and offer nonagricultural jobs. This point is important because it refers to the complementary structure of the interests of the timber industry and the rural population, which benefits from new roads and job opportunities, as well as to the absence of government services in logging areas, which are for the most part very remote. Regrettably, the authors fail to look more exactly into this complementary interest structure, although it is important precisely for understanding the deforestation dynamics of settled rural areas of the Amazon region (one of the most important future suppliers of tropical timber). For Africa and Asia it has been found that deforestation by farmers takes place along the roads opened up by the timber industry; in the Amazon region, on the other hand, these are often parallel processes. Since there are no concessions, smallholders and *fazendeiros* often sell logging rights; the *fazendeiros* in this way finance the rehabilitation of degraded rangeland (use of machines for soil-conditioning, seeding fodder plants, fertilizers, and pesticides), while smallholders are able to sell only very small amounts of wood.

But the authors – like the IMAZON studies already discussed – look at farming, ranching, and forestry as competing, not as complementary, forms of land use. This means that the models used to calculate the cost-benefit functions of decision rationales are undercomplex to the extent that they do not depict the multiple rationales that are encountered in reality. The same is true of the cost-benefit calculation of land conversion for farming uses: it is usual to assume a permanent conversion instead of including the economic and ecological utility functions of rotating fallow-cropping.

2.5.5   Tropical-forest Exploitation and Protection from the View of Allocation Theory: Studies from the Kiel *Institut für Weltwirtschaft*

Since the beginning of the 1990s the Kiel *Institut für Weltwirtschaft* has been concerned with the exploitation and protection of tropical forests from the angle of allocation theory.[38] The authors' main goal was to work out cost-benefit calculations for national and international tropical-forest protection measures; the need for protection of the tropical forests was explained with reference to the risks of climate change due to CO_2 emissions, loss of biodiversity, and the regional and local ecological services provided by tropical forests.

This means that the analyses of the Kiel authors, like those of the World Bank and the Barbier group, set out at a point below the paramount objective of "determination of the elements of a sustainable regional development strategy for the Amazon region as a prerequisite for global sustainability." This paramount objective is not reflected as such; instead, the authors permit themselves a shortcut by assuming from the very outset that an absolute reduction of the rate of deforestation is the most important goal, one to which all other goals are subordinate.

The general equilibrium model used by the authors to evaluate the costs and benefits of policy measures is the approach which entails the highest degree of abstraction from empirically observable reality and is thus fraught with the greatest methodological risks. These risks can be illustrated particularly clearly with reference to the findings of Wiebelt (1995), who used the example of the Brazilian Amazon region to simulate the effects of a devaluation policy, the reduction of subsidy-related market distortions, and the effects of land taxation on deforestation.

–   Macroeconomically, the author simulates not the positive measures (stable, realistic exchange rate, capital influx) but the impacts of devaluation policy on agriculture and forestry and the exports stemming from them. Devaluations of an exchange rate increase the competitiveness of exports. This leads the author to conclude that agricultural and timber exports increase in phases of devaluation, stimulating high demand for land and encouraging deforestation. If the pressure to devalue stemming from macroeconomic reforms (reduction of inflation and the budget deficit) ceases, *"we can expect not only stable, positive economic growth but also a considerable reduction of the dynamics of deforestation."* (Wiebelt 1995, p. 555)

– Without any additional microeconomic regulatory instruments, however, deforestation cannot be stopped; these instruments include reduction of subsidies in agriculture and cattle-ranching, which are in fact tax-free compared with other economic activities, and increase of the land tax with an eye to slowing down speculative land purchases. The simulation of the overall economic and sectoral effects of these measures shows that their macroeconomic impacts (on GNP, exports and imports) can be neglected; significant regional economic impacts in the Amazon region can be expected only in connection with an increase of the land tax by 10 %. The latter would reduce the output in the various sectors affected by a maximum of 1 %, thereby reducing the deforestation rate in the short and medium term by 3 - 7 %. Employment, however, would decrease by 3.3 % in the short term and 2.5 % in the medium term.

The author concludes from these findings that the costs that Brazil would face in giving up its free-rider role in international environmental policy are not especially high and that therefore no compensation payments are required.

The author's approach deserves to be criticized at different levels:

– Is it, in view of the known complex interrelationships between economic growth and deforestation rates, which have been demonstrated by Amelung (1997), permissible to proceed on the assumption of environmentally positive effects from macroeconomic reforms? Beginning in mid-1994, the *Plano Real* brought Brazil both a stable (overvalued) currency and enormous inflows of capital from abroad; land prices in the Amazon region fell by roughly 60 % as a result of a decline in speculative land purchases. At the same time a number of major investment projects were reinvigorated or relaunched in the Amazon region. Most investments have been going into the expansion of infrastructure, mining, and the large-scale, export-oriented cultivation of soybeans. Timber exports, too, have risen immensely in spite of the drawback represented by a strong exchange rate. Deforestation increased extremely precisely in 1995 following stabilization, as INPE data demonstrate.

–   The microeconomic instruments called for by the author are doubtless appropriate. But how will the regions affected by them respond?[39] What we have seen since 1994 is not a reduction of subsidies but new ones, also for small landowners, who had until then been left out in the cold.[40] But it must be at least noted that the tax rate for untilled, deforested land was sharply increased. The latter measure has placed medium and large landowners under pressure; this can, for instance, stimulate the conversion of the last remaining forest reserves to farmland for soybean cultivation.

In view of the changes that have occurred in Brazil since mid-1994, the prognostic power of Wiebelt's model must be seen as low. That, however, obviates the advantage that the model is supposed to have compared with partial analyses. In my opinion, the weakness of this approach must be sought in its insufficient consideration of the actual decision rationales of the economic agents.

Any adequate consideration of these rationales requires empirical study of the behavioral patterns of the actor groups to be investigated – and how they have emerged over a longer period of time – to recognize the strategies that were to be used to cope with uncertainties and risks of this kind. The gain implied by an approach of this sort would be the ability to use precise knowledge on the dominant behavioral pattern involved in the exploitation of a resource across one or more sectors to be able to better estimate how these actors would respond to changes of incentive structures and/or what changes the desired behavioral modifications would be most likely to entail.

3   Alternative Approaches to Economic Action from the Fields of Sociology and Evolutionary Economic Theory

If, instead of defining economic action as rational (or instrumentally rational) per se, we analyze more exactly how this action comes about and what forms it takes on, we can turn to approaches concerned with social action as such. The discipline in question is sociology. Evolutionary economic theory has also developed a somewhat more differentiated and contextualized concept of economic decisions and action. The following chapter deals with these two fields, sociology (3.1) and evolutionary economic theory (3.2), in order then to formulate the methodological approach pursued by the present study (3.3.).

3.1   Sociological Approaches to Economic Action

According to the premises of ecological economics, economic activity, viewed in terms of its energetic or ecological dimension, is bound to certain conditions in space and time; economic activity is not a reversible process, even though it may, from the monetary standpoint, seem to be one. In principle, one might conclude from the fact that economic activity is bound in this way to the material sphere that decisions on economic allocation are also tied into to specific constellations in space and time. These decisions would have to be explained with reference to the specific conditions under which they are taken, and not merely – as in the analyses presented in Chapter 2.5 – by placing them under the proviso that such decisions are in any case rational decisions between different options made on the basis of a monetary cost-benefit rationale.

It is possible for sociology to analyze social action in this way. The following section (3.1.1) looks into sociological thought, exemplified in Anthony Giddens' theory of structuration, with an eye to its applicability in our context (Giddens 1984).

We will then, in a second step, discuss why it is that sociology, as compared with economics, was relatively late in providing contributions on the relation between society and nature (3.1.2). The present study will advance the thesis that this "abstinence from nature" on the part of sociology stems from the theoretical-methodological tradition that began with Comte's positivism and lead to Durkheim's principle of 'explaining social matters only through social facts'. This principle reflected the then methodological state of scientific research; it was intended as a means of marking sociology off from other disciplines such as history and philosophy and grounding a scientific claim that could stand comparison with the claim to objective knowledge raised by the natural sciences. The most important representatives of the discipline have sought their orientation in this principle; present-day analyses widely represented in current sociological literature, be they constructivist or cognitivist, or of a Luhmannian systems-theory bent, focusing on the relation between society and nature, amount to contemporary applications of this principle (Durkheim 1980; Luhmann 1986; Brandt 1998).

3.1.1   Rational Action and the Determinants of Social Action

Anthony Giddens' theory of structuration (of social action)[1] rests on a basic epistemological outlook precisely the opposite of that embraced by mainstream economic theory: Giddens, pointing to the reflexivity and contextuality of social action, which apply for acting "laymen" and observing social scientists alike, rejects any general statements on the laws of social action that can be derived from the elements and structures of action.

> *"There are no universal laws in the social sciences, and there will not be any – not, first and foremost, because methods of empirical testing and validation are somehow inadequate but because ... the causal conditions involved in generalisations about human social conduct are inherently unstable in respect of the very knowledge (or beliefs) that actors have about the circumstances of their own action. (...) The theories and findings of the social sciences cannot be kept separate from the universe of meaning and action which they are about. (...) There is no clear dividing line between informed sociological reflection carried on by lay actors and similar endeavours on the part of specialists. (...) The point is that reflection on social processes (theories and observations about them) continually*

enter into, become disentangled with and re-enter the universe
of events they describe." (Giddens 1984, pp. xxxii f.; the following page numbers refer to this edition.)

Giddens concludes from this reciprocal relation between necessarily
context-bound action, observation, and communication over observed
action *"that there is no such entity as a distinctive type of 'structural*
explanation' in the social sciences; all explanations will involve at least
implicit reference both to the purposive, reasoning behavior of agents
and to its intersection with constraining and enabling features of the
social and material contexts of that behavior." (p. 232 f.)

The epistemological position on which this view of social science is
based stems from Giddens' critique of the orthodox basic consensus of
postwar (American) sociology, a critique enriched by impulses derived
from his reading of interpretive sociology.[2]

The critique of mainstream sociology is important in that it sets out the
direction which Giddens' later theory of structuration is to take. To
facilitate an understanding of this critique, Giddens starts out by sum-
ming up the basic elements of mainstream sociology (Müller 1992, pp.
154 f.):

- The view underlying mainstream sociology, positivism, is based,
  first, on the postulate of the unity of the natural and social sciences,
  which, as there is only one reality, must both subscribe to the same
  methodological criteria of scientific knowledge, second, on the
  conviction that reality exists independently and can in principle be
  grasped empirically (empiricism), and, third, on the claim that it is
  possible to use deductive-nomological models to come up with
  lawlike knowledge of social and natural systems. This, it is
  claimed, enables sociology to generate unbiased and instrumentally
  usable knowledge.

- Individual action unfolds under the constraints of unanticipated
  conditions and unintended consequences. But functional explanations are given for these constraints. That is, constraints do not result from the intertwinement of individual strands of an action, individual freedom of action is instead restricted as a means of ensuring that the overall system will function. The social system is in

a state of equilibrium maintained with the aid of the functional contributions made by institutions. Hence functionalism does not explain social action at the macrolevel but instead gives way to an objectifying system-thinking that has very little room for intentional action.

– Since scientific knowledge of sociological relations depends on a mastery of the methodological canon, and the sense of the systemic limitations on individual action can be inferred not from action itself but only from a (scientifically generated) view of the overall social system, *"sociological knowledge is ... not only a more systematic formulation of the implicit knowledge of agents, it is genuine and emergent."* (Müller 1992, p. 155)

According to Giddens, this thinking has "collapsed;" which is not to say that there is no more positivist and functionalist thinking in the social sciences but that theories grounded in this way have lost their hegemony, even though no new consensus has emerged. The attack on the orthodox consensus was launched by the schools of interpretive sociology, whose findings and concepts Giddens recombines in an unbiased, eclectic fashion, thus stepping over their self-imposed boundaries.[3]

Giddens' attack on the basic assumptions of mainstream sociology is based on the following insights of the interpretive schools:[4] First, the view that there is only one standard of rationality according to which day-to-day action can be judged is given up in favor of the idea that there are different rationalities that agents use and that can be used to interpret social behavior.

> *"The criteria of rationality that operate in the [social sciences] ... – for example, that concepts should be precisely defined, as generalized as possible, and 'context-free' – are not those which interest lay actors. The lay actor, as practical social theorist, manages to order her or his experience so as to support the supposition that the world (both natural and social) is as it appears to be (...) The attitude of the social-scientific observer is the opposite of this, involving the suspension of the belief that things are as they appear, and is (ideally) not influenced by the pragmatic demands that dominate*

the 'natural attitude' [i.e. of the lay actor, I.S.]. The two atti-
tudes, that of the scientist and the layperson, do not merge into
one another, but are radically discrepant (...) Social life, as
lived by its actors, is thus to be seen not as a series of feeble
attempts to match up to standards of rationality as specified by
the 'scientific attitude' but, quite on the contrary, as a series of
dazzling performances to which these standards are essen-
tially irrelevant." (Giddens 1993, p. 41)

This position can also be used to explain the division between natural and social sciences:[5] The use of scientific concepts in day-to-day life has no repercussions for the validity of natural laws, while social concepts arise from day-to-day life and can also change it retroactively. In contrast to nature, social structures are neither independent of action and the notions of agents nor of unlimited duration in space and time. This means that sociology is unable to perform any stringent tests to validate its hypotheses, because every test situation is itself a special social situation artificially set in contrast to real life. The findings of the social sciences are thus valid only under certain marginal conditions and cannot be used to make predictions.

Second, since the social world is conceived as an active performance of humans, Giddens emphasizes the linguistic mediateness and reflexivity of the social world with reference both to the linguistic turn in Wittgenstein's philosophy and, in particular, to day-to-day language in ethnomethodology. Understanding imparted by language is conceived as the central presupposition of every social interaction; language and its terms are thus explained as stemming from social processes and are at the same time seen as the means by which acting individuals communicate and reproduce these social processes.

Third, social researchers and laypersons alike derive what they know from the same stock of knowledge; sociological concepts are based on the lay pre-understanding of everyday terms. Language, or the process of taking up and interpreting these everyday terms as the means and precondition of interaction, in this way moves into the methodological center of sociology.[6]

Giddens derives from these findings the concept of a dual hermeneutics to which the social sciences are subject: *"The object of sociology – the social world – is itself a context always pregiven by frames of meaning; the first step to accessing the social world therefore leads through valid frames of meaning, mutual knowledge, and everyday terms. In the second step sociology can form frames of meaning of its own, technical knowledge, and scientific terms, though these always remain related back to the social world in a complex manner."* (Müller 1992, p. 161)

This implies that it is neither necessary nor possible to presuppose or define rational action in the form of a model in order to view it as rationally explainable action. The form assumed by social action as a means of gaining certain ends is instead bound to particular contexts defined in temporal, spatial, and social terms. The social definition of the action context makes up the greater part of Giddens' theory. He develops the concept of the "duality of structure" as a means of illustrating that social structures cannot exist independently of action and exercise constraint on social action but that social structures are maintained by action and both enable it and restrict the latter.[7] For Giddens this points the way out of the dead end of structuralist and functionalist approaches, which place the dominance of the social whole over the action autonomy of the individual agent, but without being able to sufficiently explain the stages of mediation between the two levels. Giddens likewise speaks out against subjectivist approaches of hermeneutics and interpretive sociology, which aim at the subjectively intended meaning of actions but lack a satisfactory concept of social structure. But he does accept the positions of hermeneutics inasmuch as he acknowledges that scientific description of social action presupposes that the describer must be familiar with the ways of life expressed in social action.

The key terms in Giddens' theory are reflexivity, discursive and practical consciousness, routine, structure and structuration, and the significance of space and time.[8]

Just as Giddens presupposes that social action is rationally explainable, he also presupposes that agents are conscious of their actions and the reasons for them and are in a position to exercise a controlling influence on the process of social life. It is this basic characteristic of social action that Giddens refers to as reflexivity. He defines action itself as a continuous 'behavioral flux' that is situated in space and time and consists not of individual, distinct intentions, reasons, and motives but of a flow of interrelated actions (p. 3). His concept of action has connotations that deviate from those of traditional action theory (Müller 1992, p. 170): He refers to the concrete day-to-day actions of agents and not to abstractly rational or typified action models; action is the conscious and reflexively monitored doing of actors, and it is embedded in the continuous flux of events in the social world; it consists of temporally ordered and spatially situated practices and it involves the capacity to actively and effectually intervene in the course of social events. Action is not regarded here as a discrete action or as an intentional decision that depends primarily on the individual's aims and ends but as a recursive practice that is embedded in social relations and constraints.

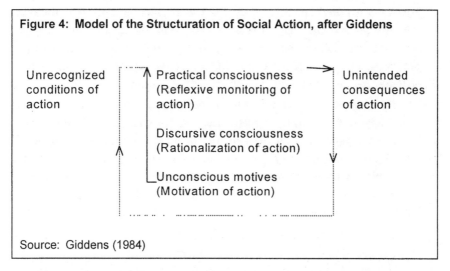

Figure 4: Model of the Structuration of Social Action, after Giddens

| Unrecognized conditions of action | Practical consciousness (Reflexive monitoring of action) | Unintended consequences of action |

Discursive consciousness (Rationalization of action)

Unconscious motives (Motivation of action)

Source: Giddens (1984)

The practical consciousness consists in the practical knowledge of actors about the rules and tact of day-to-day life; it enables them to get along in day-to-day affairs, i.e. to exercise a reflexive control of their action. The term *discursive consciousness* is used to designate the capacity to put this knowledge (and other states of affairs) into words, in this way rationalizing action. The key fact for Giddens is that while social action presupposes practical consciousness, it does not rely on discursive consciousness: we know why we do the one thing and not the other in a given situation, but we do not need to explain to ourselves "consciously," i.e. verbally, the reasons for our action <u>before</u> we act. Nor do we need to know all aspects of the reasons for an action, e.g. the physical laws that compel us to perform a certain, given sequence of movements if we are to succeed with this sequence. The lack of discursive consciousness does not impair our ability to behave adequately (i.e. in an understandable or result-oriented manner). Giddens, borrowing from Freud, refers to the third and deepest layer of action as that of the unconscious needs and wishes on which action rests, though the actors have no exact notion of them.

90 % of day-to-day behavior is performed on the basis of practical consciousness in the form of routines: *"The rationalization of action ... is ... a routine charateristic of human conduct, carried on in a taken-for-granted fashion."* (p. 3 f.) Giddens' use of the term routine includes both the psychosocial presuppositions of individual action and the specific intertwinement between individual action and institutionalized practices, i.e. practices that are stable across space and time. This is possible in that a routine is effective at different levels:

– At the psychosocial level the predictable routines of day-to-day life – which the child first learns from the reliable care of its parents – impart the "ontological security" that the individual needs to develop trust and confidence in himself and others. This trust, together with social manners and tact, represents the basic mechanism of the security system that every individual needs to exist in day-to-day life (p. 50).

– At the level of the social relationships in which the individual acts, the routines of day-to-day action intertwine the individual life with the social system in which it exists, while at the same time maintaining the social system. In the course of a routine the valid social rules are applied and confirmed. While routines are based on tradition, custom, and usage, they are not thoughtlessly repeated: the actors reelaborate them again and again in adapting them to altered conditions (p. 85). One example of this would be the routine of dividing up one's daily time between work and leisure or domestic reproduction, which has to be adapted to life with a partner and the birth of children, but without questioning, in the same measure, each of the rules behind these acts – e.g. engaging in wage labor away from home as a means of earning an income, the gender-related division of labor, etc.

Routines are maintained, first, to safeguard the confidence- and tact-based security system and the ontological security that rests in it and, second, so as not to endanger the integrity of the social system. The concept of routine thus takes on a significance that comes very close to that of structure.

Since Durkheim social structures have been seen in structuralist sociology above all as moments of constraint on the action of individuals; structural constraints were, as it were, regarded as an impersonal, causal force that sets narrow limits to individual action, though within these limits individual action is characterized by a maximum of freedom. Giddens counters with a definition that ascribes to structures, due to the immanent relation between structure and action (and action and power), both an enabling and a limiting character (p. 169). Freedom and structure are thus, in the view of the individual, not opposites: they condition one another.

For Giddens, structures are properties of social systems that are stable over longer periods of time and greater geographic distances. These properties occur in the form of rules (norms; ascriptions of meaning) and in the form of resources (authoritative resources used to coordinate human action and allocative resources which provide control over material goods) (p. xxxi). Social structures do not exist in isolation from human consciousness in that individuals are by definition social beings (e.g. the socially mediated emergence of individual ontological security), they are maintained by individuals. In this sense Giddens distances himself explicitly from Durkheim's concept of structure: structures are not emergent properties of social systems which, due to the aggregation of individuals, arise, as it were, "behind their backs." They are instead the result of the continuous intertwinement of individual actions over time and space.[9]

For Giddens structure[10] has a dual character. It is produced and reproduced in contexts of interaction by consciously acting persons with reference to rules and resources. *"The constitution of agents and structures are not two independently given sets of phenomena, a dualism, but represent a duality. According to the nature of the duality of structure, the structural properties of social systems are both medium and outcome of the practices they recursively organize.[11] Structure is not 'external' to individuals: as memory traces, and as instantiated in social practices, it is in a certain sense more 'internal' than exterior to their activities in a Durkheimian sense. Structure is not to be equated with constraint but is always both constraining and enabling. This, of course, does not prevent the structured properties of social systems from stretching away, in time and space, beyond the control of any individual actor."* (pp. 25)

For Giddens constraint occurs in three basic forms: as material constraint *"deriving from the character of the material world and from the physical qualities of the body,"* in the form of negative sanctions, i.e. *"constraints deriving from punitive responses on the part of some agents towards others,"* and in the form of structural constraint, *"deriving from the contextuality of action, i.e. from the 'given' character of structural properties vis-à-vis situated actors."* (p. 176) The scope open to actors in given situations is thus restricted by material conditions, by the sanctioning power of others, or by the given action context.

Due to this complex concept of structure, which is keyed to mediation processes based on durable institutions and interaction, the action of actors gains special significance in Giddens' theory: with reference to institutionally anchored rules and resources, the actors structure social space, the encounters in which action takes place. They do this in the framework of the given action options, although, due to the recursive character of structural moments, they also have the chance to change the latter. This is accomplished, according to Giddens, by reflection of action and its conditions, by the entrance of reflective consciousness into the everyday world, which provides at least the chance to change the definition of rules and the distribution of resources, and thus also not only to adapt routines but to reshape them. *"The only moving objects in human social relations are individual agents, who employ resources to make things happen, intentionally or otherwise."* (p. 181)

Action is accordingly not only mastery of the challenges of day-to-day life in an external, pregiven framework, which, in the structuralist or functionalist view, leads to results in conformity with the system; it is at the same time structuring action in the sense of a constant restoration or alteration of the framework of meaning for action.

Giddens' idea of structuration may thus be summarized as intending to explain the production and reproduction of social life in terms of action theory by directly linking it to the level of individual action (duality of structure), and not by interposing institutions as "objectifying" agencies of mediation geared to systemic results. Giddens views the link between interaction at the level of individual actors and social structure in analogy to language: language as an abstract set of grammatical rules is on the one hand the condition required for communication through speech acts; on the other hand speech acts reproduce and modify these rules over the course of time. The relation between speech acts and the rules of a language corresponds to the relation between individual action and social structures, since *"social structure is both constituted by human agency and yet is at the same time the very* medium *of this constitution."* (Giddens 1993, p. 128 f.)

Giddens illustrates this with reference to the three components that are part of every interaction and their correlates at the level of structure, to which they are linked by modalities of structuration (Giddens 1993, p. 129):

Interaction	Modality	Structure
Communication of meaning	Interpretive scheme	Signification
Mobilization of power	Resources (facility)	Domination
Reproduction of morality	Norms	Legitimation

The structuration of interaction or social situations is accomplished simultaneously in these three dimensions, which both have present meaning and refer back to prior frames of meaning, thus perpetuating them.

For Giddens the constitution of social structures is thus formulated, and resolved, as a problem of form. The question is no longer, as it was for Parsons, the compatibility of individual freedom and social order, the question is how linkages of action and interaction can be given "structure" (i.e. durability) across space and time. The development of institutions ensures that social systems are integrated (group reciprocity); strategic action serves the end of social integration (reciprocity of actors who reflexively monitor themselves).

The "situatedness" of social action in time and space is thus a central element of Giddens' theory. It is in developing these considerations that Giddens comes closest to the question as to the relation between social action and the natural environment, although he is not interested in this dimension in the same sense that ecological economics is. On the contrary, Giddens explicitly distances himself from its view of the relation between nature and society:

–   T. Hägerstrand (1975), whose time geography is referred to in positive terms by Giddens, formulates the hypothesis that *"sources of constraint over human activity [are] given by the nature of the body and the physical contexts in which activity occurs."* (p. 111) Giddens accepts as moments of constraint the fact that the bodiliness of human beings restricts their faculties of movement and perception as well as the fact of the finality of life and the impossibility of attending to two tasks at once (since each task has its duration) or the fact that no two persons can be in exactly the same place at the same time. In the view of the individual the volume of space and time is thus limited and presents barriers to the performance of projected actions. Giddens rejects Hägerstrand's more farreaching hypothesis that *"allocation of scarce resources of the body and its media has some sort of determining effect upon the organization of social institutions in all types of society."* (p. 117) Giddens accepts this only for the present, in which the scarcity of

natural resources does in fact dictate that we deal with them efficiently. This, however, does not apply for past epochs.

– Ecological constraints, too, which Giddens enumerates with reference to Carlstein (1978), concern only the fact that matter, organisms, and human populations exist only 'embedded' in a certain order of time and space, that activities take time, and that human beings must live in population systems (p. 116). No consideration is
given to ecological matters of the kind formulated by ecology and
thermodynamics.

What is important in Giddens' view is that *"locales refer to the use of
space to provide the* settings *of interaction, the settings of interaction in
turn being essential to specifying its* contextuality. *(...) Locales provide
for a good deal of the 'fixity' underlying institutions, although there is
no clear sense in which they 'determine' such 'fixity'. It is usually possible o designate locales in terms of their physical properties, either as
features of the material world or, more commonly, as combinations of
those features and human artefacts. But it is an error to suppose that
locales can be described in those terms alone (...) A house is grasped as
such only if the observer recognizes that it is a 'dwelling' with a range
of other properties specified by the modes of its utilization in human
activity."* (p. 118)

Social action takes place in concrete locales in space and time; social
systems likewise extend through space and time. Here Giddens formulates an idea that is further elaborated in his later studies on modernity
and globalization (Giddens 1990): Until the 19th century the media of
communication were identical with the means of transportation; a
horse, for instance, could serve a courier or the sender of the message
himself as a vehicle; the arrival of message and man was in both cases
bound up with the fact that a given distance had to be traversed in a
given period of time. A great spatial distance at the same time meant a
great temporal distance. Once the electromagnetic teletypewriter had
been invented, the means of communication were radically divided
from the means of transportation: human interaction is now no longer
dependent on bodily presence or spatial proximity but is made possible
by means that "overcome" space and time.

What is attractive in Giddens' approach is that it makes it possible to look for explanations for social action in specific, context-related factors and in doing so to use a great variety of partial theories that can be used to explain these factors. The question of the action autonomy of individuals can for Giddens not be answered universally but must be addressed above all by analyzing the specific contextual conditions and routines that have come about in the context under investigation and shape day-to-day behavior.

3.1.2   Is Sociology "Blind to Nature"? Nature in Giddens' Theory of Structuration

As we have already noted, Giddens attaches great significance to the spatiotemporality and contextuality of social action, though this interests him only to the extent that the actors and, mediated through them, social systems deal with and overcome these physical and ecological constraints. He rejects the notion that natural conditions have any independent power over social action, the institutionalization of social systems, and their chances of reproduction (see the critique of Hägerstrand referred to above), or grants the notion at best in a limited form (*qua* material constraint, of equal rank with sanctioning power and structural constraints); in Giddens' eyes they are not worth any particular consideration.

There are a number of theoretical reasons for Giddens' neglect of the relation between nature and society in social action – a surprising fact in view of the author's explicit reference to the embeddedness of social action in space and time – reasons that can only be touched upon here:

– Giddens developed his theory against a determinist understanding of social phenomena, which for him includes structuralist and functionalist thought patterns that seek to both locate moments of constraint in external forces inaccessible to individual action and at the same time to characterize these moments as causal mechanisms of social action. Giddens rejects this analytically imprecise entanglement of external constraint and cause by "endogenizing" structural constraints, i.e. by tracing them back to social action itself.

External constraints given in natural conditions have no place in this line of argument. But Giddens at least does not seek to solve the problem by placing the category of external constraint within the social system (e.g. with reference to constructivism, which knows nature only as a linguistic, social construct), preferring instead to leave the question open.

– Giddens also rejects evolutionism in the social sciences, noting that it too seeks deterministically to discover evolutionary laws for social systems, for instance in the form of a process of constantly increasing differentiation of social subsystems and functional areas. Giddens' definition of social systems as recursive and reflexive social formations is diametrically opposed to evolutionary or dichotomistic thought, which – as in the case of Coleman or even Habermas – distinguishes between modern and traditional societies. Evolutionary models are often inspired by biology and use biological concepts as metaphors to "explain" functional contexts (e.g. Luhmann's use of the concept of autopoiesis).

– Giddens defines structure as institutionally anchored rules and resources of social action, existing outside of space and time. This concept thus has an inner tension that cannot – like the structures and structural moments of social systems – be resolved by conceiving of it as the outcome of a context-bound process of social action. This inner tension exists between the – postulated – constant, noncontextual existence of rules and resources on the one hand and their institutional anchoring on the other. It seems as though Giddens, in using this concept, had something fixed, immutable in mind that is not exposed to social reflexivity to the same extent as the other forms of structure. This fixed element is in turn differentiated only socially: what is meant are standards, ascriptions of meaning, and control over humans (authoritative and allocative resources). What is important is that things here appear only as objects of human disposal and use, and have no logic of their own.

– Giddens turns the concept allocative resources against the definition of economic resources as determined by the struggle for scarce resources which, on account of their scarcity, are central for the reproduction of the social system. The basis of the economy must instead be sought in the existence of allocative resources (control over objects, goods, and material phenomena); the distribution of the power of disposal, Giddens claims, plays the central role for the constitution of social systems. Giddens uses this proposition to draw the line between himself and materialist approaches, though this is achieved at the expense of the concept of (resource) scarcity.

– Finally, Giddens proceeds at the epistemological level, borrowing from hermeneutics, on the assumption of a fundamental division between the world of nature and the world of the social. The reason for this is that all agents are defined as (practically or discursively) knowing actors who use their knowledge to constitute and to maintain social systems. Giddens cannot later invoke this immediate intertwinement of knowledge, action, and existence with reference to the sphere of nature, which is the reason for the division.[12] He would then implicitly have to concede that nature – due to the fact that it is not immediately accessible – can indeed set absolute external constraints.

Despite the – generally conceded – spatiotemporal embeddedness of social action, Giddens sees no need to deal explicitly with the relation between nature and society; the utilization of nature is subsumed under the logic of social systems and their institutions.

3.2   Theories of Technical Change: Innovation, Evolutionary Processes, and Path Dependency

The concept "routine" plays a major role in evolutionary economic theory, where it is used to understand the innovation behavior of firms and industries. Learning and innovation are fundamental elements presupposed for any reorganization of economy and society along ecological lines. The discussion of this approach is the last element of the theoretical preliminaries from which the methodology used in the present study has profited.

The following section first presents an overview of the most important theories of technical change and their basic concepts (3.2.1), in order then to look at somewhat greater length into the concepts of routine (3.2.2) and evolution (3.2.3) with an eye to working out in more detail their proximity to sociological views on economic processes. The section will in particular deal with overlaps with and contractions to Giddens' theory of structuration.

3.2.1   Systematic Overview and Basic Concepts

The theories presented in the following section have emerged since the 1960s and were conceived to analyze technical change as an endogenous component (and not an exogenously determined framework condition) of economic processes and explain its significance for economic growth, the differences of economic power among firms and countries, and international trade.[13] Following a chronological classification by Vernon Ruttan (1997), we can distinguish three main strands of the discussion:

–   Theories of induced technical change. This strand breaks down into three currents: first, one dealing with the significance of the demand for inventions (Schmookler 1966; Griliches 1957); second, a current rooted in growth theory and dealing with the stability of factor shares despite rising wage costs (Kennedy 1964; Samuelson 1965); and, third, a microeconomic current dealing with the role of relative factor prices, i.e. with the question whether innovations are used to economize on factors with rising prices (Hayami, and Ruttan 1971 and 1985; Binswanger 1978).

–   Evolutionary theories. Starting out from Schumpeter's studies on the significance of innovations for economic growth, these theories deal with the behavioral patterns of firms (routines) and the mechanisms of selection to which innovations are subject (Nelson and Winter 1982; Dosi, Freeman, Nelson, Silverberg and Soete 1988).[14] In concentrating on the factors that influence entrepreneurial decisions on changing routines and the (successful) introduction of innovations, these theories close the gap left open by the earlier, microeconomic studies of Hayami and Ruttan, who had left learning and innovation processes themselves out of consideration.

- Theories of path dependency. The "economization" of technical change shows that that this process can consist neither of an automatic takeover of new technical knowledge nor of pure historical accidents. In describing the order followed by technical change, the authors focus on different areas. While Arthur (1994) and David (1985) underline the chance character of initial decisions between competing technologies, which are positively reinforced by increasing returns, the evolutionary theories tend more to emphasize the structuring effect of entrepreneurial routines that determine the definition of problems and the direction to be taken by the search for new solutions. The concepts developed here include technological trajectories (Nelson and Winter 1982) and technological paradigms (Dosi 1984).

From a sociological perspective the evolutionary approaches offer a great variety of highly fruitful starting points for an interdisciplinary analysis of economic processes, and for this reason the following presentation will focus on this current. Although the authors concerned (like those of the other two currents mentioned above) bow to the methodological criteria of mainstream economics, placing great importance on formalizing their theory with the aid of mathematical models in order not to lose touch with their own discipline, they do develop a set of conceptual instruments that can be used to grasp quite exactly the qualitative dimensions of economic action and the complex interaction processes that determine technical change. The evolutionary approach is conceived broadly enough to be able to encompass topics involved in the other strands as well – the role of demand and relative factor prices and the significance of path dependency.[15]

The basis of evolutionary theory is a comprehensive critique of the premises of the neoclassical equilibrium model, and above all of the assumption of perfect information, a globally valid general production function, and given preferences or means. The critique focuses on the following points:[16]

- All empirically substantial information is sacrificed to the need to maintain the degree of abstraction called for by formal mathematical models, which increasingly insulates economic problems from reality;[17]

–   with an eye to modeling subjectivity, uncertainty, and change, complex formulas are included in the models that lack solid and empirical grounding: *"orthodoxy builds a rococo logical palace on loose empirical sand"* (p. 33);

–   conventional economics concentrates on the decision-making processes of firms, though both decisions and their practical implementation are bound up with uncertainty;

–   firms do not pursue clearly defined, coherent, unchanging goals; decisions emerge instead from social negotiation processes with changing coalitions within and between different management levels; altered framework conditions require "renegotiations" in which the "more rational" view does not necessarily win;[18] under these conditions entrepreneurial decisions can no longer be described as utility maximization;

–   finally, orthodoxy's reifying view of technical knowledge and skills (static input/output coefficients; neglect of the time factor; technical knowledge, as a blueprint or skills of engineers, is always available as a public good) is criticized,[19] defining it with reference to an empirically graspable definition of knowledge as an *"attribute of the firm as a whole, as an organized entity, and ... not reducible to what any single individual knows, or even to any simple aggregation of the various competencies and capabilities of all the various individuals, equipment, and installations of the firm."* (p. 63)

The positive basic assumptions of an evolutionary theory of technical change include the following:

–   Methodologically, the theory looks into the processes of emergence that are behind empirically observable phenomena: This means that such a theory relies on dynamic, if need be historical, explanations; functionalist explanations are rejected.

–   The theory is based on the actions of the agents involved (what they do and why they do it), and these need to be identified and explained; that is – with the exception of the metaobjective of earning profits – the theory does not proceed on postulated assumptions on "rationally" acting agents and their given preferences but includes in its inquiry the motives and goals of economic action, since the concern is always to explain specific (for Giddens: spatiotemporally embedded) action.

Evolutionary theory sees several reasons for actor heterogeneity and – in connection with this factor – innovations:

– The actors have only imperfect information on the present and future setting of their action; accordingly, the initial assumption must be bounded rationality. Due to imperfect information and path-dependent learning agents take different decisions, even under the same market conditions.

– It is at the same time assumed that agents are always in a position to develop new technologies, behavioral and organizational patterns, i.e. that the emergence of innovations must always be reckoned with.

– Finally, the interaction processes between agents (inside and outside markets) have the effect of selection mechanisms on the behavioral patterns and the innovations of agents, i.e. they influence the economic efficiency of "bearers" of various routines, technologies, and strategies.

– Since the aggregate economic results of individual actions (growth patterns, industrial structures) are mediated through the interplay between them and collective interaction processes, Dosi speaks of them – as did Durkheim a century earlier – as emergent properties of economic systems.

Technical change and/or technical learning in firms is understood as an interactive process due to the experiences made in different departments of a firm (internal sources of learning) and the experiences and demands of customers, suppliers, licensees, universities, laboratories, and so on (external sources). Learning processes may be either institutionalized (e.g. in the form of search processes in the R&D departments of firms or in special contract labs) or informal (e.g. in the form of exchanges with suppliers or users). The speed and the direction of learning processes are influenced by the (various) stocks of knowledge and problem-solving capacities that firms have; these differences also have to do with the cumulative character of technological learning processes.

On the whole, entrepreneurial learning is influenced by four factors:

> *"first, (the changes in) innovative opportunities (strictly speaking, the 'sources' of technical change pertain to this domain); secondly, the incentives to exploit those opportunities themselves; thirdly, the capabilities of the agents to achieve whatever they try to do, conditional on their perceptions of both opportunities and incentives, and, fourthly, the organizational arrangements and mechanisms through which technological advances are searched for and implemented."* (Dosi 1997, p. 1532)

These four factors result together in relatively stable patterns of technical change – as regards input coefficients (the concern of Hayami and Ruttan) and product features (the concern of the product-cycle theories of Posner, Vernon, Hirsch) – that are based on relatively unchanging, for the most part incrementally growing, stocks of knowledge of the firms concerned. For these firm- and industry-specific stocks of knowledge – technical knowledge concerned with the search for innovations and organizational procedures used to test and take over innovations – Dosi has coined the term technological paradigm.[20] The technological paradigm determines both the knowledge-based ("conceivable") possibilities of future technical progress and the limits facing substitution between production factors.

Despite the possibilities and limits of technical change, in large measure endogenously determined as they are, there are also effective external influences which take on four forms: changes of relative prices and demand and supply conditions – i.e. incentives – influence first the direction and second the intensity of the search. But price changes also have an impact on constant search processes, specifically by influencing which search results are chosen: whether or not a new technology is introduced can be influenced by altered relative prices; the choice of the new technology thus alters the initial conditions for the next stage of search and selection. This third form concerns the interaction between external influences mediated through price signals and the inherent dynamics of search processes:

> *"Even if opportunities do not change and agents do not perceive variations in relative prices as incentives to change their search rules* (this is what is meant by the first two forms, I.S.), *it is enough that relative prices enter into the criteria of choice between what has been found by search and what is already in use, in order to determine – in probability – 'induced' changes in the patterns of factor use, at the level of individual firms and whole industries."* (Dosi 1997, p. 1537)

The fourth form becomes effective even when the agents abide by their routines and there is no search for innovations: under these conditions the market will at given prices prefer those companies whose "better" technology allows them to invest in expanding their capacities.

Evolutionary theory does not aim at a one-sided analysis of external (price-related) incentives for entrepreneurial innovations but is instead – since it cannot assume any fixed response patterns – forced to investigate endogenous interaction between the incentive structure on the one hand and the learning capacities of firms on the other.

Once we proceed on the assumption of endogenous interaction patterns, it is not far-fetched to imagine learning processes in terms of paths. These paths are – as was noted above – grounded differently: while Nelson and Winter assume paths determined by routines, i.e. by behavior, which can be reinforced or weakened by market-mediated sanctions, Arthur and David are interested less in the behavioral dimension than in the diffusion of technologies and innovations. The latter model focuses on feedback processes that are set in motion by the choice of a given technical solution to the incentive structure for the other firms or users of the technology. Both models underline the significance of the historical analysis of innovation sequences (because of the long-term effect of original decisions) and the risk involved in sticking with outdated technological solutions due to routines and the long-term lock-in of capital.

In spite of the repeated emphasis of economic constraints and market-mediated incentives for the search for and selection of innovations (i.e. the incremental or radical alteration of routines),[21] the observer is struck by the great significance of historical action processes or development paths which evolutionary theory ascribes to the understanding of economic phenomena. It in this way questions the methodological consensus of mainstream economics, with its logically coherent, temporally invariant models of economic decisions on the utility-maximizing allocation of scarce resources arrived at on the basis of stable preferences. With reference to the price system, mainstream economics ascribes to the market the function of an unbiased mechanism of coordination and integration within the framework of an economic system marked by division of labor, differentiated in functional terms, and borne by individual agents.[22]

In contrast to the conventional view, evolutionary theory develops an understanding of economic action marked by inexact decisions, which are themselves subject to processes of social negotiation; these decisions can claim validity for only limited periods of time, since the knowledge horizon against which they are taken is inevitably clouded by uncertainty and unknown variables. If prices are interpreted by conventional theory as clear-cut signals themselves in need of no interpretation whatever, evolutionary theory proceeds on the assumption that the interpretations made by economic agents against the background of their experience-based knowledge are the decisive factor involved in lending meaning and direction to their projected actions.[23] If this is the case, we cannot proceed on the assumption that the coordination works of market and price system are sufficient to ensure social integration. It is more likely that the routines of economic agents will contain a number of conscious and unconscious interpretations of the action of other agents, part of which is mediated through the market, part situated outside the market. Economic action is in this sense seen far more as an element of the general logic of social action than both conventional economics and sociological systems theory are willing to concede.[24]

3.2.2   Economic Action as Action in Routines

The concept routine was developed by Nelson and Winter to designate *"regular and predictable behavioral patterns of firms"* or *"a repetitive pattern of activity in an entire organization, ... an individual skill, or, ... the smooth uneventful effectiveness of ... an organizational or individual performance"*. (Nelson and Winter 1982, pp. 14 and 97, the following page numbers refer to this publication.) Routine has two components or dimensions: the skills of firm members and, analogously, the organizational skills and behavior forms at the firm level.

Skill is defined as *"a capability for a smooth sequence of coordinated behavior that is ordinarily effective relative to its objectives, given the context in which it normally occurs."* (p. 73) The exercise of skills is bound to three presuppositions that give rise to their routine character (the overlaps with Giddens' concept of practical consciousness are obvious here):

– Skills are performed as a unit, not unlike computer programs; they are complex, rapidly occurring, serial processes. Rapidity and automatic performance are the marks of the skillful performer, who need not concentrate on individual steps, since he has each movement, each separate event, "at his fingertips."

– Part of a skill consists of tacit knowledge, i.e. of skills that, while mastered, cannot be fully explained or formulated. The degree of tacitness differs; many skills can be taught better by verbal instruction, others by practical experience, since language is an imperfect instrument for transferring knowledge, one that does not obviate trial-and-error processes (p. 80). The ability to articulate knowledge by language runs up against three limits that determine its degree of tacitness: *"the feasible time rate of information transfer through symbolic communication"* (especially problematical with rapid sequences), *"the limited causal depth of the knowledge"* (mastery of a skill often requires more psychomotor skills than theoretical knowledge), and coherence (language, with its linear organization, and the human short-term memory are unable to present all necessary details in their context). *"In short, much operational knowledge remains tacit because it cannot be articulated*

fast enough, because it is impossible to articulate all that is neces-
sary to a successful performance, and because language cannot
simultaneously serve to describe relationships and characterize
things related." (pp. 81 f.)

– There is a tension between the performance of skills and conscious
decisions: conscious decisions are taken only to a very limited extent and refer for the most part to the choice of an appropriate action sequence, which is then performed automatically. This choice
is itself determined by bounded rationality (or the number of options are limited), which is grounded in the skills themselves as
well as in the prevalent technological paradigm. The advantages of
paradigms must thus be sought in their suppression or obviation of
conscious decisions: action takes on the form of clear-cut routines
involving no time delays. The risk is that routine behavior may be
incorrect, ineffective, and irrelevant when the framework conditions have changed (pp. 84f.).

The complexity and the tacitness of skills make it difficult to estimate
an actor's actual skill (what is he really capable of?) and to describe it
exactly (what does the skill consist of?). This means that it is not possible to predict accurately what someone in possession of a skill will
actually be able to achieve. An additional factor is that the environment
in which the skill was acquired or learned as a rule differs from the
setting in which it is to be applied; to avoid these frictional losses,
firms, at least in knowledge-intensive industries, develop an interest in
training and employing young workers or increasing the length of their
employment.

At the level of organizational skills and forms of entrepreneurial behavior, Nelson and Winter are concerned with the essence and the origins of the continuity of stable routines, especially in large corporations
in which internal dynamics are of great significance. Routines display
three functional modes that ensure their continuity: they act as an organizational memory, as a truce, and as a target.

Routines operate as an organizational memory to the extent that *"the*
routinization of activity in an organization constitutes the most impor-
tant form of storage of the organization's specific operational knowl-

edge." (p. 99) Organizations remember by being active, not unlike the individual, who retains his skills by exercising them every day. Exercising a routine is a process of social coordination: the members of an organization must be familiar with and able to perform its subfunctions; to achieve this, they must take in signals and messages from their environment and interpret them with reference to their area of activity so that the flow of activities is kept up. This information is also mediated verbally; firms tend to form linguistic codes of their own that distinguish them from other firms and that are adapted to the specific organizational and technical requirements posed by the processes in the firm.

The formation of routines in a firm focuses operational knowledge (the knowledge, experience, and memory of individuals) in the social context in which it has emerged and in which alone it is meaningful; routines make this complex knowledge accessible for regular application. A routine works because it is based on shared experiences that interlink individual knowledge, giving rise to a detailed and specific communication pattern that carries routine behavior (p. 104 f.).

Routines can be conceived as a truce in that their operation requires a compromise between all actors involved, that is, between the formal and functional expectations which the organization places on its employees and their motivation. What is concealed behind this explanation of why employees remain with a firm is the view that their remaining is not attributable solely to structural moments of constraint to which the individual is subject (e.g. the constraint to work to earn wages), it may also be based on voluntary decisions. Here the analogy to Giddens' concept of structure as at the same time enabling and constraining is especially evident; his view of power, according to which dependent persons also have power over their superiors, plays a role here as well. Nelson and Winter refer to the truce as the origin of the symbolic cultures that emerge in firms and ensure compliance with rules and routines by means beyond conventional sanction mechanisms. Changes of routines question this truce, are bound up with uncertainty, and are thus avoided as long as possible (p. 112).

Routines function as a target when they no longer operate on their own (i.e. when the two mechanisms mentioned above no longer work). This is the case especially when disorders due to altered framework conditions crop up or when a new organization is being built up. In the first case control is used to attempt to screen out undesired change: everything coming in from the outside must be subjected to selection, modification, and monitoring in order to adapt it to the demands of routine, i.e. it is homogenized. New personnel is also trained in such a way as to place limits on new innovation spaces. In building new organizations or imitating successful routines from other organizations, the concern is less control than it is to mobilize creative potentials within the organization or external potentials by, for instance, enticing personnel away from competitors.

The control of a routine or a truce clearly points to possible reasons why organizations may abide by routines that have proved successful in the past. It also shows that, in analogy to the automatic execution of individual skills, an automatic performance of organizational routines limits the possibilities available for conscious decisions, making organizations cumbersome: the price exacted by the high level of effectiveness of practiced routines is a low level of flexibility.

What is the relationship that exists between routinized behavior and the optimization of entrepreneurial decisions in the sense of profitability? According to the evolutionary view, firms operate along the paths of routines that prove their worth under the constraints of the market. In view of the heterogeneity of firms and their routines, we can speak here only in a very relative sense of optimizing economic activity. Changes to a routine due to innovation can be regarded as an approximation to optimizing action. Such innovations may emerge from the routine itself when the usual routine is used to solve a problem, and the cumulative knowledge of the problem-solver (e.g. from the repair and maintenance department or the marketing department) gives rise to new findings on the causes of the problem that can then be applied to change the routine used to avoid the problem. In addition, existing routine elements can be recombined or new subroutines can be introduced (organizational innovations) without fundamentally changing the overall arrangement. *"Reliable routines of well-understood scope* (without any operational and semantic ambiguities, I.S.) *provide the best components for new combinations".* (p. 131)

Even the search for innovations takes place within routines, a fact particularly often observed in large corporations with R&D departments of their own. Various heuristic instruments are used here: management is geared in terms of its general corporate strategy, the details of which are worked out by lower-level and specialized departments on the basis of their own routines. We clearly see against the background of this view why Japanese management routines were bound to appear revolutionary in the eyes of the US and Europe: in the Japanese system the members of the organization were forced a) to pay far more attention to higher-level operational targets which are otherwise located downstream (total quality management), b) to integrate the logic of other departments into their direction of search or behavioral routines, or c) to look at least for constant exchange with other departments in order to be better able to deal with problems ocurring at the interfaces (Meyer-Stamer 1997 and Lingnau 1996).

To sum up, an organization's ability to exercise *"a distinctive package of economic capabilities of ... relatively narrow scope,"* above all through its routines, is caused by the tacit knowledge contained in the routinized cooperation of organization members and the "truce" between management and these members (p. 134). Nelson and Winter view firms, above all large corporations, primarily as conservative institutions inclined to retain their routines. *"Highly flexible adaptation to change is not likely to characterize the behavior of individual firms"* (p. 135), since, first, the economic success of this routinized action speaks in its favor and, second, changing routines in a firm calls for expensive new bargaining processes with an uncertain outcome. Nelson and Winter conclude from this that in the future firms will probably continue to act as they do today; changes are more likely where resistance is weakest.

But how does change occur, and how is it dealt with by firms? Evolutionary theory answers this question by applying the process of evolution (including mutation and selection) to economic processes.

3.2.3   The Process of Economic and Technical Change as an Evolutionary Process

Evolutionary economic theory is strongly marked by the new concept of evolution that has supplanted the old one (Allen 1988). The old concept proceeded on the assumption of evolution as a goal-directed process aimed at an equilibrium between functionally superior individuals and organizations and their environment. But this resulted in a methodological problem: to investigate causal relations (evolutionary selection mechanisms) in complex systems it is necessary to reduce this complexity to simple models that consist of typical elements and that can be used to determine and/or simulate the average behavior of systems and their elements. All variables and parameters fluctuate around these average values. Concentration on average values, however, masks the deviations and mutations on which the process of evolutionary change is based – microscopic diversity vanishes behind macroscopic regularity. The new concept of evolutionary theory proceeds on the assumption of self-organizing systems in a state of disequilibrium. In such systems *"basic physical non-linearities (...) in fact amplify fluctuations of variables and lead to symmetry-breaking instabilities in which structure and organization appear or, if already present, evolve qualitatively."* (Allen 1988, p. 101)

According to this view, two essential characteristics determine the evolutionary processes:

–   Since the process concerned is a continuous one, the populations preferred will tend to be not those with perfect reproduction but those whose reproduction displays mutations and variability, because only the latter give rise to the novel creations needed by evolution. Evolution does not lead to optimal behavior, since what it needs is organisms that are not only efficient but also variable. Diversity at the microscopic level is part of the evolutionary strategy of the survivors.

–   Since the process is constantly influenced by chance mutations or variations, it is a nonlinear process whose individual stages can be intensified by feedback effects. Permanent bifurcation of the evolutionary path is possible. This means that the notion of a unidirectional process with an essentially predictable goal must be abandoned. Applied to firms and their routines, this means that it is not optimal behavior (or optimal routines) but the ability to introduce change by learning that is the best guarantee of survival.

The new concept of evolutionary processes makes it plain that evolutionary economic theory is not guilty of the Giddensian verdict that it adheres to a determinist concept of social development. Giddens' critique of evolutionary theory is colored by the old concept which, if it was to retain its claim to validity, had to express itself on the goal of evolution – and affirm it in the sense of accepting an observable reality as one that has emerged from natural (i.e. objective) processes of selection. Giddens is compelled by his view of social systems as the outcome of recursive and reflexive social action to reject this line of thought. In Giddens' eyes action processes do, it is true, rest on routines and are embedded in a flux of behavior that conveys structural constraints from the past to the present; but the structural constraints are just as open to change as their emergence is based on chance events and decisions.

The new concept of evolution as an open, self-organizing (i.e. recursive) process is far more compatible with Giddens' definition of social action and his dual concept of structures. And for this reason the approach represented by evolutionary economic theory is fundamentally compatible with Giddens' theory of structuration, even though some differences do remain.[25]

Giddens' idea of the embeddedness in time and space of social action and the emergence of moments of social structure that bind present action, thus reproducing social systems and their characteristics across space and time – in evolutionary economics this idea corresponds to the notion of routines as the outcome of cumulative, communication-based learning processes of members of firms, which are framed by the demands presented by the technological paradigm, the specific firm concerned (i.e. previous routines), and the structural constraints of the market (i.e. of the action of other firms and competitors).

Complementing Giddens, evolutionary economic theory shows us the way to a better understanding of processes of change at the microlevel.

Giddens instead is interested in change at the far more highly aggregated level of social systems (from feudalism to capitalism, etc.).

In economics the basic evolutionary subprocesses are search and selection. Search processes of existing firms or the market entry of new firms (with novel products and production processes) lead to innovations which are termed, in analogy to the field of biology, mutations. The search differs from routine activities: the search for new information gives rise to additional costs when compared to simply continuing on with a routine: this amounts to taking a new, irreversible step. This step does, to be sure, entail uncertain outcomes; it is also contingent in that it is bound to a specific historical state of knowledge. *"Search processes are historical processes, not repetitive and not readily separable from other processes of historical change."* (p. 172)

What further characterizes search processes is that they are geared to problems to which a solution is needed, and that they get underway in the proximity of the problem symptoms. These symptoms define the direction of search, above all for incremental improvements of technologies in use. The decision whether or not to introduce innovations is influenced by the assessment of technical staff and management's estimate of the economic potentials of the proposed innovation; each group has only rough knowledge of the specialized field of the other group. Since, due to the uncertainty associated with innovations, it is unclear ex ante which decision is the "right" one, personal and organizational differences in judgement and perception also play a significant role. Thus a firm's routines (and how compliance with them is monitored) play an important role in the search process. This in turn means that a firm's factor intensity tends to remain the same across time.

The search process (or R&D) is described by Nelson and Winter as a dynamic, open process that generates more than merely precisely definable inventions, in that it broadens the knowledge base available for use in new attempts to solve problems. Technical progress is thus a cumulative process that builds on previous stages, and its direction is roughly determined by existing routines. This direction is referred to by Nelson and Winter as trajectories, and these are influenced by the ideas of technical personnel, by technical bottlenecks and economic, physical, and other constraints.[26]

The setting in which a selection is made consists of a number of elements: firm-specific costs and benefits stemming from the introduction of an innovation; consumer preferences; legal restrictions; the relationship between profit and expansion or contraction of the firm itself and its mechanisms of learning and imitation (p. 262 f.). There are two mechanisms for the diffusion of profitable innovations: an innovation is introduced by a pioneer firm that makes use of it in several products and processes, increasing its market share (expansion, edging out of competitors). The consequence is that the innovation is imitated by other firms. If the innovation we are looking at is, for instance, an improvement to a machine or the development of a new one, the manufacturers will be interested in, and actively promote, its diffusion.[27]

Dosi and Orsenigo (1988) define the path more exactly: *"Given sufficient stability in technological paradigms and institutional conditions, an evolutionary path (...) is likely to lead to a relatively stable evolution of the system."* (Dosi and Orsenigo 1988, p. 23) The incentive to introduce an innovation is the higher profit that can be achieved through cost-reducing innovations or product innovations for which consumers are willing to pay prices that are higher than the costs. A successful innovation thus means higher profits and with them the possibility of financing expansion, and doing so at the expense of noninnovators, until the latter manage to imitate the innovation. The stability of evolution must thus be sought in the fact that innovation rents are continuously eroded on the one hand by adjustments in terms of price and quantity made by other firms and on the other by imitations aimed at closing the gap. *"In general, the stability of an evolutionary path (...) is likely to rest upon those technical conditions of opportunity, appropriability and cumulativeness characteristic of each technological paradigm and on the permanence of the institutions governing behaviours and expectation formation."*[28]

The selection mechanism rests on the totality of the routines of all firms, and they thus influence the environment both for themselves and for their competitors. Evolution and selection are interdependent processes. The different profitability of routines (genotypes) determines which routines will dominate in the long term. Profitability, however, for its part depends on market prices, which affect all firms with similar routines. But market prices are in turn influenced by routines (the demand for inputs), i.e. by all individual routines. A firm's environment can for this reason not be regarded as exogenously determined, even though it may appear this way from the perspective of the individual firm.

What explains long-term economic change is not the profitability of a firm (or of a product or branch of industry) but the interaction of the evolving system with the *"truly exogenous features of the environment, (...) product demand and factor supply curves."* (p. 161) Nelson and Winter here advance a dual model of the selecting corporate environment. The influence of company routines (i.e. their specific production functions) on competing firms is on the one hand direct: firms attempt to learn from leaders, through imitation, industrial espionage, recruitment of competitor personnel, reverse engineering, and the like; or firms invest in an independent search for technical improvements. Since this dimension is very important, evolutionary theory places great emphasis on the non-market-mediated relations of firms. On the other hand company routines have a direct impact on other firms – by influencing, through their demand and their supply, prices and thus the market mechanism, whose decisive functional characteristic is to exercise impersonal constraint.

The market is, however, not only a constraint, it is at the same time a forum for experimental action: *"The market system is (in part) a device for conducting and evaluating experiments in economic behavior and organization."* (p. 277) What is given is only the physical possibilities on which entrepreneurial action rests; every firm must take a decision on its own specific combination of production factors, and do so under uncertainty. Firms develop a variety of solutions and routines, competition makes this variety possible and rewards those decisions that have proven meaningful in practice.

In this way, driven by search processes and the pressure of selection, a firm moves from one provisional equilibrium to the next; and the phases of equilibrium can be so brief that in the end the assumption of a dynamic disequilibrium is justified.

Based on search and selection, Nelson and Winter formulate a growth theory of their own based on technology-related profitability and productivity differentials between firms and the dynamics set in motion by innovations. *"Firms differ in their awareness, competence, and judgements in choosing to adopt or not adopt new techniques."* (p. 237) This theory also makes it possible to explain differences in welfare levels between countries with reference to different levels of technological competence, instead of arguing, tautologically, with reference to divergent sizes of capital stocks. This proposition is used in later studies by Dosi, Pavitt and Soete which deal with the effects of technical change on international trade and the economic efficiency of nations.[29]

The crucial methodological difference between conventional neoclassical economics and evolutionary economics is that the latter sees search processes as set in time; since these processes are stochastic, nonlinear processes, they are not reversible. Here evolutionary economics' critique of neoclassical theory, with its mechanistic, Newton-style concept of laws of motion (Dosi, Pavitt and Soete 1990, pp. 3, 21), sees eye to eye with the critique formulated by ecological economics. Georgescu-Roegen had accused neoclassical economics of failing to consider the dependence of economic processes on ecological and physical processes involved in the transformation of energy and matter and of failing to give sufficient attention to their social embeddedness. He critically notes in particular that (Georgescu-Roegen 1975, pp. 316 - 325, 344 - 346):

–   conventional economics doggedly clings to abstractions that have proven inappropriate: not the fact that economics proceeds on the assumption of abstract individuals is objectionable, since abstraction from the concrete is part of scientific thinking; but the assumption that "utility and self-interest" are the motives driving economic agents has proven to be a proposition infertile in analytical terms;

–   the satisfaction of individual wishes is assumed to be possible only by means of individually appropriated goods and services, and individuals are therefore assumed to tend, in the end, to make irrational use of collective goods;

– rational economic action is generally equated with profit-maximizing behavior, though there is no reason to assume this.

With the social and natural embeddedness of economic processes and their dependence on historical, irreversible time sequences in mind, Georgescu-Roegen came to the conclusion that economics must rethink the instruments it uses with an eye to analyzing above all constantly variable processes.

In spite of these many points of intersection, the two schools seldom engage in exchange. One can only surmise the reasons. One strong reason can probably be found at the metalevel: thanks to its assumption of absolute physical limits, ecological economics assumes a position of pronounced skepticism vis-à-vis technical innovations, one that is intensified by the fact that the latter were advanced by their opponents to prove that there are no such limits. In recent years ecological economics has placed more emphasis on intensifying energy efficiency and thus started to inquire into the origin of technical innovations (Weizsäcker, Lovins and Lovins 1995; Schmidt-Bleek 1994).

Evolutionary economics asks above all how innovations come about, in devising in this connection a model marked by certain assumptions on the technological and economic restrictions involved for entrepreneurial decisions. This model is based on the interactions between economic agents; apart from the implicitly noted material dimensions of technology, there are no external, i.e. nonsocial, reference variables. This places evolutionary economics within the tradition of the social sciences to regard nonsocial facts as irrelevant. In addition, evolutionary economics has no other possibility to assess innovations than to look at them from a purely economic angle or at the level of entrepreneurial action rationality. It has no possibility to pose the question as to the rationality of the aggregate outcome on the basis of higher-level, exogenous (e.g. ecological) criteria. What this means is that evolutionary economics is unable to consider problems of technical progress such as the substantial increase in the destructive force of potent technologies in the absence of any effective institutional restraints. It is apt to be this pronounced difference in the manner in which economic processes are perceived and the effects of technical change are judged that diminishes the common theoretical ground shared by evolutionary and ecological economics.

Another factor was that while Nelson and Winter (1982) regarded search processes as bound in time and irreversible, this was, for them, not the case for routines. The latter were seen as circular processes that can be endlessly reiterated (the environment permitting). Here Nelson and Winter clung – at least in part – to a neoclassical premise on which ecological economics' critique of neoclassical thinking centers.

This was corrected in later studies; Dosi and Nelson, in a 1993 conference paper, apply their evolutionary model to all forms of methodic activity. The reason they give is that the rationality expectations of neoclassical theory can hold true only for the rare situations involving a perfectly familiar and predictable context, though this condition is as a rule given neither in economics nor the world as a whole. *"Our basic assumption is that agents pursue different forms of rule-governed behavior that are context-specific and to a certain extent independent of events (in the sense that actions are invariant as regards minor changes in information concerning the environment). On the other hand agents can also conduct experiments and discover new rules, in this way again and again introducing new modes of behavior into the system."* And further: *"Are there not good reasons to assert that firms or humans (...) go through evolution when they learn from experience and sift or adapt their plans, strategies, and behaviors? Thought out further, learning and adaption can be conceived as a change of the probability distribution of the actions available, as a discovery of new possibilities of action that result from conclusions drawn from actions that have already taken place and their consequences."* (Dosi and Nelson 1994, pp. 210 and 197)

3.3   Conclusions for the Methodological Approach Pursued by the Present Study

This section will start out by setting out the conclusions that can be drawn from the strengths and weaknesses of the theoretical bodies discussed as regards the methodological approach pursued by the present study (3.3.1). The next section presents the individual steps followed by the empirical study as well as the data sources used (3.3.2).

3.3.1   Conclusions

The normative consequence of the debate over conceptions of **sustainable development** is that the economy (production, trade, and consumption) must be given binding rules for environmental and resource protection. There is broad agreement on the formulation of rules governing the use of renewable and nonrenewable natural resources, which for a number of authors includes the assimilative capacity of the environment (soil, water, air) for the wastes and by-products of production and consumption. It is unclear how these rules governing economic activity (including international trade) can and/or must be changed in such a way as to adequately take into account the biophysical limits of economic growth.

At the end of a critique of its theoretical approach as well as a look at some of the studies dealing with tropical deforestation, not much remains of the claim of **natural-resource economics** to provide information on general economic laws governing resource use. Its methods (cost-benefit analysis, calculation of the net present value of a natural resource with competing utility functions, determination of the willingness of the public to pay for environmental and resource protection, and so forth) can, however, be used to analyze resource use under market constraints, though without being able to draw any conclusions on ecological optima. These methods are also suited as aids in coming to decisions on policy alternatives, though with the following restrictions: The presupposition is a monetary valuation of (unknown) stocks of resources and the life-support system, but without any clarity as to how this is to be possible in view of changing preferences and technologies and a time horizon which must be assumed as unlimited. An additional factor is that aggregate individual economic preferences necessarily carry more weight than any such objective as intertemporal justice (preservation of stocks for future generations), which fact in turn further obscures the connection between the ecological and the economic optimum.

Ecological economics points to three important aspects that must be considered if the environment and natural resources are to be given an autonomous status in economic processes:

- economic processes must be analyzed as embedded in space and time, as irreversible processes with cumulative interactive effects on the environment and the economic system;
- this includes consideration of the biophysical limits of economic activities, e.g. in the form of ecological circumstances in the locale where economic activities are conducted;
- finally, ecological economics points to the basic problem that further quantitative growth of the economic subsystem is no longer compatible with the maintenance of life-support systems at the global level.

The mainstream of ecological economics emphasizes the need to embed economic activities in natural cycles; but it has little to say on the problem of embedding them in social processes and structures. Sociological theories and theories of technical change are more concerned with this question.

Sociology need not answer the question posed by the relationship between nature and society in the form of general laws, but it can place them in the context of historically specific relations in society, economy, culture, and religion.

The theory of structuration avails itself of concepts and figures of thought that can be used to understand social action – as does ecological economics – as generally bound to concrete temporal and spatial contexts. These concepts include the spatiotemporal organizational pattern of social action, routines of day-to-day action and the constraints under which these routines develop, and the practical and discursive consciousness which agents possess and which permits them to master and reflect, and if need be to change, their day-to-day life. These forms of consciousness give rise to considerations as to the extent to which the experience of having failed in the face of nature's resistance, an experience repeatedly made by human beings, is recognized as such and how these experiences are reflected: What factors are made responsible for this failure? What concepts, what knowledge are available for the purpose? What encourages social "environmental learning"?

With reference to the subject of the present study, we can turn to advantage a number of the concepts developed by Giddens. The task is to explain the pattern according to which the timber industry in Pará utilizes the resource "tropical forest" and the role played in the process by external trade relations. According to Giddens, an analysis would have to take consideration of the following dimensions: the spatiotemporal organizational pattern of forest use, timber-processing, and the timber trade, the routines that mark the pattern of resource use, and the material, contextual, and sanction-related constraints under which the routines are formed. Once we had this information it would be possible to determine the structure of resource utilization as it has emerged and is constantly reproduced by the actors involved. An analysis of the discursive consciousness of the agents – which could, for instance, be conducted via qualitative interviews – would make it possible to gauge the extent to which practical and discursive consciousness are congruent or the level of the latter makes it possible for the agents to grasp changes in contextual conditions, recognize possible crises, and discover new types of solutions.

The spatiotemporal organizational patterns of the social activities associated with the tropical-timber industry extend across different localities: What has to be considered here are the forest areas in which the timber is cut, the places in which the sawmills and plywood factories are located, the places of shipment of these wood products, and, finally, the places at which they are sold. These places are as a rule remote from each other, since a good share of tropical timber is demanded in the markets in the south and southeast of Brazil as well as abroad – Europe, Asia, the US, the Caribbean. What has to be explained is the significance of the spatial distribution of logging and processing as well as the fact that the latter has changed markedly over the past 35 years.

The routines to be investigated extend to the usual methods of logging, transportation, and processing as well as to processing depth and sales markets. Here, too, it is important to establish whether these routines have remained constant over time and what factors have led to change.

This consideration leads us to the constraints under which the routines are formed: The first thing to be analyzed is the physical constraints, which in the case of the Amazon region stem from the given spatial factors (distances, infrastructure development, and the like). In the second place, it is necessary to determine the influence of the potential and real impacts of legal sanctions, which can be inferred from the legal regulations, i.e. the concern here is the practical significance of environmental and forestry legislation, taxation systems, and – in the case of timber exports – trade policy. In the third place, we have to determine additional contextual factors that present themselves to the actors as "given structural moments," i.e. factors that have to be taken into account if the activities of the actors are to achieve their ends. These include the macroeconomic framework conditions and economic development in the region itself, the trends in timber markets and demand sectors, and changes in other economic sectors that affect the actors involved in the timber industry. These include in the Amazon region in particular agriculture, since logging is closely intertwined with the expansion of agricultural activities and many sawmill owners invest in land. One other structural moment has grown in significance since the beginning of the 1970s: the unique character of the Amazon ecosystems has, in Brazil itself as well as in most industrialized countries, sharpened the awareness of the population for the necessity of maintaining these ecosystems. Since then the damage incurred in connection with the development and exploitation of the natural resources of the Amazon region have been attentively registered both at home and abroad. The Brazilian government is regularly called upon to limit or prevent this damage. Local actors are also forced to come to terms with this demand and give place to the criticism voiced by the environmental movement.

This enumeration of the dimensions that an analysis of the object of inquiry along Giddensian lines would have to embrace makes it clear that the spectrums considered would have to be far wider than those normally used in the economic approaches discussed above – including ecological economics. The advantage of this approach is clearly that it does not require any sharp reduction of the complexity of the subject matter of the sort we observed in the studies presented by the World Bank or the Kiel authors. Giddens' approach offers resources that can be used to order the complex reality involved in such a way as to gear it to the structurations undertaken by the agents themselves in their own action contexts. This approach thus meets the criterion of "grounded theory" that the method of observation must be oriented as closely as possible to the object under observation in order to avoid preconceived, falsifying, auxiliary categories or abstractions.[30]

Among the theories used to explain technical change, **evolutionary economics** offers a number of points of departure that make it possible to look into the utilization of natural resources under the aspect of constituted constraints (market) and as forms of routinized day-to-day action. This approach refers routines of entrepreneurial action and technological trajectories to the technologies and organizational patterns used and their specific restrictions, in this way defining them more exactly than the theory of structuration. Entrepreneurial learning processes are, in the view embraced by this approach, subject to the (perceived) economic chances offered by innovations, the incentives in the corporate environment, the skills of the companies concerned, and the organizational arrangements and mechanisms that favor (or discourage) the adoption of innovations. The approach also explains how conservative attitudes inimical or skeptical to innovation come about: changes in entrepreneurial routines entail costs, so that improvements will tend more to seek orientation in the path defined by the technology in use, incremental innovations being the result. The problem of given ecological factors is not considered by evolutionary economics, though it can be integrated into the approach.

Seen in terms of the subject of the investigation, we can derive the following questions from the central concepts of evolutionary economics:

–   What are the techno-organizational elements and patterns to which the routines of entrepreneurial action in Pará's timber industry can be traced back?

–   How have these elements and patterns changed in the course of the past 35 years? What economic and institutional incentives (e.g. subsidies, environmental legislation and monitoring) have been influential here?

–   What specific constraints result from these routines for entrepreneurial learning processes? Can Pará's timber entrepreneurs be described generally as conservative and inimical or skeptical to innovation?

On the whole, the complex interface between economics and ecology can be analyzed in a sufficiently broad manner with the aid of the insights won from the theories of structuration and evolutionary economics, without unduly reducing the issue from the outset in terms of either ecological or economic considerations.

Methodologically, this means selecting an interdisciplinary and (in historical and sectoral terms) comparative approach for the investigation of the tropical-timber industry in Pará:

–   In consideration of the specific ecological factors given there, the following chapter (Chapter 4) will give a brief overview of the state of research on the ecology of tropical forests and the ecology of (sustainable) tropical forestry;

–   in consideration of the conditions in the world market and the technical changes that influence the chances and perspectives for the exploitation of tropical timber, Chapter 5 will discuss the developments in the world market for timber and tropical timber since the 1960s and the technical innovations made in the timber industry;

–   with a view to reconstructing the routines of the timber industry and the constraints under which they have emerged, Chapters 6 and 7 will discuss how logging, processing, and marketing have developed in the past 35 years under the constraints noted in Chapters 4 and 5 and how the patterns of resource use dominant today have come about;

– in order to avoid any sectoral reduction of the considerations on a sustainable development of the tropical-timber industry and the external trade of the state of Pará, Chapters 4, 6, and 7 will – at least in outline form – discuss the ecological and economic advantages and disadvantages of other forms of land use and include them in the conclusions (Chapters 8 and 9).

This methodological approach also makes it possible to answer the open questions resulting from a review of the present state of the research:

– The studies of the World Bank and IMAZON suggest three issues: first, it is necessary to more exactly explore the question as to how and under the impact of what economic incentives and institutional conditions the timber industry has developed since the infrastructural development of the Amazon region in the 1960s.

– Second, it is essential to clarify the question as to the empirically observable motives behind the actions of the actors in the timber industry and to what extent we can proceed on the assumption of a self-contained functional differentiation between farmers, sawmill owners, and cattle ranchers involving long-term rationales and professional perspectives. Stone's study additionally poses the question of how rapid a change in traditional action patterns may be assumed to be and how this can be determined empirically.

– Third, in this context we are confronted by the question of the factors and constraints which, beyond log prices and property rights, have influenced the routines in the timber industry.

– The studies by Homma and the group around Barbier show that the tropical-timber industry and trade must be investigated within the framework of the general development of the timber market and recent technological trends in order to take account of substitution trends and – in the sense of Nelson and Winter and Dosi – to draw comparisons between the different development paths in the timber industry. This means that the development of Brazil's timber industry must be considered as a whole.

Table 2:	Basic Data of Firms Interviewed in Pará and Amazonas					
Firms[a]	Main activity	Year of foun- dation	Origin of owner	Formal training of owner / general manager	Turnover (US$ millions)	Profit (%)
A	Exports of sawnwwod	1983/84	Denmark	Degree in business adminis- tration	21.8	0
B	Exports of sawnwood	1985	France	Degree in forestry	15 0	3 - 4
C	Exports of sawnwood	1972	USA	Degree in economics	10.0	losses since 1994
D	Sawmill	1988	Paraná	Degree in forestry	3.5	losses
E	Sawmill	1972	Santa Catarina	Secondary school	10.0	10
F	Plywood mill	1982	Santa Catarina	Secondary school	Out of operation	0
G	Veneer mill	1956	USA	Chemist	15.0	losses
H	Plywood mill	1972	Japan	Degree in business adminis- tration	40.0	2,5
I	Sawmill	1984	Fortaleza	Secondary school	4.6	losses
J	Sawmill	1979	Paraná	Degree in business adminis- tration	2.0	10
K	Exports of sawnwood	1987	Rio Grande do Sul	Geologist	5.0	5

Firms[a]	Volume of timber traded or produced (m³)	Share of exports in production (%)	Export markets[b]	Species	Employees	Forest management plan	Afforestation
							Table 2 (continued)
A	60,000	98.5	20 % F, USA, GB, PO, Phi, Hk, Th	9 (incl. tauari)	350	no	yes
B	36,000	100.0	70 % F, 25 % Fr. Caribbean	6 (95 % tauari)	130	no	no
C	46,000	100.0	USA, French Caribbean, Philippines	60 % quaruba, 20 % virola, 10 % jatobá	48	planned	no
D	4,500	70 0	40 % USA, French Caribbean, GB, PO, SP	jatobá, curupixá, mahogany	95	yes	no
E	18,000	90.0	F, USA, GB, EU, French Caribbean	8 (mahogany, cedro, tauari, curupixá)	400	yes	no
F	36,000	90 0	n.d.	n.d.	0	no	no
G	42,000	100.0	USA	6 (30 % bajera)	650	yes	no
H	80,000	90.0	20 % J, Fr. Caribbean, GB, USA, NL, Venez.	8 (25 % virola)	1.200	no	yes
I	19,000	98.5	USA, Can, PO, SP, I, Arg., J	4 (70 % virola)	250	yes	no
J	3,000	100.0	50 % F, 30 % USA, 20 % Asia	4 (70 % tauari)	50	no	planned
K	14,000	100 0	60 % F, 15 % Chi, Fr. Carib., USA, PO, SP, J	8 (tauari)	140	no	yes

Table 2 (continued)

Firms[a]	Main activity	Year of foundation	Origin of owner	Formal training of owner / general manager	Turnover (US$ millions)	Profit (%)
L	Sliced veneer mill	1990	Germany	Degree in business administration	10.0	0
M	Kitchen articles and furniture made of wood	1986	Rio Grande do Sul	Degree in business administration	12.0	n.d.
N	Sawmill	1980	Espírito Santo	n.d.	3.3	5
O	Plywood mill	1990	Espírito Santo	n.d.	7.7	5
P	Exports of sawnwood	1992	Paragominas	n.d.	1.26	5
Q	Exports of sawnwood	1993	Paragominas	n.d.	3.0	5
R	Sawmill	1994	Switzerland	Degree in business administration	7.16	losses
S	Plywood mill	1982	Rio Grande do Sul / Germany (25 %)	Degree in business administration	16.0	0

Firms[a]	Volume of timber traded or produced (m³)	Share of exports in production (%)	Export markets[b]	Species	Em-ployees	Forest manage-ment plan	Af-fores-tation
L	9,000	74.0	50 % G, USA, Asia	mahogany, curupixá, cedro	230	no	no
M	n.d.	25.0	USA, GB, F, G	7	320	no	yes
N	24,000	10.0	95 % F, J, Chi, G	6 (70 % tauari + curupixá)	170	no	yes
O	24,000	50.0	95 % F, French Caribbean, USA	15-20	418	no	yes
P	3,000	100 0	80 % F, J, USA, B	80-90 % tauari + curupixá, 20 % pau-amarelo	40	no	no
Q	6,000	100.0	90 % F, PO, B, NL	3 (80 % tauari)	n.d.	no	no
R	15,000	53.0	GB, NL, G, B, Chi, A, USA, Asia	39	230	yes	no
S	40,700	70.0	40 % G, 30 % USA	sumaúma, muiracatiara	900	yes	no

a) Firms: A - M are located in the greater area of Belém in Pará, N - Q are located in Paragominas / Pará, R and S in Itacoatiara / Amazonas

b) Export markets: A = Austria, Arg = Argentina, B = Belgium, Can = Canada, Chi = China, EU = European Union, F = France, G = Germany, GB = Great Britain, Hk = Hong Kong, I = Italy, J = Japan, NL = Netherlands, Phi = Philippines, PO = Portugal, SP = Spain, Th = Thailand, Venez = Venezuela

3.3.2   Stages and Sources Involved in the Empirical Study

The empirical investigation centered on reconstructing the action patterns or routines dominant in the timber industry, under consideration of the economic, material, and ecological constraints and chances provided by the publicly financed development of the Amazon region.

Six sources are used to reconstruct the dominant action patterns:

-    empirical studies on the timber industry in the Amazon region and in Pará which have been published since the 1960s;[31]
-    the results of qualitative interviews conducted between September 1997 and March 1998 with 19 timber entrepreneurs in Pará and the Amazon region;[32]
-    the results of some 40 interviews with experts and key persons from government authorities, research institutes, associations, and NGOs concerned with the timber industry in Pará and the Amazon region; these interviews were conducted during the entire course of the investigation (from March 1997 to June 1998) in Belém and other towns (Paragominas, Manaus, and Brasilia);[33]
-    finally, the Brazilian trade statistics and the database of the FAO were evaluated with an eye to documenting Brazil's timber exports and the international timber trade.

The companies interviewed are located in Pará in the greater regions of Belém (13) and Paragominas (4); in the state of Amazonas two companies in Itacoatiara were interviewed. Of the 17 Pará firms, five are sawnwood exporters, seven sawmills, three plywood factories, one a manufacturer of sliced veneers, and another one of furniture and kitchen items of wood. Six of these firms belong to a foreign investor or a foreign group; six come from the south of Brazil, two from the state of Espírito Santo and one from the state of Ceará. Only two of the companies polled belonged to owners from Pará.

In terms of sales, the companies polled varied from R$ 1.2 million and R$ 40 million (the average figure being R$ 10.3 million). The average sales per cubic meter of sawnwood or plywood were R$ 387 (min. R$ 137, max. R$ 1,111) and the average sales per employee were R$ 35.888 (min. R$ 18,421, max R$ 208,333).

These companies' exports represented some 42 % of the volume and 46 % of the value of Pará's timber exports. The most important foreign sales markets of the companies polled were in Europe (29 cases, esp. France, 9, which takes in an average of 67 % of the exports per company); the US (13, an average of 45 % of exports per company), the French Caribbean (7), and Asia (Japan 7, Southeast Asia 3, China 1). This distribution of exports is highly atypical for the large tropical-timber markets (above all Japan); it mirrors Brazil's very restricted shares in this segment of the world timber market.

The evaluation of the statistical data was rendered difficult by the fact that there is hardly any other sector (excepting perhaps gold-mining) that is as poorly documented as Pará's timber sector. There are two reasons for this: on the one hand the largely illegal exploitation of forests, which, thanks to generally low sawmill productivity, is the necessary economic condition for any profitability on the part of these companies. On the other hand the fact that timber export is increasingly tied up in the drug traffic or the money-laundering associated with it. So the sector has little interest in an exact documentation of its economic efficiency, the quantities of timber actually felled, and the size of the timber market.

The empirical studies published between 1960 and 1980 make it possible to assess the quality of the statistical data in that these studies always investigated samples that were very large and met the criteria of representativeness.

4   Tropical Ecology and Sustainable Forestry

This chapter will first discuss the given ecological conditions to which tropical forestry must adapt; it presents for the purpose the classical model of the ecology of tropical rainforests of the *terra firme* (mainland) and explains some revisions that will have to be made to it as a result of more recent ecological research findings (4.1). The second section will discuss the general principles of nature-oriented sustainable forestry and present the state of research on the Amazon region (4.2).

This will be followed by a brief presentation of the effects of sustainable forestry on business management (4.3.) and the present state of the ecological certification of forest management in the Amazon region (4.4.).

In the tropics the ecosystems are not permanently utilized for the purpose of social reproduction to the extent that they are in the temperate zones. If we analyze the reasons for this reduced use of the natural environment we run up against, among others, the question whether there are not natural limits on the utilization of tropical ecosystems which restrict their domestication to very narrow ranges and preclude any transfer of the resource-utilization pattern customary in the temperate zones.[1]

This pattern of resource utilization developed in the past 300 years in the temperate zones, above all in Europe, under the conditions of capitalism and the industrial revolution and has spread throughout the entire globe. Its core consists of two basic elements: first, economic utilization in the framework of an economy compelled to grow continuously and, second, the attempt to increasingly subject natural processes to human control and regulation in order to increase their natural productivity and adapt them to the constraints of economic utilization. This core of the relation between society and nature has come under increasing fire in the past 30 years. Research results on the risks of the overexploitation of renewable and nonrenewable resources and the cumulative effects of the rapid accumulation of various waste materials which the natural environment is able to assimilate only at a very slow pace have shown that the present pattern of resource utilization must be changed. At the UN Conference on Environment and Development in 1992 in Rio, the international community committed itself to take measures to maintain the world's natural life-support systems, and in particular to protect both the climate and biodiversity.

One especially explosive issue addressed in connection with the debate on the conflict between environmental protection and socioeconomic development is the question as to how the tropical ecosystems should be utilized. The main question is whether the characteristics of these ecosystems permit their domestication at all, i.e. to what extent the

ecological and economic costs involved here are offset in the short and
long term by benefits, both at the global and at the local levels.

As regards the Amazon region, different scientific disciplines provide
different answers based, implicitly or explicitly, on differently defined
natural limits:

– In the field of anthropology, the school of cultural ecology seeks to
  include the limiting ecological factors in the reconstruction of the
  paths of cultural development. Pioneering studies by Steward
  (1948), Meggers (1954), and Harris (1959) focused first on the low
  calorie outputs there due to low-nutrient soils in the *terra firme*,
  later on turning their attention above all to protein deficiency
  (Meggers 1971, Gross 1975, Roosevelt 1980). While the group
  around Betty Meggers points to this factor in explaining why the
  Amazon region has apparently never produced enough surplus
  food to make possible a social division of labor and the development of complex social structures, the group around Ana Roosevelt
  derived from these findings the question of specific forms of social
  organization that were necessary in the *várzea* (flood plain) and the
  terra firme adjoining it to overcome these limits. Reports from the
  first Spaniards who explored the Amazon region in the 15th century indicate the existence of hierarchically structured societies
  with substantial food reserves; more recent archeological findings
  made by Roosevelt suggest that settlement, domestication of plants
  for cultivation, and the invention of cultural techniques such as ce-
  ramics first occurred in the eastern Amazon some 10,000 years ago
  and then spread into the Andes region (Hurtienne 1988; Meggers
  1984, 1994; Roosevelt 1991; Johnson 1982; Dieguez and Silva
  1997).[2]

– Analyses conducted by social scientists of the consequences of
  agricultural settlement programs and large-scale industrial projects
  in the Amazon region in the 1970s and 1980s were concerned with
  the problems that resulted from the import of unadapted institutional structures and patterns of economic utilization to ecosystems
  that are different, more fragile, and less well known than those in
  which the imported systems and patterns were developed. The conclusion was often that this fragility sets limits to the domestication

of these ecosystems, and that they thus have a structurally low carrying capacity for human settlement (Altvater 1987; Bunker 1985; Moran 1982, 1993; Moran et al. 1996; Hall 1989; Hecht 1983).

– The field of ecology, whose findings provide the groundwork for the above-mentioned disciplines, was long dominated by a model of the ecology of the tropical rainforest that entailed stringent restrictions on any human utilization of the rainforest, limiting such uses to gathering, hunting, and farming with fallow cycles of at least 20 years. These forms of utilization were bound up with two conditions: a permanently low population density and a low standard of living (i.e. permanent exclusion from industrial society) (Odum 1997; Jordan 1985a and b; Norgaard 1981).[3]

This ecological model influenced many analyses of human production systems in the Amazon region concerned mainly with smallholder agriculture and the difficulties involved in settlement programs along the Transamazônica and in Rondônia (Coy 1987; Mahar 1988; Moran 1981). The classical model of tropical ecology could not even support forestry, since the postulated fragility of the ecosystems seemed to indicate that any intervention was fraught with risk.

4.1   Features of Forest Ecosystems in the Tropics

Tropical forest ecosystems occur in a relatively broad band between the equator and the Tropics of Cancer and Capricorn, i.e. in Africa (mainly in the Congo Basin), in Asia (mainly in Indonesia, Malaysia, and other Pacific islands), and in Central and South America. The Amazon Basin contains the largest closed tropical forest, over 50 % of the world's stands of tropical forest in an area 26 times larger than Germany. As in the temperate zones, there are pronounced differences between tropical and subtropical forests due to different habitat conditions (altitude, fluctuations in rainfall and temperature levels, soils) and the different plant and animal populations these imply.

The literature distinguishes between tropical moist forests, seasonal semi-evergreen tropical forests, and moist deciduous forests. The first group has no dry season (i.e. no one month with a precipitation rate <

100 mm), the second group has a dry season of two to three months, and the third is characterized by a dry season of up to five months (Whitmore 1975; Walter 1973).[4] This classification remains relatively controversial.

Box 2:   Smallholder Agriculture and Ecology in the Amazon Region

In many analyses small family farms are identified with shifting cultivation, which follows the classical pattern encountered on the agrarian frontier: Small agricultural settlers migrate in the wake of the logging companies through previously untouched primary forest areas to the agrarian frontier. But thanks to their lack of capital, low education levels, and risk aversion they have no real chance to build up competitive farms on an ecologically and economically sustainable basis and are supplanted by big landowners (Fearnside 1993; Almeida 1996; Serrão and Homma 1993).[5] Roughly half of deforestation is caused by big cattle ranches; the fallow-cropping practiced on small farms accounts for only some 30 % of deforestation, while these farms generate a stable secondary growth on roughly 50 % of their land (Browder 1988; Costa 1992; Walker et al. 1993).

Fallow-cropping is, however, often seen in a negative light due to its environmental impacts, above all regular burning off of secondary growth with an eye to preparing the land for tillage and fertilizing it with the ash generated in this way. This causes CO_2 emissions and nutrient losses; the loss of primary forest areas diminishes biodiversity. Smallholder agriculture is for the most part, erroneously, equated with shifting cultivation. This view overlooks the fact that family farming does not necessarily contribute to the progressive degradation of ever more new primary forest areas but can also stabilize in a defined area. It is growing population density – due to population growth and migration – that leads to spatial expansion.

The relative stabilization of small farms in large settlement areas in the Amazon region, e.g. the Transamazônica, Marabá, and the northeast of Pará, stands in contradiction to both the view held on the low economic and ecological chances of survival of small family farms and the classical model of the ecology of tropical rainforests (EMBRAPA-CPATU-GTZ 1991; CAT 1992; Costa 1995; Walker et al. 1995; Moran et al. 1996; and Scatena et al. 1996). Stabilization means that such farms have succeeded in surviving economically, diversifying their production systems, and developing adapted management methods.[6] These family farms are encountered both in areas with a relatively large stand of primary forest and in areas marked chiefly by secondary vegetation.

The findings on tropical forest ecosystems referred to here stem from empirical studies which were conducted in a limited number of locations and then served as the basis for generalizations. According to these studies, tropical forest areas have the following features in common (Hurtienne 1988; Lamprecht 1989; Weischet 1980; Sommer, Settele, Michelsen et al. 1990; and Bruenig 1996):

–   Temperature: Nearly constant all year; there are no seasonal changes like those in the temperate zones. The temperatures can, however, fluctuate considerably in the course of a day; fluctuations increase with increasing altitude. Days in the tropics are of equal length nearly all year long.

–   Precipitation: It generally rains throughout the year; the annual precipitation ranges from 2,000 to 2,500 mm (max. one-month dry season) and more. These high precipitation levels are as a rule associated with high humidity. Dry seasons can either occur sporadically or be restricted to a few months. For the Amazon region it has been found that 48 % of the precipitation that falls between Manaus and Belém stems from the so-called "micro-hydrological cycle," i.e. from the evapotranspiration of the forests, in certain places this figure may even be as high as 80 %.[7]

–   Soils: Tropical soils are often marked by nutrient poverty. The factor responsible for this is their great age as well as weathering and rain-wash, expedited by high year-long temperatures and precipitation levels. The nutrient scarcity is exacerbated by a low level of clay minerals, which determine the soil's cation exchange capacity and thus its capacity to absorb fertilizers.[8] The humus content of these soils, 1 - 2 %, is very low. To compensate for low-nutrient soils, tropical forests have developed closed above-ground nutrient cycles (microorganisms, ants, and other insects constitute the major share of their animal biomass; they break down leaf litter and deadwood; aerial roots directly absorb the degraded litter, a process which is accelerated by mycorrhiza; the nutrients contained in rainwater are absorbed by dense leaf canopies covered with algae and mosses). On account of this specialization in above-ground nutrient cycles many trees have developed shallow root systems whose most important function is to anchor the trees in the ground.

–   Biodiversity: A high level of biodiversity developed in the course of evolutionary processes of millions of years involving adaptation to low nutrient soils. Rainforests contain far more plant species than forest stands in the temperate zones.[9] The existence of various species with different nutrient needs, a low number of individuals per species, and a great number of specialized ecological niches increases the efficiency of the nutrient cycles. The forests in the Amazon region can support only small numbers of large herbivores and carnivores (= protein storage) because the plants there produce only small quantities of fruit and leaves that can be consumed by animals. The major part of the energy taken in is used to produce wood, which stores nutrients more efficiently than leaves (slower rotting process) and protects them from herbivores. Many leaves are hard and contain toxic substances as a means of discouraging herbivores; seeds and kernels are small, low in number, and often packed in very hard, and thus inedible, shells.

This classical model, with its focus on nutrient poverty of soils and biodiversity is in need of some enlargement and differentiation: in-depth studies have shown that climatic conditions, soils, and the reproductive behavior of plant and animal communities can vary widely. This of course has consequences for the human utilization of tropical ecosystems.

Some important new findings and differentiations:

–   Soils: Although it is true that many tropical-forest soils are less fertile than others, large-scale comparative studies have found that the humus content of tropical forest soils is just as high as, if not higher than, of forest soils in temperate zones. This is very important in that some of the organic substances in humus protect nutrients against leaching while at the same time keeping them available for the plant; i.e. they constitute functional equivalents to (scarce) clay minerals.[10]

–   Root systems: Empirical studies of the root penetration of soils have shown that the depth and density of roots may be greatly influenced by specific habitat conditions and species inventories; there appears not to be any general dominance of shallow root systems.[11]

Studies conducted in the eastern Amazon region, to which Pará belongs, came up with similar findings. This explains how it is possible for evergreen forest formations to grow in this area even though it is marked by dry seasons lasting up to five months. The studies showed that plants compensate for the water deficit in the dry months by using deep roots to draw water from deeper soil strata. It is likely that this water circulation in the soil also transmits nutrients upward from deeper, less weathered strata, making them available to plants.[12] Thanks in part to this compensation for water deficits in the dry months, the secondary vegetation that grows in fallow periods of 7 - 10 years displays evaporation rates comparable with those measured for the primary forest; it would thus appear that even young secondary forest formations can largely assume the function of the primary forest in sustaining the hydrological cycle (Hölscher 1995).

The most important conclusion to be drawn from these results is that there are greater structural similarities between forest ecosystems in all climatic zones than has been assumed until now. A comparative study of the dynamic characteristics of forest ecosystems conducted on the basis of a comprehensive database with information for 120 habitats from all continents also came to this conclusion (Reichle 1981). Some common structural features:

–   In all forest formations, especially in boreal coniferous forests in Siberia, the efficiency of wood production decreases with increasing age;[13]

–   the higher the average tree height, the higher the biomass production; the thicker the stem diameter, the lower the density; wood production increases as a function of net primary production (see below) and intensity of solar radiation (O'Neill and De Angelis 1981, p. 435).

The difference between tropical forest ecosystems and those in the temperate zones is thus to be sought above all in high levels of biomass production and biodiversity, not so much in nutrient cycles.[14]

High, even temperatures, intensive solar radiation throughout the year, and high precipitation levels lead to an extremely high energy throughput in tropical forests, and this results in a gross biomass production higher in absolute terms than that in temperate forests, i.e. these forests store very large quantities of carbon dioxide (see Table 3). It is this sink function for carbon dioxide that makes the protection of tropical forests important to any attempts to prevent worldwide climate change due to increased CO_2 levels.[15]

Table 3: Biomass Production and Losses in Forests (annual balance in tons of dry mass per ha)				
Stock	**Beech forest (Denmark)**		**Tropical Rainforest (Thailand)**	
	Absolute value	in % of GPP	Absolute value	in % of NPP
Annual increase of stock	6.9	35	3.13	2
Leaves	0		0.03	
Twigs and stems	5.3		2.9	
Roots	1.6		0.2	
Annual litter	3.9	20	25.5	20
Leaves	2.7		12.0	
Twigs and stems	1.0		13.3	
Roots	0.2		0.2	
Annual respiration losses	8.8	45	98.9	78
Leaves	4.6		60.1	
Twigs and stems	3.5		32.9	
Roots	0.7		5.9	
GPP=NPP+R	19.6	100	127.5	100
GPP=NPP-R	10.8		28.6	
ECPP	2.23		1.29	
ECPP = economic coefficient of primary production, GPP = gross primary production, NPP = net primary production, R = respiration losses				
Source: Larcher (1994), p. 134				

The higher net primary production of tropical forests must, however, not be equated with a higher yearly incremental growth of the stands, since a far greater percentage of this production per year ends up as litter. Furthermore, the tropical rainforest consumes a far higher percentage of gross primary production for heat-related respiration (98 % as opposed to 45 % in a Danish beech forest). Still, compared in terms of net primary production (NPP), the rainforest has values almost three times higher than those of the beech forest: 28.6 t/ha as opposed to over 10.8 t/ha.

Box 3: Gross and Net Primary Production of Plants

The biomass increase of a stand of plants resulting from transformation of carbon dioxide into plant body mass is referred to as primary production. It is measured in terms of dry organic substance per hectare. Gross primary production (GPP) refers to the overall quantity of carbon absorbed by a given inventory of plants. Deducting respiration losses (R), we come up with net primary productions (NPP), i.e. the actual increase of biomass plus the organic mass lost due to litter and consumption.

The reason for respiration losses is that plants breath off a substantial share of the amount of the carbon that they acquire through photosynthesis (absorbing oxygen and emitting CO_2). In respiration carbohydrates and fats are broken down, a course of events that involves winning energy for the metabolic processes in plant cells. This energy is not available for forming phytomass.

The coefficient resulting from gross primary production and respiration is referred to as the economic coefficient of primary production (ECPP), an average value calculated over protracted periods of time.

Source: Sommer, Settele, Michelsen et al. (1990), p. 146

Comparison between the biomass produced by a European beech forest and a tropical rainforest shows that the incremental growth of stands in the temperate zones can be higher not only in relative but also in absolute terms than it is in tropical forests. According to Jordan (1989), the annual increase of wood in the tropical forests of the Amazon region, Puerto Rico, and Ivory Coast is between 3.9 and 4.9 t/ha/year; only in the dipterocarpaceous forests was a value measured (6.4 t/ha/year) that approaches that noted for the Danish beech forest. By comparison: plantations with fast-growing species reach annual levels of 20 - 40 tons per hectare in tropical and subtropical areas (Lamprecht 1989).

When we speak of high levels of biodiversity we mean plants and organisms that play an important role in nutrient cycles as degraders of litter and other waste products. One issue that remains controversial is the extent to which each of these species must be seen as essential to the stability of ecosystems or whether we can proceed on the assumption of "redundancies." What role these species play – whether, for instance, they constitute a fallback position for the system as a whole for the case of external changes or are more apt to be residues from older states of equilibrium that can now vanish without causing any major damage – is an issue that has not been settled unambiguously (McGrath 1987, 1997).

Table 4:	Biomass Production of Primary and Secondary Forests in the Zona Bragantina, Pará*			
Parameter	Primary forest	Secondary forest (5 years old)	Secondary forest (10 years old)	Secondary forest (20 years old)
Number of trees per ha	1,155	1,096	1,880	1,612
Number of species per ha	316	39	61	82
Biomass (t/ha)	265.7	13.1	43.9	80.5

* Only trees with a DBH > 10 cm (primary forest) or DBH > 5 cm (secondary forest) were counted; the figures for biomass refer to superficial biomass (without soil rootmass)

Source: Salomão, Nepstad and Vieira (1996), p. 46;

The causal relation that exists between the stability of an ecosystem and its succession, biodiversity, and level of primary production is generally unclear.[16] There is agreement on the fact that greater succession means higher primary production, though it is unclear whether biodiversity continuously increases as a function of succession or stabilizes and/or declines again. Nor has any consistent relation been noted between increase of biodiversity and primary production (Odum 1980; Whittaker 1965).

Measurements of biodiversity in secondary forests in Cameroon indicated a higher number of timber types and trunks per hectare than in primary forest, though the latter displayed a greater wood mass. Other measurements made of the animal world in Asia showed that animal species have far fewer chances of survival in secondary forests. In Malaysia it was found that selective logging completely uproots sensitive species, while others withdraw to undisturbed areas in the vicinity.[17]

Comparative measurements of gross primary production and biodiversity in primary and secondary forests are available in the Amazon area only for the Zona Bragantina, the oldest settlement area in the northeast of Pará, in which fallow-cropping has been practiced for about 90 years. The values found show that the number of species initially declines enormously, in order then, however, to increase constantly, as does biomass production. And it must be noted here that for reasons of settlement age the biomass values for the secondary vegetation in the Zona Bragantina are lower than in areas with a record of more recent and less intensive utilization: in Paragominas, which has been settled only 30 years, the average biomass values measured were 51 tons/ha (4.5-year-old secondary growth) and 74 tons/ha (8-year-old secondary growth) in lightly utilized areas; the values were 19 tons/ha and 29 tons/ha for the corresponding moderately utilized areas (Salomão, Nepstad andVieira 1996).

The number of trees per hectare rises as secondary vegetation increases in age. It reaches its highest values in 10-year-old secondary forest and then declines again. At the same time, however, the average stem diameter also increases, so that the biomass values do differ considerably from those for primary forest. The number of species increases constantly with growing secondary-vegetation age, though this figure remains distinctly below the level for primary forest. Individual species respond differently to forest clearance (Vieira, Salomão, Nepstad and Roma 1996): while 268 species were counted in a reference area of primary forest, the figures found for the secondary forest area were 62, 84, 108, and 112 species (secondary forest areas aged 5, 10, 20, and 40 years). 50 - 60 % of these species corresponded to the species found in the primary forest. The authors regard some 43 % of all primary-forest species as endangered in that they occur in secondary forest areas in very low densities and have difficulty in reproduction. The proliferation of 35.4 % of primary-forest species is favored by agricultural utilization; these species are the ones with the highest numbers of individuals. They reproduce through seeds that are spread by fruit-eating animals or via shoots from tree stumps; the latter are hampered by fire clearance in their ability to produce shoots. Animal species also initially decline in secondary forest (57.5 % of the species found in primary forest are also found in 10-year-old secondary forest), in order then to increase again (81.6 % was noted in 20-year-old secondary forest).

Not only is secondary vegetation allowed to grow for seven or eight years as a means of nutrient storage that can be used for agricultural purposes, it is also utilized by farmers in this period: fruit is harvested, medicinal plants gathered, and wood – especially from fast-growing pioneer species – is harvested for use as fuel or to make charcoal.

The most important finding of these investigations is that even after five to eight fallow-cropping cycles (consisting of two years of cultivation and five to ten years of fallow), i.e. after 35 - 96 years, the forest does regenerate in the form of secondary-forest formations. These secondary formations serve important ecological functions: they absorb carbon dioxide (one hectare of five-year-old secondary forest accumulates four million tons of CO_2 per year in its above-ground biomass); they form the basis for permanent agrarian landscapes; they contain one third of the tree species of the primary forest and over one third of primary bird species.

What these findings indicate for an assessment of different forms of land use from the ecological perspective is that fallow-cropping is clearly preferable to any permanent land use without secondary vegetation (cattle-farming, mechanized soybean and maize cultivation without any fallow period).

What are the conclusions that must be drawn from the special features of tropical forest ecosystems – high primary production with relatively slow wood growth and high levels of biodiversity – for the field of forestry? This topic is the subject of the following section.

4.2   Sustainable Forestry in the Tropics

The Emergence of Nature-oriented Sustainable Forestry

Prior to dealing with the special conditions of forestry in the tropics it may be best to sketch the emergence of the principles of nature-oriented sustainable forestry (Hatzfeld 1996; Bode and Hohnhorst 1994). The presentation will start out by looking into some controversies in forestry in Germany, which in the 19th century brought forth some of the world's leading forestry experts as well as models that have influenced both plantation forestry, which is today experiencing marked growth, and various methods of tropical-forest utilization developed in the 20th century.

In the second half of the 18th century it had become evident that the degradation of Germany's forest stands and forest soils due to rapidly growing consumption of wood for energy and construction and the exploitation of other forest products (including litter and forest fruits for fodder and fertilizer, bark as a tanning agent). The emerging modern system of public administration therefore also looked into the possibilities of introducing new legislation and public authorities to restore forested areas and safeguard timber production. The first half of the 19th century experienced the founding of the Tharandt Forestry Academy near Dresden and the establishment of forestry as the discipline concerned with systematic and rational timber production (Hatzfeld 1996, p. 22).

The model for rational timber production was the so-called age-class forest or industrial forest, which is sometimes also referred to as timber plantation: the overall forest area was divided up into compartments – so-called coupes – that consisted of a homogeneous, even-aged stock of trees which could thus be harvested at a predictable point of time (the end of the felling cycle).[18] The planting of these coupes was planned in such a way as to ensure that, in principle, one coupe could be harvested per year, in his way guaranteeing a sustainable timber supply. The economic rationale for this form of operation was provided by M.R. Pressler (1815 - 1886) in the form of a theory of soil rent that sought its orientation in other economic principles similar to today's models for discounting future returns from renewable natural resources (Pressler 1858): the aim was the maximum possible return on all capital invested in the forest. The basis used to calculate the soil rent was the cleared area; the interest on the timber supply was subtracted from the forest rent. If a forestry operation was to be managed as a profitable enterprise, capital expenditure and the rotation period (i.e. costs for planting, care, and harvest as well as for the time needed for the trees to mature) had to be reduced as far as possible, and this meant that the timber volume, the harvest time, and the labor required had to be accessible to planning and rationalization.

For this type of "timber-farming" pine and spruce proved ideal because of their short rotation periods and their ability to grow well in many different soils. At the beginning of the 19th century this timber-farming was at first conceived as a means of afforestation of large waste areas, *"but the initial successes of the coniferous-timber cultures on cleared areas were impressive, the expectations of economic returns high, and the chances of marketing the products in burgeoning industrial society favorable; thus plantation forestry gained more and more ground, and thus was the forest turned into a timber factory."* (Sperber 1996, p. 43)

As early as in the 19th century the ecological and economic vulnerability of artificial timber cultivation became clear: insect infestation, the spread of fungi, massive damage due to storms, snowbreakage, and forest fires led to the destruction of large forest areas and the capital invested in them. Since these types of damage were unknown in natural forests, individual foresters and forestry specialists began, as early as the mid-19th century, to develop interest in the ecological mechanisms of forests and to introduce more nature-oriented forms of forest management.

As opposed to the theory of sustainable timber production in the form of the age-class forest, with its primary orientation to economic goals, nature-oriented forest management is geared to the self-regulation mechanisms of natural forest formations. The point of departure of nature-oriented forest management is to gain knowledge of these mechanisms (i.e. habitat-adapted selection of species, structures, and functions of living and dead elements of the ecosystem and their forms of reproduction) and thus to gain experience of the responsiveness of the forest ecosystem to internal and external changes and to use this knowledge for the purposes of forest-tending and promotion of wood growth, without endangering the reproduction of the ecosystem as a whole. The goal of timber production is flanked by aims such as species protection, protecting the hydrological cycle and soil fertility, and maintaining the natural beauty of forest landscapes and their function as recreational areas: the forest is viewed as a multiple resource.[19]

This perspective gave rise to the criteria according to which it is possible to distinguish between forest and plantation on the basis of the management system involved: forests are management systems that make use of, and sustain, the growth processes of natural forest ecosystems, while plantations are artificial ecosystems that achieve high rates of timber production in short periods of time with the aid of external energy inputs (fertilizers, pesticides).[20]

In spite of the above-named ecological and economic advantages of nature-oriented forestry as opposed to plantations, the past two decades have experienced a distinct increase of plantation areas (see Chapter 5 for more details); in the developing countries alone the area accounted for by plantations doubled between 1980 and 1995 from 40.2 million ha to 81.2 million ha (FAO 1997, p. 14) .

This trend is assessed differently in the literature; many proponents of nature-oriented forest management regard it as a passing phenomenon that will reach its limits in the medium term – as is already the case in Germany. Others regard expansion of plantations, above all in the southern hemisphere, as the essential condition that makes it possible for nature-oriented forest management to prevail in Europe (Mather 1997). Assuming continuously growing demand for wood fiber, nature-oriented forest management, with its natural growth cycles and without any need for external energy inputs, will not be in a position to meet the world's demand for timber. If this should turn out to be the case, we are faced with a growing necessity to take a hard look at the ecology of plantations at various locations and to seek to limit as far as possible the damage to which they give rise. This will, however, not alleviate the fundamental pressures driving the exploitation of natural resources.

Sustainable Nature-oriented Forest Management in the Tropics

The beginning of the modern tropical forest management coincided with the emergence of forestry in Europe: in 1847 the German foresters Mollier and Nemnich were entrusted by the Dutch colonial administration with the task of building a forest administration in Indonesia; in 1848 the German botanist and forestry specialist Dietrich Brandis was employed by Great Britain to look after teakwood production in India. Brandis developed a forest-management plan for teakwood in Burma, "invented" the Taungya system used to take advantage of the fallow period to plant teak trees, and built up the Indian forest administration.[21] The British colonial administration attempted to transfer to Africa the experiences it had made in Asia; in Central and South America the Spanish and Portuguese colonial administrations had undertaken no efforts aimed at a systematic forest utilization. In Surinam Wageningen University operated test areas in the forest from the 1960s to the 1980s that were kept up and scientifically observed for a number of years (Lamprecht 1989, pp. 18 f.; Bruenig 1996, pp. 135 ff.).

There is as yet no agreement on principles to which any sustained use of tropical forests would have to be oriented, which is not surprising in view of the limited scope of our present knowledge of tropical forest ecosystems. One of the fundamental controversies concerns the assessment of biodiversity: If the latter is seen as essential to the reproduction of the ecosystem, forestry interventions must be reduced to a minimum to cut the risk posed by loss of species. But if, on the other hand, we proceed on the assumption of species redundancy and gear our activities to maintaining the basic functions of the ecosystem, seeking to identify and protect so-called keystone species, we would be free to "domesticate" the forest and promote the regeneration of commercially valuable species at the expense of "worthless" species.

Various forest-tending systems have been developed for the tropics in the 20th century.[22] Although these systems are on the whole not very labor- and cost-intensive and attempt to ensure the stability of the original forest ecosystem, in this way minimizing risks, they have not prevailed in the tropics. Instead, the practice here is selective logging or land conversion to set up fast-growing plantations. The reasons cited include the economic risks of forest management, the slow growth cycles, the difficult working conditions in forests, and the risk of invasion by the peasant population, which would undo the success of forest-tending measures.

Bruenig (1996), based on decades of empirical research, above all in the forest formations of Sarawak, also notes that forestry in the tropics is encumbered with high risks and uncertainty. His conclusion, however, points in the opposite direction of plantation forestry: owing to the complexity of tropical ecosystems, a forest use relying on natural regeneration and geared to disturbing it as little as possible is the most promising and economically surest method of timber production. Precisely in the tropics the likelihood that plantations will fail is high; the sustainable yields between 20 and 50 m³/ha referred to in the literature are possible only in first-class sites and under optimal production conditions (Bruenig 1996, pp. 57 and 222). A good part of the plantations in developing countries is thus to be found in the subtropics; this is particularly clear in Brazil, where 93 % of such output is accounted for by plantations in subtropical and temperate zones.

Bruenig's findings confirm the assumption that tropical ecosystems are complex structures that are determined by nonlinear processes and oscillating equilibria and cannot, using the knowledge available to us today, be imitated by largely artificial systems like plantations. Levels of biomass production similar to or higher than that of the primary forest can be attained only with the aid of high levels of external energy inputs in the form of fertilizers, pesticides, and the like.

From the perspective of forestry, the most striking features of tropical forest ecosystems include the following:

–   The growth rhythms of the trees in evergreen tropical forests are oriented to specific habitat conditions, less to the species of the individual trees. *"The unexplained and unpredictable variation of biological net production (...) and the lack of simple linear relationships between growth and growth factors are the enigma of forestry growth and yield research and management planning. It is largely solved in temperate forests, but progress is slow in tropical rainforest research and practice."* (Bruenig 1996, p. 67)

–   The ways different tree species are grouped together (floristic structure) is not constant but changes over time: *"The statistical probabilities for a number of neighbouring tree species to form a persistent association in the form of a calculable 'eco-unit' are very slim."* Measurements conducted in Liberia and the Philippines showed *"constant oscillation and change between states of order (structurally complex mature phases) and disorder (structurally simpler, more chaotic decay and regeneration phases) in a small-scale, shifting mosaic pattern on a very heterogeneous soil and often also heterogeneous micro-relief (landform-soil units)"*. Bruenig concludes that this oscillating structure facilitates the coexistence of many tree species (Bruenig 1996, p. 48 f.).

– Historical pollen analyses of ancient rainforest areas from different geological ages indicate that the species composition of the vegetation cover changed relatively rapidly in response to changes in temperature and precipitation and tectonic shifts, but without displaying any regular pattern: *"The indication is that the present pattern of species distribution and the presence or absence of regeneration are poor indicators of the direction of stand dynamics. So many site and chance factors interact (...) in such a diverse manner that no consistent picture of species distribution, association and succession manifests itself in the pollen diagrams and in the living vegetation."* (Bruenig 1996, p. 22)

– Patterns of succession are not recognizable at the level of specific species compositions, though they can be identified in terms of functional aspects: in a logged area the regeneration of the forest starts out with fast-growing light-hungry pioneer species which later disappear when nutrients become scarce due to growing competition; these features remain constant, although the species themselves may change. Functionally equivalent configurations can be formed by different species.

– Due to the natural life cycle of trees as well as to external disturbances (storms, natural conflagrations) the structure of the forest is not static but highly variable even in small areas. The spectrum and the diversity of existing species likewise change in response to these disorders; species may disappear locally and then reappear. *"Constant changes of the floristic and spatial structure of the ecosystem seem to improve its resilience, adaptability and flexibility, while simple natural monocultural forests are more vulnerable to persistent damage."* (Bruenig 1996, p. 23)

Exact knowledge of the reproduction and growth behavior of species and the floristic and succession structure of forest formations constitute the basis of all types of forest management. The difficulties involved in diffusing this knowledge in the tropics and putting it into effect in the form of management rules make it imperative that the greatest possible care be exercised in performing interventions with irreversible consequences.

The state of today's knowledge does not, however, indicate that all forms of forest utilization in the tropics should be banned. We may instead proceed on the assumption that the resistance developed by certain tropical forest formations is greater than had been thought until now. Generally, high levels of biodiversity must not be regarded as proof of the particular fragility of tropical forest ecosystems. It can, instead, be argued that great biodiversity increases the responsiveness of forest ecosystems to external disturbances.

Forestry Methods in the Amazon Region

The FAO was responsible for the introduction of forestry methods in the Amazon region: in 1951 the Brazilian agriculture ministry reached agreement with the FAO to scientifically investigate the Amazon forest ecosystems to determine their suitability for forestry uses. The FAO opened up a branch office in Belém that conducted a series of expeditions between 1956 and 1961 and presented the results to the Amazon development authority, SPVEA (later SUDAM). The results of these expeditions were first published in a final report; only ten years later was the original report translated and made available to the public (Heinsdijk and Bastos 1963; SUDAM 1973b). Until the 1980s these studies constituted the basis for all projects, programs, and policy proposals advanced by SUDAM in the field of forest-resource utilization.

On the occasion of a trip to the Amazon region in 1950 Pierre Terver, the first FAO representative in Brazil, drafted a report on the difficulties of any commercial exploitation of the forest resources in this region, determining the direction that the work of the FAO mission in Belém was to take (Heinsdijk and Bastos 1963, p. 7). With a view to forestry, Terver specified the following problems: the unknown market value of forest stands and lack of any adapted forest-use techniques and regularized forestry system.

This latter point of criticism may at first seem surprising, since there was at that juncture no regularized forestry anywhere in Brazil and there was no need to exploit the timber stocks of a region that was basically inaccessible, since the araucaria forests in the south and the Atlantic coastal rainforest offered sufficient stocks of timber. This point becomes understandable only when we realize that the French and British colonial administrations had already set up forestry administrations in the tropical forests of Africa and Asia with an eye to utilizing and managing the timber stocks there. By comparison, forest utilization in the Amazon region must have appeared very backward from the angle of an FAO official.

The expeditions conducted by the FAO between 1956 and 1961 covered an area of 19.09 million ha, 1,500 km long and 500 km wide, that extended from the northeast of Pará, along the Amazon, almost to Manaus and included, beside a *terra firme* forest area near Curuá-Una (between the rivers Tapajós and Xingú), above all *várzea* forests. In addition, the expeditions studied two other *terra firme* areas to the south of Belém: along the road then under construction between Belém and Brasilia and the mahogany-logging area in the south of Pará. A second special study investigated virola stands in the Tocantins delta to the southwest of Belém.

The results of the FAO studies show that despite all habitat differences the species composition of the forests was relatively homogeneous: a comparison of two hectare samples located 1,200 km apart, one in the Rio Madeira area, one in another area to the south of Belém, showed agreement for almost half the species noted. All told, the studies identified 400 species from 47 botanical families in the 20 million ha they investigated.[23] This meant lowering – at least for the areas investigated – the figure of 1,500 - 2,000 tree species assumed by Huber and Ducke at the beginning of the century on the basis of botanical studies of individual habitats.

What is crucial in forestry terms is the occurrence of individual valuable species and the volume of timber accounted for by the different species.[24] In this sense, the studies noted that the species valuable in terms of their technical properties occurred only in smaller numbers per ha and that the average wood volume of a log of the same species varied from habitat to habitat. The data gathered by the FAO mission were, however, not enough to permit the construction of a general model of the Amazon rainforest, which sharply restricted the possibility of making any prognoses on the market value of individual forest areas.

A further shortcoming must be seen in a lack of data on the growth and reproduction behavior of the forest or of individual species, which are the *sine qua non* for any statements on the minimum length of sustainable logging cycles. Since no time series were available, and it was not possible to prepare one in the brief period of five years, the FAO experts tried to manage by identifying the distribution of individuals of several species to different breast-height-diameter classes (DBH classes) and then drawing conclusions from there on the species' assumed regeneration dynamics, but without being able to indicate the relevant time axis. The implicit assumption was that a tree's height is an indicator of its age. It was furthermore assumed that there is in the tropical rainforest a tendency toward a stable distribution of species across DBH classes, although, as the mission determined, the distribution across the individual classes varied sharply. Only for the Brazil-nut tree did the experts note a relatively even distribution of individuals per ha across the various DBH classes.

Based on the empirical data collected in the different habitats, the FAO mission worked out timber-production tables for the DBH classes between 25 - 34 cm and 45 - 54 cm, respectively, which indicated the average volume reached by each species. These tables abstracted from the differences in habitat. We know today that the growth dynamics of the individuals of a species can differ markedly and that habitat factors (light entry, precipitation, soil quality) and the proximity of other species play a role here. In addition, the age and height of trees do not correlate: small trees may be older than larger trees of other species in the same habitat. This has to do with the different forms of species reproduction: seeds, shoot formation, or new plants, which may wait for years until the right growth conditions have materialized, e.g. through the formation, artificial or natural, of a forest clearing (Uhl et al. 1990). Having conducted the investigations, the FAO, together with the natural-resources department of SUDAM, concentrated on experiments with systems of artificial regeneration with a view to domesticating the forest. These experiments were conducted at the Curuá-Una station near Santarém; the FAO was present there until 1968. In 1976 Brazilian forestry experts, above all from the forestry faculty of FCAP in Belém, took over operations on behalf of SUDAM.

From 1975 on EMBRAPA-CPATU also prepared floristic inventories and conducted forest-tending measures and measurements in experimental areas in the forest conservation area of Tapajós (Floresta Nacional - Flona Tapajós) as well as on the rubber plantations abandoned by Henry Ford in Belterra (both sites are also close to Santarém).

One striking factor is that the summaries of the results of these experiments fail to make reference to the studies conducted by the other institutions; IMAZON, an independent research institute, also publishes its empirical findings on forest degradation and the regeneration behavior of forests in use without comparing these data with the data from older studies.[25] In spite of the highly limited local base of their studies, all authors arrive at generalizations on recommendable forest-use methods for the overall Amazon region, though these propositions cannot be regarded as viable due to the high level of local diversity of the ecosystems involved. The author of the SUDAM study is much more optimistic in his conclusions on permissible depths of intervention than the EMBRAPA-CPATU authors, who call for great care and a maximum of restrictions on interventions in forest ecosystems.

In the 1960s FAO and SUDAM cooperated in experimenting with the so-called Tropical Shelterwood System (TSS) and clear-felling with a view to determining the most suitable method of domestication for the region's primary forests. Under TSS the seed trees were at first left standing; the undergrowth was removed as soon it was noted that the natural regeneration of the desired species was making no headway. As soon as regeneration was noted, the seed trees were harvested as well (TSS 1). In a different area, after the undergrowth had been removed, experiments were conducted involving planting commercial species with an eye to enrichment (TSS 2). Visits and measurements performed in 1978 and 1987 in the experimental areas and in untouched reference areas yielded the following findings:

- The enrichment plantings had to be regarded as failures in that the additionally planted species had completely disappeared in 20 years; mechanized clear-felling proved to be a very expensive method of area clearance, since fire was not used in order to be able to use the timber cleared.

- With TSS 1 and clear-felling, 20 years after the interventions the experts counted 33 - 28 species per ha, roughly one third fewer than in the reference areas (44 - 55 species/ha); over 90 % of the base area was in both cases concentrated on trees with a DBH between 5 and 45 cm, i.e. a size class of little interest for commercial exploitation.

Despite these rather sobering results SUDAM proceeded in this study on the assumption that extensive interventions are required in forest management to stimulate timber growth: this was concluded above all from the fact that the base areas of TSS 1 in 1987 were on the whole greater than the base area in the untouched reference areas. The study failed to take account of both the distribution of the base area across the DBH classes and the fact that in TSS 1 as compared with primary forest only one species was dominant, i.e. the phenomenon observed tends more in the direction of species impoverishment.

The EMBRAPA-CPATU studies were conducted in two different areas in the Flona Tapajós and in two secondary-forest areas in Belterra (40-year-old secondary forest) as well as in the vicinity of the Jari River (4-year-old secondary forest). Compared with SUDAM's findings in Curuá-Una we can note here both pronounced differences and correspondences, which point above all toward the great influence of specific habitat conditions on species structure and growth behavior of forest formations. Some of the most important individual findings of the EMBRAPA-CPATU studies:

- The number of species determined for the primary- and secondary-forest areas hardly differed at first glance: for the former it fluctuated between 106 and 172 species, for the latter between 103 and 154 species. However, the number of species indicated was for the entire area and not per hectare, and these differ considerably: the experts investigated 5 (Belterra) and 35 (Jari) ha in the primary forest, in the secondary forest the figures were 132 (Belterra) and 400 ha (Jari).

– While an average of four individuals per species were counted in the primary forest, the figure for the secondary forest was three individuals per species. Especially in Belterra the species were distributed very unevenly over the overall area. This means in all cases extremely heterogeneous forest formations.

– The timber stock per hectare of the areas differed greatly: in the primary forest it fluctuated between $96.7m^3$ and 220 m^3 (DBH > 45 cm); in the latter case the share of commercial species was $113 \text{ m}^3/\text{ha}$. In Belterra the general timber stock was 77.7 m^3, the inventory of commercial species roughly $45 \text{ m}^3/\text{ha}$.

Measurements and simulations of natural regeneration following mechanized clearance in the Flona Tapajós led the EMBRAPA-CPATU experts to come to conclusions that fundamentally contradict those of SUDAM.[26] The study was of an area that had been completely registered in 1975 and intensively cleared in 1979, with 73 m^3/ha having been harvested. This volume is distinctly higher than the level of the selective logging usual in the Amazon region and was in line with the then SUDAM call for intensified felling patterns. Between 1981 and 1987 the natural rates of regeneration were noted every two years in fixed test plots of the same area.

The results of the measurements and the computer simulation of continuing growth behavior indicated that natural regeneration alone would not permit a second profitable harvest after 30 years had elapsed (in 2009), if the yardstick was simply the stock of species marketable at present. Harvesting potential species – which would have had to be introduced to the market in the 1980s – would have been the only profitable option.

In contrast to SUDAM, Silva localizes the reasons for the insufficient natural regeneration in a specific succession dynamics that he observed *in situ* following the intensive clearance. It is from this dynamics that he derives forest-tending rules, which are needed because of the disruptions caused by the intervention (and are not due to a "per se" slow rate of natural regeneration, as SUDAM writes):

- Competition: After the clearance the competition for light and nutrients through vines and palms increased visibly (in 1975 81 % of the test parcels were free of vines, 93 % were free of palms; in 1985 the corresponding figures were only 12 and 57 %). This means that thinning operations are needed to eliminate these competitors in order to facilitate the regrowth of the species desired.

- Susceptibility: After the clearance the number of trees felled by storm increased distinctly, since felling-related damage had weakened the remaining trees and the protection afforded by the density of the forest stand had declined (SUDAM had also noted this, but explained it with reference to the unusual strength of the storms that occurred during the period under observation).

- Number of trees: Although the number of trees with a DBH > 60 cm had increased between 1981 and 1987 from eight to ten per hectare, this was seen as inadequate since a higher mortality rate (50 %) had to be assumed. In addition, the number of new trees (DBH > 5 cm) of commercial species had decreased from 17 to 7 per hectare during the same period.

- DBH growth: On the average the DBH increased by 0.5 cm per year; pioneer species such as Cecropia displayed, as expected, the highest growth rates (1 cm per year). The variance between individuals was very high for all species; these figures indicate the influences of (as yet unclarified) habitat factors on individual tree growth. Three to four years after clearance growth decreased and stabilized at a lower level (this was also noted by SUDAM); Silva recommends thinning measures every five to ten years to regulate light entry, in this way increasing continuous growth rates.

- Simulation of stand development: Without silvicultural interventions only 2.6 trees/ha reach felling maturity in 30 years (with an overall volume of 12.4 m^3/ha); with silvicultural measures the figure is 17 trees (94 m^3/ha).

From these findings Silva derives recommendations for forest exploitation that are geared to the principles of nature-oriented forest management: a light to medium logging intensity (30 - 40 m³/ha) with two to three thinning measures during a cycle of 25 - 30 years aimed at promoting the growth of the species desired. Essential requirements include preparation of a complete forest inventory prior to logging, preparation of a felling plan, and measurement of logging-related damage and timber growth three years after logging; it is recommended to repeat the latter measurement every five years. In addition, Silva provides some advice on decreasing forest damage due to skidding and transportation and avoiding timber losses with the aid of more efficient felling techniques.

Methods devised to directly control forest regeneration, such as enrichment planting or tropical shelterwood systems (TSS), are rejected: if logging intensity is reduced, it is safe to assume that the intensity of natural regeneration, together with forest-tending, will prove sufficient to guarantee an economically profitable growth of timber. The point of reducing logging intensity and using forest-tending measures is to limit the occurrence of pioneer species, which are strong competitors for light and nutrients, in this way promoting the regeneration of the species in particular demand.

These basic rules for sustainable forest use,[27] geared as they are to the principle of caution, appear plausible in view of the knowledge of forest ecology available today. Continuous inventories of the changing stocks of given species and growth behavior in different locations are, however, needed to verify the appropriateness of these rules. There are as yet no lengthy data series available for any location in the Amazon region on the growth behavior of undisturbed forest formations or the effects of forest-tending measures on net timber growth rates.

4.3   Effects of Sustainable Tropical-forest Management on Company Management

Conversion to a sustainable or nature-oriented forest utilization in the tropics runs up against a number of economic, technological, and organizational obstacles and therefore has far-reaching impacts on operations management (see Chapter 6). The chances and the problems facing the firms involved differ in terms of whether they produce exclusively for the domestic market or whether they also export.

Nature-oriented forest utilization demands of a logging firm felling and production scheduling that is geared strongly to a forest's sustainable timber supply and not – as usual – primarily to demand. Determining this timber supply and its dynamic development over a felling cycle of 25 - 30 years requires levels of skills and qualification that are lacking among the management personnel of most such firms; foresters capable of this are few in the region. The marketing of timber with an eye to safeguarding returns and profits is faced with the problem of having to sell far greater numbers of species in smaller quantities than is usual (see Chapters 6 and 7 for more detail). These species are sometimes known only in local markets and command low prices. In addition, only very few species of tropical sawnwood find acceptance in the industrialized countries and it takes several years to introduce new species. Moreover, the industrialized countries demand certain wood lengths, which leads to very large quantities of waste in cutting timber to length. The yield per cubic meter of stemwood in the export-oriented companies is for this reason only 35 %, i.e. 65 % of stemwood is lost.

The greater effort involved in planning for felling and transportation causes costs that do not accrue when the traditional logging methods are used; these include investments for the computer equipment needed to prepare a forest inventory and a database, for the generation of maps with markings for trees to be felled and individual seed trees, for log trails and forest roads, for the training of administrative personnel and forest workers, hiring of skilled personnel to perform the new planning tasks and supervise implementation.

If we take these additional costs into account in calculating the costs of sustainable forest management and place them over against local timber prices, we find that sustainable forest management is, at present price levels, not affordable. A calculation of this sort undertaken for the state of Acre in the extreme southeast of the Amazon region showed that the market prices for timber are on average 56 % below the costs required for sustainable production (Gama e Silva and Muños Braz 1992, p. 8).

IMAZON, on the other hand, presents a calculation containing not only additional costs but also the gains in productivity and efficiency that can be attained with planned logging (Amaral, Barreto, Veríssimo and Vidal 1998, pp. 125-135). A practice-oriented comparison of conventional logging methods and sustainable scheduling and logging methods showed that timber losses can in actual fact be cut from 10.4 to 0.4 m³/ha (this was achieved with a timber harvest of 40 m³/ha). At the same time the costs of forest road- and trail-building were lowered from US\$ 0.41/m³ to 0.29/m³ felled. Since on the whole fewer forest rides had to be cut, the use of heavy machinery per unit of time was cut by 37 %. The costs of the felling work itself were reduced from US\$ 0.31/m³ to 0.25/m³ by doing away with the usual two-man teams in favor of three-man teams, which made possible a more rational division of labor. The felled logs could be skidded most efficiently by using a large, rubber-tired skidder instead of a track-type vehicle; additional time was won by the possibility of immediately finding the logs and using predefined forest rides. Nonscheduled logging entailed skidding volumes of 23 m³/hour, scheduled 34 m³; the costs are reduced here from US\$ 1.95/m³ to 1.31/m³.[28]

Taking into account only the costs of felling and transportation, i.e. the immediate logging costs (without inventories, scheduling and forest-tending measures),[29] the production costs per cubic meter are US\$ 23.8 for conventional logging and US\$ 30.3 for scheduled logging. Thanks to productivity gains, however, the net returns for scheduled logging are US\$ 9.7/m³ as compared with US\$ 6.2/m³ for conventional logging. If we assume rising costs for the purchase of logging rights per hectare, the reduction of felling-related timber losses has immediate cost-cutting effects, which are accompanied by higher returns per hectare, compensating for the additional costs of planned logging. An additional factor is the enhanced regeneration capacity of cautiously logged forests, which makes greater timber growth rates possible within shorter periods of time than is the case with the conventionally exploited forest.

The introduction of sustainable forest-use systems is important not only in terms of ecological and business-related considerations but also for marketing reasons. The member states of the ITTO, for instance, committed themselves in 1990 to restrict their trading in tropical timber to products obtained through sustainable forest management starting in the year 2000 *(Target 2000)*; many local authorities, retail chains, and private consumers in the industrialized countries are committed to using only tropical wood whose sustainable origin is proved by certification from independent institutions. In a setting of this kind conversion to sustainable forest-use systems, certified as ecologically and socially sound, turns into a strategic challenge for the firms involved.

Comparison of the criteria for certification of sustainable forest management with the rules named above shows how far the latter still are from any ecological, economic, and social sustainability of forest utilization in the comprehensive sense of the term defined above.

4.4   Ecological Certification of Forest Management

At the beginning of the 1990s the idea caught on that it might be better to protect tropical forests with the aid of the voluntary instrument of independent certification of the ecological, economic, and social compatibility of forest management than to renounce the use of tropical timber, a state of affairs tantamount, in its extreme form, to a ban on the exploitation of tropical forests.

The introduction of internationally recognized ecological certification systems was backed by a number of international initiatives concerned with the development of principles, criteria, and indicators for sustainable forest management: the UN Earth Summit held in 1992 in Rio de Janeiro adopted conventions on biodiversity and climate change, the Forest Declaration, and Agenda 21. They were the basis for three follow-up processes (Helsinki, Montreal, and Tarapoto) in which some 150 governments reached agreement on principles of forest use. In 1994 these follow-up processes also facilitated the signing of the second international tropical-timber agreement which saw the members of the ITTO commit themselves to ecological certification of forest management as a central instrument that was to be used to achieve *Target 2000*. The tropical-timber-producing countries had until then refused to sign the agreement, arguing that the countries with forests in the temperate and boreal zones should, to avoid any trade-related discrimination, in turn commit themselves to sustainable forest management. In Helsinki in 1993 the European countries agreed to concentrate more on ecological aspects of their forests (biodiversity, soil protection, hydrological cycles), and to regularly monitor them. Montreal in 1993 was the first conference to bring all of the countries from the temperate and boreal zones of both hemispheres together; after a total of six conferences they agreed, in Santiago de Chile, to a number of criteria for sustainable forest management. It was likewise in 1995 that the eight Amazon Pact countries adopted similarly comprehensive criteria for the utilization of the Amazon forests. The Declaration of Santiago and that adopted by the Amazon states go beyond the ITTO principles and the Helsinki process both in ecological and in socioeconomic terms.[30]

In 1993 the *Forest Stewardship Council* (FSC), an organization consisting of environmental groups, scientists, firms from the timber industry and trade, indigenous organizations, and labor unions, was founded with the intention of developing principles and criteria for the sustainable management of natural forests and plantations and to accredit organizations with a right to certify such forest management in the name of the FSC. The initiative was based on the idea of gathering all of those concerned with forest utilization around one table and focusing the interests of all actors with an eye to linking ecological as well as economic and social goals. The general principles agreed on in 1994 have since then been concretized and adapted, at the national and in given cases at the local level, to specific local factors in the form of indicators and inspection criteria (Scholz et al. 1994).

Toward the middle of 1998 10.2 million hectares of forest had been certified in accordance with the FSC criteria, some 79 % in industrialized countries and 21 % in developing countries. In Brazil 383,549 ha of land owned by six companies have been certified. Four of them operate eucalyptus and pine plantations for the pulp and particle-board industries (78 % of the total area certified); one company operates a 300-ha-large teak plantation, another manages a primary forest of

80,571 ha in the state of Amazonas (21 % of the total area certified) (FSC Brazil 1998, pp. 9 f.).

The FSC is today the only internationally recognized accreditor of certifying organizations; importers from the industrialized countries and exporting producers are increasingly looking to the FSC for orientation as a means of avoiding the loss of any further shares to substitute products in a market marked by ecologically sensitized consumers (see Section 5.2). Aside from the FSC there are also other initiatives: the *Organisation Africaine de Bois* (OAB), with members in western and central Africa, is developing, with French support, a regional certificate of its own; Malaysia and Indonesia are currently working out national certificates oriented toward the FSC and the environmental standards of the ISO.

The wood-processing industry has thus far been the least cooperative partner; one exception is the pulp and paper industry, which, following a Greenpeace campaign in the 1980s, learned to develop constructive strategies. In Germany there are some individual furniture producers that are converting to environmentally sound management and as a rule no longer process tropical timber.[31]

The attractiveness of the instrument of certification lies in its flexibility and the many different effects it engenders:

–   At given demand levels certified companies can create a new market segment in which they can command higher prices for their products, justifying the latter with reference to the demonstrably higher ecological quality of their wood products. In the ideal case these higher prices cover the costs arising from more ecologically sound methods and their decision to do without timber cut in areas particularly worthy of protection or used by indigenous groups.

–   Consumers have the chance to promote sustainable timber production with their demand for certified products and to exert a constructive influence on the market. Previously, consumers could only send more or less diffuse signals to the market by personal abstention or by acceding to boycott appeals.

- Processing industry and trade alike are developing for the medium term a pronounced interest of their own in assuring that certificates are awarded only in connection with serious, credible, and transparent procedures, since they must otherwise fear that environmental organizations and the media will unmask the misuse of certificates, harming in this way the market chances of tropical-wood products.[32] Internal controls must also be used to prevent free-rider behavior as far as possible.

- In the ideal case a communication process may come about between committed firms, entrepreneurs, certifying institutes, critical consumers, and monitoring environmental groups and authorities. This process serves not only to ensure that certification works and is credible, it also helps to constantly improve inspection criteria and the methods of forest utilization. Moreover, this process also entails possibilities to address, and publicly debate, such fundamental questions as the ecological limits of consumption.

- Once this process of communication and mutual monitoring has got underway, the legislative and the public administrations in the countries of origin of tropical timber and the consumer countries can concentrate on reforming and shaping the legal parameters for forest management in such a way as to provide incentives for continuous improvement of operational methods in keeping with the most recent ecological and technological state of the art. It is also important to widen the possibilities open for an active participation of the local populace in tropical-forest regions in the sustainable utilization of forest resources as well as in the certification and monitoring of them.

Since the instrument of certification is a voluntary one, it is also well suited for a joint approach by actors from different countries operating on rules they have themselves established. In this way – assuming sufficient interest on the part of the most important economic actors – certification can deal more quickly and flexibly with abuses than would be possible on the basis of international conventions or treaties alone. Moreover, certification is a lever that can be used to implement forestry legislation, however demanding and irrelevant in practical terms the latter may be, since it provides an economic incentive (higher market prices).

At present eco-certification is faced with five kinds of limitation: First, forestry experts are not in agreement on principles and indicators of sustainable forest and plantation management; this has proven particularly difficult for ecosystems as complex as tropical forests. Second, in view of the difficulties involved in influencing forest utilization directly and quickly, certification runs the risk of seeming to have an alibi function; this risk is heightened by abuse of certification. Third, the market for certified wood products is on the one hand limited in terms of both its volume (some 10 - 20 % of the European and North American wood markets) and the possibility it affords to command higher prices.[33] Fourth, the limited number of certified tropical-wood-producing companies are, on the other hand, already overstrained by demand: in view of the technical difficulties named the consumer must not expect any processes of change in the tropical-forest countries in the short run, so that the only possibility open to him is to cut his consumption if his wish is to consume only certified wood. Fifth, and finally, there is at present a lack of adequately trained certifiers, a factor which is driving up the costs of certification.

The diffusion of certification in the industrialized countries in the temperate and boreal zones (Sweden and Poland have each had over a million hectares of forest certified) and the in any case declining market shares of tropical timber have the perverse effect that ecologically minded consumers may switch to wood products from the North and abandon the tropical forests to destructive exploitation by Malaysia, Indonesia, China, and Japan, with these countries then turning to Africa and Latin America once Asia's primary forests have been depleted (see Chapter 5).

Criteria and Indicators of Sustainable Forest Management in the Amazon Region

In 1998 the FSC's Brazil working group presented a proposal on criteria and indicators of a sustainable management of *terra firme* forests in the

Amazon region.[34] A proposal on the utilization of *várzea* forests is to be prepared as soon as field tests with the *terra firme* forests have been conducted and it has been determined whether the firms concerned are interested in certification.

The proposal was disseminated via the Internet for comments and proposals for amendments; toward the end of 1998 a number of workshops were held to discuss the proposed amendments. Between November 1998 and January 1999 field tests were conducted, and they were followed by a further consultation process via the Internet, which was concluded in May 1999 with a workshop held to prepare a final draft. The final version was set to be presented to the FSC in June 1999.

The criteria and indicators are organized in conformity with the FSC's ten Principles, though the last principle, referring to plantations, was left out of consideration. The present section will present the FSC Principles and then outline and discuss the FSC proposal for applying them to the conditions encountered in the Amazon region. All of the subjects addressed in this section are presented at more length in Chapter 7 of this study.

Principle 1: Compliance with laws and FSC Principles
Forest management shall respect all applicable laws of the country in which they occur, and international treaties and agreements to which the country is a signatory, and comply with all FSC Principles and Criteria.

In considering all laws and regulations dealing with forest management, FSC Brazil demands in particular

– submission of forest-management plans,
– evidence that an operator is not involved in illegal logging,
– compliance with the provisions of the Convention on the International Trade with Endangered Species (CITES), the ILO conventions, the convention on tropical timber, and the biodiversity convention,
– compliance with labor and tax laws, and

- operator commitment to disseminating sustainable methods of forest management as well as training and advanced training for forest workers.

If violations of these principles are noted, certified operators lose their certification.

The criteria at present exclude the majority of Amazon timber companies from the circle of potentially certifiable firms. The reason for this is not the abstract nature of the criteria but the traditional forms of forest use practiced in the region since the colonial era.

Principle 2: Tenure and use rights and responsibilities
Long-term tenure and use rights to the land and forest resources shall be clearly defined, documented and legally established.

In the Amazon region legally documented land ownership is for the most part highly untransparent and often conflicts with traditional land-use rights, which themselves are in part recognized by the land law in force:[35] If a person has continuously used a piece of land for thirty years, he acquires a right to a land title. The matter becomes problematical when in this situation a previous owner appears and presents a document establishing older claims. The situation is further complicated by the fact that forest utilization is legally conditioned on the private ownership of the land in question; forest use is thus in many cases bound up with land conflicts. For this reason the FSC demands that

- the operator not only present a land title but prove that he is not involved in any formal or informal conflicts with other claimants; should there be any such legal conflicts, the operator must prove that he is not obstructing a clarification of the situation;
- the operator commit himself to the use of peaceful and participatory mechanisms to solve any future conflicts over claims to use rights;
- the use rights of persons dwelling in the greater area to be utilized be respected and adequate compensation be paid; or
- consensual solutions be reached with local residents without any legal claims to the land, and that these solutions ensure these per-

sons a livelihood as a means of avoiding squatting campaigns and the like.

Compliance with these criteria also poses a considerable obstacle in Pará in that land conflicts there have traditionally been solved by violence or threats of violence and recourse to all possible legal and illegal means (forgery of documents, etc.). Arriving at a consensual solution of conflicts as a means of finding solutions to future problems is not only unthinkable for most landowners, it also meets with skepticism on the part of smallholders and landless people because they have had very little positive experience with such procedures.

Principle 3: Indigenous peoples' rights
The legal or customary rights of indigenous peoples to own, use and manage their lands, territories, and resources shall be recognized and respected.

The FSC working group requires from operators exact information on indigenous and traditional groups living in the forest-management area or its vicinity. The intention is to conclude agreements with traditional groups living in the area that provide them with direct control over resource use and involve them as partners in the planning and implementation of forest management. Places of special historical, cultural, ecological, economic, or religious significance for these groups must be respected; procedures for use conflicts resulting from this provision must be developed. If the traditional knowledge of such groups regarding the use of forest species or management systems in forest operations is used for forest management, these groups must be adequately compensated.

Principle 4: Community relations and workers' rights
Forest management operations shall maintain or enhance the long-term social and economic well-being of forest workers and local communities.

Here, too, the FSC is aiming for a reversal of the traditional relations between firms and local communities and workers: firms are expected to provide for opportunities for income, employment, and training for the local population; they are furthermore expected to continuously train their workers and improve working conditions (in particular work-place hygiene and safety), respect workers' freedom of assembly, and refrain from interfering in the formation of labor unions.

Principle 5: Benefits from the forest
Forest management operations shall encourage the efficient use of the forest's multiple products and services to ensure economic viability and a wide range of environmental and social benefits.

Forest management should strive for economic viability, while taking into account the full environmental, social, and operational costs of production and ensuring the investments necessary to maintain the ecological productivity of the forest. This means that the companies concerned are required to present realistic economic and investment plans and introduce methods and equipment geared to reduced-impact logging. Forest degradation and timber losses due to logging operations and processing are expected to be kept to a minimum.

The operators are called upon to use new tree species and introduce them to the market as well as to use nontimber forest products with an eye to diversifying both forest management and the local economy. The introduction of new species is a costly process that would in all likeli-hood overstrain individual firms, though joint efforts might prove suc-cessful, especially if they receive support from big exporters and their parent companies in Europe and the US.

The use of nontimber products is a more difficult matter: the actual diversity of nontimber products in local ecosystems can differ greatly. These are often perishable products that are known, and salable, only in local markets. As the supply increases, market prices will fall.

Principles 6 - 8 refer to particulars of forest management. At present hardly a single company in the Amazon region would be in a position to meet these standards, though most of them are not really complex and difficult to meet. The main problem will be to move the firms to embark on this path in the first place and to find enough experts to deal effectively with the planning, monitoring, and training tasks ahead.

Principle 6: Environmental impact
Forest management shall conserve biological diversity and its associated values, water resources, soils, and unique and fragile ecosystems and landscapes, and, by so doing, maintain the ecological functions and the integrity of the forest.

The following measures must be provided for in forest-management plans:
– protection of rare, threatened, and endangered species,
– protection of basic ecological functions (regeneration and natural succession of the forest ecosystem by conserving seed trees and maintaining the original forest structure),
– protection of a representative sample of all ecosystems present in a given area,
– documentation and implementation of measures designed to protect water resources, prevent erosion, and diminish forest degradation due to felling and ride-building operations,
– information for workers and residents on the importance and the methods of sustainable forest management as well as on avoiding any waste of wood resources and making use of waste materials,
– use of environmentally sound pesticides; agents designated by the WHO as dangerous and agents based on chlorine gas and transgenic agents are banned,
– environmentally sound disposal of receptacles and residues of pesticides, propellants, and lubricants outside the forest,
– careful planning, implementation, and monitoring of exotic trees used for enrichment plantings or fire protection.

Principle 7: Management plan
A management plan – appropriate to the scale and intensity of the operations – shall be written, implemented, and kept up to date. The long term objectives of management, and the means of achieving them, shall be clearly stated.

The FSC working group here sets out *en detail* the provisions that a forest-management plan must contain: management objectives, description of the forest area to be managed (maps with information on water resources, soils, topography, hydrological cycles, present land use, etc.), description of the forestry system in use and its scientific basis (forestry method used for felling and tending, mechanisms used to monitor the regeneration of the forest, species-protection measures), planning of skidding and transportation routes, camp sites and bridges to be built, measures used to prevent forest fires, and cost and investment plans with information on sources of funding.

This plan must be constantly monitored with an eye to gaining and using information on forest regeneration and adapting the plan to changed ecological, economic, and social framework conditions.

The basic elements of the management plan must be published and made available to local residents. Local residents must be invited to visit the area and familiarize themselves with forest management.

Principle 8: Monitoring and assessment
Monitoring shall be conducted – appropriate to the scale and intensity of forest management – to assess the condition of the forest, yields of forest products, chain of custody, management activities and their social and environmental impacts.

The frequency and intensity of monitoring activities must be in keeping with the scale and intensity of forest-management operations; environmental-impact assessments must be documented and made accessible to the public. The parameters of monitoring must include at least harvest volume and forest-tending measures, growth, forest damage, changes to flora and fauna, environmental impacts (incl. fire, changes to waterways, soil compaction), and the actual costs of forest management. The final assessment should include recommendations for forest-management methods, reduction of costs, and increase of yields.

Principle 9: Maintenance of high conservation value forests
Management activities in high conservation value forests shall maintain or enhance the attributes which define such forests. Decisions regarding high conservation value forests shall always be considered in the context of a precautionary approach.

Since the greater part of the Amazon region is still covered by primary forest, the FSC working group focuses on the question of the cases in which conversion for plantation, farming, or ranching uses is permissible. Conversion of unforested areas influenced by human activities is to be supported, if these areas were earlier wooded, if they are reforested with indigenous species, and if the goal is to create a forest formation that resembles the original one. This means that plantations in natural savanna regions (*campos naturais, cerrado*) are not permissible. What should be supported in particular is reforestation of the forest-conservation areas which every landowner in the Amazon region is obliged to create on 50 - 80 % of his land.

5   The World Market for Tropical Timber

This chapter looks into the dimensions, structure, and development of the world market for tropical timber. The section will also discuss the development of German tropical-timber imports and timber exports from Brazil and Pará (5.1). The chapter concludes with a look at changes in the technology and organization of timber-processing (5.2).

For about ten years now some far-reaching changes have been emerging in the world timber market, changes that are likely to increasingly restrict the competitive position of the countries that produce tropical timber. These changes are emerging in three different areas and have thus far had different impacts on forestry and the timber industry in the individual producer countries; the changes tend in part to converge or complement one another, though they may in part also clash. These three areas are (Mather 1997):

–   advances in technology and internationalization of the organization of production in the timber-processing industry,

–   the altered demands on timber production in forests and plantations resulting from this situation, and

–   new models of forest and plantation management of the sort presented in Chapter 4.

The future of the world timber market will be characterized by growing demand for wood fibers that are processed to manufacture technology-intensive reconstituted wood panels; these fibers can be produced most cheaply in plantations that are favorably situated in terms of transportation facilities and enjoy bioclimatic advantages (above all in the southern hemisphere). This implies a shift in the crucial comparative advantages of timber-producing countries from an inherited endowment with stands of native timber to a *man-made* resource base in the form of plantations with high productivity and low production costs.

This development can already be traced on the basis of the growth rates of the different segments of the world timber market.[1] Between 1990 and 1997 the most expansive segments were those based on fiber production: fiberboard (6.2 % annually), pulp (4.7 %), and paper (4.8 %). While the growth of the fiberboard segment in the 1980s was borne above all by plywood, i.e. the product that traditionally has the highest share of tropical wood, the dynamic shifted in the 1990s to novel products such as MDF (middle-dense fiberboard) and OSB (oriented-strand board) that are manufactured with fiber or particles.[2] Sawnwood is also experiencing a shift toward plantation production: the growth rate of the deciduous timber traded internationally, the classical natural-forest product, has been declining continuously for almost 20 years now. If the rate was still 5.6 % annually in the 1970s, the figures for the 1980s and 1990s were 1.4 and 1.5 %, respectively. By contrast, the growth of the trade in coniferous sawnwood, more and more of which has been produced on plantations for roughly 20 years now, has increased from 1.1 % annually in the 1980s to over 3 % in the 1990s.[3]

5.1   Quantitative Developments in the World Timber Market

Production of and Trade in Timber Products

All in all, at present over 80 % of world timber production and trade is concentrated in the industrialized countries, though since the 1960s the developing countries have experienced enormous increases in their shares in individual segments.

The following section is based on an analysis of FAO data, although in its statistics the FAO lists only producer countries, distinguishing between coniferous and deciduous timber and singling out, starting in 1990, only roundwood as an example for the industrial processing of tropical timber. It is therefore not possible to determine exactly the overall percentages of tropical timber in production and trade. In tropical developing countries output and exports of eucalyptus plantations are classified along with the production of natural tropical forests as deciduous timber products. This is the case in Brazil, too, where any interpretation of production and trade data is made difficult by the parallel existence of a modern, plantation-based pulp and paper sector based on eucalyptus plantations and a sawnwood sector based above all on tropical timber.

Table 5:	Distribution of World Timber Exports among Products and Main Exporting Countries, 1996 (%)		
Product	Share in world export value 1996	Share of five main exporting countries in world export volume 1996	
		Industrialized countries	Developing countries
Industrial roundwood	8	33	5
Tropical industr. roundwood	2	0	100
Sawnwood	19	55	1
Wood-based panels	12	27	20
Pulp	13	62	0
Paper and paperboard	48	40	1
Source: FAO Forestry Statistics			

When the present study refers to tropical timber, it means only timber from natural tropical forests; pine and eucalyptus timber grown on plantations is not covered by this term.

In international terms, the developing countries are experiencing disproportionate growth in both the production and export of timber products. These countries have increased their share of the world's produc-

tion above all in deciduous stemwood, deciduous sawnwood, and veneers and plywood; in regional terms this development is due above all
to strong growth experienced in the countries of Southeast Asia, based
on the exploitation of tropical forests.

Compared with production, the developing countries have managed to
even further increase their share of world trade in tropical timber (see
Tables A-1 to A-4 in the Appendix): in the 1960s and 1970s their
sawnwood exports increased sharply and the growth in their plywood
exports continued into the 1980s. In the 1990s, however, the most dynamic sectors in the developing countries were pulp and paper and veneer panels; their exports of deciduous sawnwood declined and the
figures for plywood indicate a historically low growth rate (3.3 % annually).

In the sawnwood and board segments (excepting veneers) the export
shares of the developing countries have thus declined despite their
higher share of world output between 1990 and 1997. In this period the
developing countries' export content of plywood fell from 74 % to
52 %. The South's share of pulp and paper exports has soared, a consequence of the growing internationalization of the production structure
in the corporations that dominate these segments (see Section 5.2 for
more detail).

The furniture exports of the developing countries rose in the period
1980/81 - 1990/91 from a total of US$ 1.3 billion to 4 billion annually.
Today their share of the world market is roughly 13 %. The by far most
important exporter among the developing countries is Taiwan, whose
production is entirely based on timber imports, and which exported
US$ 1.5 billion in 1990/91, accounting for 39 % of the exports of the
developing countries and 5 % of world exports. Indonesia and Thailand
export furniture worth over US$ 300 million; the figures for Brazil and
Malaysia were US$ 220 million and 55 million, respectively (UNCTAD
1996, p. 16 f).

Table 6 presents an overview of the growth of timber production in
developing countries.

Table 6:	Share of Developing Countries in Physical World Timber Output, 1961-97 (%)				
	1961	1970	1980	1990	1997
Industrial Roundwood	13.5	16.2	23.3	23.2	30.1
Sawlogs	13.4	18.0	25.4	23.4	29.1
Coniferous	5.6	7.0	11.5	9.8	14.7
Non-coniferous	37.0	46.7	58.0	58.0	57.8
Sawnwood	10.6	12.9	20.0	21.9	26.4
Coniferous	5.4	6.8	10.2	10.8	14.2
Non-coniferous	28.1	32.5	48.4	53.3	57.8
Wood-based panels	5.6	9.0	13.9	20.8	30.7
Veneer	15.1	29.1	35.7	52.9	56.8
Plywood	6.0	12.2	21.3	32.6	50.8
Pulp	2.5	3.4	6.0	7.6	11.7
Paper	6.8	6.9	11.6	16.8	22.7
Source: FAO Forestry Statistics					

In 1990 the world trade in timber had a volume of US$ 98.4 billion; the share of the developing countries in this trade was US$ 14 billion. The dominance of the industrialized countries is above all linked with the importance of pulp and paper exports, which together account for 60 % of the value of the world trade. The shares of the developing countries in these segments is merely 7.6 and 5 %, respectively. The value of sawnwood exports was somewhat more than US$ 17 billion, and the developing countries' share of this was 16 %. The developing countries had a 43 % share of board exports (plywood, veneer, fiber- and particle boards), which in 1990 amounted to some US$ 10 billion.

As far as the processors of tropical timber are concerned, we find that they were able to transform the natural advantages associated with stands of tropical forest into competitive advantages in the world market. This was true for Asian countries with stands of tropical forest.

In the 1990s at the latest this technological development path came to an end, with the shares in the traditionally strong segments sawnwood and plywood declining, and it is only for veneer production that we note an increase. And yet the fact is that the shares of the countries with tropical forests in the timber imports of the most important industrialized countries (except Germany) developed very unevenly between 1990 and 1995 (see Tables 7 and 8).

Table 7: Share of Tropical Timber Imports in Total Imports, 1992 (1000 m³)

	Plywood		Sawnwood (non-coniferous)		Veneer	
	Total	Tropical	Total	Tropical	Total	Tropical
USA	1447	1220	912	435	409	205
Japan	2766	2619	1699	931	313	246
Italy	269	53	1946	550	147	46
Netherlands	601	235	987	598	36	7
Great Britain	1101	519	743	354	69	7
France	318	150	554	324	80	14
Spain	n.d.	n.d.	784	392	77	6

Source: FAO Forestry Statistics

Table 8: Share of Tropical Timber Imports in Total Imports, 1995 (1000 m³)

	Plywood		Sawnwood (non-coniferous)		Veneer	
	Total	Tropical	Total	Tropical	Total	Tropical
USA	1802	1346	699	194	415	211
Japan	4667	4203	1550	940	275	186
Italy	270	51	1367	276	134	41
Netherlands	591	105	707	441	22	3
Great Britain	1062	351	669	300	58	3
France	290	127	564	420	71	26
Spain	n.d.	n.d.	660	335	54	6

Source: FAO Forestry Statistics

In **Japan**, the world's largest importer of tropical timber, these imports are showing a slight decline: plywood imports rose in all by 69 %, though the share of tropical timber in this plywood declined from 95 to 90 % because tropical-plywood imports grew only by 60 %. In contrast, veneer imports declined on the whole by 12 %, tropical veneer imports by even 32 %. The share of tropical veneer in overall veneer imports thus declined from 79 to 68 %. Sawnwood imports declined only slightly, and tropical-sawnwood imports held their own, thus increasing their share from 55 to 61 %. Due to a declining log supply on the part of its traditional Asian suppliers, Japan is experiencing a variety of substitution developments, including growing log imports from Africa, greater demand for coniferous timber and reconstituted wood panels such as MDF and OSB (Marchés Tropicaux, Oct. 25, 1996).

Sawnwood exports to the **US** have declined by a total of nearly one third, the share of tropical timber falling from 48 to 28 %. Veneer imports stagnated, as did the share of tropical timber in this segment. Plywood imports increased markedly by 25 %, while the share of tropical timber here fell from 84 to 75 %.

The trends in the most important **European countries** differ greatly: the most clear-cut trend is a decline in sawnwood imports, though here overall imports are as a rule declining faster than tropical imports. France is an important exception in this segment: it shows a high and increasing share of tropical sawnwood. A similar trend is evident for veneer imports: overall imports are on the decline, while the tropical countries are holding their absolute export volume. In Italy and the Netherlands the share of tropical timber is declining visibly, while in France it has doubled. It is only for plywood imports that a countertrend can be made out: overall imports are growing, while tropical imports have declined by 23 %, most sharply in the UK and the Netherlands. The market share of tropical plywood declined in these countries from 47 to 33 % and from 39 to 18 %, respectively.

Detailed analyses of the European markets confirm this trend:[4] in the mid-1990s all markets for timber products were affected by the downturn in economic growth in western Europe. High real interest rates, monetary turbulence, and the pressure to cut public budget deficits hampered investment in the building sector, dampening demand. The most important changes on the supply side are the palpable depletion of natural timber reserves in Southeast Asia (Malaysia and Indonesia), declining timber output in Russia,[5] sharply rising timber output in the Baltic countries and some eastern European countries, e.g. Rumania. The sizable supply of deciduous sawnwood from the temperate zones and growing MDF capacities are depressing the European market for sawnwood.

Between 1986 and 1996 European tropical-log imports declined from 2.9 million m^3 to 1.5 million m^3; only in France, which, in part due to its veneer industry, currently accounts for close to 50 % of European imports, have import figures remained high. The most sharp decline in log imports was noted for Germany.

Between 1986 and 1996 consumption of sawn hardwood declined continuously; imports of tropical sawnwood decreased in this period from 3 million m^3 to 1.7 million m^3. The weakening supply from Southeast Asia (1986: 2.2 million m^3, 1996: 517,000 m^3) was not yet compensated for by supplies from Africa (1986: 603,000 m^3, 1996: 905,000 m^3) and Latin America (1986: 195,000 m^3, 1996: 345,000 m^3). But on the other hand the volume of imports of sawn hardwood from the temperate zones has grown, increasingly replacing tropical timber: US sawn hardwood exports (chiefly oak) reached a record level of 2.8 million m^3 in 1996, and have shown a rising tendency since then.

As far as panels are concerned, European tropical imports of plywood are also steadily declining (1986: 1.6 million m^3, 1996: 1.35 million m^3). Nor have African and Latin American imports made up for the decline in Southeast Asian imports. All told, plywood prices have declined on account of weak world demand and devaluation in the Asian supplier countries. The increasing difficulties involved in getting logs needed for plywood production in sufficient quality and quantity are placing limits on Malaysia's and Indonesia's plywood output; since the devaluation at the end of 1997 the rise in the price of bonding agents has become an exacerbating factor.

As far as fiberboard is concerned, in 1994 close to 70 % of European consumption consisted of MDF. Between 1990 and 1995 European

MDF production rose from 1.8 million m^3 to 3.8 million m^3, and for 1997 a capacity of 5 million m^3 was anticipated. In the same period the price declined by 20 %. While only 12 % of European MDF output is exported, growing investments in production capacities have been noted outside Europe.

On the whole, a clear-cut differentiation in terms of species can be observed in the European market for tropical logs and sawnwood. While the UK has specialized in mahogany (83 % of world mahogany imports), 62 % of Dutch imports are accounted for by meranti. In these countries, as in Germany and Italy, most timber exports stem from Asia and Africa. In France, Spain, and Portugal Brazilian species (tauari, curupixá, jatobá, tatajuba, and pau amarelo) belong to the most important timber types.

A more exact analysis of the development of German timber exports (Brockmann, Hemmelskamp and Hohmeyer 1996, pp. 44 - 62; annual reports of the German Association of Timber Traders [VDH] and the German Federal Ministry for Food, Agriculture and Forests, [BMELF]) shows that the latter have followed the above-named general trend since the beginning of the 1990s (Table 9): all in all, the only reason why the volume of imports remained constant between 1960 and 1994 is that a drastic decrease in log imports is made up for by just as drastic increases in veneer and plywood imports as well as, since 1990, imports of end products such as furniture.

Table 9: Development of Tropical Timber Imports to Germany, 1960-94					
	Roundwood	Sawnwood	Veneer, Plywood etc.	Finished goods	Total
1960-64	1,525	128	20	0	1,673
1965-69	1,492	183	64	0	1,742
1970-74	1,347	431	161	46	1,988
1975-79	883	724	287	93	1,987
1980-84	579	781	330	101	1,789
1985-89	414	742	453	161	1,770
1990-94	272	493	762	543	2,070
Source: BMELF (1997), p. 11, figures in 1000 m^3 of roundwood equivalents					

Since 1993 German imports of primary goods of tropical timber have been cut by half: all told, in 1997 imports of sawnwood, plywood, and veneer were 480,000 m^3; in roundwood equivalents this amounts, roughly estimated, to one million m^3. By 1997 imports of tropical logs fell in absolute terms by 40 %, while imports of deciduous tropical logs reached a new low of roughly 189,000 m^3. Germany's plywood imports have increased slightly, though this figure is currently dominated by imports from Finland, the volume of which was greater than that for Asia in 1997, and the US. In 1997 80 % of German plywood imports came from Europe and North America, only 18 % from Asia and Brazil together. Imports of finished goods, above all garden furniture of tropical wood, have increased.

Price Development

Since the 1960s the real price level for tropical timber has remained relatively stable; since 1980 prices have declined somewhat on the whole, though at the beginning of the 1990s they showed a slightly upward tendency.[6] The development of the prices for tropical timber thus corresponds roughly to the development of the price index for timber products on the whole, which declined by some 25 - 30 % between 1963 and 1993.

While until 1993 deflated prices for logs (coniferous and deciduous) remained roughly 10 - 15 % below the 1980 level, prices for tropical stemwood showed a marked upward tendency, reaching 1980 levels in 1993; since then log prices, particularly in Southeast Asia, have risen, by 50 - 100 % between 1990 and 1997.[7]

Sawnwood is the only product group that shows a price increase in real terms, higher for deciduous timber and tropical timber than for coniferous timber, with the differentials between the three timber types widening. Between 1973 and 1992 the average world-market price for a cubic meter of coniferous timber rose from US$ 74 to 159, while the corresponding price of deciduous sawnwood from the temperate zones increased from US$ 114 to 380, and the price for tropical timber climbed from US$ 100 to 293. In the mid-1990s the FAO registered a price rise for Asian and Brazilian sawnwood, though it was not clear whether this trend would continue in view of the stronger orientation of demand in terms of logs or processed wood products. Between August 1997 and August 1998 a decline of 36 % for tropical hardwood was noted (Die Zeit, Sept. 24, 1998).

Deflated prices for plywood fell by 50 % between 1963 and 1980; between 1980 and 1990 they remained roughly constant, in order then to decline again in the mid-1990s. The sharp competition between the three big tropical exporters Indonesia, Malaysia, and Brazil as well as the pressure stemming from substitute products has been contributing to this negative price development.

Particle-board prices have also declined sharply: in 1993, following a slight increase, they still remained below 1980 levels. Fiberboard prices declined by 25 % between 1963 and 1980 and then began to rise again, a development that reflected the initially higher prices for MDF boards.

If we look at changes in absolute prices, we find distinct competitive advantages for particle boards and fiberboards, compared with both sawnwood and plywood. The former are more expensive than coniferous sawnwood, but they offer technical properties that are similar to those of high-quality deciduous sawnwood and they are more accessible to further processing than tougher tropical timbers.

Table 10: Average World Market Prices (US$)		
	1973	1992
Sawnwood (coniferous)	74	159
Sawnwood (non-coniferous)	114	380
Sawnwood (tropical)	100	293
Plywood	212	394
Particle board	90	231
Fiberboard	93	291
Source: FAO (1995)		

The Position of Brazil and Pará in the World Timber Market

Analysis of Brazil's timber exports shows that the dynamics between 1970 and 1997 was marked above all by strong growth in pulp and paper exports; as far as processed timber is concerned, the value of sawnwood exports decreased in absolute terms, while exports of ply-wood and semi-processed goods (strips, doors, windows) grew. Brazil also exports small quantities of particle board and fiberboard. Until the mid-1990s the level of these exports stagnated at the levels of the early 1980s and was very low as compared with sawnwood and plywood.

There are two sources available to determine Brazil's position in the world timber market between 1960 and 1997: FAO data and IBGE data, which are based on the external-trade statistics of the Banco do Brasil (see Tables 11 and 12).

Table 11:	Growth of Brazilian Physical Timber Exports, 1961-97								
	1961	1970	1980	1970/80	1990	1980/90	1997	1990/97	1970/97
	1000 m^3	1000 m^3	1000 m^3	%	1000 m^3	%	1000 m^3	%	%
Sawlogs	54	84	7	-22.0	0		0		
Conifer-ous	0	0	0		0		0		
Non-conif.	54	84	7	-22.0	0		0		
Sawn-wood	1,115	1,075	809	-2 8	479	-5 1	1,640	19.2	1.6
Coni ferous	1,095	927	187	-14 8	50	-12.4	530	40.1	-2.0
Non-conif.	20	147	622	15.5	429	-3.6	1,110	14.5	7.8
Wood-based panels	14	106	324	11.8	616	6.6	1,164	9.5	9.3
Veneer	9	33	40	1.9	53	2.9	180	19.1	6.5
Plywood	3	29	99	13.1	303	11.8	626	10.9	12.1
Pulp	3	39	890	36 7	1.033	1.5	2,250	11.8	16.2
Paper	0	1	198	69.7	840	15.5	1,220	5.5	30.1
Source: FAO Forestry Statistics, figures in % refer to annual geometric growth rates									

Table 12: Monetary Growth of Brazilian Timber, Pulp and Paper Exports, 1970-95

	1970 R$ million	1975 R$ million	1980 R$ million	1970/80 %	1985 R$ million	1990 R$ million	1980/90 %	1995 R$ million	1990-95 %	1970-95 %
Timber	653.9	547.9	1126.4	5.6	843.4	426.1	-9.3	1056.7	19.9	1.9
Sawnwood	460.3	304.8	248.6	-6.0				379.8		-0.8
Semi-pro-cessed goods	12.2	35.4	373.1	40.8				229.8		12.5
Veneer	98.4	37.9	100.5	0.2				70.2		-1.3
Plywood	33.9	27.6	143.6	15.5				259.9		8.5
Pulp	33.8	118.1	1066.8	41.2	894.3	599.6	-5.6	1475.4	19.7	16.3
Paper	3.4	107.9	456.6	63.2	716.7	613.4	3.0	1229.5	14.9	26.6
Total	691.1	773.9	2649.8	14.4	2454.4	1639.1	-4.7	3761.6	18.1	7.0

Source: IBGE, Anuário Estatístico, figures in R$ of 1996, annual geometric growth rate in %

Comparison of the growth rates in terms of volume (FAO) and export value (IBGE) shows that as a rule volume grew more strongly between 1970 and 1997 than export value, one exception being paper exports. On the whole, the export value of sawnwood declined by -0.8 % per year between 1970 and 1996, while the volume grew by 1.6 % in the same period. Growth per volume and value are furthest apart for veneers and plywood: the annual growth rate for the value of veneers was -1.3 %, a negative value, while volume reached an annual 6.5 %. For plywood the growth rate for export value, 8.5 %, was roughly half that of the growth rate for volume, 12.1 %. For pulp and paper volume and value showed parallel development: the corresponding annual growth rates were 16.2 and 30.1 % for volume and 16.3 and 26.6 for export value.

The composition of Brazil's timber exports mirrors the different growth rates. Between 1970 and 1995 the share of primary timber products declined from 95 to 28 %, while the share of pulp grew from 4.9 to 39.2 % and the figure for paper rose from 0.5 to 33 %. Within primary timber products, sawnwood (36 %) and plywood (25 %) are dominant. In 1990/91 Brazil's furniture exports amounted to US$ 55 million and then soared to a figure of roughly US$ 300 million. This unprecedented growth is explained by Brazilian producers with reference to declines in supplies from eastern Europe.

For the period between 1970 and 1983 the IBGE has provided more detailed figures on the composition of timber exports that demonstrate the process of transition from the use of the araucaria forests in Brazil's south to the exploitation of the tropical rainforests of the Amazon region (see Table A-6 in the Appendix):

–   The transition was accompanied by a drastic fall in export values, which was made up for only by stepping up mahogany exports in the 1980s;

–   veneer exports were associated with a conversion from jacarandá to mahogany; these involve considerable fluctuations in the volume figures from year to year, which point in the direction of major problems in conversion;

- beginning in 1979 tropical-timber-based plywood exports soared to a volume of over R$ 100 million; for fiberboard, which is made of plantation timber, this jump occurred in 1978, then the dynamics in this segment declined.

Pará's timber exports have been documented in more detail by the Pará federation of timber exporters, AIMEX, which was founded in 1973 (see Table 13). Between 1973 and 1995 the structure of exports changed to the extent that now instead of logs only sawnwood was exported: this change is due directly to the 1974 export ban on logs. The shares of veneer have declined, while those of plywood and semi-processed goods have increased. This structural shift entailed an eight-fold rise in the average export value per cubic meter (in current prices) and an increase of the export volume by 34 % in absolute terms, an increase that was achieved in favor of sawnwood and plywood.

Table 13: Structure of Timber Exports from Pará, 1973 and 1996				
	1973		1996	
Logs	429,516 m^3	60.5 %	0 m^3	0.0 %
Sawnwood	232,331 m^3	32.7 %	544,195 m^3	66.3 %
Veneer	42,084 m^3	5.9 %	32,356 m^3	3.9 %
Semi-processed goods	3,881 m^3	0.5 %	19,597 m^3	2.4 %
Plywood	2,589 m^3	0.4 %	224,839 m^3	27.4 %
Total volume	710,403 m^3	100.0 %	820,987 m^3	100.0 %
Total value (fob)	US$ 31,266,000		US$ 300,860,000	
Value/m^3	US$ 44		US$ 366	
Source: AIMEX				

Comparison of the data for overall Brazilian timber exports shows that Pará was strongly involved only in the rise in sawnwood and plywood; exports of semi-processed goods on the other hand have been concentrated in other regions of the country. Due to the dominant position of less dynamic segments, the share of Pará's exports in the overall value of the exports made by Brazil's timber industry (i.e. without pulp/paper and furniture) between 1989 and 1996 remained constant at around 30 %, with a slightly downward tendency.

The first half of the 1990s saw stabilization of the following trends in Pará's timber exports (see Table A-5 in the Appendix):

- Following temporary rises, the share of sawnwood is holding its own at a level of 66 %, mahogany and virola have lost their prominent position to a more broad distribution of species;

- the share of plywood has settled at a level of 27 %, while the in any case low share of veneering has declined and semi-processed goods have risen somewhat;

- the roughly 20 % rise in the export value is due above all to increases of the value of veneers and other processed wood products; the average price for a cubic meter of sawnwood has declined.

The structure of overall Brazilian timber exports appears to be changing again in the 1990s, this time in favor of sawnwood, particle board, and semi-processed goods (see Table A-8 in the Appendix);

- on the whole, the value of the exports of the timber industry has risen by 16 % per year, in absolute terms from US$ 551 million to 998.8 million;

- the share of sawnwood in the value of exports increased by 21 % from 1992 to 1996, growing from 29 to 35 % in absolute terms;

- growth in this segment is due primarily to pine: mahogany (1992: 63 %) was supplanted by pine as the dominant species, pine sawnwood accounting in 1996 for 24 % of the export value of sawnwood and 22 % of volume; mahogany's share declined to 14 % of the value of exports; exports of other tropical species grouped together grew by 38 % annually, indicating a trend towards diversification;

- the share of particle board in the value of exports increased most sharply, by a figure of 51 % annually, though its share in overall export value is only 2.3 %;

- aside from sawnwood, the most important export products are plywood and semi-processed goods; but plywood experienced only

below-average annual growth of 13 %, while semi-processed
goods reached an annual figure of 20 %.

The development of exports in recent years presents a diffuse picture:
exports of both traditional, low-processed products like sawnwood and
more technology-intensive products like particle board and semi-
processed goods have been stepped up; increased exports have been
achieved by both the conventional sawmills in the north and those in
the south, which are increasingly switching over to industrial processing of plantation timber. This database by itself is not sufficient to re-
liably assess current changes, additional information on qualitative
changes in the world timber market are required for the purpose.

5.2   Qualitative Developments in the World Timber Market

The reason why the developing counties' shares of world production
and trade have increased is different for each product group. Up to the
1980s countries in possession of large natural forest stands could use
instruments of trade policy to either create national timber-processing
industries or to exert a certain influence on the locational decisions
made by foreign industrial timber-processing firms. It is mainly in this
phase that the developing countries increased their share of sawnwood
and plywood exports. This changed when the growing importance of
plantations (and thus of man-made timber supplies) and advances in
technology- and capital-intensive fiber-processing made way for a new
internationalization strategy of the timber and wood corporations.
Products of this phase include pulp as well as novel particle and fiberboards. This situation saw the development of a competition between
potential new locations, which lent far greater weight to economic and
legal framework conditions conducive to direct foreign investment.

Instruments of Trade Policy

In the 1970s and 1980s trade-policy instruments were used to set up
tariff and nontariff trade barriers aimed at either protecting or developing sites for the timber industry. The most important instruments were

progressive tariffs for processed wood products in the industrialized countries and, as a response to this, bans and/or restrictions on log exports in the developing countries that aimed at providing an incentive for foreign corporations to build factories or to entice domestic investors to invest in processing there.[8] In the 1990s these instruments lost much of their significance due to the agreements reached in connection with the Uruguay Round on across-the-board tariff cuts and the new trade rules associated with the foundation of the WTO.[9] By the year 2005 the Uruguay Round provides for average across-the-board tariff cuts from 3.5 - 1.1 % for the industrialized countries and 4.6 - 1.7 % for developing countries. The tariff escalation (with tariffs rising in keeping with a product's degree of processing) was abolished for pulp and paper products, though it was retained for timber products. The industrialized countries impose an average tariff of 6.5 % on boards, the highest rates being encountered in Japan, the US, and the EU.

In the 1970s the response of the developing countries to the progressive tariffs imposed by the industrialized countries consisted of export barriers aimed at lowering the profitability of log exports compared with exports of processed wood products in order in this way to promote domestic timber-processing. The assumption here was that their most important comparative advantages lay in their lower wage costs and control over their forest resources; processing logs into sawnwood and plywood would at the same time reduce weight and thus freight costs. This was intended to make up for developing-country-specific disadvantages (lack of qualified manpower and infrastructure). Criticism of this strategy focused on two points: first, the developing countries, it was claimed, had comparative advantages in log production thanks to their large forest stands, but lacked them in processing. Second, it was noted, log exports were not enough to safeguard sales of primary timber products (sawnwood and plywood); what was needed for this purpose, the argument ran, was competitive production, since otherwise other log suppliers would move into the markets.

This gives rise to two questions: Do log-producing countries have comparative advantages in producing and processing logs? Are the import barriers imposed by the industrialized countries the most important obstacles to the competitiveness of the developing countries?

Aside from Ghana no African country has managed to build up significant timber- and wood-processing capacities; the import-substituting industrialization strategy pursued in Latin America entailed refocusing production on the domestic market. The case in Southeast Asia is different. These countries aimed from the very beginning at export markets, above all Japan. Once the log-export restrictions had been imposed in Indonesia and Malaysia, plywood production in Singapore, Taiwan, South Korea, and Japan declined perceptibly, while at the same time increasing in Indonesia and Malaysia. A 1985 FAO study explained this development with reference to the fact that Indonesia and Malaysia were successful in blocking access to raw materials for existing big producers of plywood. However, they neglected to build comparative advantages in processing. Output comparisons with Japan had showed that the crucial edge enjoyed by Indonesia and Malaysia lay in low log prices, in other words, in an absolute advantage. Together with low wage costs, this absolute advantage led these countries to neglect the task of stepping up their productivity and quality (FAO 1988, pp. 84 - 94; Takeuchi 1983).

Without export bans on logs the Southeast Asian countries would certainly not have succeeded in starting out with timber-/wood-processing and increasing their market shares in the industrialized countries.[10] But this alone was not enough to ensure them a dominant position in the world market in the long term; the productivity of their factories remained low due to low conversion rates and insufficient utilization of capacities (Repetto and Gillis 1988). An additional factor was their unsustainable use of their timber resources: as soon as timber scarcity began to drive log prices up, it again became more profitable to export logs than to process them domestically into plywood or sawnwood. This situation occurred in Indonesia and Malaysia in the 1990s and was intensified by a condition imposed by the IMF that required Indonesia to rescind its export restrictions on logs.[11]

Technological Innovations and Substitution Pressure

Wood being a commodity, there are strong economic incentives to invest in applied research with an eye to widening the physical limits imposed by the size of natural forest stands on the production, processing, and use of timber. The age-class forest developed by European forestry in the 19th century was a first step in the direction of systematizing and planning timber production, one that constituted an important precondition for industrial mass processing. The end of the 20th century is also experiencing a number of technological innovations that make it possible to gear timber production more closely to the technical and economic needs of industry:

–   genetic research has further shortened the maturation time of fast-growing species; under suitable bioclimatic conditions (high solar radiation and precipitation) and the proper use of fertilizers and pesticides, it is possible to shorten the rotation cycles for eucalyptus to 5 - 7 years and that of pine to 20 - 25 years, while at the same time increasing timber growth to 30 - 45 m^3/ha per year;[12]

–   sawnwood and plywood are increasingly being replaced by reconstituted wood panels manufactured from wood fibers, in part by adding to them bonding agents or other materials under pressure and heat; the result is resistant, coated, or decoratively lined boards of a new type;

–   these reconstituted wood panels are technically superior to sawnwood or even plywood, and are cheaper to produce;[13] their technical features make them better suited to the fast and flexible production of small series oriented to specific customer wishes.

This development has far-reaching ramifications for forestry:

> "Instead of having to balance quality against quantity, modern timber merchants can aim for quantity alone, and rely on processing to make up the losses in strength, appearance and durability." (Dudley, Jeanrenaud and Sullivan 1996, p. 37)

The consequence is that forest management is being optimized under the aspect of fiber production, since fiber is now the homogeneous base material of a number of different products that can be manufactured flexibly in keeping with market demands. Concentration on fiber production increases the profitability of dense, homogeneous plantations (pine, eucalyptus) with short rotation cycles as well as the practice of clearing natural forests whose natural stands are suited to fiber production, e.g. birch in boreal forests, and which can be opened up inexpensively for exploitation.

This has sharply increased the substitution pressure on massive wood from natural forests as well as on the traditional primary products sawnwood and plywood. But sawnwood production is also undergoing change under the pressure of innovations in processing technology: modern computer-controlled precision saws, which can be used to improve conversion efficiency, require a large throughput of logs as homogeneous as possible if their use is to be profitable. This, too, makes plantations and/or less diverse forests more economically attractive.

Internationalization

Since the 1980s the timber industry has been going through a process of concentration associated with the establishment of an international network of corporate timber-production and wood-processing sites.[14] The technological innovations described in the section above have made this process possible by "exempting" the timber industry from the constraints imposed by natural forest stands – and promoted it inasmuch as the vertical integration between fiber production and fiber-processing has become a crucial competitive factor. The development of plantations as well as investments in new processing plants are, however, highly capital-intensive, i.e. out of reach for medium-scale enterprises. A new element in this process of concentration and internationalization is the growing significance of new, nontraditional locations with more favorable bioclimatic growth conditions than those encountered in the boreal forest countries; these include Spain and Portugal, Chile, New Zealand, the south of Brazil, and the US.

Corporations from the traditional forest locations have sought to use their internationalization strategy to compensate for the relative impairment of their dominant position in the world market. The condition required for this is the process of concentration: while in the US, Sweden, and Japan the timber industry has long since been dominated by large corporations, the other countries involved have been marked by a more medium-scale industrial structure with dispersed forest ownership. The 1980s saw the onset of a country- and continent-wide wave of mergers that above all strengthened the market position of the big corporations from the US, Japan, and Sweden in the pulp and paper industry, at the same time bringing forth new actors in the industry. In the course of this wave the corporations involved diversified their activities, acquired large plantations, and launched timber-processing and sales operations.

Developing countries have also been able to profit from this corporate internationalization strategy: *"Bulk wood or fibre production, and the associated processing industries increase more rapidly in the South than in the North."* (Mather 1997, p. 13) Their share of world trade and their export content has on the whole risen continuously over the past 30 years; since the 1980s large plantation stands have been built up by private investors in Chile, Indonesia and South Africa, and these investors have now started building the corresponding industrial processing plants. In this way the South has also experienced the emergence of corporations that are developing into global, or at least regional, actors: Chilean corporations have formed joint ventures with New Zealand and US corporations and are investing in Brazil and Argentina; Malaysian and Chinese corporations were also involved in the privatization of New Zealand's publicly owned forests, corporations from Hong Kong, Japan, and the US have purchased blocks of stock from New Zealand pulp and paper processors.

Challenges

The technological innovations and their consequences for the organization of timber production and processing are giving rise to a number of challenges for industrialized and developing countries alike, challenges that are also affected by the changes in the postindustrial model of forest and plantation management outlined and discussed in Chapter 4 (Mather 1997, p. 16 f.). These new models are mainly concerned with the compatibility of an economically profitable and nevertheless environmentally and socially sound utilization of forests and plantations; in looking in particular at plantations we become aware of a contradiction

involved in the goal of optimized fiber production. The coming decades
will be marked by the following challenges:

– The industrialized countries have two options to make up for their
  locational disadvantages in timber production, both of which can
  be combined: On the one hand they can extend their technological
  edge in machine-building, the development of new technology-
  intensive, so-called engineered wood products, and industry-related
  services (plant construction, market analysis, and the like): Finland
  is the pioneer in this approach; in the past 30 years it has converted
  its exports from primary goods to high-quality paper, specialized
  machines, and engineering services.[15] On the other hand they can –
  in view of the exhaustion of natural forests and unfavorable conditions for fast-growing plantations, e.g. in Canada – secure their access to timber resources throughout the world and build a network
  of production sites.

– There is a risk that nature-oriented forest management may win the
  day in the industrialized countries at the expense of an expansion
  of industrial, unsustainable plantations in developing countries.
  What is needed here is work on international standards for profitable, ecologically sustainable, and socially compatible plantation
  management. The effectiveness of such standards and market-
  oriented instruments such as ecological certification can be stepped
  up by customer demands for more environmental quality in products and production processes and close scrutiny of the relevant
  corporations by the media and environmental organizations
  (Scholz 1993, 1996b).

– The developing countries are faced with the challenge, both in the
  use of their natural forests and in plantation management, of skip-
  ping the phase of industrial mass production and directly introducing methods of sustainable management. This is necessary especially in the plantation economy in that the latter, under the aegis
  of globally active corporations, often has something of a colonial
  smack to it: it is as a rule linked with purchases of large areas of
  land, which often means that small and medium-scale landowners,
  in many countries even indigenous population groups, are crowded
  out; modern processing is more capital- than labor-intensive, and

hence income effects are restricted to small segments of the populace and broad-based development effects do not automatically
materialize.

– The process of deforestation underway above all in the tropical
developing countries and the boreal forest areas must be stopped.
To what extent the establishment of plantations (or managed forests) can contribute to this end will largely depend on the political
will to push through legal regulations aimed at restricting the exploitation of natural forests. In Europe, 200 years ago, as timber
scarcity began to make itself felt, the first steps toward reforestation were undertaken; several European countries have now experienced growth of their forests, including plantations. Whether deforestation of the tropical regions can be halted will depend not
only on environmental-policy measures but also on whether agriculture can be stabilized and jobs can be provided in the urban areas of the regions affected, e.g. in the form of an ecologically
sound tourism.

– One means of stopping the destruction of the tropical forests would
involve developing medium-term perspectives for factories that
process tropical timber. These perspectives would have to concentrate on increasing local shares in timber-processing and the development of demanding niche markets abroad; they should provide
approaches of interest for both modern, export-oriented companies
and for smaller-scale workshops.

How must Pará's timber industry be judged against this background?
What chances and problems does it face if it is to survive and develop
in rapidly changing domestic and external markets? Chapters 6 and 7 of
the present study will look into possible answers to these questions.

6   The Timber Industry in Pará and in Brazil in the 1990s

Toward the end of the 1990s Pará's timber industry is at a crossroads:
on the one hand the zenith of its development over the last 40 years
seems already to have been passed. Exports have, it is true, been in-

creasing since 1994, but at the same time the economic significance of this branch of industry has declined, above all due to a growing number of shutdowns.[1] On the other hand a number of investments by big Malaysian corporations (acquisition of run-down plywood factories and large forests) appear to signal an impending drastic upturn for the industry, one that has been anticipated by optimists for some 30 years now:[2] Now that the forests in Asia and Africa have been severely depleted, the world demand for tropical timber will be concentrated on the Amazon region, because this region contains the world's largest closed tropical forest area.[3] This assumption was used again and again in the Amazon region since the 1960s and 1970s to justify the belief that the timber industry would soon develop into one of the most dynamic and high-yielding branches of the region's economy. This development has, however, thus far failed to materialize.

The present study supports the thesis that the development chances of the timber industry in the Amazon region are defined by the specific interlinkages between Pará's timber industry and the national timber industry on the one hand and the world timber market on the other. That is to say that the development and the present state of the Amazon timber industry must be analyzed in the context of Brazil's policies aimed at opening up and developing the Amazon region, and trends in the world market, which in the case of tropical timber is determined mainly by the Asian countries supply and the industrialized countries' demand. The present study concentrates on the entrepreneurial action patterns that have emerged in the Amazon region since the 1960s and are characteristic of the timber industry. As was pointed out in Chapter 2, analysis of these action patterns will cast light on the field of tension in which social action takes place: On the one hand the action patterns mirror the structural framework encompassing the timber entrepreneurs, i.e. the economic, ecological, social, cultural, and spatial framework conditions; on the other hand they show how the actors, through their specific response patterns, in turn affect these framework conditions by either strengthening or altering them.

The interlinkage between the Amazon timber industry and the Brazilian economy and the world market is not given, in the functionalist sense of the term, by factor prices and comparative advantages, the actors instead have options that permit them to influence this interlinkage. The outset is a given initial situation that is encountered by the actors, who are already equipped with certain experiences and problem-solving routines; in the case of the Amazon region the initial situation was characterized by a no more than weakly developed presence of state institutions empowered to enforce political rules and legal standards. Public investment in infrastructure development and subsidies for land purchases and subsequent forest clearing created the preconditions for migration to the Amazon region, where the individual had an enormous degree of freedom to appropriate for himself a share of the abundant resources occurring there.

This initial situation led to a chain of actor decisions on how to use the timber resources encountered in the region; this chain of decisions can be described as a cumulative process that gave rise to a certain development path or trajectory the impact of which was either to structure or to restrict future decisions. This development path can only remain stable as long as the original conditions can be reproduced. When this is no longer the case, a crisis arises.

The chances of the timber industry to overcome this crisis depends on three factors:

– the capacity of firms to introduce or adapt innovations,
– the trends in the world timber market, where demand for tropical timber is falling and
– the dynamic development of the timber industry in the South of Brazil, based upon cost advantages of plantation timber; this region attracts 85 % of all foreign direct investment in the Brazilian wood-processing industry, investments focus on the production of pulp, paper and reconstituted wood panels (Siqueira 1997).

The subject of the following two chapters is the dominant action patterns encountered in Pará's timber industry, the factors determining these patterns, and the resulting ability of companies or the industry as a whole to respond to, or indeed shape, these three factors. This is done in three steps:

–   The first step is a description of the situation of the Pará timber industry in the 1990s based on existing empirical studies and an evaluation of the author's qualitative interviews (Chapter 6);

–   in the second step a historical reconstruction of the timber industry from the 1950s on (Chapter 7) is used to depict and analyze the stages of the development of these action patterns that mark the way in which the natural resource tropical forest in Pará is used. This historical reconstruction includes contemporary empirical studies by the FAO and the regional development agency SUDAM as well as an evaluation of statistical time series compiled from economic censuses and annual statistical reports of IBGE and FAO. With a view to better assessing the efficiency of Pará's industry, the study also presents specific data on the timber industry across the nation and in Paraná, the center of Brazil's timber industry.

6.1   The Economic Framework Conditions

The economic framework conditions relevant for the subject of the present study concern on the one hand the economic reorientation that gained ground in Brazil in the 1990s in the *Plano Real* and on the other the great regional disparities that mark Brazil on the whole and are impeding the economic development of the peripheral regions, including the north, of which Pará is a part.

Economic Reorientation: the End of the Import-substituting Industriali-
zation Strategy, Consequences for Entrepreneurial Action

In the 1980s and at the beginning of the 1990s the Brazilian economy was marked by stagnation and pronounced macroeconomic imbalances, above all high and rising rates of inflation. Between 1980 and 1992 GDP grew by an annual average of only 1.25 %; in the same period per capita income decreased by 7.6 % (Levy and Hahn 1996, p. 17). Persistent balance-of-payments deficits, high inflation rates and public budget deficits were an expression of the fact that the economic power of a development strategy of industrialization based on import substitu-

tion had run out of steam; yet the political majority needed for structural reforms was not to materialize in these twelve years (Baer and
Paiva 1996).

Prior to the *Plano Real* a total of five stabilization plans were introduced, all of which failed within months. This increased economic instability and accelerated inflation. Due to the complicated system of
price-indexing and the speculative instruments developed by the banking system, however, even high and rapidly rising inflation rates led not
to a collapse of the economy but to a situation of precarious equilibrium
in which, starting in 1993, increasing growth rates were noted: in 1992
GDP decreased by 0.8 %, in 1993 it grew by 4.2 %, in 1994 by 6.0 %,
in order then to decline to 4.3 in 1995 and 2.9 % in 1996 (Conjuntura
Econômica, Nov. 1997, p. xviii).

The development of business productivity also showed a similar course:
while it grew by less than 0.4 % between 1981 and 1989, it increased
by an average of 7.35 % per year between 1991 and 1995 (Bonelli
1996, p. 621). This positive economic development is interpreted above
all as a response to the opening up of the Brazilian economy that was
gradually carried through beginning in 1988 and which compelled
companies to modernize their technology and cut costs. Competitive
pressure from imports was intensified by the *Plano Real* starting in
1994/95, which brought inflation, which had reached a figure of
2,000 % in 1993, under control.[4] The introduction of the real at a nomi-
nal dollar exchange rate of 1:1 made possible a sharp increase of imports in connection with the program of trade liberalization.

Unlike the other stabilization programs that preceded the *Plano Real*,
and had, within a period of months, collapsed, leaving behind huge
economic burdens (recession, intensification of income concentration)
(Macedo 1996), this plan did not fall back on surprising shock effects
but consisted instead in three previously announced stages the sequence
and timing of which were adhered to. First, the government budget was
provisionally balanced with the aid of a special fund. In March 1994 a
stable artificial accounting unit, the *Unidade Real de Valor* (URV – real
unit of value), was introduced and set at a level of max. one to a dollar;
the URV was made into the reference value for all payment contracts.

On July 1, 1994, the URV was converted into the new currency, the *real*, and the old currency was abolished.

Subsequent to the currency reform inflation fell by 50 % per month to 3 %; it was 14.8 % in 1996, 9.3 % in 1996, and 6.5 % in 1997. In the first 12 months following the reform GDP grew by 8 % and industrial production by 11 %, above all due to higher demand for consumer durables that could be purchased on installment.

Following an upward adjustment of the real in October 1994 (the dollar declined to R$ 0.84) and, a short time thereafter, the Mexico crisis, which led to a severe drain on Brazil's currency reserves, real interest rates were raised (temporarily up to 70 % p.a.) and a more flexible exchange-rate policy was introduced: following a devaluation by 5 % in March 1995 a policy of irregular and unannounced devaluations was introduced that was geared roughly to the inflation differential between US wholesale prices and a mix consisting of Brazilian price indices. At the same time import restrictions were imposed in order to limit the balance-of-trade deficit, which had increased sharply due to the strong real; in the first half year of 1995 imports were on the whole twice as high as they had been in the first semester of 1994. For a number of consumer goods, above all automobiles, import tariffs were therefore raised and import quotas imposed. The Asian crisis at the end of 1997 again led to outflows of short-term foreign capital deposits; interest rates were again increased and, in addition, a series of measures were adopted to restrict the government budget deficit. Since 1995 economic growth has declined to under 5 %; in 1997 the figure was 2.8 %.

Brazil's new development strategy is based on active integration into the world market, which, together with a liberal trade policy, is intended to create incentives for domestic industry to modernize its technological base and increase its productivity; these measures are intended to make it possible for Brazil to close the technological gap, becoming in this way an important industrial location for globally active corporations.[5] Foreign direct investment has in fact increased sharply since the *Plano Real*, above all in the auto industry. At the same time the policy of liberalization has also led to a situation in which foreign factories have sharply increased their shares of imported parts and other inputs with an eye to lowering their costs and enhancing their competitiveness.

To shore up this strategy it was necessary to add further reforms to the *Plano Real*; these included various measures aimed at reducing the budget deficit and cutting back the apparatus of state (incl. reform of the social security system and public administration), privatization of state-owned enterprises, and deregulation. While great progress was made with privatization (by 1996 over US$ 9 billion in proceeds, in 1998 the telephone company Telebrás was sold for US$ 19 billion), reform of social security and public administration was again and again bogged down in parliament. Thus it will prove difficult to limit the budget deficit and use the scarce remaining funds for alternative purposes such as targeted poverty reduction and development of the education/training system and a functioning public heath-care system.

These reforms changed the economic environment for private enterprises. Many, it is true, started modernizing their production facilities as early as 1990, importing capital goods toward this end;[6] but it is the advent of monetary and exchange-rate stability that confronted them with the challenge of introducing effective methods of cost calculation and cost reduction and the need to adjust to international standards in production management and marketing.

In the preceding decades entrepreneurs had, under the pressure of high inflation, been forced to make decisions with a large measure of uncertainty over the future development of prices, interest rates, and exchange rates. It was difficult to arrive at any exact cost calculation, i.e. one corrected by the factor of monetary instability, and the task required *"so much effort that many companies, above all small ones, did not even make the attempt and thus necessarily operated on the basis of relatively inexact approximate values and calculations."* (Porst 1996, p. 292) Under the conditions of growing expectations of inflation, inexact cost calculations lead to regular price markups and an increasing importance of financial management. The companies concerned spent a considerable part of their time deploying the various instruments offered by the banking system to counter the decline in the value of money; loans and foreign-currency revenues were used speculatively and not deployed productively, since the profitability of long-term – as opposed to short-term – investments was difficult to calculate and fraught with risk.

Regional Disparities and Regional Development Promotion

Brazil is marked by pronounced regional socioeconomic differentials: over 74 % of GDP is produced in the south and southeast of the country, 55 % alone in the states of São Paulo, Rio de Janeiro, and Minas Gerais (Braz de Oliveira e Silva at al. 1996). The north as a whole contributes only 4.8 % of the national economic product, Pará 2.3 %. If we look into the regional composition of GDP by sectors, we find that the only sector in which the dominance of the south and southeast is not so pronounced is agriculture, with 61.4 % of the value of overall output. As far as industry and the service sector are concerned, the share of both the south and the southeast accounts for over 70 %.

The sectoral composition of the GDP of the individual regions and states differs above all as concerns agriculture, which in the north and northeast contributes over 20 % to regional GDP (the Brazilian average being 12.6 %), and the public sector, which accounts for a share of 10 % and thus, here too, is above the national average. The north's industrial production is completely in line with the national average, while the service sector, with its 11 %, is below average. The latter fact is due above all to financial services, which are highly underdeveloped in the north.

Population concentration is somewhat less clear-cut: according to data from the population census conducted in 1991, 58 % of Brazil's 147 million inhabitants live in the south and southeast, 41 % of them in the states of São Paulo, Rio de Janeiro, and Minas Gerais. Only 6.8 % of the population lives in the north (3.4 % in Pará), i.e. in roughly half of the country's territory.

Within the northern region Pará has the strongest economic position; 47 % of the region's GDP is produced in this state. Pará is most dominant in agriculture, which accounts for 58 % of the regional sectoral product; this position is the result of the promotion of settlement in the northeast of Pará at the beginning of the century[7] and the use of tax incentives to develop huge cattle ranches and promote programs designed to attract small farmers to the Transamazônica in the 1970s and 1980s (Moran 1981, 1990; Moran, Packer, Brondizio and Tucker 1966; Bunker 1985; Walker et al. 1995; Homma and Walker 1996). As an important mining area and site of the aluminium industry, Pará contributes a share of 47 % to regional industrial production.

The great economic imbalances between Brazil's regions also lead to great disparities in living conditions. According to the *Human Development Index* (PNUD and IPEA 1996), Pará, with its HDI value of 0.699, ranges just above the median development level (0.632). Compared with all of Brazil's 26 states, Pará has a middle position (16), though as far as the states of the Amazon region are concerned it holds, ahead of Acre, the next-to-last position; the only states that are worse off are those in the northeast.

The picture of Pará's economic strength is sharply qualified when we look at the individual elements of the Index. One striking fact here is that there are no data on the living conditions and incomes of the rural population, because the IBGE surveys in the north generally take only the urban population into account. The rural population in Pará, however, accounts for some 60 % of the overall population.[8] 55 % of Pará's urban population is poor; this is the highest figure for any of Brazil's states: the average value for Brazil as a whole is 28 %, for the northeast 44 %.

According to the Human Development Report, the average per capita GDP in Brazil was US$ 2,920; the figure for Pará was US$ 1,960. This is the second lowest value in the north; it is only slightly higher than the average northeast figure of US$ 1,426. Due to the high level of income concentration in Pará as well as the great share of mining, which is low in labor intensity, in Pará's GDP, it must be assumed that this average figure conceals far lower real per capita incomes, above all in rural areas.

As a state Pará has 1.2 million km² of territory and is thus roughly four times larger than Germany, though its population density, some 4 inhabitants per km², is very low. Half of the population live in the metropolitan region of Belém; the other half is distributed across the northeast and south of Pará, along the road to Brasilia or Marabá and along the Transamazônica in the west and the island region along the Amazon up to Santarém.

One great handicap for regional and socioeconomic development is the fact that the existing road network and power grid are no more than rudimentary. Though a large part of the 35,000 km of navigable waterways in the Amazon region is to be found in Pará, shipping is very slow and in many regions concentrated in the hands of a few firms. The lack of a reasonable road network that can be used throughout the year is an obstacle to the transportation and marketing of agricultural produce and the emergence of decentral (agro)industrial production sites, which would be in need of a workable transportation system to get beyond the very limited local market. There are in Pará only a limited number of properly paved roads (2,500 km of a total of 7,100 km), the most important roads are the highway to the capital Brasilia, a distance of over 2,000 km, the road between Marabá and Mato Grosso, and the road leading to the northeast of Pará and of Brazil. The unpaved roads include the Transamazônica and the Santarém-Cuiabá road (Mato Grosso). The ways linking smaller farming settlements and the highways are for the most part dirt roads, and it is necessary to call on local politicians or entrepreneurs again and again to provide for their maintenance.

88 % of Pará's power supply is covered by a hydroelectric power plant located in Tucuruí on the Tocantins; this power plant, which generates 4,000 MW, was built in the 1980s to provide power to the aluminium factory in Barcarena. Subsequently a number of towns that were connected to this grid have been able to shut down their power plants, which were run on diesel generators. But broad areas are still without power, or continue to cover their needs with the aid of diesel generators that are as a rule over 20 years old and often break down. The largest town on the Transamazônica, Altamira, was first connected to the power grid in June 1998.

The most important branch of industry in Pará is mining, followed by agriculture and the timber industry; agriculture and industry together are more export-oriented than the Brazilian average. Since there are no exact data on the regional economic product for 1994, apart from rough estimates made by IPEA (agriculture 28 %, industry 32 %, services 40 %) (Braz de Oliveira e Silva et al. 1996), export statistics for Pará are used to draw conclusions on the significance of the individual branches of industry. In 1994 the value of Pará's exports amounted to US$ 1.8 billion; that means an overall export content for agriculture and industry of roughly 40 %. Referred to Pará's overall GDP, the export content is 25 %.[9] If we follow the export statistics, 68.7 % of the value of exports stems from mining and the ore-processing industry, 22.7 % from the timber and pulp industries, and only 6.7 % from agriculture. The most important export products are iron ore (31.8 %), alumina (25.3 %), and timber products (17.8 %). This means that Pará exports mainly raw materials and industrially processed primary products.

As far as their moorings in the regional economy are concerned, there are substantial differences between the three most important exporting branches of industry: while the timber industry displays a broad spatial dispersion and is present in at least half of Pará's municipalities, iron-ore production and the aluminium industry form enclaves. Iron ore is mined by the mixed corporation *Companhia Vale do Rio Doce* (CVRD), which was privatized in 1997, has large landholdings in the Carajás mining areas to the southwest of Marabá, and has built its own large-scale housing development, located on company land, for its employees. The aluminium industry consists of a factory run by ALBRAS, a consortium made of CVRD and Japanese corporations, which is located in Barcarena in the region of Belém. The bauxite processed there is extracted on the Rio Trombetas.

Since the 1960s Brazil has experienced the conception and implementation of a number of regional-development programs, most of which were devised to benefit the northeast and north of the country. The debt crisis at the beginning of the 1980s sharply curtailed the public funds available for investment, leading basically to a paralysis of support for regional development. The issue of the effectiveness of these programs is a controversial one, since they failed to substantially alter regional socioeconomic disparities. The slight decline of the southeast's dominance as an industrial location would probably not have materialized without regional promotion, though the rankings of and differentials between the regions changed only marginally (in 1960 the south's share in the gross output of industry was 77 %, in 1994 60,5 %; the north's share increased from 0.9 to 4.5 %, that of the northeast from 7.8 to 11.5 %, and that of the south from 13.3 to 18.9 %).[10]

In 1995 the environmental ministry responsible for the Amazon region sought, in its "National Integrated Policy for the Amazon Region" (*Política Nacional Integrada para a Amazônia Legal*), to present a draft regional-policy project to fill the vacuum that had come about in the wake of the termination of the traditional centralist regional-development programs. In addition, the *Política Integrada* was to constitute a framework for regional, national, and international efforts aimed at a sustainable development strategy for the Amazon region. The development plan for 1996/99 presented by SUDAM, the regional development agency, for the Amazon region was relatively closely geared to the *Política Integrada*.

The conditions for regional policy have changed in connection with the above-mentioned reorientation in economic policy, which restricted the state's scopes of action vis-à-vis the market, the 1988 constitution, which granted greater autonomy to the states and municipalities, and the growing national and international pressure to pay more attention to the ecological conditions prevalent in the Amazon region. The strategies presented by the environment ministry and SUDAM take these points into consideration:

–   The normative frame of reference is "sustainable development," which is defined as safeguarding the intergenerational right to use natural resources and improving the income situation and standard of living of the population of the Amazon region;

–   methodologically, the point of departure is participatory development planning and implementation in which the state unfolds its coordinative and regulatory activities in a relationship to society defined by partnership (MMA 1995; SUDAM 1995).

The plan presented by SUDAM makes it plain how sharply it diverges, at least on paper, from traditional strategies: durable growth is to be

achieved by rationally managing natural resources, strengthening regional R&D capacities, and enabling small and medium-scale enterprises (so-called SMEs) to absorb techno-organizational innovations.
Even though the plan welcomes the location here of foreign corporations as a means of promoting the transfer of technology, we cannot fail
to note that it, realistically, takes the strengths and weaknesses of the
existing productive structure as its point of departure in conceiving a
growth scenario. In view of the limited public funds available the investment program is left with the development of waterways and
pavement of existing highways – this, too, an assessment of the options
open to the public sector that is more realistic than that of previous
decades.

The criticism of the traditional institutional model of regional promotion is also clear:

> *"The administrative model of centralist planning conceived in the
> second half of the 1960s, installing SUDAM as the central organ
> of the federal government's planning system in the Amazon re-
> gion, was never really put into practice and has today completely
> lost whatever functionality it may have had."* (SUDAM 1995,
> p. 6)

SUDAM's lack of power to achieve its interests vis-à-vis other federal
agencies, the fact that, for reasons of party politics, alliances and cooperative relationships have been inaugurated without inclusion of
SUDAM, and the growing criticism of its clientelist obligingness toward local elites in the past 10 years have forced the institution, in its
own interest, to open up and operate in a more transparent fashion.

In practice not much of SUDAM's regional-policy strategy has been
implemented; the firms that enjoy favorable loans and tax exemptions
are still as a rule big industrial corporations, mining projects, and cattle
ranches, though the latter are promoted only if they are located outside
the primary-forest areas of the Amazon region.[11] Owing to traditional
action patterns and a generally lower technological level, SMEs in Pará
do not include the dynamic firms that could place SUDAM under pressure, in this way obtaining subsidies. One example of this lack of lobbying power is Pará's timber industry.

6.2   The Timber Industry in Brazil and in Pará

General Data on the Sector's Size and Structure

The timber and furniture industries are not dominant branches of Brazil's economy; only the pulp and paper industry and individual fiberboard-producing firms are seen as part of the relevant economic spectrum for reasons of their size and level of technological development.[12]

The current data available on the timber industry are on the whole very poor. In 1994 IBAMA had commissioned some regional studies on the forest sector and the timber industry in Brazil; but the studies proved to be highly fragmentary in that IBAMA's company registers are not updated and the data from the federal statistics office, IBGE, on the industrial sector are available only up to 1985 and are not very trustworthy for logging. The funds available to the forest development agency IBDF, restricted since 1981, and the disbandment of this agency in the framework of IBAMA, which was established in 1989 and focuses its activities less on resource utilization than on resource protection, also meant that statistical documentation of and research on this sector were neglected. The economic censuses that were set to be conducted by IBGE between 1985 and 1995 were cancelled for lack of funding. Only some of the data collections of the industrial federations are accessible; since there are no reliable official data available, it is as good as impossible to assess the quality of these data. The Brazilian Forestry Society (*Sociedade Brasileira de Silvicultura*, SBS) mainly collects data on plantation production.

There are three reasons for the poor state of the data available: First, the timber industry in Brazil in general and in the Amazon region in particular has never belonged to the branches of industry receiving priority economic support. Second, the industry is characterized largely by informal or illegal structures as far as the procurement of logs is concerned (the big exception being the pulp industry, which is based on plantations). Third, in the 1970s and 1980s the main research on the Amazon region was focused on the branches of industry that were held chiefly responsible for the dynamics of deforestation: cattle-ranching, farming, mining, and the energy sector (Mahar 1978; Browder 1988;

Kohlhepp and Schrader 1987). The few recent studies dealing with the
timber sector in Brazil therefore use FAO or ITTO data. It is often not
pointed out that these data are based largely on estimates.

The limited amount of data available indicate that the number of wood-
processing enterprises increased dramatically between 1985 and 1997:

Table 14: Number of Enterprises in the Timber, Furniture, Pulp and Paper Industries, 1985 and 1997		
Industry	**1985**	**1997**
Logging	n.d.	9,077
Sawmills	9,064	18,004
Carpenters	4,710	10,010
Veneer mills	230	1,106
Plywood mills	174	520
Furniture	13,075	14,524
Pulp and paper mills	315	269
Total	27,568	53,510
Source: 1997 IBAMA (after STCP 1997), 1985 IBGE Censo Industrial		

The low quality of these data becomes clear when we compare them
with the FAO data on the development of the volume of output between
1985 and 1997: the production of sawnwood and veneers stagnated,
that of plywood declined, while that of pulp and paper grew slightly
(the FAO gives no data on furniture). The Brazilian federation of the
plywood industry indicates for 1997 a figure of roughly 250 firms in
the board industry (veneers, plywood, particle board, fiberboard), a
decrease compared with 1985. It would thus be more realistic to assume
for the 1990s the same figures as for 1985, or lower ones, at least for
sawmills, veneer and plywood, and timber-processing. One striking fact
is that the greatest data uncertainty is found for the sawmills, the dominant segment in the Amazon region.

The production data of the Brazilian industrial federations deviate from
those of the FAO; the differences are, however, significant only for
sawnwood and particle board:

– Whereas the FAO indicates for 1986 - 1993 a yearly output volume of 18 million m^3 of sawnwood, the federation of the timber industry (ABPM) indicates for the same period a volume below that indicated by the FAO, though it does show a marked growth trend: from roughly 12.5 million m^3 in 1986 it rises to 15 million in 1991 and 17.5 million in 1996. In the same period the share of coniferous timber (from plantations) in overall sawnwood rises from roughly 11 to 15 % (Siqueira 1997).

– The data of the Brazilian federation of the plywood industry (ABIMCI) also differ from those published by the FAO: while the FAO indicates for plywood volumes of 1.3 million m^3 (1987 - 1990) and 960,000 m^3 (1991 - 1993), ABIMCI specifies a volume of 1.4 million m^3 between 1987 and 1989, 1 million m^3 for 1990, and 1.6 million m^3 since 1993. For particle board the FAO indicates for the entire period under consideration a volume of 660,000 m^3 per annum, while the federation indicates the same volume for 1987, but notes continuous growth from 1994 on which in 1996 led to a doubling of output to 1.2 million m^3. Only for fiberboard do the figures of FAO and the federation agree on a volume of somewhat less than 700,000 m^3 since the mid-1980s.

However, the Brazilian data on output volumes do not permit any assumption of dramatic growth in the number of enterprises, either; the more likely assumption would be a growing utilization of capacities. The high figures indicated by the IBAMA register would thus have to be explained with reference to double countings when firms have relocated as well as to a failure to strike out factories that have already closed.

The share of the industries based on wood-processing in Brazil's GDP (US$ 735 billion) was, according to estimates of the consulting firm STCP, 3.3 % for 1996 (US$ 24.4 billion); this was distributed across the individual industries as follows: primary wood-processing industry US$ 8.7 billion (sawnwood, plywood, and veneers), pulp and paper industry US$ 7.3 billion, charcoal production US$ 4.2 billion, firewood US$ 1.5 billion, other branches of industry US$ 2.7 billion.

Likewise, according to STCP data, employment in the sector was in 1996 1.5 % of overall employment; of the total of 940,000 persons employed in the primary timber-processing industry, 102,000 were active in the pulp and paper industry and 158,000 in charcoal production.

The most recent data on the leading Brazilian firms in 1990, published in the IBGE's 1993 statistical yearbook, show that the timber and furniture industries (as opposed to the pulp and paper industry) were the most unproductive industries, and had the lowest average wage costs, while, measured in terms of gross and net value added, pulp and paper are the industries without which the timber-based industry would be an insignificant factor in the Brazilian economy (Table 15).

Table 15:   Leading Enterprises of Brazil, 1990

Industry	Number of enterprises	Number of employees	Gross production value	Net value added
Total	4,110	1,334,255	227,037,399	119,035,988
Primary sector	139	46,567	11,959,425	9,554,393
Secondary sector	3,971	1,287,688	215,077,996	109,481,595
Nonmetallic mineral industry	151	50,354	4,831,749	2,841,303
Metal processing	446	168,710	35,925,555	13,990,344
Mechanical engineering	700	169,425	14,633,414	9,118,542
Timber	113	14,691	781,343	372,116
Furniture	24	3,450	235,042	140,857
Pulp and paper	120	32,174	7,687,468	4,223,268
Chemistry	369	76,214	45,296,055	22,407,417
Food	657	149,096	25,025,888	10,051,080
Beverages	73	21,703	2,225,341	1,410,144
Source: IBGE Anuário Estatístico 1995, prices in R$ 1000 as of 1996				

The Amazon region is not an important location of Brazil's timber-using branches of industry; the largest firms are concentrated in the states in the south and southeast of the country, in particular in Paraná. A list of the country's 500 biggest firms published annually by a leading Brazilian business newspaper, the Gazeta Mercantil, indicates the following picture for 1996/97 (Table 16):

Table 16: Leading Enterprises of the Timber, Furniture and Pulp/Paper Industries of Brazil, 1996/97			
Industry	Amazon	South, sgouth-east	Total
Sawmills	1	11	12
Particle board mills	2	6	8
Plywood and ve-neer mills	5	11	16
Construction tim-ber	0	6	6
Semi-processed timber products	0	5	5
Furniture	1	14	15
Pulp	1	7	8
Paper	0	22	22
Total	10	82	92
Source: Gazeta Mercantil, Balanço Anual 1996/97			

Within the Amazon region Pará was long dominant as the most important location of the timber industry. Thanks to the expansion of the road network and public- and private-sector settlement programs, Mato Grosso and Rondônia have also been opened up more and more for development, which makes them, too, important production sites of the timber industry. Table 17 provides an overview of the assumed number of timber-processing companies between 1965 and 1997:

Table 17:	Number of Wood-processing Enterprises in the Amazon, 1965-97							
State	1965	1970	1973	1975	1980	1985	1992	1997
Acre	9	20	n.d.	22	54	55	36	40
Amapá	7	10	18	29	65	62	8	15
Amazonas	25	46	54	108	145	146	57	35
Pará	147	297	183	563	1,692	1,288	630	783
Rondônia	3	7	32	76	290	313	317	509
Roraima	3	21	n.d.	13	32	27	16	25
Mato Grosso	n.d.	99	n.d	229	580	687	810	860
Total	194	500	287	1,040	2,858	2,578	1,874	2,311

Source: Ros-Tonen (1990); ITTO, IBAMA and FUNATURA (1996); Veríssimo and Lima (1998)

The figures for 1997 indicate that Pará is increasingly losing its importance as a site for the timber industry to Mato Grosso and Rondônia. The overall number of companies in the Amazon region has decreased since 1980, above all in Pará, while the figure for Mato Grosso and Rondônia has been on the rise since the 1970s. The 1997 figures are from the first empirical survey conducted since 1985 to determine the numbers and capacities of the timber-processing industry in the Amazon region. IMAZON, an independent research institute from Pará that has concentrated for years now on empirical research on forestry and the timber industry in Pará, was in charge of the survey.

The results of the survey – decline in the number of companies in Pará as a whole to a level below that of 1980 – are noteworthy in that they show that the seemingly unstoppable expansion of the timber industry in the region has, at least in the 1990s, gone an entirely different way.

There are only estimates available on the gross output of Pará's timber industry: Barreto and Veríssimo (1996) of IMAZON indicate an output value of US$ 800 million (1993) and a GDP share of 13 %.[13] According to these figures, the timber industry is, after the mining sector, the second most important industrial sector in the state, and has a share of not more than 10 % in the value added of all of Brazil's timber-processing and -working industries. The annual gross output of a typical sawmill with fewer than 30 employees is, according to model calculations conducted by IMAZON, roughly US$ 670,800; these are, in other words, small companies (Veríssimo et al. 1996, p. 61).

According to IMAZON estimates, the timber industry provides in Pará some 70,000 direct jobs and 219,600 indirect jobs (Barreto 1998). Logging alone provides 30,000 of the direct jobs; they are for the most part occupied only six or seven months a year, since logging operations in the *terra firme* are carried on only in the dry season and those in the *várzea* (flood area) can for the most part be conducted only in the rainy season. The loggers are as a rule poorly to moderately paid (2 - 4 minimum wages per month) and run high health risks. Improving workplace safety has been an issue only in recent years. Both in the big sawmill conglomerations and in the towns the larger employers often add benefits such as dwellings, schools, food rations, and, in many cases, medical care to the wages they pay.

Processing Patterns in Pará

According to IMAZON calculations for Pará, we may assume that the average sawmill processing capacity is roughly 17,000 m^3 of roundwood; the figure for Amazonas is as high as 20,000 m^3, while Mato Grosso (11,395 m^3) and Rondônia (7,600 m^3) clearly range at the bottom end of the spectrum (Table 18).

These capacities may at first seem large in view of the fact that a typical sawmill in Pará processes roughly 9,200 m^3 of roundwood per year (Veríssimo et al. 1996, p. 61). But the average figures noted above conceal the differences between medium- and large-scale sawmills and the share of plywood factories, which require between 24,000 and 130,000 m^3 of roundwood per year. A breakdown of the IBAMA register in Pará for 1990 in terms of processing-capacity size classes came up with the following results (Silva 1994): 65 % of sawmills (93 % of all companies) process between 1,000 and 5,000 m^3 per year, while 54 % of veneer and plywood factories (7 % of all companies) use over 10,000 m^3

per year. IMAZON noted in its 1997/98 survey that the greater part of sawmills own only one band saw and process between 8,520 and 12,780 m^3 of roundwood per year.

Table 18:	Average Processing Capacities in the Amazon		
State	Roundwood processed per year (m^3)	Number of mills	Roundwood processed per mill and year (m^3)
Acre	400,000	40	10,000
Amapá	300,000	15	20,000
Amazonas	700,000	35	20,000
Pará	13,500,000	783	17,241
Rondônia	3,900,000	509	7,662
Roraima	100,000	25	4,000
Mato Grosso	9,800,000	860	11,395
Total	29,500,000	2,267	13,013
Source: Barreto, Veríssimo and Hirakuri (1998)			

Within the state of Pará there are in the *terra firme* and the *várzea* different regional types of sawnwood-producing companies; aside from given ecological circumstances (the tree species available) the existence or absence of natural transportation routes (rivers), settlement age and structure and land ownership are important factors. The most important site is Paragominas, which is located some 250 km from Belém on the road to Brasilia and, with its roughly 100 sawmills, constitutes the center of sawnwood production for the domestic Brazilian market.[14] This area, which is located in the east of Pará and was originally completely forested, was opened up for farming and cattle-ranching purposes in the 1960s by building the road between Belém and Brasilia; it now accounts for the greatest share of Pará's timber production. The larger area around Paragominas contains further important locations such as Tomé-Açu and Tailândia, which developed in the 1980s and 1990s in connection with the expansion of the sector.

Belém is the center of export-oriented production of sawnwood, ply-wood, and semi-processed goods and of the main timber exporters. According to IBAMA, 8.5 % of all sawmills and 26 % of all veneer and plywood mills from Pará were located here in 1990. The logs and sawnwood processed or traded here come from all over Pará, mainly from the *terra firme*.

In the *várzea*, Breves and Portel are the main locations for sawnwood and veneer production.

Analysis of the Cost Structure of Processing

The *terra firme* is dominated by the one-bandsaw-family-operated type of sawmill. Sawmill owners are also very often landowners; in Parago-minas many *madeireiros* (sawmill owners) are at the same time *fazendeiros* (big landowners), who convert degraded forest land into rangeland for cattle or, more recently, also into farmland for growing soybeans or maize.

Until the 1990s the case was such that sawmills were operated at one place for an average of 10 years (Ferreira 1997; Veríssimo, Barreto, Mattos, Tarifa and Uhl 1996; Ros-Tonen 1993), until the timber sup-plies around them were depleted. The setting is defined by the distance between sawmill and forest and the level of transportation costs; in Paragominas the average distance has increased in the past ten years from 39 to 94 km, which means that transportation costs have risen substantially.[15] Within this period profits were as a rule not reinvested in plant and machinery but used for speculation in the banking sector or to purchase land.

According to an empirical survey, the investment costs for a small sawmill were in 1995 roughly US$ 326,000; the current average value of capital stock was US$ 120,000 at the same point of time (Stone 1997).

Sawmills which process more than 10,000 m^3 per year have one or two extra band saws; that is, capacities are expanded in an additive fashion (replication of the one-band-saw type).

70 % of the production costs of an average sawmill derive from the costs for stemwood, 20 % from wages (including incidental wage costs). The high share of costs for raw materials is due to the high conversion costs: on the average the losses incurred in processing logs into sawnwood or plywood are roughly 66 % (Veríssimo, Barreto, Mattos, Tarifa and Uhl 1996, p. 61, for 1990 and Stone 1998, p. 444, for 1995); this means that the Pará sawmills are somewhat below the average for the tropical-timber-producing countries and roughly 11 % below the average of the industrialized countries.[16]

Since all of the sawmills in Pará use very similar technology (machinery, processes, scheduling of operations, layout), their processing costs are roughly the same; i.e. they are relatively independent of location and company size. One exception is the *várzea* sawmills, which are run as family operations and thus have no wage costs in the actual sense of the term and have very low fixed and variable capital costs.

There are clear-cut differences in the costs for logging operations: as timber stands become scarce, the costs for logging rights rise. In the *várzea* they were in 1995 US$ 15/ha, i.e. very low, while in Paragominas they had risen to US$ 183/ha. In the mid-1990s the *terra firme* companies started investing in the purchase of heavy machinery (depending on company size, around US$ 20,000 to US$ 660,000 - 820,000). Companies – only large ones, to be sure – in the *várzea* also invested with an eye to being able to exploit the timber stands at higher altitudes. This mechanization enabled them to raise harvest quantities and lower unit costs.

Site differentials are clearest when we analyze transportation costs. Companies in the *terra firme* invested in larger trucks as a means of lowering their unit costs; companies in the *várzea* purchased both trucks and barges. Up until 1995 the greater part of companies of all size classes started carrying out logging and transportation operations themselves and investing in mechanization.

In other words, the companies responded to rising stemwood prices and problems in obtaining roundwood within the framework of the pattern traditional in Brazil since the 1970s: by increasing their degree of vertical integration. Stone (1996) interprets this as an appropriate and rational response pattern in that the domestic prices for sawnwood are unable to keep pace with the rising costs involved in acquiring raw materials, which are due mainly to transportation costs that have risen in absolute terms. Cutting transportation costs by means of vertical integration and increasing the share of exports with an eye to cashing in on the higher prices in the world market must therefore be seen as promising strategies.

According to model calculations performed by Stone (1998) the given technological constraints (no returns to scale in processing) and the higher costs for raw materials mean that between 1990 and 1995 profits dropped drastically at all stages of production: from 11 to 8 % in logging and processing, from 8 % to -27 % in processing (assuming no exports) or to -3 % (at an export content of 20 %). A way out of this situation was sought in an increase of the efficiency of conversion: if the latter can be raised from an average of 34 % to 47 %, overall profits increase to 20 %; if we may believe the model calculation conducted by IMAZON for the late 1980s, this profit rate is in line with the levels customary in the business.[17]

According to IBAMA, in 1990 27 % of veneer and plywood factories were located in the southeast of Pará (Paragominas, Tomé-Açu), 31 % in the south (Conceição do Araguaia, Marabá, Tucuruí, Redenção, São Félix do Xingú) and 5 % in Santarém. In other words, all in all 63 % of the sawmills were located in *terra firme* areas. In all regions the dominant type of sawmill was that with an output of over 10,000 m³ per year.[18] Stone (1996) calculated average investment costs of US$ 1.9 million for a plywood factory; in 1995 the average value of the capital stock of the plants he visited was somewhat over US$ 923,000.

6.3   Roundwood Production

According to IBGE data, between 75 and 80 % of all the roundwood produced in Brazil in the 1990s stemmed from natural forests in the Amazon region. Though these data are cited without comment by all recent studies with an eye to emphasizing the significance of the Amazon forests for Brazil's timber supply and the high degree of danger to which the forests are exposed by overexploitation (Barros and Veríssimo 1996; Ros-Tonen 1993; Kolk 1996; Uhl et al. 1997; IBAMA-FUNATURA 1996), they all the same do not seem particularly credible, above all because of the enormity of the asserted volume of timber harvested and, as was noted in the previous section, the limited processing capacities available.[19]

In connection with a survey it conducted in 1997 IMAZON for the first time prepared estimates on roundwood production from natural forests on the basis of logging and processing capacities in the Amazon region. Table 19 compares these data with those of IBGE:

Table 19:	Roundwood Production in Brazil (in m³ millions)					
Region	Primary forest IBGE 1994	Plantation IBGE 1994	Total	Primary forest IMAZON 1997	Plantation IBGE 1994	Total
North	47.2	2 6	49.8	19.5	2.6	22.1
Pará	44 5	2.4	46.9	13.5	2.4	15.9
Northeast	5 8	2.3	8.1	5.8	2 3	8.1
Southeast	0 4	22.7	23.1	0.4	22.7	23.1
South	4.8	41.4	46 2	4.8	41.4	46.2
Midwest	4.4	0.5	4.9	10.1	0.5	10.6
Mato Grosso	4 1	0.0	4.1	9.8	0.0	9.8
Brazil	62 5	69.4	131 9	40.6	69.4	110.0

If the IBGE data on the timber production of plantations are to be believed, the data, corrected in keeping with the IMAZON data on overall Brazilian roundwood production, show that the Amazon region in no respect has the dominant position in supplying Brazilian industry with roundwood that is usually attributed to it. Indeed over 60 % of Brazil's roundwood output derives from the south and southeast of the country. In all only some 40 % of the roundwood produced in Brazil comes from natural forests, which means that 60 % is from plantations. To be sure, 72 % of this 40 % is from the Amazon region; the most important producers are Pará and Mato Grosso.

According to SBS information the share of natural forests in sawnwood is declining constantly. This is in accord with foreign-trade statistics, which, for a few years now, have indicated a sharply growing share of pine sawnwood, as well as with the trend observed among pulp companies to process some plantation timber into sawnwood to compensate for sharp price fluctuations in the pulp market.[20] In Minas Gerais the modernization of the iron- and steelworks has lowered the demand for charcoal as a reducing agent; the plantation timber is processed into sawnwood and soon will be processed into fiberboard (MDF). The steel corporations that own the plantations are building modern sawmills and board factories for the purpose; the sawnwood is to be used to manufacture furniture (Gazeta Mercantil Latino-Americana, Oct. 6-12, 1997, pp. 13, 19). Also, plywood factories in the South are starting to use more and more pinewood from plantations.

Logging Patterns in Pará

The forest-use patterns in Pará differ considerably in local terms. We can distinguish roughly between three sources of logs: 1) selective logging operations on behalf of the timber industry, 2) forest clearance to convert wooded land into farmland or rangeland, and 3) intensive logging with heavy machinery and subsequent land conversion. In all three cases the timber industry is an important source of funds for the expansion,[21] stabilization,[22] or intensification[23] of agriculture.

These three logging patterns may be differentiated by forest ecosystem – *terra firme* and *várzea* – since historically different development processes have given rise to different logging methods (Uhl et al. 1996; Barreto, Veríssimo and Hirakuri 1998):

1. selective logging in the *terra firme*: In more recent settlement areas (e.g. along the Transamazônica) with primary forests that are largely intact, the sawmills are specialized in the extraction and processing of high-quality hardwood. One or two trees out of a spectrum consisting of a total of 15 - 20 species are felled per hectare (15 - 20 m^3). The operations are carried out by independent groups of loggers who receive prefinancing from the saw-

mills; the loggers purchase logging rights from either settlers or big landowners for areas scheduled to be converted into farmland and rangeland, or log illegally on public land, in national parks or Indian areas. The <u>selective felling of mahogany</u> is a special form: The mahogany supplies are concentrated in the south and west of Pará; thanks to overexploitation of the stands logging is today conducted in very remote areas, more and more in indigenous reservations and closed military areas.[24] Since mahogany logs are heavy and do not float, the companies have high costs for mechanical logging operations and road-building. This deployment of capital is worthwhile only for the most valuable species such as mahogany, even though as a rule only one individual of this species is encountered per ha (5 m^3).

2.   <u>intensive logging in the *terra firme*</u>: this use pattern came about in the 1990s in the older settlement areas along the larger roads (Belém-Marabá, Belém-Brasilia) that were built in the 1960s and 1970s and made it possible for the first time to exploit the forests of these areas, which had until then been inaccessible. Logging and transportation are carried out by the sawmills themselves with the aid of chainsaws and heavy vehicles (bulldozers for building rides, skidders for moving logs, and trucks for transportation). Logging rights are purchased from farmers and landowners for money or payment in kind, because public land has become scarce. The wooded areas owned by sawmills are regarded as strategic reserves that are not logged as long as possible. On the average 5 - 10 trees per ha (30 - 40 m^3) are felled from a pool of 100 - 200 species and then transported by truck to a sawmill up to 140 km from the site. This type of logging is referred to as intensive because it is the second or third felling cycle seven or ten years after the first harvest and the number of species harvested has expanded substantially (this is referred to as exploiting secondary species). It is the last stage of nonmanaged forest utilization before a sawmill is moved: what is required to keep up a site is that the costs for logging rights and transportation not rise in relation to sales prices for sawnwood to heights that make processing unprofitable.

3.   selective logging in the *várzea*: In Pará this traditional form of
       logging, for centuries the dominant one in the Amazon region for
       lack of roads, is encountered only in a few areas (island of Ma-
       rajó; the Amazon delta) in which the most popular species, *Vi-
       rola surinamensis*, is still found in sufficient quantities. The log-
       ging operations are carried out manually by *ribeirinhos* and the
       logs are rafted to the plywood factories (virola is used chiefly to
       manufacture rotary-cut veneer for plywood production). The har-
       vest involves cutting less than 5 m^3 per ha.

4.   intensive logging in the *várzea*: In the várzea, too, the intensifi-
       cation of logging depends on how long the region has been set-
       tled and how the forest has been used. In the Amazon delta area
       near Belém and other large urban centers 50 - 60 species are
       used, and an average of ten trees per ha (30 m^3) are felled. The
       logging and processing is done by *ribeirinhos*, who use the out-
       board motors from their boats to drive small circular saws, in this
       way satisfying the urban demand for cheap building timber; this
       activity is often prefinanced by building-material suppliers.
       Though this form of logging is intensive, it produces only small
       volumes (per year max. 650 m^3 of sawnwood per sawmill).

Analysis of the Cost Structure of Logging

The costs for logs, expressed in the price per cubic meter of stemwood
at the sawmill gate, are determined mainly by transportation costs and
the costs for logging rights (so-called stumpage fees). In the 1990s the
share of transportation costs in unit timber costs rose from 29 to 45 %
per m^3 of sawnwood equivalent; the costs for logging rights have doubled and now account for roughly 30 % of a sawmill's expenditures for
stemwood, a figure that was 15 % in 1990 (see Tables 20 and 21).

The costs of traditional selective logging (see Table 21) consist above
all of the costs involved in building access roads and skid roads in the
forest and the costs for the skidding operations themselves, because this
work requires expensive heavy machinery such as bulldozers and skidders.

Table 20:	Unit Costs of Timber Production, 1990 and 1995 (US$/m^3 roundwood equivalent)			
	1990 US$	1990 %	1995 US$	1995 %
Logging	47.48	34.8	51.76	32.4
Transport	39.38	28.9	61.28	38.4
Processing	49.61	36.4	46.66	29.2
Total	136.47	100.0	159.7	100.0
Source: Stone (1998)				

Table 21	Costs of Traditional Logging (%/ha)		
	FAO 1997	Silva 1995*	IMAZON 1998
Inventory	0	9	0
Road construction and maintenance	27	50	52
Logging	10	9	4
Riding	63	32	44
* Silva (1995) counts as inventory costs the costs incurred in developing the forest-management plan required by IBAMA.			

One other factor increasing the costs of logging is the low efficiency that is as a rule encountered here: average losses involved in unplanned logging and skidding amount to 8.8 m^3/ha, i.e. 23.2 % of the entire yield per hectare. 16 % of these losses are the result of the inability of bulldozer or skidder operators to find felled trunks. On the average roughly one trunk per ha is lost in this way (Barreto, Amaral, Vidal and Uhl 1997). Further losses are due to the inefficient use of bulldozers and skidders, which approach each trunk individually, since felling, skidding, and ride construction are not subject to planning. This gives rise to relatively severe damage to the trees in the vicinity: conventional bulldozer operations result in damage to a total of 201 m^3 per ha, 83 m^3 of which are completely destroyed trunks (Johns, Barreto and Uhl 1996).[25]

What, now, are the connections between logging patterns, processing patterns and marketing strategies? The IMAZON typology provides little information here in that the institute's inherent interest is chiefly the forest damage caused in connection with logging and how this damage may be reduced. IMAZON's view of the problem, defined as it is in ecological and forestry terms, has little room for socioeconomic variables.

6.4   Sales

Logging patterns are an expression of certain economic constraints: in Pará logging is above all demand-driven, i.e. it is geared not primarily to the "supply" that could be sustainably extracted from the forest but to traditionally well-known marketing opportunities. For lack of statistical data on production and consumption, it is generally assumed that 90 % of the timber produced goes to the domestic market and 10 % is exported.[26] There are no reliable data on the size of the domestic market; it may be assumed that the greater part of the sawnwood produced in Pará is used outside the state, above all in the building industry and, to a lesser extent, the furniture industry.[27]

In 1996 the export value of Pará's timber and pulp industry was roughly US$ 393 million; 45 % of this stems from sawnwood, 23.4 % from pulp, 19.4 % from plywood, and 6.7 % from veneers. This means that Pará had a 67 % share of the timber exported from the Amazon region and 27 % of Brazil's overall timber exports (in both cases without pulp). The Amazon region contributes a share of 40 % to Brazil's overall timber exports (AIMEX 1997). In 1995 Pará's share of Brazil's pulp exports was 9.6 % (see Table 22).

Table 22:   Pará's Timber Exports, 1992-96

	1992		1993		1994		1995		1996	
	US $ 1000	m³	US $ 1000	m³	US $ 1000	m³	US $ 1000	m³	US $ 1000	m³
Sawnwood	109,657	362,179	152,659	395,272	208,810	583,055	225,664	640,824	174,931	544,195
Mahogany		104,160		94,588		70,368		62,872		42,070
Tauarí		30,253		29,022		72,664		69,752		46,006
Virola		28,234		14,897		21,635		16,256		13,994
Quaruba		9,539		19,468		30,491		31,378		43,763
Angelim		8,328		14,341		17,583		43,310		30,626
Curupixá		22,311		38,327		71,749		50,640		19,909
Jatobá		43,887		39,529		51,085		63,378		64,018
Others		115,467		6,784		15,920		85,792		283,809
Semi-processed goods	3,293	16,087	4,623	19,275	2,711	27,017	5,047	25,225	6,683	19,597
Veneer	11,054	29,580	16,776	22,379	17,591	31,345	24,599	37,067	26,145	32,356
Plywood	41,924	178,556	78,098	228,737	85,396	280,939	77,576	246,633	76,233	224,839
Others	168		176		10,030		15,216		16,868	
Pulp	n.d.		n.d.		n.d.		142,140		91,904	
Total	166,097	526,402	252,333	665,663	324,538	922,356	490,242	949,749	392,764	820,987

Source: AIMEX

The composition of Pará's timber exports (without pulp) changed between 1992 and 1996: the share of sawnwood exports declined from 66 to 58 %, while exports of "other items of wood" increased. This could well conceal the increased export content of a large modern manufacturer of wooden kitchen articles and garden furniture.

In all, export value more than doubled between 1992 and 1996. 48 % of the increase is due to sawnwood exports, 26 % to plywood exports. The annual growth rates of the individual segments indicate that the export boom at the beginning of the 1990s was succeeded by an abrupt downturn between 1995 and 1996, when the upward revaluation of the exchange rate resulting from the *Plano Real* fully unfolded its impact. It is also clear that development in the individual segments differed greatly: while sawnwood showed high positive growth rates between 1992 and 1994, and there was at least some moderate growth in 1994/95, exports declined most sharply in 1995/96; plywood, on the other hand, had already passed its zenith in 1993.

Despite a low degree of specialization at the company level, Pará's timber-exporting sector has a high degree of concentration: 80 % of timber exports stem from the 60 firms that make up the federation of the timber-exporting industry (AIMEX). On the average, some 50 % of these firms' output is exported. 70 % of the firms are located in Belém, 30 % in Santarém, Barcarena, and Breves, i.e. in Pará's other important port towns.[28]

The degree of concentration varies in the individual segments of the timber industry: for sawnwood 27 % of the export value is accounted for by three large export firms which chiefly act on behalf of their parent companies abroad and buy up the output of sawmills throughout the entire state for export purposes; these firms themselves produce only to a slight degree. Their capital stock comes from Denmark, France and the US. 52 % of the export value of veneers is accounted for by only two firms; the smaller of the two is a direct investment from Germany and produces sliced veneer, the larger a direct investment from the US dating from the postwar era which produces rotary-cut veneer and is now switching to sawnwood. 53 % of export value of plywood stems from one firm, a Japanese direct investment dating from the early 1970s.

In Pará the production and export of pulp is concentrated in one firm that was built up in the 1960s by a US investor and taken over in the 1980s by a Brazilian corporation.

Sawnwood

Unlike the world market, the Brazilian domestic market places no particular demands on the quality of sawnwood; neither artificial drying nor exact cut to size are conditions necessary to sell such wood. This means that the marketing potentials of an average Pará sawmill with a low level of techno-organizational competence are far better in the domestic market than in the export market; thanks to the domestic market's lower quality expectations this domestic orientation makes possible both a higher felling intensity and a higher sawnwood yield per log.[29] This unexacting character of the domestic market was the condition that enabled the sawmills in Pará to survive up to the beginning of the 1990s.

The world market for tropical sawnwood places higher demands on sawmills and exporters: abroad it is possible to market only dried sawnwood of certain species that have already been introduced to the market, has no flaws, and corresponds exactly to given length and thickness specifications. This imposes technical hurdles for access to the world market.

The greater the distance of the market to the logging site, the lower the number of species accepted. These marked customer preferences reinforce the view, shaped by selective logging, of the forest as a supplier of individual valuable species and constitute a fundamental obstacle to the introduction of sustainable methods of forest management. Sustainable forestry (see Chapter 4) views logging in terms of the overall number of species occurring in an area and the need to preserve and improve the natural conditions of reproduction. Funding forest management thus requires that new species be introduced to the markets, and this in turn requires research on and documentation of the technical properties of woods with an eye to ensuring that wood dried and cut to specifications domestically will be able to achieve optimal results when it is processed abroad.

In the 1990s the species composition of Pará's sawnwood exports in fact changed, as is shown by Table 28; the number of species traded rose on the whole. The species mahogany and virola, which were dominant in the 1989s in terms of volume, were supplanted by jatobá, tauarí, and quaruba.[30]

One of the main reasons for this change was that the increasingly de-graded forest stands in the most important logging sites of Pará's timber industry, above all Paragominas and the islands of the Amazon delta, offered nothing else than so-called secondary species. How these spe-cies were finally successfully introduced to external markets is not documented. Anecdotal information notes the significance of individual initiatives, above all in the case of tauarí, a pale, soft wood from *terra firme* forests which has in the 1990s dominated the exports of many firms and is in demand mainly in France.[31] In the island region loggers have had recourse to various quaruba species, great quantities of which were demanded by Thailand and the Philippines at very low prices. Here the Amazon region has made its first experience with introducing a generic marketing designation for similar species, somewhat like the Southeast Asian "meranti," which is made up of different dipterocar-pacea species.[32]

Table 23:	Share of Selected Species in Pará's Overall Physical Sawnwood Exports, 1987-96 (%)									
Species	1987	1988	1989	1990	1991	1992	1993	1994	1995	1996
Mahogany	38.34	31.60	27.85	20.54	21.72	17.76	14.21	7.63	6 62	7.73
Jatobá	2.92	5.90	6.65	10.02	9.43	7.48	5.94	5.54	6.67	11.76
Curupixá	n.d.	0.11	0.04	0.13	1.49	3.80	5.76	7.78	5.33	3.66
Tauarí	0 01	0.58	1.33	4.89	5.14	5.16	4.36	7.88	7.34	8 45
Quaruba	0.37	0.04	0 88	1.32	0 31	1.63	2.93	3.30	3.30	8.04
Virola	22.22	17.26	20.18	8.73	4.96	4.81	2.24	2.34	1.71	2.57
Ipê	0.64	0.99	0.86	0 89	0.75	0.61	0.79	0.72	1.09	1.95
Source: AIMEX										

However, the introduction of new species has not led to a sustainable form of forest use; instead the expansion of the spectrum of species has made it possible to intensify logging. In addition, entire regions have specialized in processing the new species, chiefly tauarí, curupixá, and ipê, in this way perpetuating the old selective pattern. In the words of one entrepreneur:

> *"To manage the forest, you need to harvest more than one species. But the problem is that the marketable species do not as a rule occur together, in areas with mahogany there is, for instance, neither tauarí nor curupixá. So you have to stick with selective logging."*

The specialization in species goes hand in hand with specialization in markets; on the whole the dependence of the firms surveyed on a limited number of species and markets was far higher than what AIMEX statistical data would lead one to believe: eight of the 15 firms polled sell over 50 % of their exports in France, for four of them the figure is even 80 %. This specialization in one market is also linked with an equally pronounced specialization in two species, tauarí and curupixá; over half of the sales of five of the companies surveyed consist of these two species. The success of exporters from Paragominas was based entirely on these two species and exports of them to France. In parallel many exporting firms in the island region have specialized in exports of quaruba to the Philippines and Thailand; the sample surveyed contains two such large exporters who in 1997 made 60 and 40 % of their exports, respectively, with the sale of these species.

The market prices are far higher in the world market than they are in the domestic market and thus constitute an incentive for firms to raise their export content; the price differentials fluctuate between 17 % and 72 %, depending on quality and species (Stone 1998, p. 439). The process of artificial kiln-drying alone – a precondition for the export of sawnwood – adds US$ 100 per cubic meter to the value of sawnwood; this is an average increase in value of 25 %. In Paragominas and Santarém the export content has risen in the past years at the expense of the export firms in Belém. In Paragominas a number of sawmills have joined forces to form export firms for purposes of direct marketing, and in Santarém direct exporting is facilitated by the circumstance that for several years now foreign freighters have been sailing up the Amazon. Even export agents are making greater efforts to find suppliers in the interior of Pará. This trend will continue in the coming years as a result of the decline in forest stands in the east and south of Pará and the infrastructure development planned by the central government (expansion of waterways, paving of the Transamazônica and the road between Santarém and Cuiabá, electrification of rural areas).[33]

Raising the Degree of Processing

Despite the high growth rate of exports of wood articles there is little reason to assume that a sustained trend toward increasing the degree of processing will materialize in Pará's timber and wood exports. Due to the very low initial level, the growth rates of exports of wooden articles appears very high; export of semi-processed goods did not increase in the same period. The general growth of exports is still accounted for by the traditional segments sawnwood and plywood.

A first indication of the reasons for this stagnation is to be sought in the implicit export prices per cubic meter in the individual segments (Table 29): in 1992 and 1995 the prices of semi-processed goods, and even for plywood, which requires greater technical and financial efforts to produce than sawnwood, were lower than that of sawnwood and far below those of veneers. This has to do above all with the high prices that certain types of precious timber can command (a cubic meter of first-quality sawn mahogany can cost up to US$ 1,000). Looked at in terms of minimizing efforts, it is more worthwhile to invest in searching for and harvesting valuable precious woods, gearing these efforts to existing competence, than to invest in the production and marketing of new product segments for which no experience exists.

Table 24: Implicit Export Prices of Pará's Timber Exports, 1992-96					
	1992	1993	1994	1995	1996
Sawnwood	302.77	386.21	358.13	352.15	321.45
Semi-processed goods	204.70	239.84	100.34	200.08	341.02
Veneer	373.70	749.63	561.21	663.64	808.04
Plywood	234.79	341.43	303.97	314.54	339.06
Total	315.53	379.07	351.86	516.18	478.40
Source: AIMEX, figures in US\$/m^3, author's calculation					

A further obstacle might materialize in competition with the timber-processing companies in the south of Brazil, since the latter are technically superior and have access to cheaper raw materials. Entrepreneurs from Paragominas report having tried in vain to compete successfully against suppliers of better and cheaper pine furniture in the south of the country (Stone 1998).

6.5   Environmental Regulation of Forest Utilization and Timber-processing

Brazil has a relatively modern legal system for regulating forest utilization; between the legal norms aimed at reconciling environmental and resource protection on the one hand and economic utilization on the other with the realities of utilization there is, however, a substantial gap.

Legal Regulations

The use of forest resources is regulated by the forest code (*Código Florestal*) as well as by a number of decrees and administrative orders issued by the federal environmental authority IBAMA. Since 1990 contingents have been in effect for exports of mahogany and virola, species regarded as endangered. In 1996 the federal government published two new decrees restricting the felling of mahogany and virola and placing limitations on conversion of land by clear-felling in the Amazon region.[34] The 1974 export ban on tropical stemwood and the law on a national environmental policy, which requires licensing for environmentally harmful activities, have direct effects on the industry.[35]

The *Código Florestal* restricts the individual use rights of private forest owners: forests are defined as a public good the use of which is, for reasons of soil conservation, protection of the hydrological cycle and the habitat of animal and plant species and endangered ecosystems, conditioned on compliance with environmental-protection regulations. These regulations include a ban on logging on watercourses, lakes, and around springs as well as on hill- and mountaintops and slopes with an inclination of more than 45°. Clear-felling is prohibited on slopes with an inclination between 25 and 45°. Mangrove forests, tree stands on dunes and at elevations of 1800 m and higher, and forests that offer a habitat to rare animal and plant species are likewise protected, as are the trees along roads and rail lines.

The following regulations are in effect:

- unregulated logging is banned in the Amazon region; logging is permitted only in connection with a forest-management plan oriented to technical criteria stipulated by the public sector;[36]
- on 50 % of all land used for farming the original forest stand must be conserved as a permanent protected area (*reserva legal permanente*); these areas must be designated exactly and registered by a notary public, and even when the land is sold it may not be used for any other purpose; from July 1996 on the right of disposal was restricted to 20 % of the area in order to slow the pace of deforestation in the Amazon region;[37]
- an IBAMA permit is in any case required for the use of public or private forests, and such use is also conditioned on meeting technical criteria for ecologically adapted logging, reforestation, and forest management;
- reforestation projects with native species are given preference;
- firms that consume large quantities of wood are required, either themselves or in cooperation with third parties, to create plantations to cover their timber needs; firms that use firewood and char-

coal are required to operate plantations that cover their overall consumption;

- In approving plantation forests IBAMA stipulates that in every municipality affected sufficient land for farming and ranching must be retained;

- illegal logging of protected forests, illegal purchase, transportation, storage of wood or charcoal, and illegal production of charcoal can by punished by jail sentences between three and twelve months or fines up to one hundred times the minimum wage;

- all firms involved in forest and timber use as well as traders and owners of chainsaws must register with IBAMA.

In other words, in the Amazon region forest management has been obligatory for over 30 years. But this provision was first put into legal practice 29 years later, in 1994, in the implementing regulations of Decree 1282. Previous to this a number of different individual measures had been adopted: in 1975 selective logging was prescribed, in 1980 the minimum trunk diameter for felling was stipulated (45 cm BHD), in 1989, finally, IBAMA published a detailed ordinance on the requirements for forest-management plans. These plans must indicate felling techniques that are used to reduce forest damage to a minimum as well as planned harvest quantities and forest-tending measures and methods to be used to monitor forest growth after logging. The minimum felling cycle was set at 30 years.

Sustainable forest management in the Amazon region is defined by the Decree as "administration of the forest with the aim of deriving economic and social benefits from it, while not losing sight of the conservation mechanisms of the ecosystem to be managed," and the condition required is ownership of the forestland concerned (Decree no. 1282, Oct. 19, 1994, Article 1, § 2). The plan for sustainable forest management must take consideration of the following principles: conservation of natural resources, the structure and functions of the forest, and biodiversity and promotion of the socioeconomic development of the region. The technical parameters include preparation of a forest inventory; description of the structure and location of the forest to be utilized; identification, analysis, and monitoring of environmental impacts; pres-

entation of techno-economic feasibility, and analysis of social consequences; carrying out of logging operations with methods that reduce
impacts to the ecosystem to a minimum; retention of a forest stand that
ensures sustainable forest production; introduction of an appropriate
forest-tending system; and, in given cases, use of appropriate planting
techniques.

The following sanctions are specified for firms that fail to meet their
duties as defined in a forest-management plan: termination of operations, restoration and reforestation of an illegally logged area; fines of
up to 10 % of the market value of the timber felled; refusal of the required IBAMA transportation and storage permits, and removal from
IBAMA's register. When it notes violations of the law, IBAMA can
indict the offender and report the forest engineer responsible for the
management plan to the competent professional authority.

The general regulations on sustainable forest management were concretized in IBAMA's Portaria no. 48 of July 10, 1995; this has led to a
mix of administrative and forestry requirements that is far removed
from a practicable, coherent model for the planning of forest management in keeping with the scientific state of the art. The few stipulations
include the following: the felling cycle must be at least 30 years in duration; a maximum of 30 m^3/ha may be cut; in harvesting species on
which contingents have been imposed (mahogany, virola)[38] the operator
is required to submit a complete inventory prior to felling and to define
permanent parcels with a view to setting up a continuous partial inventory (to measure the impacts of the logging operations on species composition, growth behavior, etc.) and to comply with certain reporting
requirements imposed by IBAMA.

In June of 1997 IBAMA presented a program dealing with the economic utilization of the *Florestas Nacionais* (Flonas), the public conservation areas under its administration; the program provides for auc-
tions of concessions and expansion of the Flona areas to a total of 40
million ha in the Amazon region (O Liberal, June 8, 1997; Gazeta Mercantil, July 15, 1997). The start was to be made on 5,000 ha of land in
the Flona Tapajós in the vicinity of Santarém in the state of Pará. The
project was given US$ 1.2 million of ITTO support to prepare a forest

inventory. The program's goal is to rationalize logging: spatial concentration of logging is intended to facilitate the monitoring, planning, and modernization of logging techniques with an eye to reducing forest damage. This is intended at the same time to counter the concentration of land ownership that is at present provided for by legislation on large corporations. This proposal encountered stiff criticism on the part of public opinion, which spoke of a "privatization" of the Flonas; environmental groups pointed to the poor experience made in Africa and Southeast Asia with the monitoring of logging concessions, further noting that the demarcation of the areas for which concessions were set to be auctioned off in the Flona Tapajós displayed serious shortcomings: the program had failed to take proper consideration of the claims of the adjacent small village communities and to protect sites of archaeological findings. Once the Ministry for Public Affairs (*Ministério Público*) had declared the invitation for bids invalid for these reasons, IBAMA withdrew the project. The era of new regulatory models in forest utilization was thus, at least for the time being, terminated by a political setback.

Additional regulations bearing on forest management stem from agricultural legislation:

–   The *Estatuto da Terra* (land statute) (Statute no. 4504 of Nov. 30, 1964) stipulates inter alia the conditions under which land is transformed into private property; claim to ownership for public land that is not yet in use can be made by proving that it is being farmed; the usual means for doing this is to remove the original vegetation, i.e. to clear it. A land tax is levied on all land used in farming, ranching, and for forestry; there are exemptions for developed, unutilizable, and permanently protected forest areas (*reserva legal*). In 1996 the procedure used to calculate the land tax was reformed; since then fallow areas are most heavily taxed as a means of countering speculation and land concentration.

–   The 1991 statute on agricultural policy (Statute no. 8171 of Jan. 17, 1991) provides for a number of regulations covering environmental and resource protection, in particular measures conceived to combat soil erosion and desertification and to promote afforestation with native species; in addition, it provides for financial incentives

for landowners who conserve and protect native forests and reforest them with native species and whose free right of disposal over
their land is restricted by requirements imposed by environmental
protection. The statute exempts permanently protected areas, including forest reserves, from the land tax.

Matters concerning liability and sanctions in cases of environmental
damage are regulated by the 1981 National Environmental Policy Statute and the 1998 Environmental Crimes Statute.[39] The 1981 statute
widens the Union's competence to include protection of natural resources, specifying administrative, civil, and penal sanctions aimed at
rendering environmental protection more effective. This included the
introduction of the principle of "objective responsibility," according to
which reparation for any damage must be made regardless of fault. In
such cases it is the *Ministério Público* that is responsible for prosecu-
tion.

The 1998 Environmental Crimes Statute sets out a catalogue of forbid-
den environmentally detrimental activities aimed at strengthening the
protection of flora and fauna and containing industrial environmental
pollution and degradation; in addition, the statute prohibits the destruction of protected architectural and archaeological sites. The statute furthermore holds the threat of sanctions against public servants employed
by the environmental administration who make false statements, issue
illegal permits, suppress important information in approval proceedings, and fail to meet their supervisory duties. The intention is to sanction not only the actual offenders but also those who incite them; in
other words, in cases of illegal logging it would be not only the logger
himself but the owner of the firm that commissioned him that would
be prosecuted.[40]

Division of Responsibilities in Environmental Legislation and Environmental Administration

Brazil's 1988 constitution reapportioned the responsibilities of environmental legislation and administration across different levels – the
Union, the states, municipalities, and organs of state – in keeping with

the principle of joint responsibility and federal cooperation.[41] The Union, the states, and the municipalities are generally <u>jointly</u> responsible for protecting the environment and combating environmental pollution (Article 23 – *competência comum*); the principle valid for environmental legislation is <u>concurrent</u> responsibility of Union, states – the municipalities being exempted here (Article 24 – *competência concorrente*). Concurrent responsibility means that the Union defines general norms which are adopted and modified by the states in keeping with local factors; if there are no norms for a local special case, the individual state has the general legislative competence. In cases of conflict between the Union and the states the Union's laws have precedence.

The constitution also provides for a state-level chamber for environmental protection and resource utilization which is to advise parliament in adopting statutes, rules, and procedural regulations; civil society is also supposed to be represented in this chamber.

For the municipalities, some of which in Pará are as large as European states or German *Länder*, this means that they have the normative competence only for local special cases, and strictly within the framework defined for the Union and the states. Their responsibility for environmental and resource protection is thus restricted largely to the development and functioning of an environmental administration of their own. This stands in contradiction to the political, administrative, and financial autonomy granted to the municipalities by the constitution, to their right of self-organization under the formal conditions of democratic constitutional principles, and their responsibility for the economic development and welfare of their residents.

The norm covering joint responsibility for environmental and resource protection was strengthened by the Decentralization Decree of 1994 (Decree no. 1044 of Jan, 14, 1994): this decree was intended to increase the quality and scope of public services and make the use of public resources more effective, above all by reducing overlaps and duplications between authorities. Treaties and agreements were to be used to transfer the responsibility for carrying out public tasks to the federal and municipal levels; apart from health, social, and education affairs, environmental protection is one of the policy fields in which decentralization is to be given priority.

With an eye to forestry and the timber industry, we find the following distribution of responsibilities:

- the outlines of forest legislation are set out in the *Código Florestal*; a number of federal states have already adopted forest statutes of their own in keeping with the *Código*;

- As a representative of the Union, the environmental authority, IBAMA, is in charge of implementing the *Código Florestal*, i.e. for approval and supervision of forest management and issuing freight and storage papers for timber;

- The state environmental ministries and agencies are in charge of awarding the licenses required to operate a sawmill or plywood factory; the basis for this is as a rule a state environmental statute;

- the environmental agencies of the municipalities are likewise able to monitor the environmental impacts of timber-processing and issue regulations aimed at mitigating them.

Since 1995 Pará has had a state environmental statute. It does not have a forest statute of its own.

IBAMA-Pará is in charge of supervising forest utilization in this state; SECTAM (*Secretaria de Ciência e Tecnologia e do Meio Ambiente*), the environment ministry, is in charge of licensing sawmills. For auditing the forest-management plans, which must be approved yearly, IBAMA has only eight trained persons; for monitoring forestry activities in situ in the entire state of Pará it has only 18 officials with one vehicle each. Unlike SECTAM, IBAMA has neither expert personnel nor the equipment needed to evaluate satellite imagery (O Liberal, April 28, 1996, p. 5).

In connection with decentralization IBAMA is free to work out agreements transferring its responsibilities to state-level environmental authorities; since 1995 SECTAM has been seeking an agreement of this sort with IBAMA in the field of forestry. SECTAM wishes to compensate for IBAMA's scarce manpower resources by means of a network of agencies and police at the level of the Union, the states, and the municipalities with a view to improving its ability to perform its supervisory and monitoring duties.

This strategy has a number of advantages:

– it aims at putting an end to the competition and overlaps between federal and state authorities, replacing this situation with one marked by cooperation; this would heighten the reach and the clout of the environmental authorities;

– an important element of this strategy is the development and strengthening of municipal environmental agencies in certain areas of Pará in which a sharp increase of human utilization of the natural environment is anticipated in the coming years due to the expansion of waterways and road networks planned by the federal government;

– consolidating administrative responsibilities in the field of environment utilization would reduce administrative costs and contribute to efficiency gains in that all data would then be collected only by one agency, in this way regulating the exchange of data between agencies. The expensive and time-consuming duplicate preparation of documents presently required of firms would then be a thing of the past;

– cooperation could contribute to combating corruption and arbitrary behavior in granting forest-use permits or in imposing fines and other types of punishment, in this way increasing the administration's transparency and predictability;

– cooperation between different administrative areas and levels could be a way to heighten the territorial reach of environmental control; in view of the territorial distribution of forestry activities, which is great now and expected to increase, this would be the precondition for at least keeping on the trail of illegal deforestation activities.

SECTAM has already simplified its internal procedure for granting industrial licenses as a means of being better able to concentrate its scarce financial and manpower resources for monitoring companies on site. Whether this will mean not only less waiting time for firms but also an increase in the efficiency of environmental control, is a question that cannot yet be answered. In any case SECTAM has thus given evidence of its ability to reform; IBAMA-Pará, on the other hand, appears to be a slow-moving authority. Only in 1997 was the register of IBAMA-Pará converted into an electronic database, the condition required to update the register and prepare overviews of the number, state, and regional distribution of forest-management plans. It is possible to prepare more realistic calculations of logging and the relative regional economic significance of the timber industry with the aid of this database.

Problems Involved in Implementing and Meeting Legal Conditions

1996 and 1997 saw the publication of four sensational reports on the day-to-day practice of logging, reports that cast light on the enormous distance between the legal provisions on regulated forest utilization and the reality of unregulated exploitation:

– In March 1996 the public agrarian research institute EMBRAPA-CPATU published the results of an empirical study of forest management in Paragominas, the center of forestry activities in Pará, which was conducted in the framework of an ITTO project geared to "Target 2000."[42] According to the study there were no indications of any regulated forest management in the region, since the forest-management plans audited on site had no practical relevance for timber production, having instead been prepared merely with an eye to meeting the legal requirement in formal terms, as the forest owners themselves stated (Silva et al. 1997).

– On May 11, 1997, the NGO *Amigos da Terra*, the Brazilian section of Friends of the Earth, released a report evaluating the Amazon-region states on the basis of an index on illegal logging; the worst conditions were found in Pará. The index was based on the results of the audits of forest-management plans in the Amazon region that had been carried out after the most recent deforestation data were published in July of 1996. In Pará 64.8 % of all forest-management plans were suspended due to administrative irregularities and only 25.5 % of the plans could be confirmed; only 10.5 % of the fines imposed between January and August 1996 had been paid; this meant that only 56 % of IBAMA's monitoring costs were covered.

IBAMA's monitoring costs in Pará, the largest state in the Amazon region and center of the timber industry, were as high as those in Mato Grosso and Rondônia. Seen in terms of the overall Amazon region, these findings cast IBAMA-Pará in the light of an agency that is not only administratively incapable but also, on the whole, of one that is more inactive than not (FoE and AdT 1997).

– Shortly thereafter, on May 25, 1997, the newspapers reported on a secret study of SAE (*Secretaria de Assuntos Estratégicos* – an authority that developed out of Brazil's secret-service agency), claiming that 80 % of the timber felled in the Amazon region stems from illegal forest uses; in addition, the agency presented a list of the 22 foreign firms active in the Amazon region that allegedly process 30 million m^3 of timber a year, although they have at their disposal forests capable of producing only 3,000 m^3 annually.[43] This study directed the attention of the Brazilian public to the activities of foreign timber firms, in particular Asian ones, in the Amazon region. The report was regarded as a "merciless X-ray picture of the penetration of transnational timber companies in the region and evidence of the government's lack of ability to administer the exploitation of the natural resources in an area of huge dimensions." (O Liberal, May 25, 1997, pp. 6 f.) This was the first attempt of a public institution for at least 10 years to develop an overall view of the region and forest utilization in it.

– The end of 1997 saw the publication of a report by a parliamentary fact-finding committee that was set up after the SAE study had become known to look into the presence of foreign timber companies in the Amazon region. In May of 1996 and in 1997 the press had broadly documented a study by the *World Resources Institute* on the attempts of Malaysian and Indonesian corporations to gain a foothold in Surinam and Guyana; the report implicitly warned of the danger posed by financially powerful and unscrupulous actors.[44] The fact-finding committee made reference to this state of affairs and, in public hearings held in Brasilia, Manaus, and Belém, compiled information on foreign direct investment. At the same time it documented the generally predominant day-to-day practices of mainly domestically owned firms and the deforestation caused by the settlement of landless persons in order to prove that destruction of forest resources is not primarily linked to the nationality of the timber corporation in question (Viana 1997; O Liberal, Oct. 23, 1997, p. 6).

All in all, these four reports paint a picture of a timber industry in which hardly any legally operating firms are to be discerned and the methods of forest utilization generally in use are most aptly designated as destructive exploitation.

The factors impeding any legally induced sustainable forestry include the great number of rules governing logging, reforestation, processing, and trade. General noncompliance with the rules and the federal government's interest in regulation have led to a vicious circle: instead of revising the old rules, the authorities are constantly introducing new ones, many of which are devised far from the area concerned and are not in accord with local conditions; this reinforces the indifference of entrepreneurs and increases the irrelevance of laws.

The rule on reforestation (*reposição florestal*) may be cited as an example of the irrelevance of legal regulations:

A large plywood manufacturer reported that it had complied with this rule since the start of its operations in Pará; the reforestation work, undertaken in the past 25 years on the 300 ha of land belonging to the company, had no significance for the factory's supply of stemwood, which came chiefly from the island region. Some 2,500 families of *ribeirinhos* are registered with the company as log suppliers. It was only in 1993 that the company started reforesting operations with an eye to timber production; for this purpose it acquired a total of 80,000 ha of degraded land both in the island region and in the *terra firme* and is experimenting there with different native and fast-growing species, above all virola. Since the reforestation operations conducted in the past 25 years have been without any economic relevance, the firm is only now beginning, in cooperation with Brazilian and Japanese universities, to systematically compile and evaluate data on the growth behavior of species and individuals with an eye to being able to convert as soon as possible to plantation as a timber source.

One typical example for the practice of accumulating more and more strict regulations instead of revising existing ones is the 1994 decree on forest-management plans and the 1996 ban on logging permits for mahogany and virola. Instead of looking into the reasons for the persistence of selective logging of a limited number of species and taking measures aimed at a gradual transition to sustainable forestry, in both cases radical measures were initiated that heavily impacted regional economic events, without pointing in the direction of constructive ways out of the existing situation.

These interventions affected the *várzea* in particular: the forest statute of 1965 fails to distinguish between different ecosystems and forms of utilization adapted to them in the Amazon region; the rule on sustainable forest management was introduced without any concrete notions of what shape such management should take. Nor does the 1994 decree provide any information on the matter. While research has been underway since the 1960s on forest utilization in the *terra firme*, there is hardly any information available about the forest ecosystems of the *várzea* and their reproduction behavior. The rule governing forest-management plans for properly documented private land runs up against problems in the *várzea* in that the land along waterways belongs to the navy and cannot be sold to private persons. The firms that own forestland in the island region are in principle compelled to expell the traditional population living on it or to hire these people for its forest-management operations, with the strict provision that both fishing and hunting are banned there. Farming is possible only in areas that are transferred to such people and removed from a forest-management plan. The felling ban on virola finally fully pushed these firms into illegality: the traditional system of logging, which had earned the *ribeirinhos* a modest income and led to a reduction of virola stands as a response to the demands of the few firms there,[45] was in this way banned in many regions, in others it was forced into illegality. Mainly smaller sawmills were forced to close, because it is easier for IBAMA to enforce its rules with them.

In enacting Decree 1511 of July, 1996, the government had intended to set up an obstacle to deforestation and promote intensification of agriculture by limiting forest clearance to 20 % of the area of properties covered with primary forest and banning new forest-clearance permits for properties with areas already lying fallow. This decree was modified two months after its publication under pressure from farmers' organizations and the governor of the state of Pará:

– Family farms of up to 100 ha are not bound by the decree; this acknowledged the important role played by small farms engaged in fallow-cropping for food supplies;

– large-scale forest-clearance operations are to be permitted on land set by land-use plans to be converted, i.e. for the creation of oil-palm plantations or the settlement of landless farmers.

The first exception is accepted even by environmental organizations, because the decree would otherwise have in actual fact meant a ban on agriculture in the form of small farms, which in Pará account for some 60 % of the gross agricultural product. This would have driven farmers into still undeveloped forest areas and intensified the concentration of landed property.[46] The second exception contains an unknown variable: thus far land-use planning has been completed only for the state of Roraima; for political and institutional reasons it has for years been unable to get beyond the preparatory stage in Pará.

In view of this situation a number of NGOs are calling for a radical simplification of forest legislation. The formula "5/30/5" is used for a proposed reform in keeping with a simple rule: the first 5 refers to the average number of trees that may be extracted per hectare; the 30 refers to the number of years that must elapse between two logging operations in the same area; and the second 5 refers to the breadth in meters of the vegetation belt that must remain intact around logged areas to prevent the danger of forest fires. This formula would be sufficient to combat the most important factors involved in forest degradation: excessive logging repeated in too short intervals and forest fires.[47] But this formula is also unable to solve the basic problems posed by the dominant forest-utilization patterns, which continue to consist in concentration on a limited number of species, logging methods that are unplanned and thus cause substantial damage, and, at least in the medium term, the prospect of land conversion.

6.6   Innovation Pressure and Innovativeness[48]

Analysis of the economic situation of the timber industry at the end of the 1990s results in a clear-cut picture: the in any case low returns of the firms concerned decrease even further when the costs of raw materials rise; the low level of techno-organizational competence of these firms has intensified the profitability crisis in that it is, as it appears, difficult to lower unit costs by increasing productivity (e.g. by reducing wood losses incurred in trimming operations) or expanding the product line, in this way increasing the degree of utilization of the raw material involved (e.g. by further processing wood residues into kitchen articles or simple furniture); a lack of knowledge of business administration on the part of company owners makes it difficult to adapt to an economic environment which is stable in monetary terms and marked by high interest rates.[49]

How do entrepreneurs respond to this situation? In analyzing processes of technical change the literature on innovation theory distinguishes between four interlinked aspects: *"first, (the changes in) innovative* opportunities *(strictly speaking, the 'sources' of technical change partain to this domain); secondly, the* incentives *to exploit these opportunities themselves; thirdly, the* capabilities *of the agents to achieve whatever they try to do, conditional on their perceptions of both opportunities and incentives, and fourthly, the* organizational arrangements *and* mechanisms *through which technological advances are searched for and implemented."* (Dosi 1997, p. 1532) It is particularly important here to look into the price- and demand-related incentives for innovation, since they influence the perception of opportunities as well as the significance attached to the search for innovations (e.g. in the form of R&D expenditures) and the criteria governing the choice between technological alternatives (i.e. the direction of change). Technical change is regarded as an interactive (or co-evolutionary) process between changing an incentive structure on the one hand and learning capacities on the other.

The following section outlines and discusses the responses of entrepreneurs in Pará to the innovation pressure with which they are presently faced and their innovation capacity under the following aspects: starting points for innovations in Pará's timber industry; incentives to introduce such innovations; competence levels and visions which determine the entrepreneurs' perception of problems; and the institutional environment in which entrepreneurs move.

Points of Departure for Innovations

Innovative opportunities are given in Pará's timber industry at all phases of the value chain, starting with the need to secure a supply of raw materials. Introducing a regulated forest management or commitment to reforestation with native or exotic tropical species would be tantamount to a radical innovation, since it would "upend" the traditional method of planning production and marketing and stimulate a number of subsequent innovations. Instead of conceiving production from the perspective of sales of already introduced species, the entrepreneur would have to proceed on the basis of existing forest stands in a limited area and their development dynamics over a period of some 30 years. This would mean that a relatively high number of new species would need to be introduced into the market. This radical innovation would call for substantial investments in forestry- and timber-related research and the development of a new marketing network, including customer advisory services, tasks that would overstrain an individual company or export firm.

Compared with such radical innovations, innovative changes like a selective introduction of new (secondary) species, broadening of product ranges, and diversification of sales markets have to be regarded as incremental innovations, since they do not require a break with the traditional methods of production and marketing. An orientation toward more technology-intensive segments, however, is a demanding task for firms that have always invested no more than a minimum in processing.

All of the firms surveyed saw the problem of securing supplies of raw materials as a fundamental problem facing the industry; as a solution,

afforestation (nine mentions) was clearly preferred to forest management (four mentions). Only five of the companies surveyed had any
notion of the demands and chances associated with forest management,
while afforestation was at first glance intuitively plausible to every
interviewee because of its fundamental parallels to agriculture (in
which something is planted and then, after a certain maturation period,
harvested for processing).

> One exporter put the matter in the following succinct words:
> Sustainable forest management is concerned with "forest sustain-
> ability," while afforestation or plantations focus on "company
> sustainability." He therefore called for IBAMA to supervise for-
> est management, while the economic-affairs ministry should be
> put in charge of the subsidies for and supervision of plantations.

Apart from securing supplies of raw materials there are also other reasons that speak in favor of forest management or reforestation projects:

- all of the firms polled assume that "eco-certification" will be a
  matter of course in a few years, even though it will not solve the
  deforestation problem;
- often mention was made of the pressure exerted by European customers, who already require information on the origin of timber
  and are not always satisfied with the response that the documents
  comply with the legal standards as well as with IBAMA and customs audits (this does not apply for customers from the Mediterra-
  nean countries, including France); in this connection inspection
  visits to reforested areas were regarded as conducive to building a
  good image.

The following reasons for the introduction of forest management were
mentioned by one entrepreneur each:

- to head off environmental regulations,
- to diversify output and increase the degree of processing, which
  requires expanded capacities and continuous supplies of roundwood, and

- the possibility of negotiating long-term contracts with foreign customers on the basis of a timber supply marked by continuity and
  plannability.

Incentives for Innovations

The growing insight that the traditional methods of obtaining roundwood supplies will have to be altered is directly related to incentives:
monetary stability and the possibility it provides of operating without
the need to speculatively invest liquidity surpluses and foreign-
exchange revenues find firms in a situation marked by rising costs for
raw materials that cannot be passed on to customers because of the
competition in the international market due to substitute products. An
additional factor is the increasing pressure exerted by the legislative,
the authorities, national and international public opinion, and international customers to invest in the environmental compatibility of forest
utilization.

The influence of these different factors on the direction in which firms
search for a way out of the crisis differs considerably; the way the
problem is perceived by entrepreneurs is shaped by changes in the macroeconomic framework conditions in that the latter immediately affect
the maneuvering space of entrepreneurs. All of those interviewed indicated that their company was in the midst of a profitability and adjustment crisis; only half had made any profits since 1995, and these had
been at historically low levels of between 2.5 and 5 %. The two firms
that indicated a profit of 10 % are no doubt exceptional cases, the one
being active in mahogany exports and the other supplying a niche market for high-quality semi-processed goods.

The majority of the firms surveyed attribute this crisis to the changes
induced by the *Plano Real*, above all the overvalued exchange rate,
which, they claim, discriminates against them as exporters. Fewer interviewees mentioned monetary stability, which compels companies to
gear their operations to cost calculations; and declining sales prices are
increasing the pressure. It is possible to distinguish roughly three crisis
scenarios:

–   Companies that had decided in favor of specializing in the felling
    and export of mahogany were hit by the decline in stand sizes at
    the beginning of the 1990s, which substantially raised extraction
    costs; and then in 1996 a number of logging permits were sus-
    pended.

–   Companies that had specialized in producing timber for the do-
    mestic construction market were thrust into crisis by the scarcity of
    forest stands in the vicinity of sawmills and the rising stemwood
    prices this has entailed as well as by a recession in the construction
    market that began in March of 1995.

–   In the second half of 1994 larger companies in both groups in-
    vested in credit-financed procurement of heavy machinery used for
    logging; these companies were suddenly faced with precipitously
    rising debt-service burdens stemming from the high-interest policy
    initiated in March of 1995, and in many cases this led to closures.

In this situation the dominant response patterns of entrepreneurs are
keyed to cutting costs and raising revenues by developing new markets
and increasing their export content.

Most of the entrepreneurs polled (10 cases) started out by mentioning
cost-cutting, above all by means of layoffs and production cuts. Most
sawmills have switched from three- to one-shift operations; this has at
the same time meant binding less capital in the form of stemwood
stocks. One important point is cutting capital costs: above all the
smaller sawmills have little current capital, and borrowing it from
banks is ruinous on account of high interest rates (between 20 and
40 %). They are thus forced to rely on quick customer payment to cover
their current costs, above all for stemwood purchases. For this reason
small and medium-scale exporters prefer exporting via brokers or local
trading companies, since this assures them of fast payment; they are
forced to renounce the higher prices they could take for direct exports.
Potential solutions, e.g. developing new markets and increasing their
export content, are in most cases not in the hands of the producers but
dependent on the efforts of large exporters.

Some of the entrepreneurs interviewed are also considering the possibility of increasing the degree of processing in their output as a means

of increasing the yield of the roundwood they use and boosting revenues. This intensification strategy will gain the day if the traditional
alternative – the sale of precious sawnwood at high prices – can finally
be regarded as exhausted: up to and including 1995 the average sales
prices for a cubic meter of semi-processed goods were lower than the
average price for sawnwood, a fact due to the relatively high export
share of mahogany.

There are, however, a number of indications that mahogany stands have
declined (see Table 25): between 1987 and 1997 mahogany exports
from Pará declined by 74 %; between 1990 and 1997 the export contingents provided for were exceeded slightly only in three years, and in
four years they were not exhausted.[50] At the same time procurement of
mahogany from indigenous peoples' territories has increased; this is
seen by observers as proof of a general decline in the supplies, since
this form of procurement entails substantial risks (conflicts with the
indigenous peoples and, above all, with IBAMA, as well as confisca-
tion of shipments).

Table 25:	Quotas for Mahogany Exports and Real Exports in Brazil*(m^3)		
	Quota	Real exports	Balance
1971	-	19,401	-
1983	-	61,281	-
1990	150,000	110,488	39,512
1991	150,000	116,527	33,473
1992	130,000	113,144	16,856
1993	100,000	112,025	-12,025
1994	106,000	127,439	-21,439
1995	100,000	93,051	6,949
1996	70,000	71,166	-1,166
1997	70,000	55,730	14,270
* Quotas can be exceeded if the previous year's quota's have not been exhausted.			
Source: Statistical data from AIMEX and IBAMA, Browder (1986)			

Since the audit of forest-management plans by IBAMA in 1996 and the
ban on new logging permits for mahogany of the same year, five firms

in Pará have a monopoly on the logging and export of mahogany. It appears that the holders of logging permits are anticipating a protracted phase of high prices: only 31 % of the overall volume of logged timber permitted was exported;[51] since selling in the domestic market is less attractive because of the lower prices that can be commanded there, we can assume that logging has been reduced.

The scarcity of logs should induce entrepreneurs to look for ways out of the crisis in the direction of introducing methods of forest management or creating plantations. According to experts, there is in the whole Amazon region only one firm that is working on the basis of stemwood from properly managed and certified forests;[52] an additional company, a veneer and sawnwood manufacturer from Pará, lost its certification when it turned out that it had been procuring part of the wood it processes from third parties.

Four of the 15 firms surveyed were operating a forest-management project, five were conducting reforestation projects; four firms were engaged in no activities in this area. One firm was planning a forest-management project, another a reforestation project. The four forest-management projects indicated must be judged cautiously in view of the questionable quality of most such projects; three of the firms concerned were trading in species covered by contingents, for which regulations were being more strictly supervised.

One striking result of the survey was that the model of forestry that has gained most acceptance is the plantation, i.e. a type of economic operation that – to judge from experience – is not encountering particularly good initial conditions in the Amazon region, since monocultures are highly vulnerable to pests and disease and require relatively large inputs of fertilizers. So the natural advantage of the Amazon region, its large supply of timber, an advantage that is still mentioned in strategy papers as the factor ensuring the region's timber industry a great future (Gazeta Mercantil of May 28/29, 1997), appears to have lost its currency in the eyes of local entrepreneurs. All in all, 10 of the 15 firms surveyed were convinced that the future of the timber industry is to be sought in afforestation and not in forest management; and several interviewees made reference to the great timber yields attained on eucalyptus plantations in the southeast of the country.

The most important reason for this position is that the great natural timber supply of the Amazon regions is bound up with an equally great biodiversity and a good part of the timber available has not been introduced in potentially interesting markets. The timber firms and export companies shy away from the costs, the effort, and the risk involved in introducing a new species to markets in the industrialized countries.

The entrepreneurs interviewed and the industry federations explain the low level of commitment to forestry and forest management with reference to the fact that such long-term investments cannot be financed without tax incentives and subsidized loans. In view of the present high interest rates and the fact that soft-loan programs are available for agriculture, this expectation horizon is appropriate. The creation of the big plantations in the south and southeast of Brazil were also given start-up tax incentives between 1976 and 1987; at the same time substantial public and private funds were invested in research with an eye to maximizing the yields of the eucalyptus plantations. Brazil is one of the world's technological leaders in the production of eucalyptus for manufacturing pulp.[53]

In the Amazon region two factors heighten the risk of investment both in forest management and in afforestation with native Amazon species: in both cases the state of the research is inadequate; in addition, large areas would have to be managed, and this, in view of the constant danger of invasion by landless people, would entail relatively high surveillance costs and losses due to illegal logging and arson. While the state of the research could be improved within a few years, the danger of invasion is permanent and could be dealt with only by means of a more equitable structure of land ownership (agrarian reform) and creation of jobs in industry and the service sector, i.e. through medium-term structural change.

The costs and returns of both forms of timber production are presently difficult to compare, since the experience available remains sketchy. There is no standardized cost calculation available for plantations in the Amazon region; the IBGE's statistics indicate a higher implicit price for plantation timber from Pará (from the plantation of the pulp producer Jari) as compared with the south and southeast of Brazil. Homogeneous eucalyptus and pine plantations for pulp production can, however, not be compared with plantations stocked with fast-growing native species; the latter have different maturation periods, have other needs in terms of care, pesticides, and fertilizers, and call for a different type of cost calculation in that the aim here is to use them to produce sawnwood and plywood. In addition, experiments are being conducted with a mixed culture of different tree species and growing pepper trees or beans and corn between the rows of trees as a means of improving soil fertility and reducing the risk posed by soil erosion and pest infestation.

Entrepreneur Competence Levels and Entrepreneurial Visions

The ability of entrepreneurs to introduce innovations is limited, above all on account of their lack of knowledge of the conditions and trends encountered in the world market, of new technological possibilities, of new products in general and new potential applications in particular, and of forestry-related aspects.

Empirical studies conducted in the 1990s have all pointed to a high level of instability on the part of timber firms: their average life span is 7 - 10 years. This instability is linked with the typical cycle of sawmills, which are usually run at one place until the timber stands surrounding them are depleted. Then the company is either closed and sold to a new generation of *madeireiros* to be converted for use in other areas (cattle-ranching, urban services) or moved to a new location, i.e. to a new agrarian frontier with forest stands that are still intact.

Timber processing is regarded not as an industrial activity with any long-term perspective but as a temporary activity that is engaged in as long as the forest stands are able to withstand the advance of agriculture and cattle-ranching. The perspective of the typical sawmill owner is a limited one, in terms of both time and type of wood-processing; these two limitations reinforce each other. This does not mean that there are no families active for generations in timber-processing; but the important fact is that the long life span of a sawmill rests on continuation of destructive exploitation, with sawmills constantly relocating to areas with large timber stands.

How parabolic the rise and fall of such companies may be is demonstrated by the most recent crisis in the timber industry of Pará's island region, which was marked by two events: first, in 1996 a logging ban was imposed on virola, the most important commercial species of the *várzea*; then the Philippines and Thailand vanished as sales markets for quaruba when their currencies drastically declined in value in November of 1997. In 1996 these two countries had absorbed 25 % of Pará's timber exports. The logging ban on virola led to the closure of many small and medium-size sawmills, over 10,000 layoffs, and income losses among the river dwellers, the *ribeirinhos*, typical suppliers of even large sawmills in the region. The loss of the Asian markets led to layoffs, in Breves alone between 3,800 and 4,000 workers; one company that in 1996 was Pará's third largest exporter cut its workforce from 420 to 50 and anticipated a reduction of its sales to a fifth of what they were the previous year (Gazeta Mercantil of Feb. 2, 1998). Many entrepreneurs from the industry regard this instability as a fact of life:

> In the view of an entrepreneur from Paragominas there is an "ideal path of progress" taken by settlements in newly developed areas: it starts with the forest, whose timber is used by the sawmills until all of the land has been converted into farmland or rangeland. In Paragominas, he notes, the first economic cycle was dominated by cattle-ranching, the second by the timber industry, the profits of which were first used to modernize cattle-ranching and pepper production for exports and that will now make it possible to make investments in large-scale mechanized cultivation of maize and soybeans. This means the beginning of the third cycle, farming.

> The sales manager of a large plywood factory and sawmill in Paragominas reports that the founding family always channeled its profits into cattle-ranching; it now owns 40,000 ha of land. "As opposed to timber, it takes a long time to make profits with cattle," though the investment does pay off. Because the authorities no longer tolerate tax debts, people are now forced to pay the

property tax, and it thus makes little sense to leave the land fallow.[54]

One entrepreneur compared the timber industry with coffee farms:

> The *madeireiros* who have come here from the south do not see
> themselves in the long term as *madeireiros*, they don't like the
> forest. On the contrary, they behave like the coffee farmers in
> São Paul and Paraná did earlier: when the yield on a field went
> down, they cleared new areas of forest and relocated the farm. ...
> That is why the future of the timber industry in Pará depends on
> keeping the sawmill owners from Paragominas under control.

Relocation is the sawmill owner's *ultima ratio*, the last move before he
switches to another industry: a number of interview partners came from
families for whom timber-processing was a tradition; they came to Pará
from Paraná, Santa Catarina, and Espirito Santo when the natural timber stands in their home states were exhausted.[55]

Foreign firms also operate on this logic: a veneer factory belonging to a
German firm in the tropical-timber business had in the past 35 years
moved from São Paulo in the southeast via Salvador in Bahia to Belém;
only when the Rio rosewood in the southeast of the country was no
longer available in economically relevant quantities was processing
switched to Amazon species.

This vision of the timber industry as a merely temporary activity serving to accumulate capital to be used to switch over to different industries and land conversion constitutes a barrier to entrepreneurial growth:
there is no long-term strategy for company growth, development of new
markets, expansion, stabilization and diversification of production, for
which profits would have to be accumulated and reinvested and flanking structures – roads and a power grid, training facilities, company-
level R&D, and other service facilities – would have to be developed.
Nearly all entrepreneurs interviewed reported not having reinvested
their profits in their sawmills or plywood factories; two sawmills that,
after roughly ten years of operation, started off with plywood production can be seen as an exception. Entrepreneurs in the Amazon region
are now running up against limitations that prevent any continuation of

this path of extensive forest utilization in the framework of a family-owned company. Financially more powerful foreign investors are received with open arms, because it is generally believed that they, with their better capital endowment and technological know-how, are better equipped to come to grips with the problems involved in continuing to operate a firm under the given conditions. In Pará in recent years investments in machine maintenance or capacity expansion have in fact only been undertaken in connection with investments from Malaysia and the US.[56]

Subjectively, the typical sawmill owner does not necessarily have a consciously short-term perspective; this perspective rather finds expression in a low willingness to take new approaches to ensure the company's survival and introduce changes. The economic limitations on any continuation of the traditional methods of company management are taken for granted and thus tend to reinforce opting-out behaviors.

> An exporter from Paragominas stated that purchasing saws different from those traditionally in use was unjustified because the old saws were the most efficient technology, the one best adapted to the Amazon forest: "Modern saws are not needed for our forest;" it was, he went on, not possible to increase the efficiency of wood-processing because of the need to process each log individually. As evidence he cited a neighboring sawmill that went bankrupt after modernizing. The fact that this sawmill was taken over by a US corporation that is now continuing to invest in modernization did not change his opinion that this approach was on principle doomed to failure.

This model was reinforced by the incentive structure typical of industrialization based on import substitution (see Chapter 7). This incentive structure also explains why the investment policies of foreign companies have not differed from Brazilian policies:

> The manager of a US plywood factory reported that he was still working with machinery acquired in 1956, while the management of a Japanese firm hoped, after eight years of operation, to be able to start reinvesting, since the president of the parent corporation had spent a few years working in Pará in the past.

The Institutional Setting in which the Companies Operate

The institutional arrangements in the timber industry and its institutional environment are not particularly well suited to encourage the introduction and diffusion of innovations.

Like the Pará industry association, the federation of timber exporters, AIMEX, is also marked by a defensive position that focuses chiefly on advancing political interests and lobbying with the government. Only gradually is a professionalization of the federation beginning to emerge; this entails work as a service provider and mediator of orientation knowledge (what are the medium- and long-term changes in the world market for which Pará firms will have to prepare?) and application-oriented know-how (what means are available to come to terms with the pressure to change?). It is, in rough terms, possible to distinguish between a traditionalist and a progressive faction in AIMEX, each of which is seeking solutions in different directions.

The traditionalist faction has a defensive attitude as far as forest-utilization issues are concerned and is very interested in safeguarding mahogany logging and preventing mahogany being placed on the CITES list of internationally endangered species. At the same time it represents a liberal policy vis-à-vis foreign corporations that wish to acquire Brazilian firms and land, since this faction hopes from such developments new investments and a transfer of technology.

The progressive faction shares the openness toward foreign investors, but it has also realized that the timber sector has no development chances outside legality. In order to keep the costs of legalizing its activities as low as possible for the firms it represents, this faction wishes to adapt forest legislation "to the realities of the Amazon region." For it the risk of a bad image (identification of Amazon timber with destructive exploitation and environmental degradation; problems of certification) carries more weight than the growing scarcity of timber. More coherent and realistic laws, would, it is noted here, be easier to comply with and monitor; this could strengthen the sector's seriousness and improve its image in the world market.

In the words of one entrepreneur interviewed:

> AIMEX gives the membership orientation, it represents them with the authorities and NGOs; it shows that there are also serious *madeireiros*, because as a member of AIMEX you are different from the others who engage in illegal practices. AIMEX shows that there are also *madeireiros* who care about environmental protection and want natural resources to be conserved. A company that does not adapt to these standards has no future in any case.

The progressive faction is also concerned with strengthening the political connections of timber entrepreneurs, who are more poorly represented in political terms than the big landowners. In their view the consequence of this is that they are exposed to far more controls and sanctions:

> The best place to conceal proceeds from dubious sources is the *fazenda*, cattle-ranching is of course not legally controlled at all.

Aside from the fact that this statement unwittingly provides additional evidence for why it can also make sense for sawmill owners to acquire landed property and invest their profits in cattle-ranching, it illustrates how poorly anchored the timber industry is in Pará as an independent branch of industry. At the political level this has led to a situation in which many *madeireiros* have joined the newly founded Social-Democratic Party (PSDB), which presently supplies the president of the republic, the governor of Pará, and a number of mayors in municipalities important to the timber industry.[57]

This politicization of the industry has not contributed to dismantling the traditional reservations toward leadership personalities; when the latter make innovative proposals, this leads to reservations that the innovative leader might simply attempt to exploit the others in his own interest. All interview partners spoke about their colleagues without the slightest reservations, often insinuating that they are incompetent and adventurers.

This mistrust is associated with the competition that marks the relations of timber entrepreneurs among one another and makes it difficult to develop cooperative horizontal relations. The timber market is highly homogeneous, since there are hardly any quality differences between the products it outputs; so the competitive struggle between entrepreneurs is concerned above all with price differences and the ability to supply scarce species of precious timber. In an environment of this sort it is hardly possible for cooperative relations to develop, which is again unfavorable for the chances of innovations: horizontal cooperation would make it possible to enlarge the potential of individual firms and introduce more complex changes that would overstrain the scopes open to a single company.

Another arrangement would be to promote vertical cooperation between exporting companies and suppliers; but here, too, we encounter various obstacles. The exporters are subsidiaries of large corporations from Europe and the US that trade in sawnwood throughout the world and in part even process it. They could play an important role as a link between the spatially and culturally divided producers and consumers and as powerful actors in a market with a limited number of direct participants by placing new demands on products (quality, cut dimensions of sawnwood, accepted species) and processes (e.g. encouragement of forest management by tying exports to eco-certification), and offer their suppliers support in coming to terms with the technical difficulties emerging in this connection. Widening the spectrum of marketable species and identification of new potential applications and market niches for tropical timber would also be in the interest of the exporters as a means of again enlarging the dwindling shares of tropical timber in the world timber market.

The interviews with the export firms in Belém indicated that there exist two different strategic variants which include the various functions that subsidiary companies may fulfill for their parent corporations:

–   the conservative strategy subordinates the subsidiary to the interests of the parent corporation by assigning to the former the function of securing supplies of tropical timber, with the possibility of also dealing with other customers and under the condition of avoiding losses wherever possible;

–   the innovative strategy does not necessarily accord more autonomy to the subisidiary, though it does assist it technically and finan-

cially in investing in further processing sawnwood as well as in local value added. This makes it possible to lower freight costs and
the share of other variable costs involved in production (above all
wage costs) for the intermediate product; further processing in the
US and Europe can then concentrate on the more technically demanding phases that are crucial in determining the price of the final product.

The structure of Pará's sawnwood market favors the conservative strategy in that under the conditions of perfect competition development of
lasting cooperative relations on the one hand entails advantages only in
the medium term at the earliest and on the other hand requires substantial efforts to reduce obstacles to innovation on the part of suppliers.

There are additional supporting institutions involved in training and
research: in the field of training there are the forestry faculty (FCAP) in
Belém, which trains forest engineers, and CTM, a SUDAM training
center for skilled workers in Santarém, an institution that has existed
since the 1960s but is in the meantime somewhat down and out. Many
of the forest engineers that, as service providers, work out forest-
management plans for firms have studied at the FCAP, whose training
courses in tropical ecology and forest management are, however, not
especially good. The best forestry faculties in Brazil are to be found in
the south and southeast (Paraná, São Paulo), the FCAP has neither the
resources and framework conditions needed to attract qualified teachers
from the south nor the funds needed to conduct empirical research projects. Only a few of the teachers in Pará have an MA or a Ph.D.

EMBRAPA-CPATU (*Empresa Brasileira de Pesquisa Agrária – Centro de Pesquisas Agroflorestais nos Trópicos Úmidos*) is a public research institution for agriculture and forestry; some of Pará's limited
number of tropical-forestry experts work for this institution. But
EMBRAPA is not marked by any particular closeness to business; nor
is this any wonder in view of the dominant patterns of forest utilization.
In connection with the consolidation of the progressive faction in
AIMEX and growing pressure to change to new supplies of raw materials, the cooperative relations between EMBRAPA and some of the
larger firms in the timber industry, above all in the *terra firme*, have

improved and grown; these firms are making their forest areas available for investigations on natural regeneration behavior and forest damage and are receiving support with three reforestation projects. The smaller companies, however, are without the means needed to cooperate with EMBRAPA and are thus forced to rely on the intermediary services of AIMEX. The contact of the companies of the *várzea* with EMBRAPA has been sporadic or nonexistent, since the latter's research has thus far been restricted to the *terra firme*.

Aside from this public institution there are NGOs that have specialized in the empirical study of forestry (IMAZON, at present also IPAM) as well as training and advanced training in methods of low-impact logging (FFT). The first two institutions named are of an academic nature and offer mainly advisory and expert services; their reputation rests on the solid empirical basis of their work and the regular contact they in this way entertain with timber firms, above all in Paragominas, which make forest areas and factories available to them for their research. IMAZON has published a manual on sustainable forestry which is intended to contribute to working out more realistic forest-management plans and reducing the damage incurred in the course of logging operations. IPAM is more markedly concentrated on research on the ecosystems of the Amazon region, though one of its aims is also to makes its research findings available toward the end of a more sustainable resource use.[58] FFT (*Fundação Floresta Tropical*) is a section of the *Tropical Forest Foundation* (TFF), which was founded by the US *Tropical Hardwood Association* with an eye to advancing sustainable forestry in the tropics. TFF sees itself as an alternative more liberal in terms of trade than the FSC forestry-certification system and is, like the other NGOs, an important partner in attaining medium-range change in Pará's forest-use patterns.

The Problem Perception of Entrepreneurs and their Federation

The extent to which the services offered by these institutions are utilized depends heavily on how entrepreneurs perceive the problems involved. To what extent does the problem perception of entrepreneurs coincide with a problem description that could be derived from an analysis of the damage linked with logging, an analysis of the economic situation of the firms and trends found in the world market for timber and tropical timber? The way in which entrepreneurs view the problems facing them permits us to draw conclusions on their self-perception, on how to answer the question: How did we become what we are; how have we reached our economic success? This would mean opening up a perception both of the routines that have shaped the economic action of the actors in this industry and of the potentials which they provide for adapting their action to altered outside conditions.[59]

The interviews focused on a relatively open description of the problems with which entrepreneurs see themselves confronted as well as of conceivable approaches to coming up with solutions to them. This is regarded as an indication of the level of disorientedness on the part of these entrepreneurs, who vaguely perceive that the present crisis calls for responses that go beyond the traditional action patterns.

Unlike the relatively open analysis that resulted from the interviews, the catalogue of demands set up the federations in 1996 reflect an essentially defensive position that entails blaming the framework conditions for the crisis facing the industry and its lack of ability to find solutions to it on its own initiative. In other words, the federations show less capacity for self-reflection than the individual entrepreneurs.

What they both – individual entrepreneurs and federations – share is the view, which emerged in the phase of the import-substituting industrialization strategy, that the state possesses wide scopes of action to shape the framework conditions of the industry. The assumption is that the conditions are being intentionally exacerbated by more stringent environmental regulations and controls as a means of indulging the demands of international public opinion and the leading industrialized countries for effective protection of the tropical forests. This view is bolstered by the traditional experience that tax incentives and public investments in the Amazon region are used not to promote the region's economic development but to harness the region's potentials to the needs of the centers of the Brazilian economy.[60] The logic of this self-perception as an exploited, inferior, peripheral region at the mercy of the interests of a powerful center is in line with the view that whatever progress in development the region has attained was not reached under its own steam but is above all a result of financial support received from the center. According to this view the only way to effect an improvement of the situation is to induce the state, the representative of the economic centers of the south, to concede this fact. The fact that under the present conditions involved in the strategy of active world-market integration there are, aside from indicators influenced by the state, standards set up and mediated by the world market, standards to which the firms concerned will have to adjust creatively, is at best abstract knowledge that, in Pará's timber industry, has not passed over into a set of orientations shaping action in the area.

> Twenty years ago, one entrepreneur noted, the government wanted to develop the Amazon region and provided tax incentives for cattle-ranching and the timber industry; the idea was to promote settlement and forest clearance in this way. Today the government wants to slow this process down, it now has other priorities. Earlier people were not so interested in protecting the forest, not even at the international level.

Often the perception of the real dimensions of the present relative resource scarcity is occluded by accusations aimed at the address of 'abroad'; the insinuation that foreign countries intended, for "strategic reasons," to intervene in the Amazon region and curtail Brazil's sovereign power of disposal over the region has a long tradition. This is explained with reference to the Amazon region's raw materials and environmental resources, which, it is claimed, are to be protected in the interest of the industrialized countries, thus eliminating them for Brazil as a development resource. Any foreign presence in the Amazon region is forced to deal with this insinuation, which proceeds sometimes from a leftist-nationalist position (in the case of foreign direct investment), at other times from a liberal pro-business attitude (in the case of primarily environmentally justified cooperation).[61] What these positions have in common is a complete exaggeration of the scopes of action open to foreign actors, be they private or public.

> One exporter interviewed noted that the preference for environmental protection that dominates forest legislation was attribut-

able to international pressure and Brazil's lack of interest in the Amazon region. If, he went on, the German government should tomorrow propose a complete export ban on timber from the primary Amazon forest, and offered investment aid as compensation, the Brazilian government would impose the ban.

To solve their problems, the federations of the timber industry largely rely on the action resources of the state, which was typical of the period of import substitution. The federations have made a number of demands as regards environmental, tax, and industrial policy as a means of improving the framework conditions. There is no internal debate underway over the causes of the crisis to be found at one's own doorstep or over approaches to overcoming the crisis; nor are the trends in the world market perceived which are already changing the conditions in the market for tropical timber. The federations do not see themselves as a forum for the exchange of company-related, technical, organizational, or marketing problems, or one in which a new vision could be worked out that would actually tackle existing challenges (forest management, reforestation, further processing, substitution pressure).

The most important demands of the federations are evidence for the diagnosis that their main concern is to lower legal standards, in this way making it possible to plod on with the traditional pattern of logging and processing, without assuming any real responsibility for the regeneration of forest resources. The demands include:

- relaxing the requirements for forest-management plans (above all to abolish the cycle length of 30 years, the environmental impact assessment for areas > 2000 ha; the obligation to conduct inventories prior to logging; the obligation to confirm to FUNAI that no indigenous interests are disregarded in the area under utilization; the requirement to present land titles);[62]

- publicly promoted research on forest management in the various Amazon ecosystems and reforestation with fast-growing native species; there is no mention of company participation in the costs;

- creation of concessions following the model of Malaysia and Indonesia as a means of rationalizing forest utilization and protecting forest resources from *"the intensive and unregulated advance of farming and cattle-ranching"* (Silva et al. 1997, p. x.), provision of subsidized long-term loans for the reforestation of degraded areas as well as for forestry;

– exemption of machinery imports from the import tax;

– support for exporters in collecting, preparing, and distributing market information.

It is in particular the detailed proposals on relaxation of the requirements for forest-management plans that indicate that the timber industry has a very limited understanding of the technical functioning and the economics of forestry and is above all interested in rescinding instruments of planning and control. The support for the IBAMA project of introducing concessions points in a similar direction; in view of the known personnel and material weaknesses of IBAMA and the scarcity of public resources, it must be anticipated for the future that this authority's capacities will not suffice to monitor compliance with the use regulations for the concessions. The call for exemption from the import tax for machinery imports misses the point of the problem: the high exchange rate vis-à-vis the dollar is already substantially reducing import costs; the real bottleneck preventing further local processing is to be sought in techno-organizational deficits on the part of small and medium-scale companies, productivity deficits, and the almost total lack of trained manpower. Only one of the entrepreneurs interviewed saw the lack of a technical training center for timber as a problem; all others assumed that workers would continue to be able to learn the skills they need on the job in the company employing them. The demand calling for support in marketing is a realistic one. It is here that the liquidation of the former forestry authority IBDF, which had a processing and marketing department, makes itself felt most distinctly. Since the majority of the firms active in primary timber processing are small or at best medium-size, they are overburdened in constantly monitoring foreign markets on their own, identifying and developing new niches, introducing new species, and building up an improved customer-information system. The exporter federation AIMEX has also not shown itself to be up to the task.

6.7   Preliminary Conclusions on the Dominant Action Patterns in the Timber Industry

The analysis of the efficiency, problems, and perspectives of the timber industry in Pará in the 1990s permits some initial conclusions on the dominant action patterns in this industry:

– logging and timber-processing are seen as temporary activities; after a certain period of time has elapsed, one defined primarily by the depletion of the natural timber resources in the area surrounding a sawmill that can be profitably developed, entrepreneurs tend to relocate or switch branches of industry;

– their relationship to the natural resource forest is determined by the economics of destructive exploitation; the forest is seen as a free good that can be appropriated in competition with other users and at costs as low as possible; since there is no long-term interest in the regeneration of this resource, investments in reducing forest damage are regarded as unjustified;

– investments are concentrated either on valuable precious woods, i.e. on finding the tree stands, or on the road-building needed for extraction, the acquisition of land or other property that make it possible to opt out of the industry and diversify the economic pillars of a family firm;

– there exist price incentives for investments in further processing only for companies already engaged in exports; however, the great operational problems involved in adjusting to the new macroeconomic framework conditions (which, in addition, have repeatedly changed since 1994 under the impact of three external shocks)[63] and the growing problems in procuring raw materials are closing off this path for the majority of companies.

How did this action pattern arise in the Amazon region? When did its individual elements emerge? How stable or adaptable is it? To answer these questions it is necessary to outline the emergence of this action pattern since the 1960s and to work out what external factors were instrumental and how the actors have altered or intensified external framework conditions by repeatedly changing them, in this way consolidating their development path.

7   Historical Reconstruction of the Development of Pará's Timber Industry

The timber industry in Pará started to grow in the 1970s; this growth was influenced by the depletion of the natural forest stands on the Atlantic coast in the southeast and the araucaria forests in the south of Brazil as well as by the infrastructural development of the Amazon region which began in the 1960s and made it possible for sawmills to relocate from the south to the north. In parallel, a modern, large-scale pulp and paper industry based on eucalyptus and pine plantations began to develop in the south and southeast of the country. In the following decades two branches of the industry – sawnwood and plywood on the one hand and pulp on the other – showed a more and more pronounced tendency to develop in divergent directions (Faillace, no date; Soto 1993; Jorge 1995):

– While between 1976 and 1987 generous subsidies were granted for the creation of plantations and for R&D activities aimed at genetic species improvement, no similar funds were directed into either research on tropical forestry or reforestation with comparable native species;

– while heavy subsidies were also provided both between 1974 and 1995 to expand capacities with an eye to increasing the scale of the pulp and paper factories and stepping up their technological modernization, there were no such programs for the timber industry; the investment-promotion programs for the Amazon region likewise largely left the timber industry out of consideration;[1]

– while, at the latest following the debt crisis of the 1980s, the large pulp firms started broadening their export content and introducing modern production technology and management methods, the sawmills and plywood factories tended more to gear their operations to the domestic market;

– while their external orientation very early induced the pulp corporations to take cognizance of the incipient environmental debate in the industrialized countries and register the ecological adjustment pressure generated by it on products and production processes, the Amazon region's sawnwood and plywood producers denounced this as ecological imperialism of the industrialized countries, which, they claimed, had set out to ruin the region's development chances;

− while the federation of the pulp and paper exporters has for some years been actively participating in the newly emerging international networks involved in introducing rules governing the ecological certification of plantations and forest management, the federations of the tropical sawnwood and plywood producers and exporters are encumbered by enormous difficulties in dealing openmindedly with the issue and defining an active strategy.[2]

In 1994 Brazil's pulp industry had, along with Finland's, the worldwide lowest production costs per ton of pulp; with roundwood costs that are the lowest in the world, the Brazilian industry still has options for lowering costs, above all by increasing productivity. This contrasts sharply with the backwardness of Pará's sawnwood and plywood industry described in Chapter 6.

This bifurcation of the pulp and sawnwood industries can be explained with reference to the fact that the pulp industry for two reasons saw itself forced in the 1960s to switch over to a new technological development path:

− until the 1960s this industry too had supplied its needs from natural forests, in this case araucaria stands; the growing scarcity of this timber, which commanded rising prices at home and abroad, compelled it to develop a low-cost alternative source of raw materials. Tropical timber from the Amazon region was not an option in that the technology for pulp production in use at that juncture was keyed to processing long-fiber woods; tropical timbers are, however, dominated by species characterized by short fibers. A 1965 FAO study thus concluded that it would be necessary to set up plantations with fast-growing species in the Amazon region, also with an eye to supplying the pulp factories planned for operation there.[3] In this situation the best solution was to set up plantations in the developed south and southeast of the country. That is to say that, subsidies or no, the pulp industry started including timber supplies from plantations in its calculations of production costs and its strategic planning. Interestingly, it at an early point of time also looked to eucalyptus, with its short fibers, as a solution: this species had been used since the turn of the century to reforest some 470,000 ha, above all in the state of São Paulo, and the experience made had been systematically evaluated and documented.[4]

– Exports of short-fiber pulp increased tenfold between 1976 and 1990, while capacities increased only fourfold between 1970 and 1990; capacities for long-fiber pulp increased sevenfold. This points toward a greater significance of foreign markets than was customary in Brazil in the era of industrialization by import substitution. When, in the 1980s, world-market prices for pulp were 64 % higher than those in the domestic Brazilian market, it was possible to prevent growth in exports only by means of corporatist export controls, which were introduced in response to pressure exerted by the federation of paper manufacturers.[5] The pulp industry was therefore early to show interest in a global marketing strategy and thus also in adopting international techno-organizational standards.

In contrast to this state of affairs, the sawnwood and plywood industry, in its role as the "stepchild" of the timber-processing industries, could carry on with the conventional action pattern by overexploiting the forests in the Amazon region. But here too there are regional differences: the companies that remained in the south (mainly in Paraná) or southeast had to reorient their operations to procuring roundwood from distant sources, above all from Mato Grosso, and stepping up their productivity as a means of compensating for the higher costs for raw materials. The companies that relocated in Pará, on the other hand, were in a position to benefit from the advantages of extremely low costs for raw materials. As is shown by the analysis of the statistical data presented further below, while the companies located in Pará managed to treble their monetary returns per worker between 1970 and 1975, returns stagnated for the following 20 years and remained, at least up to 1985, below the level reached in the state of Paraná. Here the average returns declined by 20 % between 1975 and 1985, though on the whole the level of returns constantly increased between 1970 and 1985.

In reading contemporary reports on the development of the timber industry in São Paulo and Paraná in the first decades of the present century and the manner in which it fell upon the primary-forests stands, one is strongly reminded of reports on logging in the Amazon region in the 1980s;[6] so it can be assumed that the migration of sawmills to the north entailed the introduction not only of machines and equipment but also of the traditional action pattern, and this was to prove to be an obstacle to any dynamic development of the industry.

The following section traces the development of Pará's timber industry since 1960 with a view to reconstructing the introduction and formulation of this action pattern characteristic of the industry:

–   It starts out by outlining the economic framework conditions, i.e. the conditions encountered in the Amazon region in the 1960s and the changes brought about by the regional development policy subscribed to in the 1970s and 1980s;

–   it then outlines the development of Pará's timber industry, its structure and size, processing patterns, roundwood production, logging patterns, and sales;

–   the next step is a presentation of the forestry models involved in promoting the timber industry as well as environmental regulations and the modifications they have gone through in the course of the decades;

–   finally, the section works out the central elements of the dominant entrepreneurial action pattern and the development path of Pará's timber industry.

7.1   The Economic Framework Conditions

In 1960 Brazil's overall population was somewhat over 70 million inhabitants; the Amazon region's share of this population was 3.6 %. Pará, with its 1.1 million inhabitants, was the most populous state in the northern region. In the decade between 1950 and 1960 the Amazon region's economic structure was marked by agriculture and extractivism and an industrial development that lagged far behind that of the country as a whole, as is illustrated by the following figures (SUDAM 1967, p. 145):

– In 1960 the share of the north's population employed in industry was only 0.6 %, while the figure for industrial employment on the national level was 25 %;

– between 1950 and 1960 the number of industrial firms increased by a mere 4.7 %, while the average national growth figure for the same period was 32 %;

– the average company size in the north in 1960 was 7.2 workers, and their productivity was only 16.1 % of the average figure for the country as a whole. The average wage level was roughly 50 % of the figure recorded for the south of the country.

Industry was based primarily on processing products derived from agriculture and extractivism (SUDAM 1967, p. 146). Timber was of no particular significance. For 1960 INPA indicated a volume of logged timber of 257,000 m^3 for the Amazon region; in terms of their value, the yields of the timber sector lagged far behind those for Brazil nuts, rubber, and mallow fiber and were only somewhat ahead of inelastic natural rubbers (Knowles, 1965, p. 16).

After the end of the second-World-War-related rubber boom from the 1940s to the 1950s (Wagley 1953; Ross 1978; Hurtienne 1988; SUDAM 1973b), the rural economy in the Amazon region was marked above all by small family-run farms which practiced a type of mixed agriculture consisting of food cultures (manioc, maize, beans, and vegetables) and extraction of forest products (rubber, balata, copaíba resin, virola seeds, timbó roots, and timber)[7] and supplemented their diet with fish and game. It was not a pure subsistence economy in that the farmers always sought to optimize their monetary income. If, for instance, the rubber price rose, people at times abandoned farming to devote themselves wholly to tapping rubber. Harvests, minus the quantities needed for household consumption, were also sold to local traders to earn the money needed to purchase everyday consumer goods and tools.

The trade relations between farmers and gatherers, middlemen, and the trading companies based in Belém were structured along the lines of a credit system known as *aviamento* (Santos 1980; Wagley 1953): most farmers and gatherers had debts with the traders who purchased their harvests, since they were forced to buy food on credit at the start of the rubber season. For their part, these local traders had debts with the big trading companies in Belém which took their rubber and other produce against supplies of tools, food, and other items of everyday use. During the rubber boom *aviamento* was literally used to bleed the rubber tappers: these people were highly dependent on the traders for whom they tapped rubber and who in turn supplied them with food etc. This barter was conducted at exorbitant prices to the detriment of the tapper, who for this reason had as good as no chance to escape from the debt trap into which he stepped as soon as he had taken the first advance provided by a trader (travel costs and initial supplies of food and goods of everyday use). This enabled the traders to secure for themselves the lion's share of profits and to ensure themselves of a constant supply labor in the forest at the lowest possible costs (the police also guaranteed that this labor supply remained in the forest by apprehending tappers on the run).

When the rubber boom was over, the *aviamento* system became less stringent, though it did survive in the form of long-term, practically indissoluble credit relationships between traders and farmers/gatherers, relationships that were also consolidated by a strong social component.[8] When in the 1970s logging became the dominant and dynamic segment of extractivism, the *aviamento* system was reinvigorated and adapted to the new circumstances.

The Development of the Amazon Region: From the Model of National Integration to the Concept of the Amazon Region as a Producer of Raw Materials

Following the end of the rubber boom in 1912 the economic development of the Amazon region and that of Brazil as a whole were gradually delinked in relative terms up to 1964, when the military regime devised a policy aiming to open up and integrate the Amazon region.

Apart from the geographic isolation of the region, which could be reached only by air or water, the reasons for this were that the profits made with rubber had not gone into an industrial production structure in the region but had instead been used to finance the beginning of the industrialization of São Paulo.[9]

The 1950s experienced a resurgence of the interest of Brazil's central government in the Amazon region, because the plan to found an international research institute there under the auspices of UNESCO was seen as an attack on the national sovereignty over the (as yet largely unknown) Amazon resources (Nascimento 1985). 1953 saw the foundation of the first development agency for the Amazon, the SPVEA. It devised some ambitious regional-development plans, but was unable to implement them.[10] SPVEA had more success in the field of infrastructure; in 1957 work was begun on the first land link between the Amazon region (in this case Belém) and Brazil's core economic and political regions.[11] Road construction brought with it changes in the economy of the Amazon region and Pará in particular: less costly agricultural produce could now be trucked in from the south, and this shook the position of local small farmers; this applied as well for consumer goods and local industry. At the same time a track was driven into the broad areas of the *terra firme*, which until then had been accessible only via rivers and *igarapés*. Ranchers and smallholders soon began to develop these areas.

The most important development-promotion measures were carried through between 1964 and 1985; then the debt crisis put an end to public investment in this marginal region until the mid-1990s.

After the military coup in 1964 development efforts were stepped up in the framework of national development planning and *"Operação Amazônia"* was launched: in 1966 SPVEA was transformed into SUDAM on the model of the development agency for the northeast (SUDENE) and given greater competences for planning, coordination, and implementation. The tax incentives for investors were extended to foreign firms and additional sectors and now fostered activities in cattle-ranching and farming as well as exploitation of natural resources. In addition, the Banco do Brasil granted subsidized loans aimed at facilitating in every respect the development of agricultural and industrial enterprises in the Amazon region. BASA (*Banco da Amazônia*), also modeled on the Development Bank for the Northeast (BNB), was created at the same time.[12]

The motto of *Operação Amazônia* was "*integrar para não entregar*"; the socioeconomic integration of the Amazon region into the national territory was supposed to prevent foreign powers from occupying the region and its mineral resources. I.e. the program also had a strong geopolitical component. What was planned in economic terms was the creation of "development poles" in the framework of import-substituting industrialization (this amounted to transferring the regional development model from the Brazilian northeast to the Amazon region), the geopolitical goal was to settle the region by promoting immigration, above all in the border areas.

The institutional core of *Operaçao Amazônia* was to consist of five-year development plans designed by SUDAM and the law on tax incentives, which was expected to attract foreign and domestic investors to implement the plan. The law stated that this plan *"was to promote self-sustaining development of the economy and the social welfare of the Amazon region in a harmonious fashion and in step with the national economy."* The public sector was responsible for development planning, exploration of natural resources, and investment in social and economic infrastructure, while the private sector was expected to invest in industry, farming and cattle-ranching, trade, and profitable services.[13]

It soon turned out, however, that SUDAM's actual instrument of power was not its position as representative of the federal government[14] but its assessment of private investment projects, which meant control over awards of tax incentives and means from the investment-promotion fund for the Amazon region, which received funds from the federal budget and the income taxes refunded to firms that planned to invest in the Amazon region.[15] The control over the use of these funds was, however, only indirect, since the definition and implementation of projects was a matter of private initiative. The investment projects that SUDAM developed as "blueprints" for investors in different sectors proved to be not particularly relevant in practical terms.

Even the first five-year plan (1967 - 1971) revealed the weaknesses of the model: since SUDAM itself controlled only 12 % of the public funds provided for the Amazon region (88 % was in the hands of other authorities or the private sector, in the form of tax refunds), it was not able to channel the necessary investments into the priorities provided for by the plan (infrastructure, agriculture, industry).[16]

In the 1970s regional-policy activities were reinvigorated because it was recognized that, unlike the northeast, the Amazon region was not an impoverished, structurally weak area but a region rich in natural resources (*fronteira de recursos*) the exploitation of which called for specific strategies.

Promotion of agroindustry was upgraded to the level of a regional-policy model for the north and northeast in the framework of the Program of National Integration (*Programa de Integração Nacional - PIN*). The construction of the Transamazônica and the road between Santarém and Cuiabá was intended as a means of opening up the interior of the Amazon region for settlement by the surplus rural population from the drought-plagued northeast. The first national development plan (*Plano Nacional de Desenvolvimento - PND*) from 1972 to 1974 made reference to the PIN and underlined the complementarity of the economic development of the Amazon region and the northeast. The development plan for the Amazon region presented for the same period by SUDAM (*Plano de Desenvolvimento da Amazônia - PDA*) went far beyond the complex models of the first five-year plan, subordinating the Amazon region to the development needs of the industrial centers.

Integration of the economies of the country's north on the one hand and the southeast and south on the other, it was argued, was beneficial to the national economy, because *"the industry in the south would stagnate in the future if it did not have easy access to the regions producing raw materials. Furthermore, integration will lead to an expansion of the domestic market for the goods produced in the south."* (Mahar 1978, p. 35)

Thus it was that the perspective of an economic development of the north was linked to promotion of agricultural production and the provision of raw materials either to be processed in the south or for sale in the world market. Promotion of agriculture was to be geared to the model of modern, large mechanized farms and cattle-ranching; this meant that the new settlers along the Transamazônica were to be chiefly farmers from the south and southeast who had been displaced by the expansion of large-scale mechanized cultivation of maize and soybeans.

In the second national development plan (PND II) and development plan for the Amazon region (PDA II) for the years 1975 - 1979 the new program POLAMAZONIA again served to underline the region's function as a supplier of raw materials and thus the abandonment of import substitution as a development model for the north: the planning provided for a total of 15 farming-, ranching-, and mining-related development poles; the largest of these was the *Programa Grande Carajás* in Pará, which was to develop in a short period of time into Brazil's major iron-ore production area (Hall 1989).[17] PDA II above all emphasized the Amazon region's function as an earner of foreign exchange from the export of raw materials and proposed creating a number of forest-conservation areas in which a modern timber industry based on rational timber production was to be located.

This role assignment for the Amazon region must be seen in the context of the first oil-price shock of November 1973: since 80 % of Brazil's oil consumption was then covered by imports, the quadrupling of the oil price had a disastrous impact on the country's balance of trade and foreign-exchange reserves. Instead of simply accepting a cutback of economic growth in this situation, the military government decided in favor of retaining its growth course and financing it via external credit.

"The 'Second National Development Plan' (PND II) entailed the launch of a comprehensive investment plan intended to boost production in the primary-commodity industries and a rapid expansion of infrastructure. However, the choice of the growth option at the same time implied a dramatic rise in the foreign debt. Without credit from abroad Brazil could not have paid the higher bill for oil imports and at the same time continued to import intermediate products for industrial production, in particular for the large-scale investment programs of PND II. This growth-through-debt could be justified by the

fact that later foreign-exchange savings due to the investment programs would finally make it possible to achieve trade surpluses sufficient to service the national debt." (Baer and Paiva 1996, p. 69)

In this altered overall economic situation the more socially motivated program components of the development policy for the Amazon region had to give way to the components aimed at a rapid expansion of the exploitation of natural resources in the region. De facto this meant that the colonization programs were abandoned in favor of large-scale cattle ranches and subsidies for hydroelectric power plants and ore mines.

The second oil-price shock of 1979 and the increase of the LIBOR rate undid Brazil's calculation, ushering in the debt crisis of the early 1980s as well as a phase of accelerated inflation and low growth which persisted until the beginning of the 1990s. In this period Brazil came under strong international pressure to rethink its development strategy for the Amazon region. The social and ecological costs of the programs more or less implemented by then had become clear and were exacerbated by the critical overall economic development experienced in the 1980s:

–   Settlement of the Transamazônica was advanced largely without the flanking measures planned (including expansion of social and physical infrastructure, provision of agricultural extension services, and assistance with marketing) and remained far behind the goals set; lack of ecological knowledge and an inadequate endowment with equity capital on the part of most settlers led both to high emigration rates and spontaneous immigration, as a consequence of which land conflicts between big landowners and settlers were more and more often settled by force (Schönenberg 1993).

–   The tax incentives granted by SUDAM fostered above all the creation of big cattle ranches that absorbed little labor and deforested large areas, without engendering any significant economic returns (Hecht 1982, 1983; Browder 1986, 1988): the creation of new rangeland led to rapid losses of soil nutrients and a decline in fodder-plant resources, the consequence being that prior to their abandonment the ranges sufficed to keep a maximum of 0.5 head of cattle/ha; the lower returns made it difficult to invest in an intensi-

fication of ranching (e.g. by building fences with an eye to range
rotation, cultivation and fertilization of feedgrass, and selection of
better-adapted cattle breeds).

– Linking the region to the highly productive agricultural and industrial centers of the southeast and south had displaced local producers and restricted investment in the processing industry to the food
industry and the extraction and at best primary processing of mineral resources and timber.

Since PDA II SUDAM's promotion policy has been oriented to the
model of an "export enclave" (Mahar 1978, pp. 142 f.). The Amazon
region was to absorb industrial products from the country's economic
centers and export raw materials; over three quarters of the investments
approved by SUDAM were concentrated in the primary sector and the
large-scale projects Jari (pulp) and Carajás (iron ore, bauxite, and aluminium). The weak points of this model included its lack of linkage
effects (neither intermediate products nor machinery were produced in
the region, further processing was also done outside the region), low
employment effects, and the dominance of a small number of big corporations. The royalties on mineral resources were very low and were
disbursed to the municipalities in whose territory the mining area was
located; the state of Pará thus experienced no growth of its funds available for public investments. No royalties whatever were exacted for
logging operations. For this reason little of the returns of the raw-
materials-processing industry remained in the region.

In the 1980s it became clear that the development-related measures had
entailed a number of undesired consequences that could be dealt with
neither by the responsible government agencies nor by private actors.
The negative socioeconomic and ecological impacts of cattle ranches,
large-scale projects, and gold-mining, by which Pará, as one of the
centers of development policy, was especially hard hit, moved into the
foreground. The cattle ranches in the south of Pará had proven unable
to use rangeland productively on a sustainable basis; since then these
areas have experienced conflicts with landless people who wish to settle the fallow areas. The big projects also, albeit to a lesser extent, entailed destruction of primary forest areas; but above all in the develop-

ment phase they attracted great numbers of unskilled workers, who were laid off when the projects were completed and then either swelled the slums in the big cities or settled as small subsistence farmers. The gold finds in the Amazon region set off a huge wave of migration concentrated in Pará on the Serra Pelada near Carajás, Tucumão in the southwest, and the rainforest areas around Itaituba and the Tapajós, at the end of the Transamazônica (Mathis and Rehaag 1993).

At the end of the 1980s ecological aspects were therefore given more attention in development plans, though they had little influence on practice. Scopes for intervention and formulation of policy had been narrowed down by the debt crisis, rising inflation, and recession to such an extent that there were hardly any chances to effect the change of environmental course that was called for (Ros-Tonen 1993, p. 45 f.).

In Brazil the 1980s were mainly marked by low growth rates, high inflation, and declining real incomes. Many programs for monetary stability were set up, they usually failed within a short period of time and thus increased the uncertainty and the risk bound up with economic decisions. This situation led to a flight into tangible assets, above all real estate, and short-term speculative investments in financial assets with an eye to reducing losses due to inflation, uncertain market trends, and economic- and monetary-policy surprises sprung by the government.[18] Under these conditions economic decisions were geared to extremely short terms; investments in company-level technological modernization, new products, and the development of new markets entailed incalculable uncertainties and were generally suspended until, when trade liberalization began in 1990, a permanent reorientation of economic policy began to emerge. Even though it was at that time unclear when this would make itself felt in the domestic business cycle (the boom following *Plano Cruzado* I in 1986 and the *Plano Collor* in 1990 had made it plain how great the positive demand effects stemming from an effective control of inflation could be), above all the larger corporations in the southeast and south at that time began making initial modernization investments.

One important change compared with the two previous decades was that the influence exerted by regional and local élites on SUDAM's funding policy increased substantially in connection with democratization efforts. Since the days of SPVEA the regional élites had been regarded as obstacles to development in that they, as big landowners and traders, were not in line with the model of modern industrial capitalism. Under democratic circumstances these élites now joined forces in political parties or alliances and took advantage of their economic power to secure for themselves a greater share of SUDAM's funds. Subsequently these funds, which now were dwindling, again flowed into cattle ranches and other big agricultural organizations (e.g. large-scale orange plantations in the northeast of Pará). One important instrument used by local élites to exert more influence on the way SUDAM awarded its funds was and is the Council of Amazon Governors, which assembles several times a year to ratify the list of audited and approved investment projects.

7.2 Pará's Timber Industry between the 1960s and 1980s

7.2.1 The 1960s

In 1963 Heinsdijk and Bastos, in a report prepared for the Brazilian government and the FAO, described the Amazon timber industry as follows:

"The present organization of the Amazon timber industry leaves much to be desired. It is possible to obtain data on exports, but not on domestic consumption and production costs. It is possible for one and the same firm to make both profits and losses; the workers and traders from the interior of the country have no notion of these things because timber processing is only one of many activities in which they engage. (...) In logging as in the sawmills obsolete and costly work methods are employed. The industrialists never themselves fell the timber they need, instead relying, with few exceptions, on placing their orders with the actual producers, the caboclos, *who live in their sphere of influence and, depending on necessity, work both in logging and in rubber extraction."* (Heinsdijk and Bastos 1963, p. 81)

The typical sawmill of that period worked only on order, keeping not even quantities of between 5 and 10 m^3 of sawnwood on supply. The customers ordered timber for a specific purpose from a sawmill, which financed the logging of the species required via middlemen. These middlemen paid the *caboclos* mainly in food and provided the tools and transportation vehicles needed (saws, boats, or, in rarer cases, trucks and tractors) (Heinsdijk 1966, p. 17).

It is thus not surprising that the Amazon region in the 1960s had a tiny share of Brazil's timber industry; with the exception of up to three plywood and veneer factories, the firms in the region were all sawmills and artisanal furniture-producing companies. Only in Belém was there one firm that manufactured furniture in series.

With its 54 % (1959) and 76 % (1970) of all Amazon sawmills, Pará dominated the region; Pará's share of Brazil's overall stock grew from 0.09 % (1959) to 0.6 % (1970). The latter phenomenon is due less to the higher number of sawmills in Pará than to a decrease of sawmills in Brazil on the whole, from 11,191 to 3,535. Between 1953 and 1962 the average sawnwood output in Pará ranged between 90,000 m^3 and 120,000 m^3 annually.

The industry in Pará is dominated by small unproductive sawmills: according to an empirical survey conducted by an FAO expert, in 1962 54 % of such companies employed between 1 and 9 persons, with only 9.8 % employing over 25 persons. Roughly half of all of Pará's sawmill operations were family-run companies with two to three additional workers; their output was small and geared to the local market. Production was often at a stillstand, either for lack of demand or on account of a seasonal lack of roundwood supplies. The next highest group, employing an average of 10 - 24 persons (36 %), used its output to supply both local and export markets; they were older family-run operations with little interest in further expansion. The major part of timber exports came from the ten "big companies," which employed a third of the labor at work in the sector (leaving out of consideration the family workers in the first group) and showed *"a lively interest in modernizing and expanding productio."* (Knowles 1965, p. 11).

In Pará the timber-processing companies were concentrated in the region of Belém (46 %), in the Tocantins delta (27 %), in Breves and the area around it in the west of the island of Marajó (9 %), and on the islands in the Amazon delta (2 %) (Knowles 1971, p. 28). As early as in the 1960s the timber reserves in the immediate vicinity of the sawmills were depleted; this increased competition for logs, thus boosting prices as well, which forced many sawmills to close, even though it was at that time possible to add higher costs from raw materials to final consumer prices (Knowles 1964, pp. 12 - 13, and 1971, p. 27).

The average production capacity was less than 2,000 m^3 per year; only two sawmills produced some 4,500 m^3 annually. Pará was thus not far below the national average output volume: an IBGE survey from 1958 indicated for 1957 an average yearly output of 1,633 m^3 for sawmills (IBGE 1959). The average monetary returns of Pará's mills were, however, far below those of the Brazilian average, which is probably due to the lower sales prices in the region (Knowles 1965, p. 9).

In most sawmills the installed production capacity as a rule exceeded actual output needs by 50 %; the lower capacity utilization was due chiefly to the age of the machines, inappropriate saws, an unfavorable layout, and poorly trained workers, who caused great losses in terms of time and raw materials (Knowles 1965, p. 21).

The Amazon region had begun to produce veneers and plywood only in the 1960s. In 1971 there were three firms operating with modern machinery and technical support from their parent or partner firms: a factory in Manaus that produced sliced and rotary-cut veneer; a factory in Portel that produced rotary-cut veneers for the US market; and a Dutch factory in Macapá that manufactured rotary-cut veneers and plywood. All of these firms chiefly used woods light in weight and color for export (chiefly virola); their capacity utilization was as a rule 70 %.

Furniture was manufactured by artisanal workshops on order. These companies had to compete with furniture produced industrially in the south of pine and veneers manufactured of tropical timber. Beginning in the 1970s there were some attempts made at series production of furniture from tropical woods with modernized design; but the competition in the south as a rule produced better and cheaper furniture.[19]

Patterns of Processing

The production activities of the sawmills were characterized by a number of technical inefficiencies that sharply curtailed their productivity and quality. The result was high production costs that not infrequently exceeded market prices. These technical inefficiencies included inappropriate and poorly maintained machines, inefficient layout, processing of non-dried timber, lack of trained workers, insufficient knowledge of the technical properties of woods, and a problematical power supply.

–   Machinery: While there were efficient machines from the south available to process soft wood, there was a lack of efficient domestic machines for processing hardwood. Most companies lacked the funds needed to import machinery and therefore used domestic machines to process hardwood. Most saws were obsolete circular saws, only in Belém and Santarém were there a few modern band saws. More modern saws produced in Brazil were more expensive and technically inferior to models from Europe and the US. Generally the saws were improperly maintained; there were above all problems in sharpening the sawblades. An additional factor was low utilization rates for the machines; longer waiting periods for spare parts that had to be procured from the south or abroad and a lack of raw materials during the dry season were often the cause of protracted outages.

–   Layout: The inefficient setup of individual machines caused the loss of considerable working time in moving logs and boards from operation to operation; in addition, this caused material backlogs in front of the machines. Because of the heat, the workshops consisted of open, roofed halls; this fact and the lack of regular disposal of wood residues and sawdust encouraged the proliferation of mildew, leading to material losses.

–   Drying of timber: Drying was for the most part done in the sun, and only after boards had been cut; the boards were set up in a scissor-like pattern. The loss of moisture often caused them to contract or crack, which led to losses of material and made it impossible to comply with the dimensions specified by foreign customers Most domestic customers, even furniture workshops, do not demand dried wood in spite of the known quality problems involved in this case. As for the use of drying chambers, there was a lack of exact know-how on the degree of shrinkage of the individual species and the level of relative humidity required if the wood was to be exported to other climatic zones. At the time of his survey, Knowles saw only one drying chamber in operation, in a factory in Portel, which produced sawnwood for export to the US.

– Lack of experienced and trained manpower: This lack was felt above all in transportation (truck and tractor operators) and in processing (saw operators and persons capable of classifying sawnwood as per quality), since there were as good as no training facilities in the region and experienced workers as a rule migrated to other states with better living conditions.

– Knowledge of the technical properties of woods: Here the workers generally had a lack of the technical knowledge that would have enabled them to avoid losses in cutting to size and planing; lack of knowledge on the part of sawmill owners prevented the introduction of new species to the market and thus any modernization of forest use.

– Power supply: In the 1960s there were only very few watermills and steam engines, which were operated with wood residues and sawdust; but on the whole conversion to diesel generators won the day, a development which was induced by the availability of diesel engines from ships and the ease and low costs involved in procuring fuel and spare parts. It was above all the trouble involved in procuring spares for obsolete steam engines, as well as the danger of fire, that led to their replacement with diesel generators. It was only the big sawmills that had workshops of their own which continued on with the cheaper steam power.

Cost Structure

According to studies by IBGE and Knowles, somewhat over 40 % of production costs are due to stemwood costs and 8 - 18 % to wage costs.[20] Moreover, Knowles calculated, on the basis of average unit costs and export prices, a theoretical gross profit of 57 % of sales revenues (Knowles 1965, pp. 67 f.). In real terms, however, the profits are apt to have been lower in that as a rule only a maximum of 20 % of the volume of output was exportable, an additional 50 % consisted of low-quality timber that was sold at very low prices, and 30 % was residues that were often sold below the cost price. Knowles' calculation did not include depreciation costs.

Compared with the national industry, Pará's timber industry in the 1960s was thus clearly underdeveloped. The reasons for this included the low level of industrialization of the region and its low level of techno-organizational competence, poor marketing opportunities, geographic isolation, and a clear-cut lack of knowledge on the technical properties of woods and appropriate methods for avoiding losses incurred during processing.

7.2.2   The 1970s and 1980s[21]

The development dynamics of the timber industry picked up distinctly during the 1970s. The Amazon region's share of Brazil's timber industry increased: in 1970 the Amazon region's share of Brazil's sawnwood production was 6 % and its share of plywood production 11 % (Bruce 1976, p. 8).[22] All told, there were, according to the count undertaken, at that time 287 sawmills in the Amazon region (without loggers and more simple shops that worked only with axes and handsaws) as well as 5 plywood and veneer factories; in the spring of 1979 there were already 793 sawmills, 9 veneer factories and 8 plywood factories.[23] Compared with 1965, this means for 1970 a rise of 45 % for sawmills and 150 % for plywood factories; eight years later this stock of sawmills had again grown by 176 % compared with 1970, and the stock of plywood factories had jumped by 240 %.

Compared to 1962, the output volume had risen tenfold, reaching a level of 1.2 million m^3 of sawnwood per year, and by 1978 this figure had doubled to 2.68 million m^3. Average company size had grown between 1962 and 1972: in Pará the share of firms with max. 10 workers had declined from 54 to 40 %. In 1979 company size had again increased: 514 sawmills were producing less than 5,000 m^3 per year, these companies employed up to 25 persons; 233 mills were producing between 5,000 and 10,000 m^3 and 56 over 10,000 m^3. The latter normally had between 100 and 200 workers, though the number of workers varied considerably even in sawmills with the same output.

The output volume of veneer and plywood factories also grew very rapidly: in 1972 the industry produced a total of 121,000 m^3 of veneer or plywood, in 1978 the figures were 205,000 m^3 of plywood and 70,000 of rotary-cut and sliced veneer.

On the whole the state of Pará was able to retain its dominant position in the region's timber sector: in 1972 70 % of sawmills and 60 % of plywood and veneer factories were located in this state; 75 % of the timber harvested stemmed from Pará, as did 67 % of sawnwood output, 89 % of sawnwood exports, and 75 % of supplies to the domestic Brazilian market. In 1979 Pará's percentage of sawmills in the Amazon region had dropped to 65 %; these output 67 % of the sawnwood produced in the Amazon region.

Unlike the 1960s the industry is marked by high volatility and a high percentage of firms of extraregional origin: in the 1960s the most important locations in the state of Pará continued to be the region around Belém (204 firms, 36 %), the island of Marajó (79 firms, 28 %), and the delta of the Rio Tocantins. These firms do not, however, resemble those of the 1960s: 74 % of the firms in business in 1973 had been built up after 1965. Moreover, since 1967 a migration of sawmill owners from other states can be noted: in 1973 9 % indicated that they had already operated a mill in the south, 12 % in other areas of the Amazon region, while the remaining 79 % came from Brasilia, Espírito Santo (a traditional timber-processing region), Goiás, and Mato Grosso.

The average real production capacity of the sawmills had more than doubled and was now 4,100 m^3 per year; in the Belém region and in Marajó, however, 58 or 54 % of the sawmills were producing less than 2,600 m^3/year and thus continued to operate at the average level of 1962. The percentage of larger sawmills had, however, distinctly increased by 1972: 16 % of the sawmills in Belém and 22 % of those in Marajó were producing between 6,700 m^3 and 13,000 m^3 per year; 4 sawmills, or 6 % of the total, were even above this figure (Bruce 1976, p. 33).

In the 1970s 80 % of all firms operating in the Amazon region had only one production site; only a few firms indicated having several mills in the Amazon region or in the south and southeast of Brazil.

Labor productivity varied sharply: on the average 13 manhours were needed to produce one cubic meter of sawnwood; the smallest sawmills needed 17.7 hours for the same output, the medium-sized mills 11.8 hours, and the large ones 21.5 hours. The medium-sized sawmills had the highest productivity, producing between 5,400 and 13,000 m^3 of sawnwood per year with 11.5 - 11.8 manhours per m^3 (Bruce 1976, p. 41). There were also factors other than plant site that influenced productivity:

- The key problems already enumerated for 1962 – obsolete machinery, inadequately trained manpower, problems in obtaining spare parts and ensuring an uninterrupted power supply – continued to exist, according to information provided by the entrepreneurs interviewed. Wood continued to be dried in the air and without compliance with recognized standards on residual moisture contents; in 1979 fewer than 5 % of sawmills had drying chambers.

- The entrepreneurs also mentioned new problems that indicate, compared with the 1960s, an altered problem perception, a dynamization of the industry, and an interest in partaking in general economic growth. These problems include lack of access to reasonable loans needed to expand production by setting up larger-size stemwood storage facilities (production continued to fluctuate seasonally) and purchase new machinery and a high rate of worker rotation. On the average in Pará only 60 % of production capacities were utilized because of seasonal fluctuations (Mercado 1980, p. 52).

- The efficiency of conversion (ratio of stemwood to sawnwood) was in Pará below the average for the Amazon region of roughly 1.8: in Marajó it was lowest (2.31), and somewhat higher in Belém (1.94) and southern Pará (1.90) (Bruce 1976, p. 34). These efficiency differentials depended on log diameter (the smaller the latter, the higher the losses).

– The different daily output volumes depended on the hardness of the timber sawn, i.e. it was not necessarily an indication of absolute low productivity. When only hard woods were sawn, the daily output might decline to 79 % of the normal output, though when soft woods were involved the figure might rise to 142 % (Bruce 1976, p. 35).

Apart from construction timber, most sawmills in the Amazon region also produced sawnwood of different qualities; a product specialization in different processing techniques was noted only for firms that produced wood for floors, veneers, or plywood. Only a limited number of sawmills sought to develop new product lines; as a rule they did this only when they were forced to by stable changes in customer demand, species supply, and stemwood quality (Mercado 1980, p. 51).

The plywood factories were as a rule more efficient and more strongly geared to maintaining a uniform product quality. Since demand was high, the normal practice was to work in two eight-hour shifts; the drying chambers were in operation 6 days a week for 24 hours (Mercado 1980, p. 58). All the same, only 70 % of capacities were utilized. The factories worked with modern machines from the US, Italy, and Japan. Like the sawmills, these firms had problems procuring spare parts as well as with low qualification levels on the part of their constantly fluctuating workforces.

The existence of veneer factories was something new to the Amazon region; in the decades past, suitable stemwood was shipped to the south of Brazil or abroad. In 1978 the veneer factories were distributed as follows: two works apiece were located in Pará and Amazonas and five in Rondônia. Only 75 % of the capacities of these plants was utilized owing to problems with marketing and transportation (Mercado 1980, p. 59).

The Significance of the Development of the Amazon Region for the Dynamics of the Timber Industry

The dynamic development of the timber industry in Pará that got underway in the 1970s must, in view of high general rates of economic growth (1970-80, an average of 8.7 % p.a.), be attributed to three factors: in large measure to road-building, in far lower measure to promotion by SUDAM, and to a not insignificant extent to the ban on log exports imposed in 1974.

In the 1960s forest utilization in the more inaccessible areas of the Amazon region was marked by traditional extraction activities and fallow-cropping carried out by the local population; logging played no more than a minor role.[24] At the same time powerful changes were already emerging, triggered by the development and accessibility brought about by road construction. At the end of the 1950s construction began on the road between Belém and Brasilia; between November 1959 and September 1960 this area was investigated by an FAO mission that was to submit proposals to SPVEA on the establishment of forest-conservation zones that could be utilized productively.[25] The members of the mission directly observed the spontaneously emerging utilization dynamics along a new agrarian frontier in the *terra firme*; they must have been especially impressed by the rapidity with which the forests contiguous to the new road were cleared, within a few months, to make space for agricultural activities. As agriculture proliferated, leading to a substitution of secondary growth for primary forest, the potential for fishing and hunting declined visibly. Prior to road construction logging operations were conducted only in the vicinity of São Miguel do Guamá, where the timber could be rafted down the Rio Guamá to Belém. There were at that time no other means of transportation.

The forest formations in the region were densely wooded; for this reason, and in anticipation of the dynamics of destruction unleashed by the unregulated expansion of agriculture, the FAO experts proposed demarcation of a forest preserve along the highway from Belém to Brasilia as a means of securing a permanent basis for the timber industry. This proposal was never put into practice, and what happened instead was a run on land in this area. Between 1955 and 1968 the area experienced the rise of a good number of big farms whose owners concentrated on cattle-ranching and logging and founded a new town named Paragominas (composed of the names of their home states Pará, Goiás, and Minas Gerais) (Foweraker 1981; Hecht 1983, 1984). Up to the 1980s the area was known as the "Wild West" because many land conflicts were settled here by force of arms. In the 1980s Paragominas, with its over 200 sawmills, became the center of Pará's timber industry.

The example of Paragominas illustrates the significance that the development of the Amazon region had for the expansion of Pará's timber industry. The crucial factors here included less the tax incentives granted by SUDAM than settlement programs and road-building:

–   SUDAM focused its promotion policy on large-scale projects until the end of the 1980s; since there were hardly any such projects in the industrial sector outside the tax-free zone of Manaus, it was above all mining projects and cattle-ranches that were fostered in Pará. The creation of cattle ranches meant first of all that firms purchased large tracts of land and cleared them at least partially as a means of underscoring their possession and claim to use them. Disbursement of the subsidies was made contingent on measures required for a productive utilization, deforestation being regarded as one such measure. Since these tracts of land were for the most part very remote, there was no profitable sales market for the logs produced, so most of this timber was burned. Medium-size firms that had been unable to obtain SUDAM subsidies were more under pressure to sell their timber to fund clearance operations (Browder 1988).

–   The settlement programs led to a sharp and rapid rise of the population in the rural areas of the Amazon region, which served to overcome the region's classical problem – lack of manpower. For Pará's timber industry, which was expanding into the rural areas of the state, this was a crucial factor, since its mobility depended on the availability of new cheap labor.[26]

–   Road construction opened up access both to the timber-rich *terra firme* areas (thus placing log production on an entirely new basis), 91 % of which were public land, and to the domestic market in the southeast and south of the country. This domestic market constituted the condition needed for the enormous growth that the timber industry was to experience in the 1970s and 1980s, since this market was not particularly exacting and was easy to service. Even Knowles had realistically predicted in 1965 that road construction would make the Brazilian domestic market into the most important sales market of Pará's timber industry.

Settlement programs and road-building opened up access to timber-rich areas for the sawmills and were the condition that ensured that the industry's nomadic character was retained.

"When timber supply becomes inadequate, sawmillers know that they can move their mills to new locations with access to stands of uncut timber." (Mercado 1980, p. 34)

Seen in these terms, the SUDAM tax incentives played a subordinate role for the expansion of the timber industry. In any case their effective impact in shaping the degree of modernization of the sector or its spatial distribution was negligible (see Section 7.5 for more detailed information). In the timber industry SUDAM gave preference to vertically integrated large-scale projects with a high employment effect which themselves carried out the mechanized logging and transportation and aimed for a higher degree of processing and a high export content. Such projects were beyond the financial and technical means available to the bulk of timber entrepreneurs who migrated to the Amazon region.

Analysis of the catalogue of all timber projects ever promoted which was published by SUDAM at the end of the 1990s proves the thesis of SUDAM's low degree of influence on the timber industry (SUDAM 1996a, 1996b):

–   Between 1964 and 1995 a total of 684 firms received SUDAM subsidies; 89 % of these were granted a complete 10-year exemption from the income tax and only 11 % were given FINAM funds for initial or additional capital investments. Compared with the overall number of firms in the industry, which in these decades probably numbered in the thousands, the share of subsidized firms is relatively low.

–   Between 1980 and 1989 665 applications for tax exemptions or other subsidies (i.e. 97 % of all applications placed in the entire period) were approved; 54 % stemmed from Pará and 17 % apiece from Rondônia and Mato Grosso.

– In Pará in the 1980s 44 % of the applications approved stemmed from Paragominas, 23 % apiece from the region of Belém and the south of Pará, and only 9 % from the island region. These figures mirror quite exactly the shift of timber production from the *várzea* to the *terra firme* that was made possible by the construction of new roads.

– 77 % of the investment subsidies were applied for between 1978 and 1989; between 1990 and 1995 only 4 new applications were placed. 71 % of the subsidized firms were in Pará. On the whole only 10 certificates confirming completion of an investment project were issued – between 1990 and 1994; the period that had elapsed since the initial application averaged 7.4 years.

Analysis of the firms benefiting from tax exemptions and/or subsidies shows the following composition:

Table 26:	Distribution of Wood-processing Firms Subsidized by SUDAM (%)			
State	Sawnwood	Veneer/ Plywood	Sliced veneer	Furniture
Pará	82.9	11.7	2.6	
Maranhão	81.5	11.1		
Amazonas	74.6	8.9		16.4
Mato Grosso	71.1	26.1		
Rondônia	86.8	14.0		
Amazônia	80.2	13.1	2.2	4.2
Source: SUDAM (1996b)				

SUDAM's incentive policy had no positive impact on the industrialization of Pará or the Amazon region. In Paragominas, the center of the timber industry, nearly all of the applications placed were for exemptions from the income tax; only in 1989 and 1992 did two firms apply for funds for modernization or additional investments.

Instead of the SUDAM incentives it was other factors that were decisive in the rapid growth of the Amazon timber industry. There were hardly any barriers to entry for newcomers (Mercado 1980, pp. 34 ff.):

- The initial investments ranged between US$ 40,000 (1978 market value) for a small sawmill and US$ 60 - 80,000 for a medium-sized sawmill. Newcomers often also took over bankrupt companies, or they transferred their machinery from other parts of the country, thus reducing their initial costs.

- The lack of product differentiation in the sawnwood market made it possible for new firms to demand the same prices as established ones; due to the high demand the entire output was regularly sold.

- The log supply was high and low quality standards made it possible to hire unskilled, cheap labor; the wood losses incurred in this way did not constitute a tangible cost factor in view of the extremely low prices for logs and the ease with which sawnwood could be sold.

In 1974 the Brazilian government imposed an export ban on logs; the way in which this ban came about has not been discussed in the literature, though various sources see it as having great import for the expansion of processing in Pará. At that time Pará's timber entrepreneurs undertook a number of attempts, albeit unsuccessfully, to have the ban rescinded.[27] The background of the ban will not mainly have been the desire to foster the processing industry in Pará, since this would have required manifold and long-term measures such as development of a functioning forestry administration, infrastructure improvement (road network, ports), programs aimed at heightening techno-organizational competence in sawmills and promoting marketing. This measure is also surprising in that it comes at a point of time at which the Amazon region, in the framework of PND II, had definitely been characterized as a foreign-exchange earner via exports of raw materials. High-quality logs of precious woods at that time commanded good prices in the world market, and were in any case certainly higher than those in the domestic market. It may for these reasons be assumed that the log export ban was aimed at securing supplies of raw materials for the domestic timber and furniture industries in the south and southeast of the country as well as cheap building materials for the burgeoning cities.[28]

The log export ban did not serve to foster the industrialization of Pará; the strategy of development via the buildup of resource-processing industries had just been replaced by PND II. The measure instead served to underline Pará's role as a supplier of resources to the industrialized south and southeast.

How underdeveloped the industrial sector in the Amazon region remained is illustrated by the fact that at the beginning of the 1980s the timber industry, as small and unproductive as it was, was one of the Amazon region's most important branches of industry: *"Four of the region's six states and federal territories depend on wood products for more than 25 % of the industrial output. (...) In Rondônia and Roraima, wood products account for more than 60 % of industrial output. Many new urban Amazon settlements depend on local lumber industries for their only links to the national economy."* (Browder 1988, p. 249)

In 1985 the northern region was able to increase its share in the Brazilian timber industry's gross value added to 18 %, even though the company pattern had not changed. This timber industry still consisted in its majority of small sawmills with an average of 16 workers, and though these firms accounted for a total of 21 % of the industrial jobs in the region, they accounted for no more than 9 % of the gross value of industrial output. With the exception of a large furniture factory in Manaus, the furniture industry consisted almost exclusively of small artisanal workshops with an average of six workers; their contribution to gross industrial value added was less than one percent. This artisanal structure at that time dominated the whole of Brazil's furniture production.

> *"Until today the regional timber-processing industry (as opposed to the national development in recent years) has, due to its restriction to a small number of more or less simple productive segments, not been able to connect up with more dynamic demand areas, in this way raising internal value added and entering on an intensified growth path."* (Guimarães Neto and Rocha 1992, p. 21)

In the context of a persistent stagnation of the domestic market in the 1980s[29] the plywood and fiberboard industries had introduced technical innovations and developed new markets abroad as a means of escaping the sales crisis at home. Compared with this, sawnwood exports had hardly increased at all.

Brazil's sawnwood industry was globally characterized in a SUDAM expertise as an unproductive industry that had lost touch with recent technological developments (e.g. electronically controlled cutting to size that reduces wood losses and increases precision). The situation of the sawmills of the Amazon region had hardly changed at all compared with the 1960s and 1970s: these shops continued to work with inefficient machines and layouts, maintenance was poor, there was a lack of specific knowledge of adapted processing and storage methods, since these firms had no trained production managers.[30]

According to the same expertise the plywood industry in the Amazon region was no less inefficient; this opinion was based on information of the industry federation. All told, one quarter of the plywood output in Brazil comes from the Amazon region; 85 % of Brazil's plywood industry covered its supply needs with timber from natural forests. It in general had a lower productivity level, a very low level of automation, and produced products of mediocre quality (Guimarães Neto and Rocha 1992, p. 69).

7.2.3 The Development of Pará's Timber Industry between 1959 and 1985, as Mirrored by Statistics

This section will discuss the extent to which the timber industry in Pará, compared with the development in Brazil as a whole and the development in the state of Paraná, the national center of the timber industry, proved able to increase its performance between 1959 and 1985. The following indicators are referred to: the gross production value of the timber, furniture, and pulp/paper industries, net value added per worker, and data on investments and employment in these three industries.

A general overview of the changes in the timber industry in terms of number of firms, number of workers (overall, per firm), average wage costs, gross production value per firm, as well as net value added per worker overall and per worker in production is provided by Table A-8 in the Appendix, broken down as per region and in terms of average data for Pará, Paraná, and Brazil. We find here that compared with Paraná Pará's timber industry consists wholly of smaller firms – and this applies for all reference data. One striking fact is the relatively high level of wage costs between 1980 and 1985 in the face of declining company-level gross production value and a net value added per worker in production that had been on the decline since 1975.

Gross Production Value of the Timber, Furniture, and Pulp/Paper Industries

Between 1959 and 1985 the gross production value of these three industries grew in Brazil by 6.9 %, the highest growth rates were noted for the years of the "Brazilian economic miracle" between 1970 and 1975 (18.7 % p.a.). Between 1959 and 1985 the north and the midwest always showed the highest growth rates (15.3 % and 9.8 %, resp.); Pará's position here was just below the average figure for the north. The south on the other hand was only somewhat above the national average, and the southeast was even below this figure (see Table 27).

Between 1970 and 1980 the north showed a figure of 26.6 %, the highest annual growth rate noted; Pará, with its 30 %, was even somewhat above this. Between 1980 and 1985 gross production value declined in Brazil by -2.7 % per year, in Pará by -1.8 %, while in the north the overall figure increased slightly, by 1.3 %.

In spite of this all in all positive development the dynamics of these three industries declined visibly in comparison with the development in Brazilian industry as a whole: between 1959 and 1985 Brazilian industry as a whole grew by 8.6 % per year and by 20.2 % between 1970 and 1975 (see Table A-9 in the appendix). Thus the share of the three branches of industry in the gross production value of industry as a whole declined from 7.3 % in 1959 to 5.0 % in 1985. The case was different in the north and in Pará: here the growth of the timber, furniture, and pulp/paper industries was distinctly above the average growth of industry as a whole; this illustrates the great significance of these industries for the region's industrial development.

Table 27: Growth of GPV of the Timber, Furniture and Paper Industries in the Regions, 1959-85

	1959 R$ millions	1970 R$ millions	1959-70 %	1975 R$ millions	1970-75 %	1980 R$ millions	1975-80 %	1985 R$ millions	1980-85 %	1959-85 %	1970-80 %
North	41	147	12.3	500	27.7	1,552	25.4	1,659	1.3	15.3	26.6
Pará	*26*	*75*	*10.1*	*296*	*31.6*	*1,038*	*28.5*	*946*	*-1.8*	*14.8*	*30.1*
Northeast	216	352	4.5	1,147	26.6	1,835	9.9	1,576	-3.0	7.9	18.0
Southeast	3,413	6,151	5.5	13,331	16.7	18,351	6.6	16,938	-1.6	6.4	11.6
South	1,445	3,167	7.4	7,984	20.3	11,321	7.2	8,861	-4.8	7.2	13.6
Paraná	*622*	*1,465*	*8.1*	*3,553*	*19.4*	*5,022*	*7.2*	*3,593*	*-6.5*	*7.0*	*13.1*
Midwest	45	115	8.9	396	28.1	824	15.8	512	-9.1	9.8	21.8
Brazil	5,160	9,932	6.1	23,357	18.7	33,883	7.7	29,547	-2.7	6.9	13.1

Source: IBGE Censo Industrial, figures in R$ as of 1996, annual geometric growth rate in %

The weight of each of these three industries changed in the course of the decades (see Table 28): between 1959 and 1985 the share of the timber industry declined from 35.5 % to 23.7 %, that of the furniture industry from 24.7 to 22.9 %, while the share of the pulp and paper industry, which showed by far more dynamic development than the other two industries, increased from 39.9 to 53.3 %.

Table 28:	Share of Timber, Furniture and Paper Industries in GPV of Total Industrial Production, 1959-85								
	1959		1970		1975		1980		1985	
	R$ m	%	R$ m	%	R$ m	%	R$ m	%	R$ m	%
Timber	1,830	35.5	3,485	35.1	8,425	36.1	11,105	32.8	7,017	23.7
Furniture	1,272	24.7	2,721	27.4	5,906	25.3	8,060	23.8	6,773	22.9
Paper	2,058	39.9	3,725	37.5	9,026	38.6	14,718	43.4	15,757	53.3
Total	5,160	100.0	9,931	100.0	23,357	100.0	33,883	100.0	29,547	100.0
Source:	IBGE Censo Industrial, figures in R$ as of 1996								

The regional distribution of the gross production value of three industries did not change remarkably, despite the north's high growth rates: the north's share of overall gross production value grew from 0.8 to 5.6 %, the southeast's share declined from 66.1 to 57.3 %, and the south's share remained practically constant (28 and 29.9 %) (see Table 29).

If we distinguish between the three branches of industry (see Table 30; Tables A-9 and A-10 in the Appendix), we see clearly that the growth in the north was based on the growth of the timber industry, whose share of gross production value rose from 1.9 to 17.8 % between 1959 and 1985, while the north's share in the gross production value of the furniture and pulp/paper industry, 1.5 and 2.0 %, resp., was very modest. Pará had no more than very low shares in their overall gross production value: 8.8 % (timber), 0.4 % (furniture), and 1.9 % (pulp/paper).

Table 29:	Regional Distribution of GPV of Timber, Furniture and Paper Industries, 1959-85 (%)				
	1959	1970	1975	1980	1985
North	0.8	1.5	2.1	4.6	5.6
Pará	*0.5*	*0.8*	*1.3*	*3.1*	*3.2*
Northeast	4.2	3.5	4.9	5.4	5.3
Southeast	66.1	61.9	57.1	54.2	57.3
South	28.0	31.9	34.2	33.4	29.9
Paraná	*12.1*	*14.8*	*15.2*	*14.8*	*12.2*
Midwest	0.9	1.2	1.7	2.4	1.7
Total	100.0	100.0	100.0	100.0	100.0
Source: IBGE Censo Industrial					

The development of the share of the three industries in regional gross production value again demonstrates their relatively weak dynamics as compared with general industrial development: between 1959 and 1985 their share rose from 7.6 % to 12.0 % in the north, in the south it declined from 15.9 to 9.2 %, and in the southeast from 6.3 to 4.2 %. The share of the timber industry sank even more: in the southeast and south from 1.2 to 0.5 % and 11.2 to 3.2 %, respectively, and in Paraná from 17.1 to 4.7 %. In contrast, the share rose from 6.3 to 9 % in the north and in Pará from 7.9 to 16.6 %.

The balance is that

– the dynamics of the timber industry lagged far behind general industrial dynamics,

– despite the enormous growth in roundwood production in the north, no dynamic industrial base emerged there that might have broken the dominance of the southeast and south, and

– the pulp/paper industry, the most dynamic sector, concentrated its operations in the southeast and south, since its raw-materials base and its most important sales markets were located there.

Table 30: Growth of GPV of the Timber Industry in the Regions, 1959-85

	1959 R$ millions	1970 R$ millions	1959-70 %	1975 R$ millions	1970-75 %	1980 R$ millions	1975-80 %	1985 R$ millions	1980-85 %	1959-85 %	1970-80 %
North	34	125	12.6	464	30.0	1,123	19.3	1,250	2.2	14.9	24.6
Pará	*21*	*64*	*10.7*	*283*	*34.6*	*685*	*19.3*	*614*	*-2.2*	*13.9*	*26.8*
Northeast	72	135	5.9	374	22.6	649	11.7	410	-8.8	6.9	17.0
Southeast	672	1,066	4.3	2,459	18.2	2,903	3.4	1,900	-8.1	4.1	10.5
South	1,017	2,071	6.7	4,792	18.3	5,760	3.7	3,082	-11.8	4.4	10.8
Paraná	*473*	*1,028*	*7.3*	*2,359*	*18.1*	*2,950*	*4.6*	*1,439*	*-13.4*	*4.4*	*11.1*
Midwest	34	88	9.0	336	30.7	671	14.8	375	-11.0	9.7	22.5
Brazil	1,830	3,485	6.0	8,425	19.3	11,105	5.7	7,017	-8.8	5.3	12.3

Source: IBGE Censo Industrial, figures in R$ m as of 1996, annual geometric growth rate in %

Net Value Added per Worker

For lack of physical output data for the three industries investigated, the indicator "net value added per worker" will be used here as a proxy for the development of labor productivity.[31]

If we compare net value added/worker in the timber, furniture, and pulp/paper industries, we find that the gap between the southeast and all other regions grew between 1959 and 1985: assuming a value of 100 for the southeast, we in this period find the figures for the north declining from 46 to 42, with Pará remaining nearly constant (from 37 to 38), and a decline in the south and Paraná (from 67 to 58 and from 68 to 62, resp.) (see Tables 30 and 31).

Table 31:	Growth of NVA/Employee in the Timber, Furniture and Paper Industries of the Regions, 1970-85							
	1970	1975	1970-75	1980	1975-80	1985	1980-85	1970-85
	1000 R$	1000 R$	%	1000 R$	%	1000 R$	%	%
North	9,371	16,818	12.4	23,428	6.9	22,963	-0.4	6.2
Pará	*7,396*	*16,253*	*17.1*	*23,159*	*7.3*	*20,755*	*-2.2*	*7.1*
Northeast	8,099	16,016	14.6	18,941	3.4	20,254	1.3	6.3
Southeast	20,201	30,689	8.7	39,019	4.9	55,257	7.2	6.9
South	13,509	24,268	12.4	27,406	2.5	31,868	3.1	5.9
Paraná	*13,789*	*26,250*	*13.7*	*30,104*	*2.8*	*34,533*	*2.8*	*6.3*
Midwest	9,138	15,512	11.2	18,746	3.9	14,347	-5.2	3.1
Brazil	16,236	26,153	10.0	30,846	3.4	40,102	5.4	6.2
Source: IBGE Censo Industrial, figures in R$ as of 1996, annual geometric growth rate in %								

The picture changes when we look at the timber industry alone: here the north has the highest figure in 1985, while Pará is below the lower average for the southeast and Paraná. In the southeast and south net value added/worker declined by -6.4 and -5.8 % between 1980 and

1985 (see Table A-11 in the Appendix). Yet this peak figure places the north only slightly ahead of the south in 1975.

Table 32: NVA/Employee in the Timber, Furniture and Paper Industries in the Regions, 1970-85				
	1970	1975	1980	1985
North	46	55	60	42
Pará	*37*	*53*	*59*	*38*
Northeast	40	52	49	37
Southeast	100	100	100	100
South	67	79	70	58
Paraná	*68*	*86*	*77*	*62*
Midwest	45	51	48	26
Brazil	80	85	79	73
Source: IBGE Censo Industrial (Southeast: 100)				

If we also assume a value of 100 for net value added/worker for the furniture industry in the southeast, this figure rises in the north from 40 to 71; this is due above all to the large-scale furniture industry in the free production zone in Manaus. In Pará it declines in the same period from 47 to 46, in the south and Paraná it rises from 68 to 97 and from 72 to 80, respectively. The north shows the worst figures for the pulp/paper industry: net value added/worker here stagnates compared with the southeast (= 100) at a level of 39/40, while in the south and in Paraná it rises from 75 to 97 and from 75 to 105, respectively (see Tables A-12 to A-13 in the Appendix).

As in the case of gross production value, comparison of the net value added of the timber, furniture, and pulp/paper industries with industry as a whole clearly illustrates the weak dynamics of the timber and furniture industries; only the pulp/paper industry is clearly above the average level of gross production value for Brazil (see Table A-14 in the Appendix).

Investments

The statistical data available on investments in the timber, furniture, and pulp/paper industries are very sparse, since not all of the firms interviewed provided information. What becomes visible by approximation are the following changes in the regional distribution of investments:

–   in the timber industry the north's share in investments grows from 2.4 % in 1959 to 25.3 % in 1980, while at the same time the shares of the south and southeast decline from 26.9 to 13.1 % and 63 to 42.3 %, respectively;

–   in the furniture industry the whole share of the southeast's losses (from 84.2 to 49.8 %) benefits the south (10.5 to 32.1 %) and, to a lesser extent, the north (from 0 to 7.2 %);

–   In the pulp/paper industry there are no investments in the north in 1959, 81.4 % of investments are concentrated in the southeast and 10.7 % in the south; in 1980 the southeast holds only 54.8 %, the south 28.3 %, and the north 9.2 %.

The most pronounced spatial deconcentration of investment dynamics is thus found in the timber industry. The pulp and paper industry accounts for the greatest volume of investment, though the timber industry also shows a substantial volume, showing considerable growth. This is surprising in view of the timber industry's low average company-level figures of gross production value and net value added compared with the pulp/paper industry. Qualitative data would be needed to be able to exactly assess these different capital productivities. The empirical studies on Pará's timber industry have already clearly shown that investments here have been concentrated chiefly on mechanization of logging and less on modernization of capital stock in terms of machinery used for processing, which would raise company-level value added.

Capital intensity (C/Y) and capital productivity (Y/C) can be calculated only for the years 1975 and 1980 (see Table 33). Comparison of the data for Pará, Paraná, and the Brazilian average shows that Pará's capital intensity, 0.57 and 0.69, respectively, are above the averages for

Table 33:	Capital and Profits in the Timber Industries of Pará, Paraná and Brazil, 1975 and 1980							
	Capital stock	Enter-prises	C/Y^a	Y/C^b	Capital stock	Enter-prises	C/Y^a	Y/C^b
	1975	1975	1975	1975	1980	1980	1980	1980
Pará								
Average of all industries	348,006	1,482	0.66	1.52	627,317	4,818	0.83	1.20
Timber industry	287,101	430	0.57	1.75	253,878	1,856	0.69	1.45
Single firm	53,840	282	0.36	2.78	71,507	340	0.54	1.84
Partnership	262,884	48	0.56	1.80	413,377	33	0.97	1.03
Ltd. comp.	434,233	100	0.36	2.80	596,983	343	0.57	1.75
Stock corp.	1,853,516	28	0.57	1.75	3,218,888	59	1.01	0.99
Paraná								
Average of all industries	482,971	7,272	0,36	2,79	495,922	13,714	0.25	3.98
Timber industry	402,471	1,920	0.46	2.19	367,313	2,349	0.30	3.32
Single firm	144,738	293	0.44	2.28	81,165	391	0.45	2.22
Partnership	334,900	71	0.29	3.42	453,547	32	0.20	4.96
Ltd. comp.	305,503	1,285	0.35	2.84	290,332	1,522	0.34	2.90
Stock corp.	1,107,805	283	0.30	3.29	1,582,061	231	0.24	4.13
Brazil								
Average of all industries	n.d.	n.d.	n.d.	n.d.	740,553	207,781	0.29	3.50
Timber industry	330,042	9,007	0.37	2.73	219,044	20,472	0.41	2.41
Single firm	90,233	2,395	0.36	2.79	65,983	5,921	0.59	1.69
Partnership	218,472	379	0.36	2.77	266,986	289	0.44	2.29
Ltd. comp.	235,413	5,050	0.33	3.06	225,299	9,328	0.42	2.39
Stock corp.	1,311,296	1,126	0.41	2.42	1,866,326	938	0.35	2.83

C = capital; Y = yield; a = capital intensity; b = capital productivity in production

Source: IBGE Censo Industrial 1975 and 1980, capital stock figures in R$ as of 1996

Brazil and Paraná (more so in 1980 than in 1975), though capital productivity, 1.75 and 1.45, respectively, was also clearly below the average; this trend applied mostly for the big corporations with the largest capital stock, and it had even intensified between 1975 and 1980. In contrast, in Paraná capital productivity had increased sharply, and done so in all size classes. IMAZON data for 1990 indicate for the average Pará sawmill 0.59 compared with 1980, and thus a declining capital intensity, as well as a stagnant capital productivity of 1.7 compared with 1975.

These data confirm the findings of the empirical studies indicating that in Pará high returns were achieved with a relatively low deployment of capital by focusing activities on logging precious timber species without increasing the technology content of the processing phase. In addition, these data indicate that in the 1980s the capital stock was sharply depreciated, since preference was given to investment in real estate over reinvestment.

Employment

The share of the timber, furniture, and pulp/paper industries in overall industrial employment declines in Brazil between 1959 and 1985 from 11.0 to 9.6 % (see Table 34). At the same time employment in these industries increased in absolute terms by a figure of 4 % per year. The relative share of the timber industry declined by 5.2 %, chiefly in favor of the pulp/paper industry.

Employment developed differently in the different regions: in the north the share of workers in the three industries in overall regional industrial employment rose from 16.9 to 25 %; in 1980 a peak figure of 29.1 % was reached; in the southeast this share declined from 8.2 % to 6.7 %, in the south the figure was 27.4 to 17.1 % (see Table 35). This development is also mirrored in the regional growth rates: employment growth in the north is highest: 10.1 % from 1959 to 1985; between 1975 and 1980 employment there shows the highest growth, 17.4 % per year (Pará: 19.4 %). In the southeast and south the development of employment, 3.3 and 3.9 %, respectively, is somewhat below the Brazilian

Table 34: Growth of Employment in the Timber, Furniture and Paper Industries in the Regions, 1959-85

	1959 Employees	1959-70 %	1970 Employees	1970-75 %	1975 Employees	1975-80 %	1980 Employees	1980-85 %	1985 Employees	1959-85 %
North	3,104	10.1	8,979	13.5	16,942	17.4	37,826	-0.2	37,513	10.1
Pará	*1,895*	*10.5*	*5,656*	*12.1*	*10,034*	*19.4*	*24,325*	*-2.5*	*21,392*	*9.8*
Northeast	12,170	5.2	21,282	6.9	29,752	10.3	48,513	-1.1	45,935	5.2
Southeast	102,684	3.7	152,901	5.7	202,065	2.4	227,130	1.2	241,618	3.3
South	71,569	4.7	118,250	7.0	165,877	4.7	208,370	-1.6	192,008	3.9
Paraná	*29,942*	*4.7*	*49,825*	*5.9*	*66,507*	*4.0*	*80,946*	*-2.5*	*71,293*	*3.4*
Midwest	2,691	8.9	6,883	14.5	13,549	11.4	23,283	-2.6	20,400	8.1
Brazil	192,218	4.4	308,295	6.8	428,185	4.9	545,122	-0.3	537,474	4.0

Source: IBGE Censo Industrial, annual geometric growth rate in %

Table 35: Share of Employees in the Timber, Furniture and Paper Industries in Total Industrial Occupation in the Regions, 1959-85

	1959		1970		1975		1980		1985	
	Em-ployees	%	Em-ployees	%	Em-ployees	%	Em-ployees	%	Em-ployees	%
North	3,104	16.9	8,979	22.3	16,942	24.6	37,826	29.1	37,513	25.0
Pará	*1,895*	*15.6*	*5,656*	*22.6*	*10,034*	*26.9*	*24,325*	*37.6*	*21,392*	*33.8*
Northeast	12,170	5.8	21,282	7.7	29,752	7.4	48,513	8.8	45,935	7.6
Southeast	102,684	8.2	152,901	8.1	202,065	7.7	227,130	7.0	241,618	6.7
South	71,569	27.4	118,250	25.9	165,877	22.8	208,370	21.4	192,008	17.1
Paraná	*29,942*	*43.7*	*9,825*	*43.6*	*66,507*	*38.1*	*80,946*	*34.4*	*71,293*	*27.7*
Midwest	2,691	19.5	6,883	18.5	13,549	19.8	23,283	20.5	20,400	16.7
Total	192,218	10.7	308,295	11.4	428,185	8.6	545,122	10.9	537,474	9.6

Source: IBGE Censo Industrial

average; the southeast is the only region that shows a slight increase in employment of 1.2 % during the five crisis years between 1980 and 1985.

On the whole, the share of the southeast and south in overall employment declined in the three industries between 1959 and 1985 from 90.7 to 80.7 %.

7.3   Roundwood Production

7.3.1   The 1950s and 1960s

According to FAO estimates, an annual quantity of roughly 1 million m^3 of logs was cut for the processing industry and for log exports (Knowles 1965, p. 18). If we assume for Pará a share of 60 - 70 % of the sawnwood production of the Amazon region, we arrive at a volume of cut timber of 600 - 700,000 m^3 per year for the state. Logging operations were for the most part not carried out by the sawmills themselves but by small logging teams hired by middlemen on behalf of the sawmills. It was in this way possible to lower costs for the procurement of raw materials. Larger quantities of roundwood were procured by engaging several middlemen at once. Logging was done by hand, with axes, sometimes with the aid of handsaws and wedges. As a rule a man could fell 3 m^3 per day or transport this quantity of timber out of the forest and assemble it into rafts (Knowles 1971, p. 33). Losses were incurred less in felling the timber than in cutting it to size to be transported.

The costs of logging and transportation (and thus the procurement costs for raw materials) varied sharply from one procurement site to another; the suppliers normally added a profit of 100 % to their costs. While a cubic meter of virola, which can be rafted, cost US$ 6, the supply price of a cubic meter of mahogany stemwood could be as high as US$ 30, since the stands of these trees were at least 600 km inland from Belém.

In the *várzea* the logs were rolled manually to the river and there either rafted to the sawmill or shipped on board a barge. In the *terra firme* the logs were loaded by hand on to trucks. In the Amazon region the use of draft animals was not customary either in agriculture or in forestry. The trucks were light (5 t) because the unpaved state of the roads ruled out heavy loads; this raised unit transportation costs. The barges had a capacity of up to 100 t and were for that reason the cheaper means of transportation.

In the more modern sawmills the logs, once unloaded, were sorted according to species, the volume recorded, though in most cases the logs were randomly stacked and processed in keeping with the principle of chance. *"Very often there is no control or inventory of the timber stocks whatever and, in view of the successive processing of logs in a sawmill, no method of e.g. more quickly processing timber that is vulnerable to mildew."* (Knowles 1971, p. 25 f) There was no chemical protection of the logs.

In the 1950s and 1960s a total of roughly 40 species were commercially cut and sold (Knowles 1965, p. 134). Even in this period a concentration on two species was becoming evident, virola (Virola surinamensis) and mahogany (Swietenia macrophylla King), which were to assume particular importance for the expansion of the timber industry:

– virola, a pale, easy-to-work softwood suitable for both plywood and sawnwood production, grows rapidly, and its habitat in the *várzea* and the delta of the Amazon River was easily accessible;

– mahogany, a reddish hardwood with excellent mechanical properties, is used to produce sawnwood and veneer above all by the furniture industry and commands very high prices in the world market; these very high sales prices have encouraged the extraction of these trees, which occur only in isolation (as a rule one individual per ha) and in *terra firme* forests.

Virola-logging was the basis of the expansion of the plywood industry in the 1970s; above all in the 1980s mahogany-logging was used to fund the development of sawmills, private road construction, the acquisition of heavy machinery and trucks for mechanized logging and the purchase of large tracts of land in the south of Pará to create rangeland for cattle-ranching.

In the 1950s there was a ban on felling virola (which was then known not under its Latin name but under its traditional one, *ucuúba da várzea*), because its fatty seeds were gathered and made into soap in Belém (SUDAM 1973b, p. 301). Even then, however, the wood of the virola was of great significance in the plywood industry, which had for that reason chosen to locate in the Amazon region. The FAO mission at the end of the 1950s investigated the dense virola stands in the Tocantins delta (southwest of the Amazon delta) with a view to opening up an alternative area where this important timber could be harvested. Once the FAO report was published, virola-logging in this area increased enormously; the logging ban on virola was undermined and in the coming years fell fully into oblivion.[32]

In the 1950s it was still unknown in what areas mahogany occurs in the Amazon region; it was generally assumed that this species grows in the middle-western to southern Amazon region. This is why the area in the south of Pará investigated by the FAO was characterized as an "isolated exceptional habitat" (SUDAM 1973b, p. 319). The FAO's attention was directed to the location by the only major corporation – Rio Impex – that harvested this timber there, exporting it as sawnwood via Belém.[33] The decimation of the mahogany stands that was noted even then was attributed by the FAO experts to the proliferation of fallow-cropping and uncontrolled burning. But even the richest, untouched forest formations had no more than a mahogany supply of 4.72 m³/ha; the average supply was 3.56 m³/ha (SUDAM 1973b, p. 322).

7.3.2   The 1970s and 1980s

In the 1970s some 2.3 million m³ of logs were processed in Pará, two thirds of this in Belém (34 %) and on the island of Marajó (35 %). Compared with 1962, volume had roughly tripled. Log consumption had increased far more than the number of sawmills; this tallies well with the fact that it was mainly the number of medium- and large-size sawmills that had increased. According to IBGE data, in the 1980s roundwood production had increased to roughly 16 million m³.

As in the 1960s, most sawmills covered their needs with roundwood cut by third parties: 72 % of the sawmills interviewed by Bruce derived no timber from forest areas of their own; 80 % of the sawmills interviewed procured their stemwood exclusively from third parties (Bruce 1976, p. 26). Six years later Mercado arrived at similar results. Those who used their own forests indicated that they derived an average of 57 % of their timber from them. In view of the results found by EMBRAPA as well as those of other authors writing 20 years later, there is reason to doubt this statement (see Chapter 6); since the *Código Florestal*, with its stipulation that timber must be harvested from managed forests, was then already in effect, it is more likely that the statements involved were somewhat embellished. This is also indicated by the fact that 65 % of sawmills themselves possessed no land, while 11 % owned up to 1,000 ha and 12 % held between 10,000 and over 500,000 ha (Bruce 1976). In the region of Belém and on Marajó only one fifth of the saw-mill owners interviewed by Bruce owned forests of their own.

In the 1970s the regional differences in the technologies used for log-ging began to emerge clearly: the *várzea* continued to be dominated by manual logging carried out by *caboclos* and *ribeirinhos*, while the *terra firme* experienced a very slow mechanization of logging practices (above all the use of power saws, less of tractors, bulldozers and larger trucks). The advantages afforded by mechanization consisted in pro-duction rises; the costs per cubic meter for wholly mechanized logging and transportation were higher than the average costs for manual log-ging (Knowles 1971, p. 34).[34] The power saw served above all to in-crease the amount of timber felled; the losses that continued to be in-curred in logging were accepted.

As in the 1960s, problems with log supply existed in that storing supply stocks for the dry and rainy seasons was an expensive enterprise that required considerable advance capital. In the dry season it was not pos-sible to raft timber from the *várzea* via the Igarapés; in the rainy season the dirt roads in the *terra firme* forests were impassable. The interrup-tion of log supplies due to the change of seasons was one of the greatest obstacles to a continuous supply of raw materials and reasonable levels of capacity utilization. Since 97 % of the firms polled by Bruce indi-cated that they produced throughout the year, they must, as opposed to the 1960s, have managed to overcome this obstacle. Mercado noted in 1978 that it was chiefly the smaller sawmills that were still forced to stop production toward the end of the dry season because their means were not sufficient to create reserve stocks of sufficient size (Mercado 1980, pp. 41 f.).

The regional origin of the logs processed shows that though road construction had increased the significance of *terra firme* forests, a considerable share of the stemwood used continued to originate in the *várzea* areas and the island region (Mercado 1980, p. 18). In Pará in 1978 only 15 % of logs were transported by truck, 80 % were rafted, and 5 % were transported by boat. The sawmills were very close to their sources of logs: an average of 52 % of logs were cut up to 50 km from the sawmills, though there were marked regional differences. In the Belém region 50 % of logs were felled at a maximum of 25 km from the sawmill, in Marajó the figure was 43 %. In the south of Pará 56 % of logs were felled at a distance between 25 and 50 km (Bruce 1976, p. 25).

As regards the number and significance of the species logged, considerable changes can be noted vis-à-vis 1962: on the whole six species accounted for 68 % of the stemwood processed; 90 % of the stemwood was accounted for by 23 species. The most important species were virola (28 %) and mahogany (8.7 %). Some sawmills had specialized in processing one single species, others processed a total of 25 species.

In 1976 three quarters of sawmill owners indicated that their species composition had not changed in the past three years; 12 % stated that they were now processing more species, and 13 % indicated changes in the species processed, chiefly because of supply problems. The decision on the species to process was made on the basis of the species available, customer wishes, and species marketability (Bruce 1976, p. 36).

The veneer and plywood industry processed far fewer species than the sawmills: virola alone covered 49 % of their log input, three further species together covered 41 %. Plywood factories satisfied their great demand for timber in the same way as sawmills, though the former, thanks to their generally higher sales volumes, were able to offer higher prices for stemwood and create sufficient stores for the dry season (Mercado 1980, p. 58).

Comparison with the 1960s shows that the clear-cut dominance of two species, virola and mahogany, set in at the beginning of the 1970s. Specialization in a limited number of species that either commanded high prices abroad (mahogany) or had a safe sales market (virola) was characteristic of Pará's timber industry until the end of the 1980s, i.e. for 15 to twenty years. The scarcity of these two species, which was at that time becoming palpable, was experienced as a crisis by the entire industry.

Production of sawnwood for export was intensified between 1980 and 1986 in response to high inflation, devaluation of the exchange rate vis-à-vis the US dollar, and export subsidies. This export orientation for its part intensified the specialization in the few species marketable abroad, above all mahogany. Even after export subsidies had been abolished, this specialization persisted (mahogany; export), continuing up to the beginning of the 1990s, when mahogany was becoming increasingly scarce.[35]

7.3.3   The Development of Roundwood Production between 1975 and 1991, as Mirrored by Statistics

Despite the reservations noted in Chapter 6 about the quality of IBGE's statistical data on roundwood production, this section will briefly outline the regional shifts and qualitative developments which they indicate (see Tables A-20 to A-27 in the Appendix). Since it was not possible to verify the correctness of the data for the 1970s and 1980s on the basis of other primary sources (the IBGE data are for the most part used in the literature without comment), the data presented will be evaluated only as an indication of trends.

Between 1975 and 1991 the share of the south and southeast in roundwood production (from plantations and primary forest) declined from 75 to 54.4 %; the share of the north grew from 9.2 to 33.4 % (see Table 36). The continuing strong share of the south and southeast is based on the growing share of plantations in overall roundwood production: between 1975 and 1991 this share grew in Brazil from 36.3 to 52 % (see

Table 36: Regional Distribution of Total Log Production, 1975-94

Region	1975 m³	1975 %	1980 m³	1980 %	1986 m³	1986 %	1991 m³	1991 %	1994 m³	1994 %
North	4,534	9.2	12,874	16.5	33,085	39.2	32,030	33.4	49,767	37.7
Pará	*3,942*	*7.9*	*11,674*	*14.9*	*19,493*	*23.1*	*29,350*	*30.6*	*46,894*	*35.6*
Northeast	5,256	10.6	6,852	8.8	9,499	11.2	7,837	8.2	8,038	6.1
Southeast	14,729	29.8	29,081	37.3	18,406	21.8	22,135	23.1	22,962	17.4
South	22,297	45.1	26,060	33.4	29,538	34.9	30,007	31.3	46,228	35.0
Paraná	*10,575*	*21.4*	*9,777*	*12.5*	*15,278*	*30.6*	*18,124*	*18.9*	*22,688*	*17.2*
Midwest	2,648	5.4	3,172	4.1	3,714	4.4	4,123	4.3	4,904	3.7
Total	49,465	100.0	78,039	100.0	84,474	100.0	95,938	100.0	131,900	100.0

Source: IBGE, Produção da extração vegetal e da silvicultura Vol. 9, years 1973-94 and Anuários Estatísticos do IBGE 1971-73

Table 37:   Share of the Regions in Log Production from Primary Forests, 1975-94

Region	1975		1980		1986		1991		1994	
	m³	%	m³	%	m³	%	m³	%	m³	%
North	4,534	14.4	11,483	31.7	32,008	71.7	30,755	66.5	47,159	75.4
Pará	*3,942*	*12.5*	*10,284*	*28.4*	*18,416*	*41.2*	*28,370*	*61.4*	*44,539*	*71.2*
Northeast	5,210	16.5	6,600	18.2	8,637	19.3	6,985	15.1	5,756	9.2
Southeast	2,211	7.0	1,224	3.4	1,607	3.6	558	1.2	393	0.6
South	16,924	53.7	13,743	37.9	8,486	18.9	4,416	9.6	4,779	7.6
Paraná	*8,627*	*27.4*	*5,586*	*15.4*	*4,259*	*9.5*	*2,849*	*6.2*	*3,173*	*5.1*
Midwest	2,648	8.4	3,161	8.7	3,701	8.3	3,519	7.6	4,439	7.1
Total	31,528	100.0	36,212	100.0	44,670	100.0	46,233	100.0	62,527	100.0

Source: IBGE, Produção da extração vegetal e da silvicultura Vol. 9, years 1973-94 and Anuários Estatísticos do IBGE 1971-73

Table 38: Regional Distribution of Log Production from Plantations, 1975-94

Region	1975 m³	%	1980 m³	%	1986 m³	%	1991 m³	%	1994 m³	%
North	-	0.0	1,391	3.3	1,077	2.7	1,275	2.6	2,608	3.8
Pará	-	*0.0*	*1,391*	*3.3*	*1,077*	*2.7*	*980*	*1.9*	*2,355*	*3.4*
Northeast	46	0.3	251	0.6	862	2.2	852	1.7	2,282	3.3
Southeast	12,518	69.8	27,857	66.6	16,799	42.2	21,577	43.4	22,569	32.5
South	5,373	29.9	12,317	29.4	21,052	52.9	25,591	51.5	41,449	59.7
Paraná	*1,948*	*10.9*	*4,191*	*10.0*	*11,019*	*27.7*	*15,275*	*30.7*	*19,515*	*28.1*
Midwest	-	0.0	11	0.0	13	0.0	604	1.2	465	0.7
Total	17,937	100.0	41,827	100.0	39,804	100.0	49,705	100.0	69,373	100.0

Source: IBGE, Produção da extração vegetal e da silvicultura Vol. 9, years 1973-94 and Anuários Estatísticos do IBGE 1971-73

Table 39). Plantation production was concentrated during this entire period in the south and southeast (1975: 99.7 %; 1991: 95 %), while the north increased its share of roundwood production from primary-forest stands from 14.4 % (1975) to 67 % (1991) (see Tables 37 and 38).

Table 39:	Share of Plantations in Total Log Production in the Regions, 1975-94 (%)				
Region	1975	1980	1986	1991	1994
North	0.0	10.8	3.3	3.9	5.2
Pará	*0 0*	*10.8*	*3.3*	*3.3*	*5.0*
Northeast	0.9	3.7	9.1	10.9	28.4
Southeast	84.9	95.8	91.3	97.5	98.3
South	24.1	47.3	71.3	85.3	89.7
Paraná	*18.4*	*42.8*	*72 1*	*84.3*	*86.0*
Midwest	0.0	0.3	0.4	14.6	9.5
Total	36.3	53.6	47.1	51.8	52.6
Source: IBGE, Produção da extração vegetal e da silvicultura Vol. 9, years 1973-94 and Anuários Estatísticos do IBGE 1971-73					

In the same period Brazilian roundwood production nearly doubled from 49.5 million m^3 to 95.9 million m^3. The annual geometric growth rate in this period was 4.2 % for Brazil as a whole; but the regions showed great differences: in the north it was 13 %, in the southeast 2.6 %, and in the south 1.9 %. The overall growth of roundwood production was thus based chiefly on growth in the north. However, if we distinguish between logs from plantations and primary forests, we come up with the following qualifications:

–   on the whole the share of logs from primary forest in the overall production of logs in Brazil declined between 1975 and 1991 from 63.7 to 48 %;

–   it was only in the south, the greatest log producer in the 1970s, that a process of structural change set in: the share of logs from primary forest declined from 76 to 15 %, while the production of plantation timber grew by 10 % per annum and in 1991 its volume even exceeded that of production from primary forest in 1975;

– the north's share of log production from primary forest rose from 14.4 to 66 %, while plantation-timber production stagnated between 1980 and 1991, starting to grow only thereafter.

The fact that the plantation sector as a whole had the greater dynamics is illustrated by a comparison of the annual geometric growth rates between 1975 and 1991: in plantation-timber production it was 6.6 %, in timber production from primary forest only 2.4 % (see Tables 40 - 42).

This indicates that the south and southeast had specialized in plantation-timber production with higher growth rates, while the north extracted stemwood from primary forest stands and held a declining share of Brazil's overall timber production. It is clear that it is in the plantation sector as compared with exploitation of the primary forest that the greatest potential for a rapid and inexpensive increase of production volumes exists and is already being utilized. Another indication of the competitive advantages of plantation-timber production is the implicit price per cubic meter of roundwood that can be noted in the IBGE data (see Table A-27 in the Appendix). The announced investment projects in the south and southeast in the manufacture of reconstituted wood panels indicate that the plantation area in this region will again increase in the coming years. This is likely to mean that the different specialization patterns marking the timber-processing industries in north and south will continue to consolidate.

7.4   Sales

7.4.1   The 1960s[36]

In the 1950s and 1960s Pará's timber industry was highly export-oriented; it sold an average of roughly 51,500 m^3 per year in extraregional markets. At an annual production volume of roughly 90,000 - 120,000 m^3 of sawnwood, this amounted to an export content of 43 - 57 %. 35.4 % of exports went to the domestic Brazilian market outside the Amazon region, 64.5 % to foreign markets; i.e. the share of all the

Table 40:   Growth of Total Log Production (from Primary Forests and Plantations) according to Regions, 1975-94

	1975	1980	1975-80	1986	1980-86	1991	1986-91	1994	1991-94	1975-91	1975-94
	m³	m³	%	m³	%	m³	%	m³	%	%	%
North	4,534	12,874	23.2	33,085	17.0	32,030	-0.6	49,767	15.8	13.0	13.4
Pará	*3,942*	*11,674*	*24.3*	*19,493*	*8.9*	*29,350*	*8.5*	*46,894*	*16.9*	*13.4*	*13.9*
Northeast	5,256	6,852	5.4	9,499	5.6	7,837	-3.8	8,038	0.8	2.5	2.3
Southeas	14,729	29,081	14.6	18,406	-7.3	22,135	3.8	22,962	1.2	2.6	2.4
South	22,297	26,060	3.2	29,538	2.1	30,007	0.3	46,228	15.5	1.9	3.9
Paraná	*10,575*	*9,777*	*-1.6*	*15,278*	*7.7*	*18,124*	*3.5*	*22,688*	*7.8*	*3.4*	*4.1*
Midwest	2,648	3,172	3.7	3,714	2.7	4,123	2.1	4,904	6.0	2.8	3.3
Brazil	49,465	78,039	9.5	84,474	1.3	95,938	2.6	131,900	11.2	4.2	5.3

Source: IBGE, Produção da extração vegetal e da silvicultura Vol. 9, years 1973-94 and Anuários Estatísticos do IBGE 1971-73, annual geometric growth rates in %

Table 41: Growth of Log Production from Primary Forests according to Regions, 1975-94

	1975 m³	1980 m³	1975-80 %	1986 m³	1980-86 %	1991 m³	1986-91 %	1994 m³	1991-94 %	1975-91 %	1975-94 %
North	4,534	11,483	20.4	32,008	18.6	30,755	-0.8	47,159	15.3	12.7	7.7
Pará	*3,942*	*10,284*	*21.1*	*18,416*	*10.2*	*28,370*	*9.0*	*44,539*	*16.2*	*13.1*	*8.0*
Northeast	5,210	6,600	4.8	8,637	4.6	6,985	-4.2	5,756	-6.2	1.8	-0.7
Southeast	2,211	1,224	-11.2	1,607	4.6	558	-19.1	393	-11.0	-8.2	-5.8
South	16,924	13,743	-4.1	8,486	-7.7	4,416	-12.2	4,779	2.7	-8.1	-5.4
Paraná	*8,627*	*5,586*	*-8.3*	*4,259*	*-4.4*	*2,849*	*-7.7*	*3,173*	*3.7*	*-6.7*	*-2.9*
Midwest	2,648	3,161	3.6	3,701	2.7	3,519	-1.0	4,439	8.0	1.8	1.8
Brazil	31,528	36,212	2.8	44,670	3.6	46,233	0.7	62,527	10.6	2.4	2.9

Quelle: IBGE, Produção da extração vegetal e da silvicultura Vol. 9, years 1973-94 and Anuários Estatísticos do IBGE 1971-73, annual geometric growth rates in %

320 ACTION PATTERNS OF THE TROPICAL TIMBER INDUSTRY

Table 42: Growth of Log Production from Plantations according to Regions, 1975-94

	1975	1980	1975-80	1986	1980-86	1991	1986-91	1994	1991-94	1975-91	1975-94
	m³	m³	%	m³	%	m³	%	m³	%	%	%
North	0	1,391	n.d.	1,077	-4.2	1,275	3.4	2,608	26.9	n.d.	3.4
Pará	*0*	*1,391*	*n.d.*	*1,077*	*-4.2*	*980*	*-1.9*	*2,355*	*33.9*	*n.d.*	*2.8*
Northeast	46	251	40.4	862	22.8	852	-0.2	2,282	38.9	20.0	12.3
Southeast	12,518	27,857	17.3	16,799	-8.1	21,577	5.1	22,569	1.5	3.5	-1.1
South	5,373	12,317	18.0	21,052	9.3	25,591	4.0	41,449	17.4	10.2	6.6
Paraná	*1,948*	*4,191*	*16.6*	*11,019*	*17.5*	*15,275*	*6.7*	*19,515*	*8.5*	*13.7*	*8.4*
Midwest	0	11		13	2.8	604	115.5	465	-8.3	n.d.	21.8
Brazil	17,937	41,827	18.5	39,804	-0.8	49,705	4.5	69,373	11.8	6.6	2.7

Source: IBGE, Produção da extração vegetal e da silvicultura Vol. 9, years 1973-94 and Anuários Estatísticos do IBGE 1971-73, annual geometric growth rates in %

timber produced that was sold abroad was between 28 and 37 %. It accounted for less than 5 % of overall Brazilian timber exports.

The quantities supplied fluctuated considerably from year to year; between 10,700 and 30,000 m^3 for the domestic market and between 13,500 and 60,400 m^3 for foreign markets.

As far as the domestic market is concerned, different states of the northeast were the most important purchasers of Pará's timber, above all for use as construction timber; these states purchased an average of 74 % of the timber exported within Brazil (13,500 m^3). Rio de Janeiro, São Paulo, and Minas Gerais absorbed an average of 25.8 %, chiefly decorative and furniture wood (4,700 m^3). On the whole Pará's sales in these markets contained 64 % sawnwood for the construction industry and 20 % sawnwood for the furniture industry .

The foreign sales markets[37] were heterogeneous:

–   Portugal, with its 14 % of exports, was the most important and constant sales market, though at that time it showed no signs of dynamic growth; this market demanded only selected, high-quality logs of a limited number of species (sucupira, macacaúba), though it paid a preferential price 25 % above the world-market level; the same went for sawnwood.

–   The US was a sharply fluctuating market, but one that absorbed constantly growing quantities of virola (sawnwood and rotary-cut veneer); this market was difficult to serve because of the high demands it placed in terms of the quality and aesthetics of the timber it imported.

–   In Europe (except Portugal) it was possible to market more species, and smaller deliveries were also accepted, though here, too, there were higher quality standards. Germany, the UK, and the Netherlands were the most constant customers.

On the whole some 16 species were exported; the only new species that had consolidated its position was virola. Most firms that supplied the traditional export markets in Portugal and the south of Brazil did nothing to change the spectrum of the species marketed, while new firms, above all those that processed virola for the North American market, were actively looking for other species with properties resembling those of this pale, soft wood.

The sales prices exerted no clear-cut pressure in the direction of a higher degree of processing; they instead tended to intensify the search for precious woods that could be sold at high prices as logs or sawnwood (Knowles 1971, pp. 60 ff.). In 1969 the average price for a cubic meter of durable construction timber was US$ 54 and for furniture wood US$ 108. The highest prices for logs were US$ 85 for jacarandá do Pará and muiracatiara. One m^3 of sawnwood of these two species commanded US$ 139; a cubic meter of mahogany sawnwood commanded a price of US$ 120. To compare: a cubic meter of virola stemwood cost only US$ 21, in the form of sawnwood US$ 29,84, in the form of veneer US$ 44, and in the form of plywood US$ 117. The advantage of processing virola into veneer or plywood was thus to be sought in the effects to scale of mass production, which ran up against natural limitations with e.g. mahogany extraction because of the great isolation of and distance between individuals.

7.4.2   The 1970s and 1980s

At the beginning of the 1970s the export orientation of Pará's timber industry had grown as compared with 1962: according to empirical studies by Bruce (1976), in 1972 61 % of the timber produced was exported, 28.9 % sold in local markets, and only 10.2 % marketed outside the Amazon region. Pará then had a share of 90.4 % of Amazon timber exports and 75.1 % of Amazon sales in the national market (Bruce 1976, pp. 41 – 54).

The growth in exports was due to the rapid increase of exports of logs and plywood. The former had increased fivefold by 1972 as compared with 1966, the latter tenfold (see Table 43).

Foreign markets were supplied with a volume of 502,670 m^3 in 1972, the local market receiving 237,930 m^3 and the national market 84,090 m^3; roughly 42,000 m^3 went to the northeast and 33,600 m^3 to São Paulo and Rio de Janeiro. This meant that the quantities sold had increased more than tenfold.

According to Brazilian foreign-trade statistics, the Amazon region's shares of Brazil's timber exports between 1966 and 1972 had increased for logs and sawnwood; as far as veneers and plywood are concerned, however, the Amazon region's shares had declined in spite of sharp growth in absolute terms.

Table 43: Share of Amazonia in Brazilian Timber Exports, 1966-72				
	1966		1972	
	t	%	t	%
Logs	21,251	38.4	107,923	92.3
Sawnwood	24,318	46.9	80,000	57.7
Veneer	7,668	80.4	20,562	70.9
Plywood	557	91.0	10,000	54.4
Source: SERETE (1973), pp. IV.149 - IV.154				

The sawmills had taken up a specialization pattern involving concentration on only one of these submarkets, with 65 % of these sawmills supplying only one market. On the whole the local market was the dominant market for 50 % of sawmills, and in view of the high export content this figure clearly shows that these must for the most part have been small sawmills. Only 24 % of them focused exclusively on export, 11 and 7 %, respectively, served the local or national market in addition to foreign markets. Only 6 % of sawmills served all three markets.

In 1972 64 % of the output of plywood and veneer factories went into exports, 29 % to the local market, and 8.3 % to the national market, above all to the states in the southeast.

This development casts light on the background of the export ban on logs: between 1968 and 1972 the Brazilian economy was in a growth phase that was sustained even following the first oil-price shock; under these conditions firms could anticipate growing demand for timber from the construction and furniture industries.[38] To satisfy this demand, the flows of goods had to be rechanneled from foreign markets to domestic markets in the southeast and south. The expansion dynamics of the timber industry in the Amazon region was so great in the early

1970s that the logs accumulating due to the export ban could easily be absorbed by it (Bruce 1976, p. 67).

Expansion of the road network had created the conditions required to redirect goods to the domestic market; while in 1962 nearly the entire timber output sold extraregionally had to be transported by ship, 10 years later 76 % of sawnwood deliveries for the national market left Belém by truck (Knowles 1965, p. 93; Bruce 1976, p. 45).

Mercado's study (1980) points to the effects of the log export ban: in 1978 the share of Amazon sawnwood exports had declined drastically. Only 12 % of output was exported; 55 % was sold in other regions of Brazil, and 33 % was sold in local markets of the Amazon region. In Pará, which, with its 2.6 million m^3, produced over half of the Amazon region's sawnwood (4 million m^3), production for the national market was dominant (1.66 million m^3); at the same time Pará supplied 268,000 m^3 of sawnwood for export, half of all the sawnwood exported (479,000 m^3) (Mercado 1980, p. 65 f.). On the national market, the northeast (43 %) and the southeast (40 %) were the most important customers.

In the plywood industry the sales structure had also changed radically, probably on account of the strong domestic demand: instead of 64 %, only 20 % went into exports, the national markets absorbed 71 % (previously 8.3 %), and local markets 9 %. The most important national markets were São Paulo and Rio de Janeiro; abroad it was the UK (55 % of exports) and the Netherlands (24 %) that imported plywood for their construction industries and for furniture production (Mercado 1980, pp. 69 f.).

The case was different in the veneer industry: 89 % of rotary-cut veneer was exported, mainly to the US (72 %) and Europe. The reason for this pronounced export orientation was that there were only a limited number of factories and these were for the most part subsidiaries of foreign corporations, and their output was either marketed worldwide by the parent corporation or further processed into manufacture plywood. 56 % of the sliced veneer used by the furniture industry as well as to produce radio and television housings were exported, mainly to Spain, the UK, and Venezuela.

The marketing organization was not particularly well developed, since, as in the 1960s, most sawmills produced on order (in 1978 this was true of 85 % of sales; Mercado 1980, p. 53) on the basis of delivery terms coordinated individually with every customer. This is why production was not geared to internationally valid product standards, a fact which further hobbled the growth of exports. Still, the producers indicated having no marketing problems (Bruce 1976, pp. 9, 54; Mercado 1980, p. 52).

The middlemen for the national sales markets were wholesalers and brokers; the brokers arranged for sales, receiving in return a commission of 5 - 10 %, depending on whether or not they collected the sum due from the transaction.

Exports were brokered mainly by foreign importers, who got directly in touch with the sawmills. A second approach to the world market was mediated by foreign brokers who resided in Belém and monitored production on behalf of importers, classified the sawnwood, and arranged for delivery. Only large sawmills were able to directly approach foreign markets and themselves transact exports (Mercado 1980, pp. 68 f.).

A total of 44 species were exported (see Table A-29 in the Appendix), though eight species accounted for 90 % of the volume of exports (virola, mahogany, and andiroba alone accounting for 83 %). In local markets it was a total of 39 species that accounted for 90 % of sales. There are no data on the species composition of exports immediately following the export ban on logs.

It is generally assumed for the 1980s that some 90 % of Amazon timber was sold in the domestic market; 88 % of the Amazon region's timber exports stemmed from Pará. In Pará itself the export content was probably higher; an empirical study conducted in 1988 on 71 firms around Santarém and in Belém came up with an export content of 43 %. Even factories with an annual output between 500 and 2,500 m^3 of sawnwood had an average export share of 55 %. According to this study, the national market absorbed a total of 48 % of output, the regional market 2 %, and the local market 7 % (Ros-Tonen 1993, pp. 173 - 177). The southeast and the northeast had remained the most important markets.

Vantomme and Peixoto (1985) estimate that in the mid-1980s some 75 % of Brazil's sawnwood exports, 86 % of veneer exports, and roughly 42 % of plywood exports stemmed from the Amazon region.

At least in the sawnwood and veneer segments, the relatively pronounced outward orientation of the timber industry was directly linked with specialization in mahogany and virola; it was mainly these two species that succeeded in competing with other suppliers of tropical timber. The spectrum of species markets abroad generally continued to narrow: mahogany (45 %) and virola (25 %) represented over two thirds of exports, other important species included jatobá (8.4 %), pau amarelo (5.4 %), and andiroba (3.6 %). 94.4 % of exports were covered by ten species (Ros-Tonen 1993, p. 181). According to AIMEX, the most important sales markets for sawnwood were the US (38 %) and the UK (21 %), northern Europe (9.5 %) and the Caribbean islands (7.6 %); 92 % of veneers were exported to the US; 42.4 % of plywood went to the Caribbean, 29 % to the UK, 21 % to the US, and 8 % to Europe.

7.5   The Model for the Development of the Timber Sector

In the 1960s the FAO together with SUDAM worked out a model for the development of the timber sector which fits into the general modernization strategy for the region in the framework of import-substituting industrialization. In the 30 years that followed, this model has been adapted to the changing state of the art of forestry and the new economic framework conditions Although SUDAM's department of natural resources always emphasized the economic potential of the Amazon region's forest resources, it never succeeded in prioritizing this sector. Apart from infrastructure expansion, and due to the tendency to channel subsidies into large operations, it was for decades big cattle ranches, mining, and settlement of foreign assembly plants in the customs-free production zone in Manaus that were given precedence. The low level of subsidies granted for investments in the timber industry were concentrated on large operations of foreign and south-Brazilian provenance; a promotion strategy geared to the existing structural characteristics of the sector (decentralized small-scale production structure) was never developed.

The following outline of the historical development models for forestry and the timber industry is intended to serve to reconstruct learning processes in the institutions concerned with R&D planning. We find here that the perception of the sector has clearly changed and that various innovations have been proposed, though the latter were only partly relevant to the action patterns predominant in business practice.

7.5.1   The 1960s

SUDAM's first five-year plan (1967-72) perfectly exemplified the perception of problems dominant in the 1960s: the underdevelopment of the Amazon region was to be overcome by defining growth poles, exploring natural resources, and encouraging the immigration of qualified persons as well as by means of a technical, scientific, and entrepreneurial exchange with Brazil's south and the rest of the world. The goal was to modernize farming and ranching and to rationalize the economy of extraction by means of domestication, genetic improvement, and cultivation of products otherwise extracted.[39]

There were two competing models in the field of forestry:

- On the one hand the idea was to build up integrated industrial complexes (above all in the field of pulp production), promote the rational cultivation of the most valuable native species in deforested areas, and prepare forestry-related and economic studies on the profitability of and reasonable sites for the timber industry (SUDAM 1967, p. 102);

- on the other hand there were plans to locate small and medium-scale firms here that would further process local raw materials and create jobs (SUDAM 1967, pp. 47 f., 146).

The first model prevailed in the documents published later as well as in actual promotion policies. It rested on two pillars (See Heinsdijk 1966; Heinsdijk and Bastos 1963; Pandolfo 1969):

–   technical modernization of logging, transportation, and processing, including the required investments in infrastructure (above all power supply and road construction);
–   introduction of a rational utilization of forest resources with the aid of forest-tending measures geared to gradually transforming the heterogeneous Amazon rainforest into a more homogeneous commercially utilizable forest made up of stands of marketable species. Although the initial idea was to create plantations with native species, the dominant notion was to "domesticate" the natural forest.

In the FAO's opinion the way to safeguard timber production over the long term was to create forest-conservation areas in the Amazon region in which private firms could acquire large areas for long-term forestry use. The remaining stands of the valuable Atlantic coast forest in Espírito Santo and Bahia were to be sustainably managed, with reforestation receiving subsidies in the south.

Clara Pandolfo, head of SUDAM's department of natural resources from the 1970s until 1992, regarded the introduction of a rational forest management as the *conditio sine qua non* for any modernization of the timber sector. In her opinion, however, the domestic entrepreneurs were the least suited persons for the job in that they had always exploited the Amazon region's timber resources with an eye to short-term profits, an approach that made use of primitive destructive techniques, *"without creating the conditions for a solid and durable industrial structure."* The perennial rise and fall of even large-scale sawmills in Pará is, she noted, easy to explain: the cyclical course of business development is the *"natural fate of any large company based on extraction"* that deployed primitive and outdated technologies, had no reasonable management, and was forced to come to terms with high production costs stemming from an uncertain, expensive, and disorganized supply of raw materials (Pandolfo 1969, pp. 95, 97).[40]

In Pandolfo's view, any rational forest management would entail relocating firms in the forests to be utilized in order there to arrive at an integrated exploitation and further processing of all species encountered in forest management. The creation of such vertically integrated industrial complexes was to be made possible by foreign investors and SU-

DAM's investment incentives. These complexes were to process first-quality logs into veneers and plywood, the remaining logs into sawnwood, while the sawmill waste and the low-quality wood accumulated in connection with forest-tending measures was to be processed into particle board; these products were then to be used to manufacture furniture, doors, and windows. This output of plywood and particle board would, she argued, make the Amazon region into the most innovative and dynamic segment of the timber industry, thus triggering in the regional economy strong growth and modernization effects. These industrial complexes would, the argument continued, also induce great demand for workers in the fields of forest-tending and industrial processing; this would make it possible for stable settlements to emerge in the interior of the Amazon region that would offer people an alternative to slash-and-burn agriculture.[41] This model neglected the competitive disadvantages that would have resulted from great distances from sales markets, though.

A different, more radical variant of the integrated industrial complex that was developed by the FAO mission at the end of the 1950s set its sights chiefly on pulp production (SUDAM 1973b, pp. 437 f., and 1969). The forestry ideal behind this model was the extraction of a maximum of timber per hectare; this was to entail various processing forms, adapted to the mechanical properties of the species, producing sawnwood, plywood, and pulp. Pulp production was seen as particularly well suited to finance logging for the production of sawnwood and plywood in that it required large quantities of timber. Mechanization, i.e. an enormous boost in the productivity of logging, and the introduction of modern forestry techniques would have been the precondition for any integrated timber-processing of this type. Since, the FAO argued, the natural regeneration of forests was still unexplored, the latter should be replaced by commercially utilized forests of native species, eliminating the noncommercial species. To promote the creation of these commercial forests, the development of a pulp industry was to be given foremost priority.

At the end of the 1960s there was great optimism at SUDAM; as regards the chances of achieving a technological modernization of the production structures in the Amazon region with the aid of big foreign investors and generous tax incentives (50 % reduction of the income tax, exemption of imports of capital goods from the import tax) and subsidies. *"It is perceptible that a new entrepreneurial mentality is dominant in the region, engendering adventurous new initiatives that entail the introduction of more modern and profitable technologies."* (Pandolfo 1969, p. 104)

This optimism was based in the first place on an increase in investment in the region:[42]

–   the location of two large foreign corporations and the announce-ment of the location of a further firm, both of which were active in the production of veneers and plywood, were interpreted as harbin-gers of a major wave of investment that was generally anticipated in view of the growing consumption of tropical timber in the in-dustrialized countries and the dwindling timber resources in Africa;

–   furthermore, industrialists from the south of Brazil announced a number of investment projects in the Amazon region, the most speculative of which was the creation of a large complex that was to produce annually 45,000 m^3 of sawnwood, 6,000 m^3 of sliced veneer, and 27,000 m^3 of particle board.

In the second place, the big investment projects were as a rule linked to the purchase of large forest areas for which forest-management plans had to be prepared. Apparently confidence in the superior rationality of foreign investors was so great that there was no doubt that these plans would be implemented.

In subsequent years, however, it turned out that none of the major in-vestment projects was to prove to be the realization of the "integrated industrial complex" that SUDAM and the FAO had envisioned in the 1960s as a means of optimally utilizing a maximum of the species that occur in the region.

The Institutional Framework Conditions

In 1965 Brazil's forest legislation was modernized by adapting the old forest statute of 1934 to the new objectives and conditions (development of a modern pulp industry; reforestation in the south and development of new forest areas in the Amazon region as a means of safeguarding supplies of raw materials). At the same time in 1967 the Institute for Forestry Development (IBDF - *Instituto Brasileiro do Desenvolvimento Florestal*) was founded by merging the *Instituto do Pinho*, founded in 1941, and the *Departmento dos Recursos Renováveis*, founded in 1962.[43] Furthermore, in 1968 an institute for forestry research was founded (IPEF - *Instituto de Pesquisas Florestais*) which operated mainly on private funds and was geared primarily to the interests of the expanding pulp industry. The IPEF was concerned above all with the management and genetic improvement of eucalyptus plantations (Jorge 1995, p. 5).

IBDF was responsible for formulating forest policy as well as for directing, coordinating, and carrying out measures aimed at rationally utilizing, protecting, and conserving renewable natural resources and promoting forestry (Statute no. 289, Feb. 28, 1967). IBDF was also responsible for supervising logging and regulating the timber industry as well as the trade in timber products. In the Amazon region IBDF largely restricted its activities to collecting export taxes that had fallen due.

7.5.2   The 1970s

While SUDAM assumed at the end of the 1960s that attracting and locating big foreign corporations would contribute to modernizing and expanding timber-processing, introducing rational forestry practices and modern methods of business management, and diffusing a more entrepreneurial mentality, in the 1970s it focused on more concrete measures aimed at providing forestry and the timber industry with a "modern" base: propagation of the mechanization of all phases of production (logging, transportation, processing) and the call for a reformed forest policy that would pursue ecological, economic, and social development goals (Almeida 1978; Pandolfo 1972, 1974, 1978).

SUDAM had in mind a complex program that could use modernization of production and forest management both to increase the productivity of the timber industry and to safeguard and enhance the productive potential of forests. SUDAM's perception of the problem was at that time shaped by the following assumptions:

–   measures aimed at developing and integrating the Amazon region would lead to a rapid settlement of the region, and this in turn would threaten the continued existence of extensive forested areas;

–   the growing international demand for tropical timber would heighten the pressure on forest reserves;

–   forest protection could work only if protective ecological measures were supplemented by strategies of economic utilization;

–   only through the import of foreign know-how and by putting forest use on a new footing (concessions instead of private ownership) that provides the public sector with better control options would it be possible to modernize the mentality of the Brazilian entrepreneurs in the timber industry.

Mechanization

SUDAM's mechanization program mainly started out with logging and transportation. Rational forest-management and reforestation programs, though, were neither supported nor monitored and controlled. The obvious question as to what consequences mechanization, with the heightened logging and processing volumes it entails, would have without any forestry measures designed to safeguard permanent forest stands was not taken into consideration.

The goal of mechanization was to lower the high timber losses associated with manual logging and to increase labor productivity: while manual logging in a *terra firme* forest could produce 0.5 m^3 of timber per man-day, it was possible to produce 17 m^3 per man-day with a power saw and manual transportation and 50 m^3 per man-day with a power saw and a skidder (SUDAM 1973a, pp. 4 f.).[44]

The bias of these modernization proposals towards the hardware involved implies a complete neglect of the planning and organizational aspects of rational logging: there was no reference to the need to prepare forest inventories as a means of planning the first and subsequent felling cycles, to mark the trees to be felled as well as those to remain standing, to carefully prepare skid roads and camp sites in the forest, to plan the felling direction, or to remove the vines, which can take down other trees, causing a chain reaction and leading to an undesirably large break in the forest canopy. The failure to take these measures into account, today a core component of the rules of low-impact logging (LIL), led to a situation in which the increase of the logging volume per unit of time and the enlargement of the area accessible for logging at the same time enormously intensified the destructive power of logging.

Increasing the techno-organizational level of processing was not actively advanced by SUDAM itself. This was instead implicitly regarded as a component of entrepreneurial competence, even though, beside a few modern factories, the sawmill sector consisted of small and relatively unproductive companies.

Forestry Reform

The demands for forestry reforms aimed for demarcation of forest-use zones in which concessions were to be created, introduction of forestry methods geared to a "rational exploitation" of forest resources, and enforcement of the obligation to reforest.

Establishing concessions in forests marked for permanent forestry use was intended to place the timber industry on a foundation sound in forestry terms. This implicitly acknowledged not only that the small and medium-size timber-processing firms largely covered their timber needs from illegal sources but also that the large factories relied wholly on a system of small independent suppliers and middlemen.[45]

Supplies of raw materials were hampered by great fluctuations due to seasonal factors; this and the uncertain future supply of logs prevented most companies from fully utilizing or expanding their capacities. The small independent suppliers were not able to raise the investment capital they needed to reap the benefits of mechanized logging and transportation. A modernization-minded firm that wanted to eliminate this bottleneck would – SUDAM argued – have to make a twofold investment: in large forest stands and in heavy machinery for logging and transportation.

Long-term concessions were to provide a remedy in this situation. The holder of the concession was to be responsible for exploring and tending the forest, indeed in some cases even for reforestation measures; these concessions were to entail conditions which the state, as landowner, was to dictate and monitor. Royalties were to be paid for the use of the concession; administrative fees were to be collected to cover the costs of forest administration. In the opinion of the FAO expert who was commissioned by IBDF to prepare an expertise on concessions, this instrument would entail the following benefits (Schmithüsen 1978, pp. 13 f):

— the industry would be able to invest its capital solely in mechanizing logging operations and expanding processing capacities and would not be forced to bind it in acquiring land;

— the government could focus its scarce resources on planning the technical monitoring of the concessions;

— negotiating a concession agreement would offer many possibilities for an active forestry and industrialization policy, since by stipulating conditions on forest management an agreement of this sort could guarantee the long-term availability of a supply of raw materials, stipulate the volume and the type of timber to be cut and processed, and influence the degree of processing on site. Under the conditions of strong demand for tropical timber, investments could be attracted in this way;

— forest utilization in the framework of concessions would facilitate control of annual timber flows, which would be a relatively effective means of adapting roundwood production to the long-term development of processing capacities; this would prevent any rapid migration of the timber industry and contribute to stabilizing rural communities;

— collecting royalties and administrative fees would raise public revenues;

— awarding concessions could reduce the competition for scarce resources and contribute to a regulated development of the industry.

This line of argument had basically two weaknesses which still apply today:

- Owing to the specific conditions encountered in the Amazon region – the existence of publicly owned forests, the interest on the part of settlers to sell logs, and, as e.g. in Rondônia, the practice of handing over land to timber companies free of charge – it often proved unnecessary to purchase land to procure timber; all that was required was mechanization of logging operations to make progress in opening up the *terra firme* forests. This meant that there was no essential economic incentive to acquire concessions.

- The risk that the holder of a concession might overexploit forest resources because the state failed to meet its monitoring duties was quite large in view of the general institutional weaknesses in the Amazon region.

Owing to the economic risks of concession agreements, the report referred to them as risk contracts, thus drawing a parallel to the ongoing debate on the modalities of prospecting and exploiting oil reserves, which was to be permitted on the basis of risk contracts between the state oil enterprise Petrobrás and foreign investors. This and the justified doubts as to the ability and willingness of IBDF to fulfill its control duties led to a sharp controversy in which the government was accused of trying to give the Amazon region's forest resources away to foreigners; this was enough to thwart the concession idea.[46]

A similarly controversial debate had been triggered in 1974 by the proposal made by Clara Pandolfo, the head of SUDAM's natural resources department, to demarcate so-called production forests (*florestas de rendimento*) that would be managed by private firms in the form of joint ventures with the state as forest owner. (Schmithüsen's concession proposal took over the reasons advanced for Pandolfo's production forests, though it modified the economic-legal modalities of utilization.) Pandolfo had been able to observe the expansion of the timber industry in the Amazon region since the 1950s and was familiar with the shortcomings of the present system, and above all the risk inherent, first, in any unregulated and destructive logging process and, second, in the fact that the industrial processing of timber (and thus also investments) continued to be concentrated in the south, so that there were in the north no incentives to maintain the region's only locational advantage (supplies of raw materials) over the long term and develop it by means of further industrialization and linkage effects.

The explicit openness of both concepts (Pandolfo's and Schmithüsen's) for foreign corporations was enough to mobilize the critics of the nationalist wing, who in the 1960s had set up a parliamentary fact-finding commission on foreign activities in the Amazon region.[47] The core of this criticism, however, was targeted at the model of the big industrial corporation as the agent of development; this was countered by a proposal to set up a program which provided for cultivation of precious timber by small and medium farmers who would also receive technical support and sales guarantees.[48]

Pandolfo's ideas, which took on official shape in PDA II (1975-79), were guided by the attempt to interlink ecological, economic, and social goals. The political controversies over the means best suited to the purpose have clouded our view of a program that was, at least in its goal perspective, a progressive one in today's terms. Pandolfo was basically concerned with protecting forest resources from the advancing front of cattle ranches and agricultural settlements; she here argued on two tracks: not only was company modernization to ensure a rational forest utilization, small farmers were also to be settled in special forest-use zones and earn their living with forest-tending and timber-processing on a cooperative basis.[49] Looked at from today's perspective, we would have to note critically that the utilization of nontimber products was not taken into consideration (in Pandolfo's view, far from being capable of development the extraction economy was one of the causes of underdevelopment) and that the approach involved the undifferentiated assumption that large companies were more rational in their use of resources.

In practice Pandolfo fought, in vain and in an unequal struggle, for the recognition of forestry as a sector important in both economic and ecological terms. Her call for instruments of a long-term land-use planning (economic-ecological zoning, demarcation of conservation and forest-use zones) and a research geared to forest utilization has been reiterated and justified again and again throughout the decades, albeit without attaining any relevance in policy. Her most powerful opponent was the São Paulo federation of entrepreneurs, which had invested in big cattle ranches in the Amazon area and wanted assurances as to the possibility of purchasing further land subsidized by SUDAM. In 1976 Pandolfo had succeeded in having the Amazon council of ministers forbid SUDAM from subsidizing cattle ranches in primary-forest areas. Though nothing came of this ban, it did alarm the big landowners, who had their spokesman Meireles address President Figueiredo, demanding that he declare that the future of the Amazon region belonged to ranching, not forestry. Aside from the establishment of some national parks and reservations for indigenous peoples, Meireles' vision of the Amazon region was committed to a release of the "remaining area" for agriculture and ranching; *"he wanted to convert the whole of the Amazon region into a huge* fazenda.*"[50]* An interministerial working group appointed in 1979 by Brazil's minister of internal affairs was unable to do much to change this state of affairs when it spoke out in favor of a forest policy contra ranching interests and proposed reviving the 1974 Pandolfo proposal to award concessions in demarcated forest-use zones.

Despite the negative public response to the idea of concessions as well as the setbacks experienced in seeking to introduce a forest policy for the Amazon region, at the end of the 1970s IBDF worked out a forest-management plan for the only forest-use zone demarcated in Pará, the Floresta Nacional de Tapajós south of Santarém, which was intended to be exploited by private firms in the framework of concessions. The plan covered 1,000 ha, but interest in it was limited because the existence of large logging areas that could be worked free of charge or at low costs removed any incentives to accept logging concessions supervised by IBDF and entailing fees (Ros-Tonen 1993, pp. 144 f.). In the 1970s the idea of forest management continued to imply converting the primary forest into a more homogeneous forest with native precious species, though no longer on the basis of clear-felling and subsequent reforestation but by means of enrichment plantings with native species that were expected to induce a gradual transition (Pandolfo 1978).

This notion, which was to be placed on a scientific footing with the aid of tests with enrichment plantings conducted at the experimental station in Curuá-Una, was broadened to include the idea of expanding the spectrum of marketable species. Since the unit costs of logging can be lowered by increasing the number of marketable species cut per ha, research was to focus on the species best suited to processing and modern forestry techniques.

> *"If a broader species mix can contribute to lowering extraction costs and raising the attractiveness of logging while at the same time expanding the access of Amazon species to the national and international markets (in order to mitigate the effects of fluctuations in demand and bottlenecks in raw materials), it will be possible to stimulate greater investments in logging and processing, realize higher profits, increase the stability of the industry, and achieve a broader penetration of the forests."* (Bruce 1976, p. 69)

The reforestation obligation stipulated in the *Código Florestal* was as a rule not complied with, there was no reliable monitoring by IBDF.

> *"A concern for conservation of the forest resource – full utilization of the timber harvested and management of the forest resources to ensure sustained production in perpetuity – is virtually nonexistent."* (Mercado 1980, p. 78)[51]

SUDAM's regulations stipulated that timber-processing firms that applied for tax breaks present forest inventories and forest-management plans for their forests, that they employ forest engineers responsible for implementing the plans, that operations be audited externally on a regular basis, that logging be mechanized, and that bulldozers, trucks, and barges be purchased for the purpose (SUDAM 1973a, pp. 6, 8). The subsequent development of the timber industry sharply contrasts with these stipulations and proves that in practice they have been implemented with a bias toward mechanization but at the expense of forest management, which in practice is nonexistent. Two of these (approved) applications can be seen in SUDAM's library; they show that the application documents contain no statements on the origin of the timber to be processed or on forest-management or reforestation plans.

On the other hand, one of the applicants documented large investments in the mechanization of logging operations, transportation and road-building, and this was in fact the greatest cost factor (See AMAZONEX 1982; Ciprandi 1988).

7.5.3   The 1980s

At the end of the 1980s SUDAM undertook a last major effort to implement its then 14-year-old forest-policy program; since the World Bank was unwilling to finance it, it was doomed to insignificance (SUDAM 1988). One surprising aspect of this proposal was that it continued to proceed on the assumption of a large measure of governance capacity on the part of the state, though this capacity had been visibly curtailed since 1982. For instance, economic-ecological zoning was to make it possible to control the location of investment projects and set up protected areas for biotechnology research. The most important innovation compared with the 1970s was the clear-cut commitment to sustainable forestry; SUDAM here broke in conceptual terms with its former notions that the natural forests could be replaced by plantations or forests with a reduced number of species.

More clear-cut, though isolated, signs were set by the Amazon-related environmental measures undertaken by the Sarney and Collor governments that were designed to show the world that the Brazilian government was not inactive. In April 1989 Sarney launched the *Nossa Natureza* program, which consisted of a number of individual measures that were to be used to stop deforestation due to cattle ranches and to improve the environmental compatibility of mining (obligation to reforest). Timber-using industries were obliged by law to cover their timber needs from natural or planted forests of their own within a limited number of years; firms with low timber needs could meet this obligation by paying a reforestation fee to IBAMA. President Collor's administration initiated the first concerted action of IBAMA, instructing federal police and armed forces to ferret out illegal logging operations, combat forest fires, and destroy illegal landing strips of gold prospectors, above all in the reservation of the Yanomami. This action, which has been followed by others at irregular intervals, was intended to make it plain that the tacit tolerance of illegal and destructive resources appropriation was over, at least at the federal level. The second important measure initiated by the Collor government was to start government-level talks on PPG-7, thus signaling that Brazil was ready to engage in cooperative international measures aimed at protecting the Amazon rainforest.

7.6   Conclusions

Proceeding from a historical reconstruction of the development of the timber industry in Pará since the 1960s, we can work out the development path on the basis of which the present situation of the timber industry emerged and which influences the ability of the firms concerned to respond in an innovative fashion to today's challenges. The beginning of this development path is marked by an initial endowment with material resources and action routines; routines consist of attitudes, views, and action patterns that mirror the de facto validity of the legal and institutional framework conditions in place and the ecological and technological conditions under which available material resources can be utilized profitably. Routines change in individual firms and/or across an entire industry when changes occur that make adjustment appear either worthwhile or inevitable. This initial endowment, in combination with cumulative decisions on action which either remain within the routine or alter it, gives rise to a trajectory or path that defines the framework in which the decisions of the actors are shaped, for routines themselves in turn affect the framework conditions, thus giving shape to the competition between firms. The direction of development of this path or trajectory cannot be inferred immediately from the initial conditions on the basis of universal laws of probability; it instead emerges under specific historical conditions in a specific fashion.

In the 1960s the initial endowment of Pará's timber industry includes:

–   Large forest stands that are relatively difficult to access and have, measured in terms of overall timber reserves, a stock of trees of low commercial value;

- a weakly developed infrastructure with an inadequate power supply and a network of roads and waterways that do little to open up the region.

Its initial endowment with routines includes:

- the view that the more worthwhile forms of land use are agriculture and cattle-ranching, which means that stands of primary forest have to make way for them;
- the view that timber-processing is a temporary economic activity that goes on until the timber supplies are depleted and farming or ranching has become the dominant mode of land use;
- the orientation to a limited number of marketable species (selective logging) as well as to the demand given in markets;
- a techno-organizational level that is as a rule low and finds expression in a low degree of timber-processing, poor product quality, a poor state of machine maintenance, and a low level of willingness to alter processing methods and technologies.[52]

SUDAM's development policy entails a change in the material framework conditions in the timber industry: on the one hand road construction and colonization programs are used to open up access to new forest areas, in particular those in the *terra firme*, in this way increasing the supply of freely accessible timber; migration increases the manpower supply, thus eliminating the – until then most significant – restriction on the massive exploitation of natural resources in the Amazon region. This, on the other hand, increases the size of the timber industry's market, both local and national, in that the region can now be reached via the highway to Brasilia.

The characteristic feature of the 1970s is the enormous dynamics of demand, which invariably grows faster than the supply. This means that the producers always find buyers for their products, both at home and abroad. Facilitation of logging operations leads to a sharp rise in the number of timber-processing companies, an increase in roundwood production, and an increase of exports, which consist practically exclusively of logs; the export content rises from roughly a third in 1962 to two thirds ten years later. Under these conditions no reason is seen to alter the basic pattern of logging and processing; only incremental innovations such as power saws, tractors, bulldozers, and trucks are introduced with an eye to raising labor productivity and satisfying growing demand.

But not even power saws are introduced everywhere: in the *várzea* forests axes are still in use up to the 1980s and 1990s: *"it makes no sense for the loggers in the várzea to substitute the axe for a chain-saw (because) the axe is multifunctional. It is, for instance, also used as a hand-grip for the lumbermen when the logs are floated off the forest and as a hammer to fasten the pins through which the steel cables (of the raft) run. Moreover, it is useless to increase the productivity of felling if the productivity in log transportation cannot also be raised."* (Ros-Tonen 1993, p. 78) The only way that transportation productivity could have been increased significantly would have been by acquiring large barges.

The instrument of competition in the market is not product or price differentiation but the ability to supply given, specified quantities of timber. Stable, organized supply relations are nonexistent; the suppliers look to customers with the greatest willingness to pay.

The 1974 export ban on logs compels the majority of firms to look to the domestic market, i.e. to the traditional markets in the northeast, southeast and south of the country: the lower quality of the sawnwood into which the unexportable logs are now processed rules out sales abroad for most of the companies involved. The growth of demand in the domestic markets is, however, so great as to absorb the overall output; no drastic decline in the number of companies is noted in Pará following the ban on log exports. The techno-organizational learning process into which these companies were forced was not demanding.

The typical Pará sawmill, with its annual output of some 4,200 m³ of sawnwood, one band saw, and 16 workers, emerges in this way in the 1970s. The monetary returns per worker will change only slightly in the course of the coming 20 years.

"Evidence of inefficiencies in timber production and marketing is readily apparent, but the penalty for such inefficiencies is

> *not apparent Timber production in the Amazon region is ex-*
> *panding rapidly. There is a market for all that can be pro-*
> *duced. Product prices are relatively high; stumpage is avail-*
> *able free or at nominal cost; labor costs are still generally*
> *low; and profits are high. Under such circumstances, one can-*
> *not expect to find much concern with matters of efficiency."*
> (Mercado 1980, p. 73)

In the 1980s the framework conditions again change: domestic demand declines due to recession and declining real incomes; high inflation and uncertain economic prospects stimulate flight into tangible assets, above all real estate, as well as into short-term speculative investments. The dynamics of the timber industry in this decade rests on two segments:

– Some firms specialize in exploiting the mahogany reserves, above all for exports. Since this is the Amazon region's most valuable timber, one that can command a cubic-meter price of US$ 900 or 1,000, efforts are focused, as in the period prior to the export ban on logs, on increasing logging productivity (i.e. increasing the volume of timber) and not on improving efficiency in processing logs into sawnwood.

– Some other firms continue to produce sawnwood for the domestic construction industry, investing their returns in real estate and financial assets with the goal of opting out of the industry in a few years.

The industry had been used to high inflation rates since the 1960s: even before various indexing mechanisms were introduced in 1969 with the aim of constantly adjusting prices, entrepreneurs in Pará had safeguarded themselves against inflationary losses by means of high markups. Cost calculations were difficult under the conditions of high inflation, and in any case unnecessary because of the traditional markups and the certain prospects of sales. In the 1980s this behavior was intensified by accelerating inflation and abrupt changes in monetary and currency policy. This removed any economic incentives to raise efficiency and labor productivity that would otherwise have made themselves felt at older locations when the supply of raw materials began to decline in the 1980s, directing investments into processing instead of into logging.

The mahogany boom and the certainty of finding large timber reserves in the Amazon region continue to attract firms from the south and southeast of the country to Pará, to the new "timber frontier."

> *"Not only is the amount of timber superficially limitless, but it is available for the taking. Over 90 percent of the forests is in public ownership, but government exercises little control over forest exploitation."* (Mercado 1980, p. 78)

Although forest legislation provides stipulations on forest utilization that would have led to artificial scarcity, the lack of institutional controls for enforcing these stipulations created a situation in which the innovation potential of entrepreneurs in the 1980s and 1990s is geared to safeguarding the supply of raw materials by building illegal roads and exploiting areas settled by indigenous peoples. The latter practice takes on different forms: businessmen often decoy indigenous groups with regular deliveries of food, tools, and liquor, which are deposited at certain places and exchanged for logging rights. In other cases the businessmen simply invade these protected areas, exploring and exploiting the stands of mahogany and other species. In still other cases there are agreements that open up sources of monetary income for the indigenous groups. When the gold rush in the inaccessible areas of Pará's southwest had ended, the small aircraft that had been used to fly gold prospectors into the forest and to supply them from the air were used to transport and supply logging teams.

At the end of the 1980s there are signs of an incipient depletion of the forests around the centers of the timber industry. Big landowners in Paragominas sell logging rights for their forest reserves to sawmills and in this way finance the intensification of cattle-ranching. The species composition of exports changes; the firms begin to specialize in new species that were regarded until then as unsellable or less interesting, e.g. tauari. In this situation the firms choose, as they did following the export ban on logs, the path of least resistance and retain their specialization in a limited number of species instead of aiming at a higher number of species per company as a means of dispersing their risk. This means retaining the extremely selective pattern of forest use, which makes it difficult to look to a new long-term means of securing the supply of raw materials.

The *Plano Real* in 1994 alters the macroeconomic conditions; monetary stability, a high-interest policy since the spring of 1995, and the high exchange rate throw the timber industry's productivity gap into relief. The sector is in serious crisis; a concentration process sets in. Various ways out of the crisis begin to emerge:

– some entrepreneurs close up shop and leave the industry; the more successful of them sell to foreign investors;

– a more or less undefined share of entrepreneurs relocates in areas with scarcely developed forests;

– a small percentage resolves to invest in new machinery and the processing of products;

– exports are increasingly concentrated on the subsidiaries of large foreign timber-trading corporations, because direct exports are made more difficult under the conditions of monetary scarcity.

The second way out – relocation – amounts to an attempt to abide by the transmitted development trajectory; it is still not clear how many entrepreneurs will make this attempt.

The framework conditions have become more difficult, as the following example illustrates: In 1995 the federation of the Paragominas timber industry was invited by the government of the state of Amazonas to inspect the Itacoatiara site; Itacoatiara is surrounded by large forest areas and is situated three hours by car from Manaus on the Amazon in the vicinity of the delta of the Rio Madeira, an Amazon tributary flowing in from the south. The town already has two big plywood factories, two smaller-scale timber-processing companies, and a large sawmill, the MIL Madeireira.[53] The Amazon government had decided to build up a center of the timber industry here and to provide a training center for skilled workers toward that end.

The Paragominas entrepreneurs found in Itacoatiara a situation that did not match the action patterns familiar to them from Pará:

−   The Amazon government promised tax breaks, though it conditioned them on strict compliance with legal regulations on forest utilization, specifying as a model the computer-controlled forest-management system of MIL Madeireira;[54]

−   this forest-management system is based on the use of a maximum of 65 species; in practice somewhere between 32 and 47 species are logged yearly; the majority of Paragominas entrepreneurs regards it as wholly impossible to market this number of species;

−   a good part of the forests around Itacoatiara are in the *várzea,* which means that the logs must be transported in boats or in the form of rafts; the Paragominas entrepreneurs, however, were accustomed to exploiting *terra firme* forests, with road transportation by truck, and find this change too difficult to master;

−   finally, Itacoatiara's location required a far more marked export orientation, since the domestic markets can be served only by air or boat along the Rio Madeira to Mato Grosso, where the road network begins, and this is relatively expensive or requires large quantities to be profitable.[55]

The Paragominas entrepreneurs were unable to make much of what they found here: they neither saw the introduction of a planned forest utilization as feasible nor were they able to concentrate wholly on world-market-quality sawnwood or to build up plants with capacities that would have justified transportation by barge. An additional factor was that the government of Pará was already offering generous subsidies for the cultivation of soybeans and maize in Paragominas; this meant that for most entrepreneurs, who are as a rule already big landowners, the time had come to switch into agriculture.

This example shows that there are limits to the continued existence of the traditional timber industry even under the conditions of enormous spatial and material expansion potentials, and that these limits must be sought among entrepreneurial action patterns.

At present there is one possible alternative location in Pará: Altamira on the Transamazônica, which was connected to the power grid in July 1998 and which is adapted to these action patterns; this, the announced

project of paving the Transamazônica, and the forests along the highway, which have until now not been overexploited, constitute the precondition for again realizing here the traditional extensive pattern of the
timber industry (Gazeta Mercantil, June 3, 1998).

All told, the entrepreneurial action pattern in the industry has remained
surprisingly stable between the 1960s and the 1990s.[56] In Pará the response to changes in external conditions has been to undertake minimal
adjustments within the framework of the view that timber-processing is
a "temporary activity." This has meant reinforcing the structures that
have prevented the emergence of a sustainable pattern of resource utilization and company management.

Though logging has been modernized technologically, it has largely
retained the organizational form it had in the 1960s, one which is
geared to the *aviamento* of the extraction economy of the previous
centuries. The purchasers of the products extracted, in this case timber,
advance the procurement costs, often also finance a share of the operating costs of the logging teams (e.g. spare parts or new trucks, power
saws), and have, thanks to their position as creditor, considerable influence on the sales price of the stemwood. Processing firms conduct the
logging operations on their own initiative only when they are very large
companies, the logging areas are relatively close to the sawmill, or
when the species in question is a valuable one like mahogany.

Although most firms formally comply with the provisions of the forest
statute and submit logging plans, their plans are not relevant for actual
forest utilization, neither for firms that purchase timber from third parties nor for firms that log themselves. This irrelevance of the forest-
management rules is closely linked with the low number of species that
can be exploited commercially.

The number of species remained nearly unchanged from 1960 to 1994
(see Table A-29 in the Appendix). While at that time a total of some 40
species were utilized, this figure has now increased to roughly 250,
though fewer than 40 species have been able to hold their own in export
markets. Comparison of the species composition in the 1970s and that
of the 1990s shows that, in contrast to the claims made by the exporter
federation AIMEX, no substantial success has been made in diversifi-

cation. Instead, following the end of the virola and mahogany boom, the old state familiar from the 1970s has again gained sway.

Of the 37 species exported in 1995, 28 (76 %) were already being exported in 1972, so only nine species are actually new. The 28 species that have been present in export markets for at least 26 years have changed as follows in terms of quantities:

–   for 11 species the volume is the same as in 1972;

–   for 14 species the volume has risen, substantially for ten of them (angelim, cedro, ipê, jatobá, tauari, maçaranduba, pau amarelo, piquiá, quaruba, tatajuba); this mirrors the generally larger volume of exports;

–   for 3 species the volume has declined distinctly (mahogany, virola, andiroba).

Of the nine new species, only curupixá has an extraordinarily large volume (50,000 m^3); two have volumes between 12,000 and 13,500 m^3, three between 5,000 and 8,000 m^3, and the rest is lower. This is of course not to rule out later sharp growth of individual species.

The average size and capacity of sawmills has hardly changed between the 1970s and 1990s. As a rule the mills are equipped with one band saw; their annual output is roughly 40 - 50 % below max. capacity. The max. output capacity of a band saw continues to be 4.5 m^3/hour; Bruce (1976) calculated this volume for the 1970s, this figure still applies in the 1990s, according to information given by a Brazilian market leader for band saws at a trade fair for timber-processing machinery in Belém in November of 1997. The average real productivity of a band saw has hardly changed: in 1989 daily output ranged between 18 and 22 m^3; in the 1990s, according to IMAZON data, the figure is 17 m^3/day. This indicates an annual output ranging between 4,300 m^3 and 5,720 m^3 as compared with a max. capacity of 9,360 m^3 (Bruce 1976, p. 21; Ros-Tonen 1993, p. 66).

Another problem is a passive attitude toward processing technologies:

"The problem is not simply a lack of research effort; more importantly, the problem is a lack of adaptation to new tech-

niques and products developed at public research centers."
(Mercado 1980, p. 76)

Only some large plywood firms invest in R&D, above all with an eye to improving and reducing bonding agents, which, apart from stemwood, constitute the most expensive input. Sawmills have wholly abstained from R&D activities aimed at improving products and production processes. This has led to a situation in which their export chances have not been particularly good:

> *"Export lumber is controlled by international grading rules. (But) most sawmill operators are not even aware of them. At the present stage of development, many sawmill operators would be incapable of applying grade standards."* (Mercado 1980, p. 77)

The institutional environment has always been remote from company practice, pursuing abstract modernization ideals instead of analyzing existing firms and their strategies.[57] It is, however, questionable whether improvement proposals developed with an eye to "reality" would have better chances of realization, since the routines themselves are obstacles to increasing techno-organizational levels.

The notion dominant in the 1960s and 1970s was that the timber sector would have to develop on the model of the vertically integrated industrial corporation in order to attain a maximum of efficiency. Mercado noted that *"the general lack of vertical integration as well as the geographic dispersal of the timber products industry lead to inefficient use of wood raw material."* (Mercado 1980, p. 74) The FAO had also looked to the same model in the 1950s and 1960s; it is referred to by Knowles as well as by numerous publications of SUDAM. Even Knowles, who has a good eye for the difficulties facing any economic utilization of the Amazon forest in an age of mass production, clings to the model of the large integrated corporation. The model of efficient, smaller-scale, flexibly producing companies was only to emerge in the post-Fordist era of flexible specialization.

An example for the unrealistic nature of the recommendations on developing the timber industry are those made by Mercado, who proposes increasing capacity utilization, granting company owners cheap short-term loans to prefinance their timber stocks, and thus long-term supply contracts between logging teams, traders, and sawmill owners. Had this proposal been put into practice in the 1980s, it would probably have led to a massive rechanneling of loans to the financial sector, in parallel to the subsidized loans in agriculture, since the returns in the money markets were far higher than those in commodity markets. Long-term supply contracts on stemwood would, it is true, have constituted a condition required to raise company capacities; but capacity expansion does not necessarily mean a sustainably successful firm.

Analysis of the statistical data on average employment and the monetary returns of Pará's timber and furniture industry has shown that these figures differ little from the overall Brazilian data for these industries. Compared with other branches of industry they generally show the lowest figures; these similarities indicate that the limitations found in Pará for an industry on the "natural forest path" apply for the other Brazilian regions as well.

In the 1980s some isolated firms emerged that sought to replace the pattern of extensive expansion with a strategy of intensification (increase of the degree of processing); but these firms were, for three reasons, able neither to survive nor to initiate any process of change in the dominant action pattern:

–   On the one hand the macroeconomic conditions (inflation, recession) presented obstacles to any reorientation at the company level: day-to-day financial management became a *sine qua non*, absorbing a good share of the time available to management for tasks other than the organization of procurement and sales. What we find mirrored here is a lack of professionalization on the part of management.

–   On the other hand the fact that up to the 1990s the traditional pattern of resource utilization and company management could be successfully continued without any major adjustments was construed by entrepreneurs to mean that this action pattern was optimally adapted to regional conditions. Indications of faulty developments in raw-materials procurement and production and/or market signals pointing to the fact that this pattern was exhausted did not make themselves felt because there were no company-level instruments available for the purpose and because the entrepreneurs in any case proceeded on the assumption that their business would continue only for the length of an externally defined, "natural" period of time.

–   Finally, the models and action patterns dominant in the industry encumbered intensification: the entrepreneurial view linked technological modernization to the large vertically integrated corporation which manages everything on its own, from procurement of raw materials to processing and marketing. Even managing these different phases of production required a relatively large administrative apparatus and was very expensive (purchase of machinery, prefinancing roundwood procurement); the difficulties associated with the introduction of new products had to be dealt with in addition to technical problems in timber-processing which led to quality defects and losses. The action pattern in the industry placed obstacles in the way of any development of stable business relationships with stemwood suppliers and the task of maintaining a skilled, stable workforce. Domestic and foreign customers, accustomed to poor quality and unreliable delivery from the Amazon region, had to be convinced to purchase small quantities of processed products from a region that offered no price advantages and caused considerably higher control costs.

It was only in the 1990s that changes began to emerge that offered prospects of diversification and intensification of production: the new economic framework conditions are forcing entrepreneurs to focus less on the monetary dimension and aim for cost reductions and productivity increases. The depletion of the forests, the high costs involved in developing marginal forest areas, and the tightening up of environmental regulations will in the medium term bring about a radical reversal of patterns of resource utilization. At the same time it is growing more difficult to opt out of the industry because of the generally higher demands placed on the management and learning capacities of entrepreneurs, and this means that remaining in the old branch of industry also offers advantages.

Finally, the industry is beginning to see possibilities of specialization that open up chances of intensification even for smaller companies: the large trading companies are developing an interest in improving and diversifying the products in which they deal as a means of defending sales markets and are selectively fostering entrepreneurs who are willing to modernize and are able to focus on improving processing and leave marketing up to the trading firms. At the same time the trading companies mediate contacts with customers so that the suppliers can familiarize themselves with their needs and learn from them, not least in techno-organizational respects.

8   Patterns of Resource Utilization and Foreign Trade: Results of the Study and Conclusions

This chapter will sum up the main results from the preceding four chapters on the ecological foundations of tropical forestry and agriculture, the world market for timber, the advance of the plantation economy, and the development patterns of the tropical-timber industry in Pará (8.1). In a second step, the theoretical implications are discussed (8.2) and, finally, the resulting options for action are presented (8.3).

8.1   Results of the Study

As regards the **ecological preconditions** of any sustainable resource utilization in Pará, a review of recent research results show that both a sustainable forest utilization and a sustainable agriculture are possible if specific local ecological characteristics are known and certain principles are adhered to. In the case of Pará acknowledgement of the fact that there are biophysical limits to the expansion of the economic subsystem need not necessarily imply that the goal must be to maintain stands of primary forest as large as possible;[1] it is equally conceiveable to proceed on the basis of a mixed concept for rural regions. This concept would on the one hand have to set certain conditions for any further conversion of primary forest into areas for agricultural and forestry use and on the other hand conversion would have to be banned in conservation zones and in areas with particularly fragile ecosystems.[2] The consequences that an orientation of this sort might entail are outlined in more detail in Section 8.3.

As regards the world **market for timber**, review of the literature and analysis of FAO statistics show that the market shares of tropical timber are on the decline. This is due in some measure to altered preferences of customers, who prefer paler woods or reject tropical timber because they are unwilling to be part of the destruction of tropical forests. The greater part of this trend can probably better be explained with reference to substitution pressure exerted on tropical timber: this pressure stems both from the use of other materials (PVC, aluminium), especially as far as windows etc. are concerned, and from the process of technical change induced by new reconstituted wood panels, the technical properties of which are in no way inferior to tropical timber. The new, technology-intensive wood panels (mainly MDF and OSB) are manufactured from homogeneous wood fibers and particles stemming from sawmill waste and logs. The basic wood material increasingly stems from plantations that are being created in new locations in Europe (Spain, Portugal) and in the southern hemisphere (New Zealand, South Africa, Chile, the south and southeast of Brazil), where they encounter propitious natural growing conditions. The timber output of these plantations can be both planned and artificially enhanced, and their unit production costs are lower and production times shorter.[3] The costs per cubic meter of eucalyptus and pine are lower than the production costs of tropical timber because harvesting work can be done by machine and the distances to factories or ports are as a rule short.

As regards the **development pattern of the timber industry in Pará**, the study showed that the entrepreneurial routines in the industry are highly homogeneous and have been stable since the 1960s. This homogeneity and stability can be explained by the fact that the companies involved have again and again succeeded in using smaller, incremental innovations along the given technological path to adapt to the changing structural constraints (economic incentives and chances) to which they have been exposed. While there are, formally, regulations, above all in the form of the forest statute, these have been of little practical relevance due to major institutional weaknesses. The practical and discursive consciousness of the actors in the timber industry have made very little progress under these conditions: the new quality of the difficulties encountered by firms in the 1990s is recognized only in part, while the strategies devised to solve them as a rule move within the traditional routines. The result is that the willingness and ability of Pará's timber industry to introduce problem-solving innovations appears quite low. Entrepreneurs who break out of the traditional routines by introducing methods of nature-oriented sustainable forest management or specialize in a particular market segment as a means of improving the quality of their products and the productivity of their companies are exceptions.

The dominant pattern of resource utilization and processing – the entre-preneurial routine in Pará's timber industry – consists of the following elements:

–   The typical sawmill is a small family-owned operation with up to 16 workers that uses a band saw to produce some 4,200 m^3 of sawnwood per annum; the machinery in use is as a rule old (and may even have been taken over from bankrupt predecessors) and in a poor state of maintenance; the workers have no formal training, being trained instead on the job.

–   The productivity of these sawmills has hardly changed throughout the years.

–   Logging operations are conducted using power saws, tractors, bull-dozers, and trucks; at the same time the predominant method is still conventional selective cutting, a practice restricted to a limited number of species and carried out in an unplanned fashion in com-pany-owned, non-company-owned, or publicly accessible forest areas; logging is geared to the marketability of species and not to safeguarding a sustainable supply of timber.

–   The number of marketable species remained roughly the same from 1970 to 1994; due to the depletion of virola and mahogany the priorities have changed in favor of tauarí, curupixá, and jatobá.

–   Management focuses on purchasing logs (if the sawmill does not itself log) and marketing the sawnwood produced, which as a rule is sold in the domestic Brazilian market; there is for the most part no regular bookkeeping aimed at cost control; the overriding com-

pany objective is to accumulate profits and not to consolidate and
grow in one branch of the industry.

- logging and processing are seen as activities that are engaged in
  only temporarily – until the timber supplies surrounding the sawmill have been depleted; since the forest is regarded as a free good
  that will in any case have to make way to farming or cattle-
  ranching, investments are at best geared to increasing the productivity of logging operations by means of mechanization or to finding highly valuable stands of precious timber, mainly mahogany.

The environment of the sawmills – the constraints to which they are
subject – has changed again and again in the course of the past three
decades, but without compelling any drastic change in entrepreneurial
routines, since the new structures have tended more to be enabling than
restrictive:

- The factors triggering the growth in the timber industry since the
  1960s have been on the one hand the depletion of the primary forests in the south of Brazil and the opening up of the Amazon region, which eliminated the critical obstacles to expanding production into this region: road construction provided access to the forests of the *terra firme* and the sales markets of the richer south and
  southeast, the official settlement policy made sufficient manpower
  available in rural regions.

- On the other hand demand was marked by powerful dynamics:
  producers always found buyers for their wares; the domestic market was not particularly demanding in terms of quality, requiring
  instead only large supplies, which could be delivered thanks to the
  mechanization of logging.

- The export ban on logs imposed in 1974 drastically reduced the
  industry's external orientation, leading to export reductions of over
  60 % and production cuts of some 10 %; since the sawnwood produced here did not as a rule meet the quality standards of the world
  market, the fall in external demand was compensated for by taking
  advantage of high domestic demand.

- Instead of leading to a contraction of the timber industry, the recession in the 1980s led to growth in a subsegment, that of export-

oriented firms; these firms on the one hand benefited from general
export subsidies by at least in part using the low-interest loans they
obtained for speculation, and on the other hand profited from the
high external demand for mahogany, which persisted until the beginning of the 1990s.

Since the 1980s, however, new constraints have emerged, and they
have exposed firms to more far-reaching pressure to adjust:

– The high ecological and social costs of the settlement programs in
the Amazon region have been visible since the 1980s; this circumstance was instrumental in awakening the interest of Brazilian environmental groups and the international public in preserving the
Amazon forests; subsequently the Presidents Sarney and Collor decided on environmental measures designed to protect these forests
and for the first time lent practical relevance to the country's 1965
forest statute; it became more and more difficult to process timber
obtained from wholesale forest clearance aimed at creating rangeland and farmland.

– In 1992 the G7 pilot program on the protection of the Brazilian
tropical forests was agreed on by Brazil, the World Bank, and the
G7 states; this encouraged expansion of indigenous areas, establishment of nature-conservation areas, and the development of environmental administrations in the Amazon states.

– In the 1990s the instrument of voluntary ecological certification of
firms began to gain ground; in the international trade in tropical
timber it was the industrialized countries that first recognized the
chance offered by this instrument to constructively engage the
boycott campaigns launched by environmentalist groups; certification of forest management now came in for increasing discussion
in Pará as well.

– In the 1990s timber scarcity also for the first time made itself felt
in the centers of Pará's sawnwood production; the impairment of
forest regeneration capacity by selective logging and massive land
conversion in some areas began to force firms in the timber industry either to close, to relocate, or to look into reforestation.

- Finally, in mid-1994, the *Plano Real* brought the country a new currency that has since then been a successful tool in fighting inflation; at the same time this plan brought Brazil a higher exchange rate until 1999 and high interest rates; these changes highlighted the productivity gap in the timber industry, subsequently leading to a good number of company closures.

Most entrepreneurs responded defensively to the timber scarcity and the new environmental and economic challenges by calling for subsidies and changes to the forest statute. Although the insight is growing that exports to the industrialized countries are increasingly going to be linked to environmental stipulations, hardly any changes in practical action have made themselves felt that would indicate that entrepreneurs are committed to coming up with any realistic solutions that would offer the industry long-term perspectives.

In particular the severe consequences of traditional logging practices for continued timber production (to say nothing of the protection of forest ecosystems) have not become part of the general practical knowledge of the actors: in view of the limited number of marketable species, selective logging is viewed as the only economically rational harvesting method. In the entrepreneurs' view, the conservatism of the tropical-timber markets has become an incontrovertible fact to which the sawmills have to adapt. Entrepreneurs are still unable to recognize the natural conditions of timber production as a natural boundary set to the industry. Another consequence of this view is that the creation of plantations appears more plausible as a solution than management of forest stands that are in the end regarded as unproductive.

8.2   The Results Seen in their Theoretical Context

The theoretical problem involved in the study was bound up with three interrelated dimensions:

- How can the concepts *routine* and *technological development path* be used to analyze the emergence of patterns of resource utilization?

- What role is played here by an outward-looking orientation of the economy?
- And what is the role of the specific ecological conditions?

Routine and *technological development path* are thought concepts that refer us to the pronounced intrinsic dynamics of entrepreneurial action and decision patterns and thus to the fact that external economic constraints can be effectively filtered only through these intrinsic dynamics. Routines and development paths are also in large measure shaped by the technological solutions employed in firms or industries; technology includes the machinery and processes used, worker skills, and company-level organizational patterns. Routines are changed only when there is a concrete reason to do so, and then for the most part only within the framework defined by the development path embarked upon, since the problem profiles for which a solution is sought are also shaped by given routines. The term technological paradigm was coined to characterize the mode of perception created by a routine:

> Technological paradigms *"embody an outlook, a definition of the relevant problems, a pattern of enquiry. A 'technological paradigm' defines contextually the needs that are meant to be fulfilled, the scientific principles utilised for the task, the material technology to be used. In other words, a technological paradigm can be defined as a 'pattern' of solution of selected problems based on highly selected principles derived from prior knowledge and experience. A technological trajectory can then be defined (...) as technical progress along the economic and technological tradeoffs defined by a paradigm. Moreover, the technological paradigm also defines the boundaries of the inducement effects that changing market conditions and relative prices can exert upon the directions of technological progress. (...) The crucial hypothesis is that innovative activities are strongly selective, finalised in quite precise directions, and often cumulative."* (Dosi, Pavitt and Soete 1990, p. 84)

These concepts can be used to explain why the entrepreneurial action pattern current in Pará's timber industry has, despite its turbulent setting, remained stable for nearly four decades and why Pará's share in the world market for tropical timber has, despite the region's huge timber stands, not developed as rapidly as the shares held by Malaysia and Indonesia.

Stability: The entrepreneurial routine current in Pará consists in a constant overexploitation of the forest, persistent low levels of company productivity, and a low degree of value added. This pattern of resource utilization emerged in Brazil in the context of a mercantilist colonial economy geared to the needs of the colonial power; the Portuguese colonial economy intensified this use pattern by failing largely to develop any industrialization strategy for motherland and colony alike. The development policy pursued by the Brazilian central government for the Amazon region since the beginning of the 1970s saw the region above all in the role of resource supplier and foreign-exchange earner and accordingly fostered economic activities based on the pattern of destructive exploitation, because environmental regulations were either nonexistent or not enforced.

No changes in the routine emerged in the period covered by the present study, since there was no reason for them:

- The natural abundance of timber lasted until the 1990s in Pará's production sites, which were developed in infrastructural terms and had links to the important markets in the south of the country.
- The high demand in an unexacting domestic market made it unnecessary to introduce cost-reducing and/or quality-raising measures. The external market demanded only certain species and qualities as well as quantities that were not subject to dynamic growth.
- These specific marketing conditions amounted on the one hand to negative feedback effects: they reinforced the original routine as well as the view that the timber industry was an industry not particularly demanding in technological terms and one marked by a low level of dynamics, one in which it was easy to make high profits in the short term with a minimum of expense and effort.
- On the other hand they acted as positive feedback to the extent that they increased the potential of the forest damage caused by logging, stepped up demand, and led to mechanization of logging and

transportation, but without awakening any interest in preserving a sustainable supply of timber.

The inertia of entrepreneurial routines also found expression in the fact that the growth of the industry followed an expansive pattern containing hardly any potential for intensification. Between 1960 and 1985 the industry did manage to achieve an increase in the physical volume of output on the basis mainly of mechanization of logging and a broadening of the spectrum of the species marketed, but without catching up with the productivity level of the south-Brazilian timber industry. Since then the development of productivity of Pará's timber companies has stagnated. In addition, since the 1970s they have gone on producing mainly sawnwood. The growth of the industry is thus based chiefly on spatial expansion instead of increasing productivity and differentiation of production.

By working out industry-specific patterns of technical change, evolutionary economics provides an additional explanation for the stability of routines. Pará's timber industry belongs to the category of supplier-dominated industries, which neither induce nor engender technical change on their own, benefiting instead from innovations introduced by their suppliers.[4] Firms of this category typically produce goods using machines and processes developed externally. In their case technical change is shaped by user skills in making use of (new) processes as well as by relative input prices and the prices and performance of capital goods. Firms of this category accumulate technical skills only to the extent that they learn to operate and marginally improve their plant and machinery, i.e. adjust to the specific demands posed by their business. Capital intensity in this category is influenced by the long-term development of the price of labor; as long as the price is low, there are no incentives to raise capital intensity.

An important factor is that the dynamics between users and producers of technology are marked by mutual influences: diffusion of innovations is encouraged by improved machine performance and decreasing relative machine prices; high and rising user demand constitutes an incentive for suppliers to force technical change. Demand is on the other hand influenced by user technological competence; if neither user technological competence nor user product range is altered, the producers will have as good as no incentive for further technical developments.

This situation, a vicious circle, applies to the relationship between timber industry and the construction of specialized machinery: thanks to persistent high demand and low wage costs, the timber industry saw no reason to increase its productivity, conversion efficiency, and product quality, which would have required regular machine innovation or replacement. In this situation the simplest and safest approach for machine-builders was to continue to offer the time-tested machines. Technical innovations did not prevail because there was no demand for them.

World-market share: in 1974 the ban on log exports for Amazon timber was imposed; this is a measure that was used in Indonesia and Malaysia to encourage the export of processed wood products.[5] But in Pará the consequences were different: the timber industry converted to production of sawnwood, but it sold this wood mainly in the domestic market, which placed far lower demands on quality than the industrialized countries, which until then had purchased roundwood from Pará. The problem was thus not the change involved in sawing the timber, it was meeting the higher standards placed on the quality of processing, which would have required investment in technical equipment and manpower qualification. The consequence was a drastic decrease in export content.

Under the aspect of industrialization and foreign-exchange revenues, the log export ban must thus be seen as having failed. From the view of the producing region, however, this is a different matter: output continued to rise thanks to the high domestic demand in the south, southeast, and north of the country, mainly for building timber. These regions are located at distances ranging between 1,000 km and 3,000 km, i.e. these are exports from Pará's viewpoint. But the advantage is that there are no differences involved in language, currency, laws, marketing rules, and product standards.

The strategy of inward-looking industrialization that brought Brazil high growth rates up to the beginning of the 1980s formed the framework for the expansion strategy of Pará's timber industry and made it possible to retain traditional routines. Retention of a world-market orientation might even then have opened up for the Amazon timber industry the path taken by the Malaysian and Indonesian industries; the price for technological learning would probably have been far higher deforestation rates. The boom in timber exports in the 1980s does not contradict the thesis of a technological standstill, since the boom was based not on an increase of competitiveness but on the export of mahogany. The demand for this scarce precious wood had risen worldwide (one of the reasons being the depletion of the stands in Africa); the government subsidized exports as a means of earning hard currency to service its foreign debt. Under these conditions the exporting companies were able to earn high profits within the framework defined by existing routines.

The plywood and fiberboard industries increased their export shares in the 1980s as a means of compensating for low levels of domestic demand. Compared with Malaysia and Indonesia, the high production costs of these two industries made themselves felt drastically following the currency reform of 1994, leading to factory closures and cost reductions, though not to modernization investments.

The development of Brazil's share in the world timber market is in line with the explanation given by the evolutionary theory of technical change for different world-market shares: it is differences in technological skills and innovative capacities, embodied in variously efficient company routines and the cumulative effects of technological learning processes, and not natural (or given) factor endowments, that explain the different performance of industries and economies in international terms: *"the skills and knowledge necessary to develop, produce and sell products"* and *"the actual realisation of that capacity to generate and commercialise new and better products and productions processes"* constitute the entrepreneurial foundation of international competitiveness (Dosi, Pavitt and Soete 1990, p. 3).

Evolutionary theory thus proceeds from Krugman's (1979, 1982) new trade theory purporting to explain North-South trade with reference to the dynamic interaction between the North's capacity for innovation and the South's capacity for imitation. The North's product innovations make it possible for it to realize innovation rents, in this way financing its higher wage costs (and its higher level of development), and to continue doing so until the South has copied the product and begun manufacturing it itself at lower costs. Subsequently the innovation rents are eroded. The North can thus assert its precedence only by maintaining its technology monopoly and continuously producing innovations.

This model is broadened by evolutionary economics to include the firm- and industry-related and overall economic processes of technical change and the interlinkages between these processes that can be used to explain country-specific differences and the fact that technical change can lead to decline on the part of former leading countries and the rise of new leaders (Soete 1985). In this view the dynamic change of world-market shares is closely linked with the diffusion processes of new technologies and products that contribute to the erosion of innovation rents, in this way keeping the motor of technical change running.

A high level of technological competence (skills plus innovativeness) thus constitutes a source of absolute advantages in the world market (Dosi, Pavitt and Soete 1990, pp. 137 and 142 f.). What is crucial to securing world-market shares is the technical knowledge that permits firms to produce innovative products and to utilize process innovations more efficiently and quickly than others as a means of reducing input coefficients and increasing labor productivity.

Dominant technologies and the best practice constitute the autonomous determinants of international trade flows. These, however, must not be conceived as fixed parameters; they are in constant motion, and are so as a result of the dynamics inherent in technical change and the fact that efficiency is by definition highly contextual (entrepreneurial routines being dependent on their social context).

Against this background the current situation in Brazil's timber and pulp industry may be characterized as follows: While the south, thanks to direct investments from Chile and Portugal, is able to produce new, technology-intensive wood materials, the north is left behind. Only Asian plywood corporations that continue to bank on the path marked out by traditional methods of processing tropical timber are interested in investing in the Amazon region as a means of safeguarding the continuation of their own production in the face of the depletion of Asia's stands of tropical forest. The Brazilian pulp industry, on the other hand, at a very early point of time started looking to an externally oriented strategy, gearing its operations to the international best practice.

The **characteristics and functional cycles of the Amazon region's ecosystems** place limits on the utilization of renewable natural resources, and these are not recognized by the day-to-day knowledge that finds expression in the dominant entrepreneurial routines encountered there. The failure to take cognizance of the ecological specifics of the Amazon region has a number of different causes: first, the low level of diffusion of existing knowledge concerning local ecosystems. This is due to the low level of formal education among the greater part of the population, the low regard in which the traditional knowledge of forest dwellers is held, and a lack of professionalism on the part of forest and sawmill owners, who regard it as unnecessary to have any reasonable measure of knowledge of forestry. Second, the ecological blindness of existing routines has to do with the premise that processing timber from the primary forest is a temporary affair that will sooner or later have to make way for more productive forms of land use. The third complex of causes is connected with this last reason; it is the weakness of institutions in enforcing legal restrictions on forest utilization. If conservation is viewed merely as a cost factor with uncertain benefits, and managing the primary forest is seen as an unprofitable activity, there is no justification for investing in strengthening the institutions entrusted with these tasks. This is why not even the introduction of safe property rights will work as an instrument to be used in introducing sustainable systems of forest use.

The ecological blindness of entrepreneurial action patterns and the development policy conceived for the Amazon region has contributed strongly to the overexploitation of natural resources and the emergence of socioeconomic structures that today pose obstacles to the introduction of any sustainable utilization patterns. These structures include above all the large-scale landholdings that have specialized in extensive cattle-ranching. The rise of large landholdings was also financed by the prospering timber industry; mainly in inflationary times, profits made in the timber industry have flowed into purchases of land. This has perpetuated the ecological (and socioeconomic) problems involved in large-scale agriculture. By way of contrast, small family farms in old and new settlement areas have shown a surprising measure of innovativeness and adaptability to given ecological circumstances.

The case of the tropical-timber industry in Pará generally does not indicate any incompatibility between **economic development, an external orientation, and the preservation of life-support systems**. It has instead become clear that practical consideration of the conditions to which the reproduction of the natural life-support systems is tied is dependent on the routines and constraints that determine entrepreneurial or, in general, social action. These routines and constraints bear the marks of society and history. It is possible to recognize systematic links between economic constraints and more or less consideration of natural life-support systems, though these links do not obey any universal, that is, abstract and ahistorical, logic.

These systematic links can prove to be very powerful structural moments impeding the introduction of changes. For instance, the collapse of earlier civilizations can be explained in terms of a disparity between population growth and retention of routines in food production, social organization and division of labor, and attempts at change that came too late.[6] At present the ponderousness of the negotiation processes aimed at implementing the Climate Convention is a good example of the inertia of irrational structures.

We can, however, not rule out the general possibility of changes aimed at ecologizing economic activity, since even structural economic constraints are socially constituted and their reproduction depends on the continuity of the action patterns instrumental in constituting them.

In the end, the key factor involved in achieving the necessary ecological and socioeconomic adjustments will be the interaction between cumulative processes in politics, society and the economy, and fortuitously emerging opportunities. This formulation is no cause for optimism, though it does forbid any view defined by disaster scenarios unavoidable because they are the result of systematic causes (and any alleged inability to act on the part of the individual that serves to occlude the notion of responsibility).

8.3   Action Options

The following section deals with the action options available to foster sustainable development paths in Pará's rural areas and in its timber industry.

Sustainable Development in Pará's Rural Areas

Strategies for the economic development of and improved living conditions in Pará's rural areas must seek their orientation in the limiting ecological facts that are given there; that is to say that human interventions must not be allowed to call into question the stability of basic ecological functions. Section 8.1 of the present study thus speaks of a mixed concept for agriculture and forestry which consists in the demarcation of conservation areas and the development of guidelines for a sustainable utilization of natural resources. In Pará three factors could facilitate the realization of a concept of this sort: first, the growth of the population in the region has shown distinct signs of relaxation since the end of the 1980s; there is no reason to assume an unmitigated flow of migrants into the region. Second, for some ten years now roughly 60 % of Pará's population has been concentrated in municipalities with up to 20,000 residents, which are usually classified as rural areas in international statistics. These municipalities are found above all in the older settlement areas in the east of Pará.[7] All in all, we find that there is no reason to assume a constant pressure to expand into untouched forest areas – one of the central premises of frontier economics. Third, there are, above all in the south of Pará, extended deforested, degraded areas available that could, at least in part, be used for new production systems such as reforestation or plantations based on a combination of various native and exotic species.

What conditions should be placed on agriculture and forestry? The concern in agriculture must be to take leave of the model of the "rational, capital-intensive large-scale farm" and to foster small and medium-size family farms based on labor-intensive and diversified production systems. Such production systems as a rule combine perennial cultures with annual cultures and animal husbandry, preserving the permanent ground cover by means of permanent cultures and fallow-cropping (cyclic growth of secondary vegetation on plots used for annual cultures). It must be understood that fallow-cropping is not an inefficient form of land use but serves the purpose of maintaining soil fertility and the basic functions of ecosystems (above all the hydrological cycle). By improving the rural infrastructure in older settlement areas, including the Transamazônica, it is possible to increase the profitability of farms and the stability of rural settlement.

The concern in forestry must be to gain general acceptance for the model of nature-oriented forest management, which aims at supporting the natural regeneration of forests as a means of ensuring sustainable timber production. Clear-felling and substitution of the primary forest by plantations or stepping up timber production by means of various methods of enrichment-planting have proven to be inappropriate approaches. The above-mentioned degraded areas should be used to experiment with plantations, while methods stemming from nature-oriented forest management should be employed to exploit the timber resources of the primary forest.

The task of putting these models into practice calls for an invigoration and qualification of environmental policy and environmental authorities in the Amazon region; this would place the disputes in this policy field on a less emotional footing and gradually contribute to devising solutions to impending problems. A coherent tropical-forest policy combining ecological and socioeconomic goals would not only entail positive local and regional effects (and cause relatively low short-term economic costs), it would also enormously improve Brazil's international repute and widen its political options.

Environmental policymakers can presently rely on three worldwide trends that have emerged in the past 10 - 15 years, reinforcing one another and in this way fostering processes of social change in the direction of a more sustainable form of economic activity:

– In contrast to Inglehart's thesis on the postmaterialist values of industrialized societies (Inglehart 1977 and 1990), we find a growing international environmental consciousness also in developing countries, and there not only among the urban middle classes but also and precisely among groups in rural areas whose survival is a matter of preserving the life support systems; one piece of evidence of this is the movement of the rubber tappers in the Amazon region who are fighting for forest protection. This environmental consciousness creates political pressure demanding that legal and economic instruments be used to contain or to prevent the negative environmental consequences of social action. Furthermore, this leads to altered consumer behavior regarding certain product groups; environmentally harmful products are avoided and the demand is voiced that environmentally sound alternative products be designated as such (Scholz 1993).

– Environmental instruments, altered consumer preferences, and educational campaigns organized by environmental groups and federations are, above all in the industrialized countries, putting corporations under pressure to give their products and production processes a more environmentally compatible shape. There are similar processes underway in the developing countries, above all in the area of farming and forestry, and these processes are being intensified through world-market integration: transnational corporations and outward-looking industries can, thanks to a watchful world public opinion, less and less afford to produce to lower standards in the South than in the North. Without any active local public sphere and functioning environmental authorities, however, it is easier for such corporations to push green propaganda in the South without effecting any real changes in their actual behavior.

– Many environmental organizations are demanding that regulations and negotiations at the national level be shored up and advanced by means of legally binding agreements at the international level, in the legal framework either of the WTO or of problem-specific international environmental conventions (Scholz 1996a).

One obstacle to international environmental conventions is the political goal of creating equal conditions ("level playing field") for all actors involved in international trade. The consequence is that the industrialized countries either use their negotiating power to force on the countries of the South environmental standards that are just as high as those in effect in the North, or to lower their own standards. The developing countries advance two arguments to counter these demands: they are, first, not as responsible as the North for historically accumulated, global environmental damage and, second, they lack the technical and financial means required for the necessary investments, the result of which is that they are cut off from a (growing) participation in world trade. This can lead to blockades that impede any change at all. A strengthening and qualification of environmental policy and the authorities responsible for administering it in the countries of the South would contribute to lifting such blockades.

Perspectives of a Sustainable Tropical-timber Industry

At the sectoral level ecological conditions and new technological trends emerging in the world market are giving rise to a new model for the tropical-timber industry: the industry will have to take leave of the notion that it can compete with the plantation economy and offer homogeneous mass products (sawnwood and plywood). The perspective open to the tropical-timber industry must be sought in an attempt to reconcile the reproduction-related ecological needs of the tropical forest with its economic interests in utilizing the latter; the means to this end must be sought in a strategy of flexible specialization in niche markets. Supply of small quantities of diversified and high-quality products with complete information on their technical properties and potential uses would be an interesting and wholly new development perspective for the tropical-timber industry, which might in this way develop an interest in sustainable forest management.

The structural characteristics of tropical forest ecosystems do not lend themselves to any rational exploitation along the lines of industrial mass production; they require the development of adapted management patterns, since the reproduction behavior of tropical tree species does not permit the creation of the homogeneous industrial forests with predictable maturation periods familiar from the temperate zones. The plantation economy is a form of timber production congenial to industrial mass utilization. This is not to say that this is a desirable form of production; it is indeed probable that even plantation management will have to change if it is to be sustainable and that this will entail a reduction of the timber supply (and a lowering of mass consumption). The processing and marketing patterns of sawmills and other timber-processing companies will also have to take account of the structural characteristics of the tropical forests: due to biodiversity timber quantities of certain magnitudes can be preserved in the tropics only on the basis of greater qualitative heterogeneity. This heterogeneity could be turned to account by developing market niches that have need for the special aesthetic and physical features of tropical timber. Increasing labor productivity, product quality, and the depth of processing would make it possible to achieve higher yields and thus offer companies a durable perspective.

In Brazil the task of transforming this model into reality in the timber industry of Pará (and the Amazon region) can be promoted by retaining the export ban on tropical logs, more intensively monitoring the logging of and trade in mahogany, encouragement of certification of tropical forestry, and an invigoration of environmental policy and the authorities responsible for it. The goals of these measures would have to be to intensify the innovation pressure to which Pará's timber industry is presently, for the first time for decades, exposed due to the depletion of local forest stands and substitution by new, technology-intensive wood panels.

The export ban on tropical logs may at first glance appear to constitute an obstacle to sustainable forestry, since log prices are higher in the world market than they are domestically. But this measure is for the time being the most important dam against the encroachment of the financially highly powerful investors presently active in the market: Asian timber corporations out to obtain logging concessions in the tropical-forest regions of Africa and Latin America with an eye to supplying their plywood factories with huge quantities of unprocessed timber. In Brazil the export ban forces these corporations to develop or take over local processing capacities, thus creating (or preserving) jobs; the restrictive practices of environmental authorities in granting licenses and the economic crisis in Asia have thus far prevented any large-scale logging activities here. It must, however, be anticipated that Asia's demand for tropical logs will soon increase again. But even if the export ban is retained, it would be a grave strategic error to place one's stakes on Asian investors: they represent the ecologically unadapted and technologically outmoded development path of a tropical-timber industry specialized in the production of cheap and simple mass goods, which neither contributes to sustainable patterns of resource utilization nor increases regional welfare.

The objective of stronger controls on the logging of and trade in mahogany would be to close off the sawmill owners' option of continuing to specialize in this valuable timber, in this way making quick, high profits. It is only when this option has been shut off for good that the economic interest in sustainable forest management can gain ground. At present there are contingents only on exports of mahogany; due to the high domestic demand for this timber it would make sense to extend this measure to the domestic trade as well.

Voluntary certification of sustainable forestry management relies on the market mechanism: in Europe certified timber can on the one hand command higher prices than noncertified timber and on the other hand this makes it possible to secure sales markets over the long term, since a growing demand here would run up against a slowly increasing supply. Certification also relies on the information and participation of civil society; this means that local residents, environmental groups, and consumer organizations would check whether certified products rightly bear their certificates and whether the practice of certified firms is in accord with the standards. They can always count on media interest in uncovering abuses and improper behavior. Certification is in this way also an instrument that can be used by civil society to strengthen (and control) environmental authorities.

A campaign aimed at certification of forestry practices should start out with the export markets, in order later to focus on the domestic market as well. Certified timber can presently be sold in all European markets; a growing supply from Brazil could contribute to weakening the conservatism of the importers in the industrialized countries as a means of forcing them to meet their duty – of looking to new, ecologically oriented consumer preferences and altering their supplies accordingly. In view of the strength of the environmental movement in the south and southeast of Brazil, which has been fighting for the preservation of the tropical forests for over 20 years now, an attempt could be made to develop a domestic market segment for certified tropical timber. The better part of Amazon timber is used domestically in the building and furniture industries; the process of its replacement by plantation timber has already begun in the south and southeast. It is, in other words, necessary to develop new market segments for tropical timber in the domestic market.

Conversion to sustainable forest management and further processing of timber products will call for demanding learning processes in the companies concerned: management must learn to make use of specialized know-how and to use forest inventories as the basis of the logging and forest-tending that can stimulate the growth of species which can be marketed profitably. At the same time this type of forest use will oblige the processing companies to broaden the spectrum of marketable species by introducing new species to the markets at home and abroad and raising the productivity and quality of timber-processing. To achieve this, the companies involved will have to learn to develop horizontal cooperative relationships that can be instrumental in dealing more efficiently with the tasks facing them as well as to maintain intensive and durable relations with their customers as a means of familiarizing themselves with their needs.

One thing essential to this strategy is a professionalization and strengthening of the business environment; this applies for the federation of timber exporters AIMEX, the entrepreneurial federation FIEPA, and research institutions such as EMBRAPA-CPATU and FCAP.

The actors in Pará who commit themselves to realizing this demanding program can count on the support of international development cooperation. The approaches and tasks of development cooperation are the subject of the following chapter.

9 Conclusions for Development Cooperation

Conclusions relating to development cooperation can be drawn at two levels: at the overriding level concerned with a sustainable development strategy for the state of Pará to which the sectoral strategy would have to be adapted (Section 9.1) and at the sectoral level involving promotion of an ecologically and economically sustainable tropical-timber industry (Section 9.2). But first two preliminary remarks:

- The proposals for development cooperation presented in what follows are concerned with the exemplary case of Pará. As was pointed out in the theoretical-methodological considerations presented in Chapter 2, we cannot proceed on the assumption of any universally valid laws on the economic utilization of tropical forests. If we are to understand patterns of resource utilization, we must instead work out the specific, historically and socially constituted action rationality of the actors involved. Comparisons with other regions may provide us with impetuses here, but they will not supply us with any blueprints for development- and environment-related measures.

- Apart from those relating to the tropical-timber industry, the proposals move on a more general level, since any more precise studies on other economic sectors (e.g. mining, farming, cattle-ranching) would have gone beyond the scope of the present study.

9.1 Development Cooperation and Sustainable Development in Pará

The following section will start out with a brief overview of the scenario for Pará and then go into the points of departure offered by the G7 pilot program to conserve the Brazilian tropical forests (PPG-7) for promoting a strategy of sustainable development in Pará.

A strategy committed to the model of sustainable development is necessarily geared to the concurrent goals of ecological sustainability, economic efficiency, and social justice (Kürzinger 1997b). In Pará this model is as a rule the frame of reference of all official documents and strategy papers, though there is, as far as operational considerations are concerned, a lack of clarity on means and instruments and a certain reluctance to negotiate the tradeoffs involved here. The model has prevailed in the discourse, though in the practice of public and private actors it has far less effect.

Together with the state of Amazonas, Pará is one of the economic heavyweights of the Brazilian Amazon region, and it is also one of Brazil's most important foreign-exchange earners. It nevertheless has a number of structural weaknesses (low per capita income, high share of the primary sector in GNP) which, together with the weaknesses besetting its political-institutional system (insufficient political clout in asserting itself against powerful vested interests), lead to blockades at the regional level.

Aside from bilateral and multilateral development cooperation, the Brazilian federal government and the Pará state government also act in the capacity of investors and promoters of development activities; the federal government above all in connection with the program "Brazil em Ação," which is concerned with investing in the development of infrastructure (expanding river courses, paving highways, expanding electricity generation and the power grid). The Pará state government grants tax breaks to private investors and actively seeks to attract projects involved in processing the raw materials produced in the region, above all from the mining industry. The interest of Malaysian investors in palm-oil production and timber-processing in the region is a result of an advertising campaign launched by the state government.

The financial volume of development cooperation is far lower than the funds involved in public-private investment programs: for instance, PPG-7 provides US$ 320 million, while "Brazil em Ação" has a volume of some US$ 3 billion. According to INCRA, the settlement of 287,539 families in connection with agrarian reform between 1995 and 1999 cost US$ 5.8 billion; over 60 % of this settlement program was carried out in the Amazon region.[1] In the south of Pará negotiations are underway on the construction of a copper refinery that is projected to cost US$ 1.5 billion.

The PPG-7 is the region's biggest development-cooperation program.[2] Roughly half of the funds stem from Germany, and some 20 % is administered by the World Bank's Rainforest Trust Fund. Because of the strategic significance attached to PPG-7 as a pilot program, the following discussion will focus on it, while at the same time also looking at the activities of other, nongovernmental actors.

The G7 Pilot Program on the Protection of Brazil's Tropical Forests (PPG-7)[3]

In 1992 a decree was issued, following lengthy negotiations, that created the groundwork for the G7 pilot program on the protection of Brazil's rainforests.[4] The aim of the program is to introduce a model of sustainable development in Brazil's tropical forests, and it will therefore, at least in the medium term, influence the conditions for the timber industry. The instruments provided for include the introduction of new models of environmental management in selected areas of Brazil's Amazon states on the basis of ecological-economic zoning (land-use planning), the creation of gatherer reserves, Indian protection areas, national conservation areas, promotion of a sustainable forest and *várzea* management, promotion of science centers and applied research, and support for demonstration projects of businesses and the population, which are supported by NGOs (MMA 1997; and the present chapter).

The program, chaired by the environment ministry, is administered by the ministries of justice, foreign affairs, financial affairs, research and technology, the Secretariat for Strategic Affairs, and NGOs from the Amazon region and the Atlantic coastal forest region. The agriculture ministry and the agrarian-reform authority INCRA are not involved in PPG-7.

The governance deficits in the field of environmental policy in Pará cannot be compensated for by the PPG-7 alone. It would therefore make sense – in keeping with a thinking in win-win options – to encourage innovative policy approaches that could be used to advance the ecological adjustment of land-use systems.

In the coming five years the challenge in Pará will be to find an active role for environmental and resource protection in the process of the state's regional economic development. PPG-7 could provide a point of departure for these efforts; here five points deserve mention:

–   strengthening the environmental ministries and authorities in institutional terms at the state and municipal levels within the framework of the natural-resources policy program (NRPP),
–   demarcation of protected zones,
–   promotion of initiatives on sustainable resource utilization (demonstration projects, Pro Manejo, and Pro Várzea),
–   cooperation with nongovernmental actors.

The **NRPP** is intended to support the environment ministry and the environmental authorities in selected municipalities in the eastern Amazon region and in the west at the termination of the Transamazônica by diffusing knowledge and experience with methods and procedures geared to an environmentally oriented economic promotion and land-use planning.[5] This approach is an important and more realistic alternative to the concept of a land-use planning directed by the federal government, as provided for in "ecological-economic zoning." It would make more sense, and would be more in accord with the Brazilian constitution (the principle of cooperation and subsidiarity govern the interaction between the levels of administration), to proceed from the municipal level and conduct land-use planning hand in hand with the development of an efficient municipal environmental administration.

On the whole, the NRPP is intended to strengthen the scopes of action open to federal and municipal environmental authorities in the following areas:

–   identifying the impacts of macroeconomic policies on environmental and resource protection in the Amazon region and possible measures designed to contain the negative ecological effects,
–   identifying interfaces between PPG-7, the integrated Amazon policy of the Brazilian environmental ministry, the "Brazil em Ação" investment program, and measures that could serve to strengthen the concern of environmental and resource protection at these interfaces.

- preventing any polarization between environmental aims and the goals of economic and social policy by looking for encouraging win-win options or, should this not be possible, identifying the alternatives with the lowest ecological costs and the highest social and economic benefits.

This could be used to counter the weaknesses that have become visible in the course of the first phase of PPG-7:

- the exclusion of the agricultural ministry and the agrarian-reform authority INCRA from the PPG-7 steering committee,
- the dominance of defensive goals of environmental and resource protection, which tend to lose sight of the problems and interests of the majority of the population of the Amazon region; this has placed obstacles in the way of the development of a more broad-based political backing for the program in the region.

It will not be necessary to go into the **demarcation of conservation areas** at any length here. This is closely linked with the **promotion of sustainable resource-use patterns**. In looking at this context it is important to distinguish between measures aimed at forest protection (in the sense of conservation) and measures serving the goals of sustainable utilization and development; both are justified and necessary:

- the first group includes both the demarcation of indigenous and conservation areas and measures associated with the economic development of the towns in the Amazon region that can serve to lower the conversion pressure to which the forest is exposed;
- the second group includes measures designed to promote sustainable resource utilization, i.e. support for indigenous peoples in utilizing their resources (PD/I), the institution of concessions in publicly administered forests such as the Flona Tapajós, promotion of the timber industry in the framework of Pro Manejo (see Section 9.2), promotion of R&D in the field of sustainable tropical forestry and agriculture and the processing of agricultural and forest products (including nontimber products), and the improvement of the living conditions of the urban population.

The promotion of urban areas and economic activities is an important precondition for reducing the pressure on forests. The "resource protection through sustainable utilization" approach in any case acknowledges the economic interest in exploiting resources; but when the issue is fragile ecosystems (i.e. ecosystems with structures and dynamics too complex to be reproduced artificially, as in many parts of the temperate zones as a result of century-old developments), this approach, at least as far as the state of today's knowledge is concerned, runs up against limits that must be recognized and taken into account. It is for this reason that it is highly important to provide alternative sources of income; but since this, in the medium term, will at best just be manageable, we will have to anticipate further conversion of Amazon forest. According to the most recent findings of the research on tropical forests discussed above, this need not mean the inevitable collapse of whole ecosystems, as was generally thought even ten years ago, but the inevitable price to pay will be the loss of some endemic plant and animal species.

Promotion of sustainable land-use systems is emphasized in a paper published by KfW/GTZ during the planning phase of the PPG-7: *"Promotion of small-scale farming, in particular using agroforestry approaches, must be seen as one of the most important fields of action."* (KfW and GTZ 1991, p. 53) Promotion of integrated pilot projects at the local and/or regional level as well as promotion of cooperatives and initiatives geared to processing and marketing agroforestry products has already become reality in numerous demonstration projects (PD/A), mainly in the south of Pará, but also in the Amazon delta. This is particularly important for Pará, with its large share of population living in rural areas. Cooperation with existing bilateral farming-promotion projects is therefore an important step. In Pará this is possible with the GTZ project on poverty reduction in rural areas, ProRenda Pará, and the research projects aimed at management of secondary forests, which are being conducted by the universities FU Berlin (socioeconomic dimension), Göttingen, and Bonn (natural dimension) in the framework of the SHIFT program and receive support from the German Ministry for Research and Technology.[6] Both GTZ and the SHIFT projects are concerned with the northeast of Pará, the oldest agricultural settlement area, and thus offer some interesting points of contact.

Promotion of small family farms in particular would entail positive consequences:

- Increasing yields would make it possible to improve the incomes and living conditions of smallholders;

- an increase of yields could help to supply the towns more from local resources, which would in turn reduce the share of food supplies from the south, with their environmentally detrimental side-effects, and contribute to developing urban-rural relations conducive to development;

- another important point would be to develop food-processing industries in the small and medium-size towns, and to do so with an eye both to local food supplies and exports.

More markedly basing food supplies on the areas surrounding towns will require more than merely improving the local road network. The factors that will have to be dealt with include the market power of the southern Brazilian wholesale chains as well as institutional arrangements such as legislation on public calls for bids that specify that in matters of public procurement the lowest bid is always given priority. This means that, for instance, schools are forced to purchase food for school meals from bidders from the south, assuming that the latter are cheaper, and are unable to procure local produce.

To rule out the possibility that raising the productivity of small-scale agriculture might entail growth effects at the expense of forest stands, a land-use planning – like that provided for in NRPP – is called for that specifies and bindingly demarcates settlement areas for small farms. It would make considerable sense to link measures of this sort with a rehabilitation of degraded land in the east and south of Pará.[7] Cooperation with **nongovernmental actors**, i.e. with NGOs, will be used to encourage the participation of the Amazon population in this program. PPG-7 is therefore supporting the NGO umbrella organization GTA (*Grupo de Trabalho Amazônico* - Amazon Working Group), whose members include the association of rubber tappers (CNS), the Association of Indigenous Peoples (COIAB), the Association of Small Farmers and Farmworkers (CONTAG), the Association of Small Fishermen, and a number of environmentalist groups. With its relatively large percentage of rural population (seen in terms of the overall Amazon region), Pará is represented in GTA above all by farmers, fishermen, and gatherers of Brazil nuts. Thus far there is no participation of NGOs with an urban base, e.g. in the population groups resettled in connection with urban-renewal programs (Silva 1998).

GTA is the mouthpiece of civil society and is now recognized as a partner by Brazil's environment ministry. At the PPG-7 donor meetings GTA plays an important role, above all through its critical comments and position papers (GTA/FoE 1996, 1997; Leroy and Soares 1998). It would now be important to institute such stable and continuous consultation processes at the state level, i.e. in Pará, between the environment ministry, the municipal environmental authorities, and civil society.

GTA has a very broad makeup and represents various population groups and their in part divergent interests; this entail both advantages and disadvantages. The most important advantage is that GTA has developed a good eye for the inadequacies of PPG-7 as a sectoral environmental program and has again and again pointed to the necessity of regarding PPG-7 as part of a necessarily more broadly based program of sustainable regional development. The disadvantage is that GTA has problems in bearing up against and balancing conflicting interests; problems of this sort are often intensified by contradictions between environmental and economic policy or between agricultural policy and the vagaries of politics.

GTA's function is clear: it has the potential to critically and constructively accompany the PPG-7 measures and the development activities of the Brazilian federal government and the states of the Amazon region. It can in this connection be a critical partner of the environmental authorities and base its efforts on an alliance with progressive parliamentarians, town councilors, and representatives of the sciences. This critical accompaniment can be used to avoid mistakes in planning and implementation. At the federal level this function is exercised by civil-society organizations and individuals who have been appointed to the advisory council of the environment ministry (COEMA - *Conselho Estadual do Meio Ambiente*).

The core of GTA's criticism of PPG-7 procedures is that GTA's potential, i.e. the potential of the population groups concerned, has not been able to unfold adequately and is not used by governmental actors. The lack of inclusion of the local population has already led to disillusionment among a number of groups, which can just about be moved by their foreign partners to become actively concerned with this program, which is not particularly visible in everyday life. In the case of Pará this problem is exacerbated by the fact that small farmers are not explicitly included in PPG-7 and must make themselves heard in other ways, e.g. through demonstration projects.

9.2   Promotion of a Sustainable Development of the Tropical-timber Industry

Measures aimed at promoting a sustainable tropical-timber industry will have to include the areas of resource protection and resource utilization. The protection measures that could be supported by development cooperation in the framework of PPG-7 include professionalization of the environmental authorities in the field of forestry, above all the monitoring and sanction capacities of state and local environmental authorities. At the start of the new century the satellite-monitoring program SIVAM could create the conditions needed for a more efficient monitoring of the environment; at least three conditions will have to be met if SIVAM is to become effective:

–   data collection must be in accord with the needs of environmental policy and environmental authorities;

–   the personnel on the ground must be trained in using this new monitoring technology, above all in evaluating satellite imagery;

–   the authorities have to be in a position to reach sites on the ground in order to be able to verify a satellite message and initiate appropriate measures.

The following aspects should be taken into account in consultations on resource policy: from the perspective of resource protection it is important not to give in to business demands to water down regulations on forest utilization, though it would certainly make sense to look through the legal regulations with an eye to simplifying them and strengthening their coherence. It would also be helpful to put mahogany on the CITES list of endangered species, which would amount to a ban on international trade with this species. There should be domestic contingents for the logging of and trade in mahogany.

As far as resource use in forestry and the timber industry is concerned, the program component of PPG-7 on promoting sustainable forest management, Pro Manejo, provides a good platform. This program focuses on, among other things, the instruments of voluntary certification and forest management. The point of this is to ensure that forest owners and timber-processing companies have an incentive to put into practice the legally binding forest-management plans, in this way acknowledging the link between forest utilization and a permanent perspective for their operations. This instrument of certification will first become effective in the exporting branch of the timber industry. Domestically, "green" markets will have better chances in the south and southeast of the country, in that these areas have more affluent and environment-minded consumer groups. In view of the dominance of the domestic market for the tropical-timber industry it would make sense to invest in developing these markets.

A further approach that Pro Manejo intends to make use of is to build up programs for the local farming population aimed at using community-forestry approaches and advanced-training measures to mobilize understanding for and interest in sustainable forest management.

Above and beyond promotion of nature-oriented forest management, what is called for is measures aimed at fostering the technical competence of timber-processing companies over the medium term as a means of enabling them to come closer to the ideal of the flexible firm specialized in market niches and producing quality products. Innovation efforts should initially be geared to introducing at the company level different methods of forestry and timber processing in the following areas:

–   planning and implementation of an ecologically and economically sustainable management,

- company-level production planning that is adapted to a sustainable timber supply;
- business administration (chiefly costing and controlling) and marketing.

A customer-oriented development of products for specialized industrial, artisanal, or artistic applications is a goal that would have to be addressed at a later point of time.

All of the points mentioned call for the parallel development of an efficient business environment offering specialized services: for forestry-related planning and advanced training, business consulting, market research, and, finally, product development.

This industry strategy would have to be shored up in terms of environmental (see above), economic, and structural policy as a means of depriving the strategy of destructive exploitation and sales of simple sawnwood produced from precious timber of their status as a profitable entrepreneurial perspective. The economic-policy measures required include continued incentives that encourage firms to raise productivity and innovate. The tropical-timber industry will also have to actively seek integration in the world market, since the world market exerts pressure to adjust to ecological standards and offers higher prices for certified timber. In the 1970s a world-market orientation would have been just as disastrous as the growing demand for timber in the domestic market; but today, for reasons that include the declining demand for tropical timber, it can also entail positive ecological effects. The conditions needed in this situation include a continuation of the export ban on logs and a serious, transparent certification system.

Finally, limited economic-promotion measures could be used in the Amazon region to support the timber industry in introducing a nature-oriented forest-management system, raising productivity, and modernizing its marketing.

Notes

Chapter 1

1   Wiemann et al. (1994) for the case of India; Chudnovsky and Chidiak (1995) for Argentina; and Scholz et al. (1994) for Chile. A number of country case studies were conducted for UNCTAD on this issue at the beginning of the 1990s, but without a homogeneous approach (that would be needed to make comparative studies possible) The individual case studies and/or their results have not yet been published

2   One consequence of the neoliberal-style reforms initiated by the military dictatorship from 1973 on as well as of the structural-adjustment policy pursued from 1982 in Chile is that the apparatus of state has been drastically cut back. The limited capacity to act displayed by the executive can thus not, as in other countries, be attributed to a functionalization of the state for particularist interests (rent-seeking).

3   For a critique, see Martínez-Alier (1995).

4   For industrialized countries, see Eder (1988), Beck (1986); for an analysis of the global relationships between nature and society, see Becker (1992) and Bruckmeier (1994).

5   See the contributions in Brandt (1998).

6   Throughout the world CO_2 accounts for 55 % of the greenhouse effect.

7   Salati and dos Santos (1999). It is not easy to measure the CO_2 emissions stemming from deforestation in the Amazon region, since the carbon dioxide content of the various forest formations fluctuates in terms of specific forest biomass content: The highest levels are found in primary forests, the lowest in secondary vegetation.

8   To compare the average values for the industrialized countries and developing countries: the former have an output energy intensity of 20.2 gigajoules / US$ 1000 of GDP and a carbon intensity of 16.3 kg C / gigajoules and 0.33 t C / US$ 1000 of GDP; the latter have an output energy intensity of 37.7 gigajoules / US$ 1000 of GDP and a carbon intensity of 14.2 kg C / gigajoules and 0.54 t C / US$ 1000 of GDP (Loske 1996, p. 60).

Chapter 2

1   The best access to the broad range of literature on the topic is provided by the literature database ELDIS, which can be accessed on the Internet: http://www.ids.ac.uk.

2   The most influential studies on the timber trade and the timber industry are Repetto and Gillis (1988) and Barbier, Burgess, Bishop and Aylward (1994). On boycotting tropical timber and its effect on consumption see Brockmann, Hemmelskamp and Hohmeyer (1996).

3   See Browder (1989) on the timber industry in Rondônia and Nascimento (1985) on the same industry in Pará.

4 Barros and Veríssimo (1996) and Stone (1997) and (1998); the journals include *World Development*, the *Journal of Forestry Ecology*, and *Management and Ecological Economics*.

5 See Chapter 6 for more information on this topic.

6 In the state of Mato Grosso, which is part of Amazônia Legal but does not belong to the northern region, IMAZON noted 860 sawmills in 1997.

7 System competition with the Soviet Union also played an important role here; in the beginnings of US development economics the perceived successes of Soviet development planning were seen as a challenge for the economics and politics of the West (Hirschman 1981)

8 For a summary, see Vornholz (1993, 1994) and Lélé (1991).

9 See Goodland and Daly (1993) and Section 2.3 of this study for more information.

10 Pearce and Turner (1990), Vornholz (1993), and the final report of the Enquete Commission of the German Bundestag, "Schutz des Menschen und der Umwelt" (Deutscher Bundestag 1998, p. 46).

11 An overview of the different directions of research and the most important literature at the interface between environment and economy is provided by the annotated bibliography of Steiner and Meyerhoff (1993). The presentation in this section largely follows Pearce and Turner (1990).

12 The theoretical foundations of this new discipline were laid in the 1930s (Hotelling 1931 and Pigou 1932).

13 See Endres and Querner (1993) on the distinction between environmental and resource economics.

14 The term "satisficing" comes from the literature on bounded rationality and designates the always imperfect information horizon against which decisions on economic activities are taken.

15 On the critique, see Hampicke (1992), Kappel (1994), and Daly and Cobb (1989).

16 The inclusion of institutions and collective action in the framework of the New Institutionalism is unable to solve this problem fully, since the New Institutionalism shares the neoclassical premises on rationally acting, utility-maximizing actors.

17 Barnett and Morse (1963) and Sapsford and Balasubramanyam (1994). Falling prices mean that no signals are set by raw-materials markets that point to the scarcity problem. Accordingly, theoretical studies on development concerned with the chances of (world-market-oriented) industrialization on the basis of raw materials say not a word about the ecological dimension of this strategy (Wall 1980 and Owens and Wood 1997).

18 The invention of ocean drilling rigs increased the stocks of accessible crude oil; improvements in extraction of crude oil from oil shale may prove to be a step entailing similar impacts.

19 The classical examples include saltpeter from Chile, for which a synthetic replacement was developed in Germany during the First World War, or copper, the demand for which has declined due to the development of glass-fiber cables.

20 The following summary of findings from the field of ecology and thermodynamics is based on Barbier (1989), Chapter 2. – The orientation of economists in terms of

physics has tradition; after all, the thought models of neoclassical economics follow the principle of Newton's mechanics, according to which ecological processes are reversible processes that obey general laws, i.e. the laws of space and time.

21   This presentation borrows on studies by E.P. Odum (see Chapter 4); Trepl (1987) provides an overview of the rise of ecology as a science.

22   In Chapter 4 these functions of the feedback mechanisms are briefly explained with reference to the ecosystem tropical rainforest.

23   On thermodynamics and its use for an economic analysis of the exploitation of the environment, see Georgescu-Roegen (1975); Stephan and Ahlheim (1996), pp 25 - 43, and Binswanger (1993).

24   This section follows Binswanger (1993).

25   What is meant by ecological efficiency is that a maximum of biomass can be maintained by degrading a certain quantity of low entropy.

26   As early as in the 1980s some 40 % of the earth's net primary production (i.e. its overall net production of plant biomass) was consumed by human activities or lost (Vitousek, Ehrlich, Ehrlich and Matson 1986).

27   Costanza (1991) presents a comprehensive overview of the state of theory development in ecological economics.

28   *"In the long run we are all dead,"* noted Keynes alluding to the fact that economics is concerned with short-term rationales. Ecological economics, on the other hand, counters by advancing the argument that this "long term" could, if the economic system continues to expand, be abbreviated to a number of decades.

29   This is the basic idea behind Germany's new ecological tax reform.

30   Georgescu-Roegen and Herman Daly have strongly criticized the blindness for nature neoclassical economics and linked their arguments with a fundamental critique of mainstream economics.

31   See the remarks on issues involved in the theory of science in Section 3.1.1.

32   Homma here goes on record against the demand of rubber tappers for the establishment of extractivist reserves, which is highly popular in international development cooperation circles.

33   IBGE, Brazil's official statistics agency, annually publishes data on the physical and monetary yields of vegetable extractivism. In timber production a distinction is made between primary-forest timber and plantation timber.

34   For the World Bank, World Bank (1992) and Schneider (1995); for IMAZON, Almeida and Uhl (1995), Barros and Verissimo (1996), and Stone (1997, 1998)

35   For more details, see Chapters 6 and 7.

36   Barbier, Burgess, Bishop and Aylward (1994), p. 3 The page numbers that follow refer to this publication.

37   This close context is mirrored by the criteria of the Forest Stewardship Council (FSC) for the certification of sustainable forestry; see Chapter 4.

38   The following studies are named here in the place of a complete list: Amelung (1997); Amelung and Diehl (1992); Thiele (1996); and Wiebelt (1995).

39   The political representation of the Amazon region in the parliament and senate of the Brazilian Union is far greater than the Amazon region's share of the population

and its contribution to the economy, this often makes it possible for the *bancada amazônica* in parliament to push through additional financial transfers and exceptions from budget cuts.

40   The financial crisis of January 1999 increased the pressure to reduce the budget deficit, IMF loans were bound to strict adherence to fiscal discipline. Thus subsidies will have to be reduced

Chapter 3

1   The following discussion is based on Giddens' book "The Constitution of Society" (1984) Quotations from other works are noted separately. On the place of Giddens' works and his theory of structuration in the history of social theory, see Müller (1992).

2   Giddens identifies this basic consensus in the writings of Parsons, Merton, and Lazarsfeld. The result of his endeavors is his 1976 publication "New Rules of Sociological Method", which is quoted here after the edition of 1993.

3   This approach has attracted from some quarters the accusation of superficiality and vague imagism (Müller 1992, p. 152).

4   Of the interpretive schools, Giddens discusses hermeneutic philosophy (Gadamer), which proceeds on the assumption of a radical division between social and natural sciences, the linguistic philosophy of the late Wittgenstein; and ethnomethodology (Garfinkel), which is influenced by phenomenology (Schütz) and Max Weber. Giddens' thought also shows traces of postempiricist philosophy of science (Kuhn, Lakatos, Toulmin) and French structuralism (esp. Lévi-Strauss and Derrida) (Giddens 1993, pp. 1 - 27).

5   This line of argument follows Bhaskar (1979).

6   Here Giddens take a position in sharp contrast to that of Durkheim, for whom the scientific nature of the sociological method was bound up precisely with the non-use of the everyday terms of agents.

7   Analogously, Giddens also defines power as a dual or two-sided capacity: In the first place, power per se is not a resource but is associated with any action; in the second place, it presupposes *"regularized relations of autonomy and dependence between actors or collectivities in contexts of social interaction"*; in the third place, however, *"all forms of dependence offer some resources whereby those who are subordinate can influence the activities of their superiors "* (Giddens 1984, p. 16)

8   These concepts have consequences for the definition of traditional sociological concepts such as power, constraint, identity, role expectation, society, social systems, etc , but it will not be possible to go into them in the framework of the discussion interesting us here. Nor is it the *sine qua non* to an understanding of the use made of Giddens' theory in this study.

9   Giddens here quotes Durkheim's famous definition from the "Rules of Sociological Method," which places humans in analogy to chemical elements: the combination of different elements leads to the emergence of new, different substances in which the elements take their place, Durkheim claims that the properties of social systems, which must be distinguished from their members, are analogous. Giddens

rejects the premise of the metaphor: We can ascribe an isolated existence to chemical elements, not to human beings (1984, p. 169 f.).

10   Giddens distinguishes structure from structures and both terms from the *"structural properties of social systems"* (1984, p. 23): The first term refers to rules and resources embedded in institutions; structure exists *"out of space and time,"* in the *"absence of the subject"* (p. 25). Giddens borrowed this definition from French structuralism (Lévi-Strauss, Derrida), which understands structures as mental processes of consciousness; in principle, this is not compatible with Giddens' variant of action theory. The second term is used to designate the factors of transformation and mediation through which social systems reproduce themselves (p. 24). The third term, finally, refers to *"those institutional characteristics"* which safeguard the existence of social systems over space and time (p. 24).

11   What Giddens means by recursivity is that the *"structured properties of social activity - via the duality of structure - are constantly recreated out of the very resources which constitute them "* (1984, p xxiii)

12   The knowledge embedded in day-to-day social action is *"not separate from their [the social actors'] world, as in the case of knowledge of events or objects in nature. Testing out just what it is that actors know, and how they apply that knowledge in their practical conduct (..) depends upon using the same materials - an understanding of recursively organized practices - from which hypotheses about that knowledge are derived The measure of their 'validity' is supplied by how far actors are able to co-ordinate their activities with others in such a way as to pursue the purposes engaged by their behaviour."* (Giddens 1984, p. 90)

13   For an overview, see Ruttan (1997), Dosi (1997), Hurtienne and Messner (1994), and Meyer-Stamer (1996).

14   Hodgson (1993) presents an overview of the tradition of evolutionary thought in economics.

15   The following overview largely follows Dosi (1997).

16   What follows is a summary of the critique of orthodox neoclassic thinking as worked out by Nelson and Winter (1982)

17   This was demonstrated in Section 2.5 with reference to the discussion of the logging dynamics in tropical countries on the basis of allocation theory (Wiebelt 1995) as well as with reference to the analysis of the tropical-timber trade presented by resource economics (Barbier, Burgess, Bishop and Aylward 1994).

18   Nelson and Winter (1982) here refer to Cyert and March (1963), who show that it is less agreement on ultimate goals then on procedures that can be used to reach decisions that are crucial to entrepreneurial capacities to act.

19   Nelson and Winter (1982), p. 60, summarize the view of the neoclassical model as follows: *"Technical knowledge is articulated knowledge. It is the sort of thing that can be recorded, stored at negligible cost, and referred to when needed."*

20   See Dosi and Nelson (1994), pp. 218 f. Dosi's use of the term paradigm here is somewhat confusing in that the term is situated far below the level of aggregation with which e g. Kuhn is concerned in upheavals of scientific paradigms. Freeman and Pérez (1988) use the term techno-economic paradigm - more in analogy to Kuhn - to refer to the specific historical intertwinement of technology, economic, social, and institutional organizational features that characterize forms of society.

Dosi and Nelson (1994) use the term technological regime to approximate this level of aggregation

21 Freeman (1982) distinguishes between incremental innovations that continuously occur in the production process, increasing the efficient use made of all production factors, and radical innovations that have a discontinuous character, tend more to stem from formal research contexts, and usually lead to combined changes of products, production processes, and corporate organization. Radical innovations give rise to new branches of industry and new products.

22 The costs of coordination are acknowledged by the New Institutional Economics, which sees them as the reason for the rise of institutions, including, in the end, firms themselves

23 See also Piore (1996), who, in a review of the *Handbook of Economic Sociology* (ed Smelser and Swedenberg, 1994), which gives much space to studies on innovation theory, emphasizes that most of the authors are influenced by the new social science and its ambivalent action concept colored by linguistic sociology.

24 E.g. Luhmann (986), who traces the functioning of social subsystems back to the existence of binary codes that are in no way interlinked with one another (can generate no resonance), in this way defines away the ambivalence of social communication.

25 The most important include, first, the insistence of evolutionary economics on the market as an impersonal selection mechanism that places firms under pressure to adapt – Giddens generally rejects the concept of adaptation as void of substance when applied to social processes – and, second, the idea of the emergent properties of economic systems that arise from the aggregate interactions between individual firms, an idea that Giddens likewise rejects since he cannot imagine the actors or firms as isolated individuals.

26 This implies the question as to the extent to which a firm is capable of absorbing radical innovations that would wholly revolutionize its routines. The question can be answered only empirically, since there is evidence both for decline of large firms due to radical innovations and for the absorption of such innovations.

27 Pavitt (1984) develops a typology by distinguishing whether the industries concerned are developers or suppliers of innovations. Lundvall (1988) looks more closely at the dynamics between manufacturers and users, drawing conclusions on the significance of historical processes of the accumulation of technological competence that can be explained with reference to national specialization patterns.

28 Dosi and Orsenigo (1988), p. 24; what is meant by *appropriability* is the extent to which a firm is in a position to at least temporarily appropriate the profits stemming from an innovation without having to share them immediately with competitors.

29 See Dosi and Soete (1988) and Dosi, Pavitt and Soete (1990); Chapter 8 of the present study looks into these studies at greater length.

30 See Flick (1991), who refers to this approach as *"object-related theory formation."*

31 These include SUDAM (1973); Knowles (1965); Bruce (1976); Mercado (1980); Ros-Tonen (1993); Barros and Veríssimo (1996); and Stone (1997, 1998).

32 A tabular overview of the most important features of the firms polled (which were assured of anonymity) can be found in Table 2.

33   The authorities included the environmental ministries of Pará, Amazonas, and
      Brazil, the environmental authorities (IBAMA) of Belém, Manaus, and Brasilia,
      the customs authority of Pará, and members of the Amazon development agency
      SUDAM The associations polled included the federation of Pará timber exporters,
      AIMEX, and the Brazilian plywood and tropical-timber federation, ABIMCI. In-
      terviews were also conducted with timber experts of the advisory organization for
      small and medium-scale companies, SEBRAE, in Belém. As far as the field of re-
      search is concerned, the author also interviewed members of the University of
      Pará, the agricultural research institution EMBRAPA-CPATU in Belém, INPA in
      Manaus, IMAZON and IPAM in Belém, and French and Dutch researchers work-
      ing there The NGOs interviewed included Greenpeace, WWF, FFT, CTA, CNS,
      and FASE. An interview was also conducted with M. Simula and J. Tissari from
      the consulting company Indufor OY.

Chapter 4

1   Ecologists distinguish artificial and domesticated environments (cities, agricultural
      areas) from the natural environment (Odum 1997, p 10).

2   Until recently the dominant thesis was that the Andes region was always culturally
      superior to the Amazon region.

3   For a critical discussion of the classical model of the ecology of the topical rain-
      forest as well as recent findings, see Hurtienne (1997), to whom this chapter owes
      a great deal. The prominent German representatives of the classical model include
      Weischet (1980, 1985) and Weischet and Caviedes (1993); Sioli (1956, 1983) and
      Klinge (1983).

4   Other classifications have been proposed by Lauer (1952) and Lamprecht (1989),
      pp. 34 ff.

5   This view often draws the conclusion that only market-oriented, capital-intensive
      medium- or large-scale farms represent a viable form of agriculture. But this trend
      is not greeted unanimously; Coy (1987) sees it in a negative light because of the
      social displacement effects involved, while Almeida (1996) and Serrão and
      Homma (1993) underline the conditions required for any competitive agriculture.

6   Typical annual cultures are rice, maize, and beans; perennial cultures are often
      seen as including both semi-perennial cultures such as pepper and maracujá and
      trees with a long lifespan that are planted for their fruit or their wood.

7   Evapotranspiration refers to the overall evaporation stemming from ground evapo-
      ration and plant transpiration (Salati 1987; Schubart 1983).

8   In Latin America 65 % of all tropical soils are reported to be very low in nutrients
      (Weischet 1980)

9   In Venezuela some 42,000 plant species have been reported thus far, as compared
      with some 2,800 for Germany (Sommer, Settele, Michelsen et. al. 1990, p. 23).

10   Comparisons of 40 representative soil samples from southwest Germany with 23
      samples from tropical moist forests and deciduous forests from South America and
      Malaysia showed that the humus quantities of the soils of temperate and tropical
      areas display similar levels. Soils of tropical moist forests are not low in humus
      per se but only when they are sandy (150 - 220 t of humus/ha; min. average humus

quantity in Germany: 200 t/ha). The more clayey soils, which are far more frequent in the tropics, have humus levels similar to those found here (Sommer, Settele, Michelsen et al 1990, pp 109 - 110).

11   Investigations conducted in the *várzea* of the Rio Negro and the Amazon showed that the main mass of roots extends to a depth of 40 cm, the figure for the low-nutrient soils of the upper Rio Negro was up to 15 cm. But roots were measured in both habitats that extended further than 1 m In Surinam root depths of over 150 cm have been noted (Sommer, Settele, Michelsen et al. 1990, pp. 113 - 115). The group around Nepstad seems to have been the first to propose the thesis of the significance of deep roots. This thesis was confirmed by empirical studies undertaken primarily in Pará, but also in the west Amazon region; these samples found root depths of at least 8 m, though some extended to 18 m (Nepstad et al. 1994). Bruenig (1996) cites similar figures for Sarawak.

12   Empirical studies in an ancient agrarian-settlement area in the northeast of Pará were unable to clearly prove any decrease of soil fertility when the utilization form was rotation between farming and secondary growth. When the fallow period is long enough (min. 7 years), it is possible to achieve stable harvests using a system consisting of natural fertilization (accumulation of nutrients in the vegetation cover with a high share of leaf material) and selective addition of mineral fertilizer for longer periods of time (Hurtienne 1997).

13   This proposition is based on a sample including forest formations from all climatic zones; the authors prove this by calculating the wood production of coniferous and deciduous forests in temperate and boreal zones over a period of 144 - 500 years (O'Neill and De Angelis 1981, p. 414).

14   Bruenig (1996), pp. 24 - 29, 36 - 39 and Whitmore (1993) come to the conclusion that it is wrong to assume a dominance of above-ground nutrient cycles in moist tropical forests.

15   The exact calculation of the sink capacity of forests is a controversial issue.

16   Succession refers to the specific temporal course of development taken by the species composition with an ecosystem (Loucks et al. 1981).

17   On measurements of tree species, see Jentsch (1911); on animal species (Stevens 1968).

18   The end of the felling cycle is the period when a tree has passed its fastest phase of growth, i e when net growth per unit of time has lessened.

19   Prior to the introduction of forestry the forest was also used, and degraded, as a multiple resource: wood for fuel and building was removed from it, fruits and litter were gathered for animals and as fertilizer for field, as well as other forest products. Technical innovations lowered the economic dependence on wood; the "wooden age" (Sieferle 1988) was supplanted by the age of coal and oil.

20   In its last report on the state of the world's forests, in 1997, the FAO also used the concept of a forest bound to "natural soil conditions, not subject to agricultural practices," thereby distinguishing between natural forests and plantations; but the latter term is used to refer to areas that were never forested or to stands of non-native species. This means reversing the actual state of affairs that sees the managed forests of the industrialized countries as natural forests. While data are given to indicate to what extent forests in the developing countries are disappearing and

being replaced by plantations, this category, for the industrialized countries, is termed "not applicable" (FAO 1997)

21 Rudyard Kipling erected a literary monument to Brandis in the final story of his "Jungle Book." For more information on the Taungya system (Lamprecht 1989, pp. 144 ff).

22 See Lamprecht (1989) for the Malayan Uniform System (MUS), the Tropical Shelterwood System (TSS), CELOS and line planting.

23 Only individuals with a breast-height stem diameter of at least 25 cm were counted.

24 Both the historical studies conducted by the FAO and contemporary studies are as a rule limited to the sustainability of timber production; today an additional consideration is protection of the basic ecological functions of forest ecosystems. The view of the forest as a multiple resource whose direct economic value may be sought in nontimber products (traditional products of gatherers and genetic resources of pharmaceutical and biotechnological interest) and in the forest's recreational value (ecotourism) is gaining ground only slowly in the Amazon region. See Section 4 4

25 See SUDAM (1990) for the evaluation of the results from the Curuá-Una research station, Carvalho (1987) and Silva (1993) for an evaluation of the results from the Flona Tapajós and Belterra. See Barros and Veríssimo (1996) on the IMAZON findings

26 See in particular Silva (1993)

27 See also the descriptive EMBRAPA-CPATU brochure for sawmill operators: Silva (1996).

28 In logging operations without scheduling, the caterpillar or skidder operators have to look for each individual log; this entails the destruction of much undergrowth, and felled logs are often not recovered because they cannot be found. This method entails far greater damage to the forest canopy and adjacent trees than in the case of planned logging: the canopy damage drops from 27 to 45 % to 18 %; instead of the average of 27, only 14 adjacent trees are damaged.

29 IMAZON assumes a figure of US$ 72.3/ha as costs for inventories, felling and transportation costs and forest-tending measures; referred to 40 m^3 of felled timber, the additional costs amount to US$ 1.80/m^3

30 Fore more detail. see Evans (1996)

31 Marchés Tropicaux, August 1, 1997, and Lehmann (1993). In Germany the federation of public and private forest owners has thus far been unable to decide in favor of participation in the German FSC initiative.

32 The cases of certificate misuse discovered in Germany in the summer of 1998 were all committed by companies from industrialized countries that deal in tropical-wood products. These cases show that even a self-interest logical in itself must be defined as such in a social process before becoming effective: without the vociferous protests of environmental groups and reports in the press the short-term economic rationale of the fraudulent companies would have paid off.

33 According to Precious Woods, a sustainably managed forestry firm in the Amazon region that has been certified by the FSC, the company's products command prices in Europe for its certified wood that are 10 - 15 % above average levels.

34 The FSC Brazil working group consists of nongovernmental organizations (NGOs) active in the fields of social welfare and the environment, the union of construction workers and forestry workers, research institutes, the federations of the pulp and paper industry, the timber exporters of Pará (AIMEX), and the federation of plantation operators The environment ministry as well as certifiers also participate in the capacity of observers. The subgroup in charge of working out criteria for the utilization of *terra firme* forests is directed by IMAZON, further members include GTA, an NGO, and AIMEX. Consulting experts include representatives of two NGOs with considerable experience with indigenous, traditional forest dwellers (*caboclos* and *ribeirinhos*) as well as recognized forestry experts from EMBRAPA-CPATU.

35 The lack of clarity in matters of land ownership is a problem that not only plagues the Amazon region, it is also characteristic of the history of the settlement of Brazil as a whole

Chapter 5

1 All percentage figures are calculated from FAO statistics on world production of and world trade in forest products.

2 In the 1980s the trade in plywood grew by 9 % per year, a figure which dropped to 3.5 % in the 1990s. See Neue Zürcher Zeitung, Dec. 4, 1996.

3 See Chapter 4 on the definition of the terms plantation and natural forest.

4 See Marchés Tropicaux of Jan 1, 1996, Oct. 25, 1996, Sept. 19, 1997, and Jan. 16, 1998.

5 Liberalization of the rail freight rates increased real transportation costs for remote logging areas to such an extent that logging was no longer profitable there.

6 Barbier et al. (1994), pp 14 ff, and FAO (1995) The absolute price figures in the text are given in current US$

7 Marchés Tropicaux, Sept. 19, 1997. Following the drastic devaluation in Indonesia at the end of 1997 prices plummeted, leading to major sales problems for logs from Africa.

8 See the detailed country studies in Repetto and Gillis (1988) and FAO (1988).

9 On the general impacts on the developing countries of the Uruguay Round and the foundation of the WTO, see Wiemann (1996); see UNCTAD (1996) on the agreements for wood products

10 See here Goodland and Daly (1996), who are basically positive as far as log export bans are concerned.

11 This condition was imposed in 1998 in connection with a structural-adjustment program.

12 By way of comparison· In Scandinavia production proceeds on the assumption of a rotation cycle of a hundred years and annual timber growth of 3 m³/ha (Mather 1997, p. 14)

13 According to STCP calculations the production costs in Brazil for MDF or OSB boards are 50 and 70 % lower than the cost of 4mm plywood; this cost differential is due above all to the low share of raw-materials costs in producing such novel

panels. While for plywood nearly half of production costs are due to the raw material, for MDF and OSB they account for only roughly a quarter to a third (Simula 1997)

14 For a summary view, see Dudley, Jeanrenaud and Sullivan (1996) and Mather (1997)

15 A number of the leading consulting officies active in the fields of wood, pulp, and paper are from Finland.

Chapter 6

1 Silva et al. (1997) found that since 1994 some 20 % of the sawmills in Paragominas, one of the core areas of Pará's timber industry, have shut down. Devaluations in Asia reduced the prices of Asian timber exports, placing Brazilian exporters, whom the hardness of Brazil's currency had placed at a disadvantage, under severe pressure, in addition, the Philippines and Thailand were no longer available as sales markets This is expected to mean a decline in imports of some 20 % for 1997/98. The export-oriented timber industry experienced shutdowns and mass layoffs in the first quarter of 1998 (O Liberal, March 1, 1998)

2 On Malaysian investments in the Amazon region, see Viana (1997), Toni (1997), O Liberal, May 1, 1996, and Oct. 23, 1997, and Karsenty (1997).

3 According to FAO (1997) data, over 50 % of the world's tropical forest stands are in tropical South America; the by far greatest share of these is located in the Amazon regions of the eight Amazon states Brazil, Columbia, Venezuela, Ecuador, Peru, Guyana, and Surinam. And the largest part of these resources is in Brazil.

4 The following presentation of the *Plano Real* is based largely on Fritz (1996, 1997).

5 This is the line of argument of e.g. Gustavo Franco, one of the fathers of the *Plano Real* (Franco 1996)

6 Imports of capital goods increased in 1990 by 14 %, in 1991 by 7 %, in 1992 by 11 %, in 1993 by 56 %, in 1994 by 47 %, and in 1995 by 90 % (Bonelli 1996, p. 625).

7 The settlement of the northeast of Pará was intended as a means of stepping up local food production; the project involved enticing both landless persons from Brazil's northeast and Japanese and European settlers into the region. In the 1950s the Japanese settlers introduced pepper cultivation here, ultimately making Pará into the world's greatest supplier of pepper (Penteado 1967; Inhetvin 1991; Kitamura 1994; Costa 1992, Hurtienne 1997).

8 Rural population here includes, in keeping with the international definition, municipalities with up to 20,000 inhabitants. Brazil's popluation statistics usually proceed from a figure of 5,000 residents.

9 Author's calculations after Nosso Pará (1996), p. 63, and Braz de Oliveira e Silva et al. (1996) Brazil's average export content has traditonally been roughly 7 %, in 1994 it was 27.7 % for industry and agriculture and 12.7 % as a share of overall GDP

10 On regional imbalances and regional economic promotion, see Baer (1995), Chapter 12, Cano (1985).

11   Proceedings of the SUDAM's *Conselho Deliberativo* on projects approved, on the
      Internet under http://www sudam gov.br.

12   In the pulp industry 80 % of pulp output is accounted for by five firms; in the
      paper industry 53 % is produced by seven firms Brazil is the world's seventh larg-
      est pulp producer and its eleventh largest paper producer; 47 % of the pulp and
      33 % of the paper produced there are exported (Faillace, undated, pp. 29 - 32). The
      country's overall fiberboard output is accounted for by two firms, its particle-board
      output by six firms (Guimarães Neto and Rocha 1992).

13   Barros and Veríssimo (1996), pp. 1 f. Data on the GDP of Brazil's states have not
      been published by IBGE since 1985, in 1996 IPEA prepared a number of GDP es-
      timates for the years 1985-94, but they contain no data on the individual branches
      of industry (Braz de Oliveira e Silva et al. 1996). Maia Gomes and Vergolino
      (1997) have prepared an overview of the development and distribution of regional
      growth between 1960 and 1995 in the Amazon region, but it concentrates primar-
      ily on the spatial dimension and less on branches of industry

14   Oral communication from Brandão, Paragominas, Oct. 29, 1997; along the ca.
      450-km-long section of the road from Belém to Brasilia between Santa Maria do
      Pará and Açailandia there are some 300 sawmills.

15   Ferreira (1997). On the basis of Stone's data (1998), p. 445, we can calculate an
      increase of the unit costs for sawnwood of 17 % between 1990 and 1995; trans-
      portation costs per unit rose by 56 % in the same period.

16   On the yield of sawmills in tropical countries, see Repetto and Gillis (1988) as
      well as Brockmann, Hemmelskamp and Hohmeyer (1996). The typical yield of
      sawmills in the industrialized countries is 70 %, see Herkendell and Pretzsch
      (1995), p 19

17   See the different contributions in Barros and Veríssimo (1996)

18   Silva (1994), pp 6 and 16 Since the IBAMA register is not reliable, the data cited
      here will have to be seen as rough approximations.

19   The IBGE estimates roundwood production on the basis of the sales figures indi-
      cated by timber firms to the internal revenue service.

20   IBAMA (1998); on the sawnwoord production of pulp comapnies, see Gazeta
      Mercantil, May 7, 1998, and Marques (1997)

21   Veríssimo, Barreto, Tarifa and Uhl (1996) note with reference to the example of
      mahogany extraction in the south of Pará how the clandestine road-building com-
      missioned and financed by timber corporations to transport mahogany logs cuts
      the rides crucial to an agricultural conversion of forests. This is the only case thus
      far documented of the timber industry as a ground-breaker for farming settlements
      in Pará.

22   For many smallholders the sale of logging rights or logs to timber dealers is an
      important source of cash, since these farmers are then not responsible for trans-
      portation (one of the most crucial bottlenecks in the marketing of their produce).
      Logging rights are also often handed over in exchange for the building or mainte-
      nance of roads. According to the agricultural census of 1995/96, the revenues
      stemming from extractivism (90 % of which come from logging) make up an av-
      erage of 32 % of the gross value of farm production; the figure for 1985 was
      merely 16 %.

23 Mattos and Uhl (1994) note how in Paragominas proceeds from the sale of logging rights are used to finance the costs needed to modernize ranching (incl. erecting the fences needed for rotational use of grazing land, the use of tractors, pesticides, and fertilizers for growing fodder plants). As a result cattle-ranching becomes more profitable and may be even more sustainable, but this type of forest use is in no way sustainable.

24 GTA and FoE (1997); logging in indigenous areas is not always done against the will of the indigenous peoples, when they, as in the case of Kayapó in the south of Pará, have bargaining power enough to ensure themselves a share of the profits made through the logging operations.

25 The forest damage incurred in connection with conventional logging seriously impairs the forest's regeneration capacity and increases the risk of forest fires, since the dead vegetation dries out and is highly combustible.

26 Silva et al. (1997); oral communication from Guilherme Carvalho, the secretary general of AIMEX, and from Adalberto Veríssimo, IMAZON.

27 According to STCP, in Brazil 38 % of sawnwood is used in the building sector and 35 % goes into the furniture industry.

28 Oral communication from the secretary general of AIMEX, August 27, 1996.

29 Ferreira (1997), p. 19, found in an empirical study conducted in Paragominas that when timber is processed for the domestic market 58 % of the trunk can be used, whereas when timber is processed for export only 30 % can be used.

30 36 % of the volume of sawnwood was, according to AIMEX data, made up of six species (including jatobá, tauarí, quaruba, mahogany); the remaining 64 % was made up of 33 further species. Mahogany accordingly accounted for only 7.7 % of the volume of exports, which, at a price of US$ 800 per cubic meter, is a share of export value amounting to some 19 %. AIMEX breaks down the shares of species in sawnwood exports only in terms of volume, not export value; this masks the continuing relative importance of mahogany exports.

31 Tauarí was first looked into for its potential uses by a US forester; in the 1980s a small French-Brazilian export company specialized in the trade with new species introduced tauarí to the French market. There this wood is used chiefly to build windows, doors, and staircases. The French-Brazilian company was bought up at the beginning of the 1990s by a big French timber-trading corporation that offers windows, doors, and staircases in building-materials stores of its own in France.

32 A major timber exporter from Pará regards this as a significant innovation that has the potential to revolutionize timber-logging and the timber trade. This could make it possible to achieve effects to scale in logging and marketing that have never been possible with the traditional European-style demand for given timber species for given uses. This innovation could also intensify logging and thus increase forest destruction.

33 Once Altamira, the administrative and business center of the Transamazônica in the interior of Pará, had been connected to the power grid in June of 1998, sawmills started relocating there. The objective of this relocation is to get access to the largely intact forest stands in the west of Pará. See Gazeta Mercantil Pará, June 3, 1998

34 The outlines of the *Código Florestal* were formulated in Statute no. 4771 of Jan. 23, 1934, under Getúlio Vargas, and given their present, extended, form on Sept.

15, 1965. by the then military government of Castelo Branco. Decree no. 1282 of Oct. 19, 1994, contains regulations for the articles of the *Código Florestal* on sustainable forest management. Decree no. 1298 of Oct. 27, 1994 stipulates that the national forests administered by IBAMA can also be used for productive ends. *Portaria* no. 48 of July 10, 1995 requires presentation of a forest-management plan (*Plano de Manejo Florestal* – PMF). *Medida Provisória* (provisional measure) no. 1511 of July 25, 1996 stipulates that clear-felling is permitted only on max. 20 % of wooded property (the figure was previously 50 %) and that no further clear-felling is permissible on farms when deforested areas are fallow or being used for unproductive purposes. Decree 1963 of July 25, 1996 places a freeze on all new logging permits for mahogany and virola for two years and makes the validity of existing permits contingent on a new audit by IBAMA.

35 Statute no. 6938 of August 31, 1981 defines the distribution of responsibilities and the instruments of national envionmental policy; Decree 99274 of June 6, 1990 stipulates that licenses for environmentally harmful activities are to be granted by state environmental authorities, while this right remains with IBAMA in the case of natural resources that are under federal supervision. In 1999, IBAMA's competences were further reduced in favor of state authorities.

36 Article 15 of the *Código Florestal*; in Portugese the formulation is: "*Fica proibida a exploração sob forma empírica das florestas primitivas da bacia amazônica...*"; what is meant by "empirical" logging is unregulated logging, i.e. not guided by the theoretical principles of forestry.

37 Article 16, small and medium-size farms of up to 100 ha were later exempted for social reasons under pressure from farmers' organizations, since the regime of fallow-cropping practiced by them requires that their entire holding be used. The regrowth of secondary vegetation and the cultures planted ensure that the ground is nearly constantly covered. This is, however, only the case when the fallow cycle is at least seven years long. – In the other regions of Brazil the *reserva legal permanente* stipulated only 20 % of a landholding

38 The contingents for exports of virola, imbuia, mahogany, and araucaria (Brazilian pine) are based on IBAMA's Portaria no. 138-N of Dec. 28, 1993. Imbuia occurs in the Atlantic coastal forest in the southeast of the country, araucaria in the forests of the south.

39 Statute no. 6938 of August 31, 1981; on the statute on environmental crimes, see O Liberal, Feb. 25, 1998.

40 The proposed law was energetically opposed by entrepreneurial federations in the Amazon region, since, it is claimed, the new law "*would force entrepreneurial activity in the Amazon region into illegality* " As with other laws, this one too in fact failed to take specific Amazon conditions into account; many individual measures are clearly geared to the types of environmental damage typical of the south and southeast of Brazil.

41 The following discussion follows Horta (1994).

42 ITTO members committed themselves, starting in 2000, to trade only in tropical timber stemming from managed forests.

43 The Pará industry federation and AIMEX countered by noting that in 1995 only 949,000 m^3 of timber were exported from Pará; the 30 million claimed by SAE, as well as an alleged 50 million m^3 of roundwood, were rightly termed totally un-

founded. See O Liberal, June 22, 1997, p. 12. – According to FAO a total of 16 9 million m³ of (deciduous) sawnwood was exported worldwide in 1993

44   See O Liberal from May 1, 1996, p. 6, and May 11, 1997, p. 7. An Indonesian corporation had offered Surinam an investment sum that was three to four times the country's GDP; it wanted in exchange some 70 % of the country's area for logging operations. To circumvent the law of the land, which prohibits land purchases by foreigners of over 1500 ha, the corporation set up a network of national dummy companies. In view of the WRI report on the low returns which Surinam stood to gain through the deal, the negotiations were suspended for the time being.

45   The actual extent to which the regeneration of virola is endangered is a controversial issue While the stands in the immediate shore areas really have declined, there are also reports indicating a very good regeneration in the north of the isalnd of Marajó; a delegation of acknowedged IBAMA and EMBRAPA-CPATU experts inspected this area in 1997 and subsequently spoke out in favor of rescinding the ban on felling virola. The lack of clarity indicates that in formulating these measures the government simply pointed to the two best-known species found in the Amazon region as a means of decreasing logging.

46   The very fact of the decree shows how far removed the environment ministry is from the reality of the Amazon region.

47   FoE and AdT (1997), p 10, and oral communication from IMAZON experts.

48   The following section is based on an evaluation of interviews conducted by the author between September of 1997 and March of 1998. Quotations from the interview protocols are presented as indented paragraphs.

49   On this, see Ferreira (1997), pp 16 - 26, and Stone (1998).

50   The system of quotas has thus not proved to be an effective instrument for reducing the felling of mahogany, though it has led to a more effective control of the legality of logging and transportation. at least for exports, since exports have to be approved and the documents accompanying every mahogany export transaction are carefully audited Oral communication from the responsible customs official in Belém and different exporters, Oct 1997 Illegal logging in indigenous peoples' territories is found out in this way, and has led to increasing confiscations. In Nov. 1998, after a raid in the south of Pará, the felling and transportation of mahogany was banned until further notice, since large quantities of this timber were found at sawmills. and the timber was not from areas where logging was permitted.

51   In 1996 IBAMA had released 136,000 m³ of mahogany for logging (FoE/AdT 1997, p. 14).

52   This is the well-known Swiss firm Precious Woods that operates the project MIL Madeireira in Itacoatiara near Manaus. See Neue Zürcher Zeitung of Nov. 24, 1995, and Die Zeit of June 20, 1997. But even this firm was given bad headlines when it became known in the summer of 1998 that part of the logs delivered to the German *Land* of Mecklenburg-Western Pomerania had been bought from third parties, i e. stemmed from nonmanaged areas (FR of Sept. 15, 1998).

53   The BNDES provides large corporations with loans for reforestation projects that add 2 5 % plus a risk surcharge to the long-term interest rate The long-term interest rate, TJLP, was between 1996 and 1998 11 % p.a. Experts estimate the profit of a eucalyptus plantation at 10 - 12 % p.a., assuming a cycle of 21 years and an

initial harvest after 7 years have elapsed (Gazeta Mercantil of Oct. 20, 1997, p A-5).

54 Since the government of Pará has plans to provide generous subsidies for the large-scale cultivation of maize and, above all, soybeans, a number of sawmill owners in Paragominas, who have already purchased land, are redirecting their activities toward agriculture.

55 Veríssimo et al. (1996) investigated two important sawmill agglomerations in Pará and found that the greater majority of sawmill owners do not derive from the Amazon region, though they had already been active in the timber industry (Barros and Veríssimo 1996, Chapters 1 and 2).

56 This is not necessarily a result of any scarcity of capital; big investment funds of the public investment bank BNDES geared to promoting medium-scale firms in the Amazon region have found disbursement problems that cannot be explained only with reference to the bureaucratic obstacles involved in applying for funds.

57 The mayor of Paragominas (PSDB) owns a large sawmill and plywood factory, there are also a number of such cases along the Transamazônica.

58 IPAM became well known throughout Brazil in 1998 when it presented a map of the Amazon region containing the areas at risk from forest fire following the "el Niño" phenomenon and based on both satellite data and results from fieldwork. Furthermore, IPAM has presented a catalogue of measures based chiefly on an evaluation of the experience of small famers that is aimed at reducing the risks of fire clearance IBAMA's measures aimed at lowering the danger of forest fire – which has not yet been put into practice – is in large measure indebted to this catalogue

59 Aside from the semi-open interviews conducted in 1997, the following description of the problem perception of entrepreneurs is based on statements of the federations that were noted down at two different congresses in 1996 (Silva et al. 1997; FIEPA 1996).

60 See Chapter 7 on this point

61 Kolk (1996) provides an overview of the constantly recurring suspicion that the Amazon region is set to be placed under international tutelage, as well as of foreign influence on Brazil's Amazon policy; these positions recently reerupted in view of the Malaysian investments in the Amazon region and the again and again expressed – but seldom proved – accusations of illegal trade in biogenetic resources from the Amazon region (biopiracy).

62 In the past years illegal logging in indigenous peoples' areas and on public land has increased substantially, The intention is to legalize this practice (GTA/FoE 1997)

63 The Mexico crisis at the end of 1994, the Asia crisis a year later, and the 1998 crisis triggered by the Russian economic turmoil in September of 1998 forced the Brazilan government, if it was to defend monetary stability, to impose packages of measures that entailed drastic interest-rate hikes (the last one: 50 %). Since 1999 the exchange rate has been floating, which has entailed massive devaluations.

Chapter 7

1 The question of the influence of SUDAM's tax incentives on the timber industry is discussed further below.

2   The Brazilian pulp producer Aracruz, which has a 7 % share of the world market for eucalyptus-based pulp, was instrumental in putting together a larger delegation of entrepreneurs to attend the first international meeting of the Forest Stewardship Council, at which certification rules were to be discussed; the company made sure that independent NGOs were also included in the process. Aracruz also proposed that the Business Council for Sustainable Development (BCSD) commission the independent London-based International Institute for Environment and Development to prepare a study on future worldwide paper consumption and compare the ecological, social, and economic impacts of paper production from pulp and used paper (IIED and WBCSD, undated).

3   See Knowles (1965), p. 63. In Pará a US millionaire named Ludwig began setting up a pulp factory on the Jari River at the end of the 1960s that was to be supplied with plantation timber. This factory remained the only one of its kind in the Amazon region. Due to numerous management errors the factory took up operations only toward the end of the 1970s; in subsequent years it for the most part operated in the red. In the mid-1980s the firm was taken over by a Brazlian consortium. In the mid-1990s modernization investments were announced that were aimed at making the plant interesting for foreign investors; but sales negotiations failed on account of the excessively low offers made. In 1997 there was a fire in the factory that interrupted its power supply for six months, this plunged the entire municipality into an economic crisis (Pinto 1986; Fearnside and Rankin 1982, 1985; Fearnside 1988; Carrere 1996).

4   The charcoal demand of the railroads in São Paulo was instrumental in depleting the natural forest stands; in 1904 the *Companhia Ferroviária Paulista* started investing in eucalyptus cultivation. An agronomist named Edmundo Navarro travelled around the world studying eucalyptus species and silvicultural methods suited to accelerating their growth; he published innumberable studies on the topic which, had they been translated, would have made him the greatest eucalyptus specialist of his times. In 1911 he became director of the forest authority of São Paulo, transforming it into an agency geared to promoting reforestation with eucalyptus. The agency issued 250,000 seedlings per year. At the same time botanical research of the primary forests and their potential industrial uses was terminated (Dean 1997, p 250 f)

5   It was only in 1991 that the prices for pulp in the domestic market were liberalized (Soto 1993, pp. 28 f , 31 ff.).

6   See the classical report by the French geographer Monbeig which was published in Paris in 1953 and published in translation in Brazil in 1984. A study by the US environmental historian Warren Dean (1997) provides some interesting information on the historical patterns of forest utilization on the Atlantic coast.

7   Balata is a latex that is tapped from the maçaranduba tree; copaíba resin is a medicine. Virola seeds were used to make soap, and the poisonous timbó root was used to produce a pesticide.

8   The river trading post was a social meeting point; the trader regularly funded feasts on special occasions, he advanced small sums, and was often the godfather of the children of the famers/gatherers (Wagley 1953).

9   See Santos (1980); Hurtienne (1988) on this little-known aspect.

10   The first development plan was never approved by parliament; the funds were allocated on an annual basis and with substantial delays, which made any long-

term project planning impossible. Priority was given to agriculture as a means of increasing food security; furthermore, the region was to produce raw materials for the south of the country and for foreign markets.

11   It was only in 1974, 17 years later, that the paving of the 2100-km-long road between Belém and Brasilia was completed; this long period of time not only illustrates the practical problems of building a road in the moist tropics (the first unpaved road took five years to complete), it also casts a light on the difficulties the still marginal region has in realizing its interests in the competitive political struggle for public funds.

12   The BASA emerged from the *Banco de Crédito da Borracha*, which was founded in the 1940s, held a monopoly on rubber and was supposed to provide loans for food production and infrastructure development.

13   While in 1964 tax incentives accounted for 20 % of SPVEA's budgets, its share had reached 200 % in 1966; i.e. the tax incentives were far greater than the institutions's own funds (Mahar 1978, p. 21).

14   The federal authorities were not willing to respect the legally specified territorial sovereignty accorded to SUDAM, which would have meant a limitation of their freedom to act. This amounted to the loss of a central precondition for any successful development planning, namely a coordinated approach involving all of the major actors in the region (Pandolfo 1994; Mahar 1978).

15   The tax incentives included a 50 - 100 % rebate on the income tax for firms that located in the Amazon region, a tax exemption on imports of machines and equipment to be used in the Amazon region, and the possibility of deducting from estimated income tax between 50 and 75 % of investment sums planned for the Amazon region.

16   In 1968 SUDAM proposed that it should be given all tax revenues raised in the region for three years in order then to invest these funds in the development of infrastructure; moreover, the electrification of the Amazon region was to be financed by means of a national electricity surtax. This proposal was not approved.

17   The *Programa Grande Carajás* also included bauxite production on the Rio Trombetas and construction of an aluminium factory (with port expansion in Barcarena), construction of a rail line from the iron mine to the port in Maranhão, and construction of the dam and hydroelectric power plant in Tucuruí, which was to supply Barcarena and Carajás with power.

18   There were repeated drastic devaluations and swings between price freezes and releases; in 1990, one day after his inauguration, President Collor froze 70 % of savings accounts for 18 months (Coes 1995; Fritz 1997; Meyer-Stamer 1996).

19   Knowles (1971). p 41, definitively regards these artisanal operations as obsolete and incapable of providing a significant contribution to the region's economic development; in his opinion the artisans could be better used as skilled workers in modern furniture factories

20   In 1958 IBGE polled 4408 firms active in the timber-processing industry; at the beginning of the 1960s Knowles estimated a cost structure, since the entrepreneurs interviewed were unwilling to discuss the matter. He arrived at higher figures for wage costs than IBGE.

21   On the data on the timber industry in 1972, see Bruce (1976), on the data for 1979, see Mercado (1980) While Bruce gives separate data for Pará timber industry,

Mercado does not differentiate in this way; since 1978 Pará's share of sawmills and of the volume of production in the Amazon region was nearly 70 %, Mercado's statements on the Amazon region can also be seen as representative of Pará.

22   Eleven years after the collection of basic data on the Amazon timber industry that Knowles had conducted on behalf of the FAO, Richard Bruce conducted a further study on production and sales of Amazon timber, this time on behalf of the forestry authority IBDF and SUDAM and with support of UNDP and FAO. The federal states covered by the study included Pará, Amazonas, Roraima, Amapá, Rondônia, and Acre Bruce's research team visited 158 sawmills and four plywood and veneer factories Data on 21 further sawmills and five plywood factries were taken from IBDF's registers. The sawmill sample investigated included 58 % of all sawmills in the major region of Belém (including the east of Pará), 46 % of the island of Marajó (incl Macapá and Portel), 69 % in Amazonas and Roraima, 85 % in Acre and Rondônia, and 58 % in the south and west of Pará and in Amapá. Mercado's 1978 sample included 101 sawmills of different size classes (13 % of the aggregate) and 13 veneer and plywood factories (76 %) in all Amazon states.

23   Mercado (1980), the source of these data is the IBDF register.

24   See the FAO expedition reports in Heinsdijk and Bastos (1963), pp. 45 - 50, and SUDAM (1973b), pp. 301 - 435.

25   Glerum (1965). This report is one of the few existing sources from this period.

26   *"Amazonian sawmills   (have) a great deal of locational flexibility. New labor supply can be obtained if necessary, since unskilled workers can be trained in a few days for most sawmilling jobs ( ) Logger mobility permits mills to reach out farther for raw material as the more accessible stands are depleted "* (Mercado 1980, pp 33 f) While, thanks to the competition with the industrial firms emerging in the customs-free production zone, the timber industry in Manaus had problems in obtaining manpower, this problem did not exist in Pará due to the high unemployment there, above all in rural areas (Mercado 1980, p. 54).

27   Oral communication from Clara Pandolfo in July of 1997, who was then director of SUDAM's Department of Natural Resources.

28   Knowles (1971) estimated that in 1970 70 % of the Amazon region's timber output was sold abroad, chiefly as logs.

29   In Brazil average economic growth was 1.6 per year between 1980 and 1990.

30   SUDAM and PNUD (1988), quoted after Guimarães Neto and Rocha (1992), p. 65.

31   The physical output data presented in the IBGE economic census rule out any crossing with the data on workers Evidence is presented for the stagnation of the physical productivity of sawmills in the final section.

32   In fact hardly anyone in the Amazon region remembers the then use of virola seeds or the logging ban; one entrepreneur who processes virola into sawnwood noted in an interview that the ban was evaded by using the species' Latin name instead of its generally familar one as a means of camouflaging such logging.

33   According to information of a mahogany exporter from Pará who had again begun cutting mahogany in this area in the 1980s, this was a German company which left the region at the end of the 1960s. His logging teams still run across logs that were felled at that time but had to be abandoned because of their size and weight.

34   In a test operation conducted in 1967 at the FAO experimental station Curuá-Una. a team of 4 men using power saws cut 40 m³ of stemwood per day (over three times more than with manual logging); a tractor was used for transportation, a mechanical crane was used to load the truck. The truck drove 12 km to the river and there loaded a boat which travelled up to 110 km to the sawmill.

35   Browder (1987) studied that expansion of the timber industry in Roulim de Moura, Rondônia, in the period; he saw export subsidies as an influential factor bearing on the depletion of mahogany: Pará's mahogany exports, which accounted for two thirds of Brazil's exports, decreased significantly, however, only in the 1990s; i.e. the crucial factor was not the subsidies but scarcity.

36   See Knowles (1965), pp. 91 - 112.

37   90 % of the Amazon region's timber exports in the 1960s and 1970s derived from Pará (Knowles 1971, p. 55).

38   At the end of the 1970s the greater part of the sawnwood was sold in the Amazon region at prices determined by the producer, demand was so high that it always outstripped supply, in spite of strong growth (Mercado 1980, p. 54).

39   The fact that promotion measures were provided for extraction activities illustrates the great economic weight that this sector had at that time in the Amazon region. The measure proposed included creation of rubber plantations combined with colonizations projects, creation of plantations with trees which yield fatty seeds and pau-rosa trees as a means of rationalizing rosewood production. These proposals were not put into practice.

40   The purchase of logs at that time accounted for 55 - 75 % of the production costs of a typical sawmill, this percentage was higher for mahogany.

41   These optimistic views on strong local integration and development effects in the timber industry were in accord with the then-valid development model of the FAO's forestry department, as formulated by its head, J. Westoby (Westoby 1962).

42   Between the middle of 1964 and the end of 1967 SUDAM had approved eleven investment programs with an overall investment volume of US$ 9.4 million (current value). 42.4 % of these projects were financed with tax incentives (Pandolfo 1969, p. 106).

43   The *Instituto do Pinho* was built up in response to the depletion of the araucaria forests in the south of Brazil under the Vargas government and placed in charge of reforestation (financed by means of compulsory duties from timber exporters), modernization of processing technologies, and regulation of the trade in araucaria timber. The *Departmento de Recursos Renováveis* was responsible for administering the national parks and forest-conservation areas (Ros-Tonen 1993, p. 121; Terezo 1997).

44   Knowles (1971), p 33, indicates a productivity of 3 m³ per man-day for manual logging in the *várzea* , with transportation and raft assembly; *várzea* timber is as a rule lighter than *terra firme* timber and was cut as close to the riverbank as possible.

45   Schmithüsen (1978) mentions a factory that processed 7,000 m³ of roundwood per month and used 100 - 150 suppliers for the purpose; the timber was rafted up to 2,000 km. This system was only possible on the basis of free access to timber resources on public land, cheap river transportation, and the low standard of living of the *ribeirinhos*.

46 Valverde (1980) The criticism was strongly influenced by the practice of the timber companies in the south of Brazil of illegally logging publicly owned protected forests and getting away with it by making payments to IBDF officials.

47 Valverde (1980) and, in more detail, Kolk (1996).

48 The critics here referred to the overexploitation problems which had occurred in the concessions of large corporations in Africa and Asia and showed that logging on the grand scale need not automatically give rise to broadly effective development effects. The counterproposal had in mind the Taungya system developed in the 19th century by the German forestry expert Dieter Brandis on behalf of the British colonial authority in Burma; the system provided for cultivation of teak by farmers, who were given sales guarantees by the state (Valverde 1980; Bruenig 1996)

49 Pandolfo was influenced by the eco-development concept of Ignacy Sachs and the debates surrounding the 1972 Stockholm environmental summit (Pandolfo 1994 and 1978, pp. 2 f). Her high regard of the forest resources of the Amazon region as the base for an independent regional development stemmed from the French chemist Paul Le Cointe, with whom she had studied in the 1920s in Belém. Le Cointe was one of the first in the century to study the botany of the Amazon region and document the economic benefits that could be derived from it (Le Cointe 1945) The proposal of founding agricultural forest settlements can be found in Pandolfo (1972)

50 Personal communication from Clara Pandolfo, June 1997

51 See also SUDAM (1973b), p. 7

52 An exception in the 1960s were small farmers with artisanal skills who cut logs into beams and posts, complying with precise specifications (Knowles 1965, p. 86).

53 Nearly all of these companies are at least partly foreign-owned: a German firm holds a 25 % of share in one of the two plywood factories, the other was recently bought by the same Malaysian investor who purchased two bankrupt plywood factories in Pará One of the timber-processing companies belongs to an Austrian; the big sawmill, MIL Madeireira, is an investment of the Swiss company Precious Woods.

54 Oral communication from Mr Hummel, IBAMA Amazonas, and from the vice-president of the environmental authority, March 1998. The work of IBAMA and the environmental authority in the state of Amazonas on converting the timber industry to sustainable forest management is considerably more credible than that in Pará. Following a phase marked by intensified surveillance and fines, the authorities have now begun to reach agreements with the companies concerned on clearly defined periods of time for a gradual transition from destructive exploitation to forest management. IBAMA in Amazonas is coordinating a PPG-7 program on sustainable forest management that is designed to support firms and agricultural cooperatives that are willing to innovate.

55 Only in 1996 was work begun on expanding the Madeira waterway, above all for shipping the soy crops harvested in the north of Mato Grosso for two years now. In Itacoatiara a modern, fully automated transshipment port facility was built that transfers the soybeans from river barges to ocean freighters that travel up the Amazon to Itacoatiara.

56 This is surprising above all against the background of the process of structural change that took place in Brazil as a whole in this period.

57 See Meyer-Stamer (1996) for an explanation of the relationship between ISI and insufficiently qualified institutions involved in techno-organizational learning.

Chapter 8

1 The German development minister stated at the PPG-7 donor conference in Bonn in 1996 that the most important indicator of the success of this program, which, it should be noted, claims to be in accord with the guiding model of sustainable development, was reduction of the deforestation rate to zero.

2 The size of conservation areas should be increased, and care must be taken that these areas are respected. Projects such as the conservation area in Mamirauá in the state of Amazonas (*Estação Ecológica Mamirauá*) in which the local population is involved in resource management could lead the way.

3 To increase the yield of the tropical forest, it is necessary to log greater and greater areas and more and more distant regions; it for this reason involves rising costs.

4 See Dosi, Pavitt and Soete (1990), pp 90 - 111. The supplier-dominated industries include traditional industries, agriculture, the building sector, many service providers, and informal outwork.

5 Malaysia and Indonesia succeeded in building an industry before their native forest stands had been depleted; Malaysia's industry is now increasingly processing timber from rubber plantations, while Indonesia is specializing in eucalyptus plantations In the Philippines the dynamics of deforestation has remained high due to the smuggling of logs to Japan; the processing industry that emerged there is now forced to rely on imported sawnwood. In western and central Africa Ghana is the only country that has thus far developed a processing industry worthy of the name; it is based on log imports from central Africa because of the depletion of Ghana's forests.

6 See e.g. Harris (1980). Harris assumes that human groups or cultures change their food-security routines only when massive crisis symptoms occur.

7 Oral communication from Thomas Hurtienne, based on an evaluation of national census findings and agrarian censuses for Pará between 1950 and 1996.

Chapter 9

1 See http://www.mpo.gov.br and the Latin American Brazil Report of Jan. 5, 1999, pp. 5 f The Movement of the Landless (Movimento dos Sem-Terra - MST) questions the INCRA data, itself specifying a figure of 130,000 - 150,000 families.

2 See Kolk (1998) on the history of PPG-7; the article analyzes the coalitions of Brazilian and external actors, governmental and nongovernmental, that support PPG-7 and made it possible for the Brazilian government to change from a course of confrontation to one of cooperation. The analysis also includes changes induced by the process of internal reform in the World Bank

3 See Scholz (1997). The following presentation refers only to the Amazon part of PPG-7, the activities designed to protect the Atlantic coast forest, the Mata Atlântica, are not considered here.

4   Decree no. 563 of June 6, 1992. The pilot program was announced by then Ger-
     man Chancellor Helmut Kohl at the 1990 G7 summit in Houston

5   The corresponding subprogram of NRPP is called Programa de *Gestão Ambiental
     Integrada* (PGAI), i e. program for an integrated environmental management.

6   The results of these projects were discussed in Chapter 4

7   See the minutes of the 4th meeting of IAG, 5/29-6/9/1995, p. 12.

Bibliography

Adams, R. (1982). *Paradoxical Harvest. Energy and Explanation in British History, 1870 - 1914*, New York

Adelman, I. (1984): "Beyond Export-led Growth," in: *World Development*, Vol. 12, No. 9

AIMEX (1997): "Exportações de madeira do Pará, compilação de dados estatísticos 1987 - 1996," Belém

Allen, P.M. (1988): "Evolution, Innovation and Economics," in: G. Dosi et al. (eds), *Technical Change and Economic Theory*, London, New York

Almeida, H. (1978): "A atividade florestal na Amazônia como empreendimento integrado," Paper Presented at the III. Brazilian Forestry Congress, 4.-7.12.1978 in Manaus, SUDAM, Manaus

Almeida, O.T. de (ed.) (1996): "A evolução da fronteira amazônica. Oportunidades para um desenvolvimento sustentável," IMAZON, Porto Alegre, Belém: Edições Caravela

Almeida, O.T. de / C. Uhl (1995): "Developing a Quantitative Framework for Sustainable Resource-use Planning in the Brazilian Amazon," in: *World Development*, Vol. 23, No. 10

Altvater, E. (1987)· *Sachzwang Weltmarkt. Verschuldungskrise, blockierte Industrialisierung, ökologische Gefährdung Der Fall Brasilien*, Hamburg

− (1991): *Die Zukunft des Marktes. Ein Essay über die Regulation von Geld und Natur nach dem Scheitern des "real existierenden Sozialismus,"* Münster

− (1992): *Der Preis des Wohlstands oder Umweltplünderung und neue Welt(un)ordnung*, Münster

Altvater, E. / A. Brunnengräber / M. Haake / H. Walk (eds) (1997): *Vernetzt und verstrickt Nicht-Regierungsorganisationen als gesellschaftliche Produktivkraft*, Münster

Amazonex - Industrial Exportadora S.A. (1982): "Projeto de Ampliação," SUDAM, Belém (mimeo)

Amelung, T. (1997) *Globaler Umweltschutz als Verteilungsproblem im Nord-Süd-Konflikt*, Frankfurt a.M. etc.

Amelung, T. / M. Diehl (1992): Deforestation of Tropical Rain Forests. Economic Causes and Impact on Development, Tübingen

Amsberg, J. (1998)· "Economic Parameters of Deforestation," in: *The World Bank Economic Review*, Vol. 12, No. 1

Antes, R. (1996): *Präventiver Umweltschutz und seine Organisation in Unternehmen*, Wiesbaden

Arthur, W.B. (1994): *Increasing Returns and Path Dependence in the Economy*, Michigan

Baer, W. (1995): *A economia brasileira*, São Paulo: Nobel

Baer, W. / C. Paiva (1996): "Vom Cruzado zum Real. Die Stabilisierungspläne seit der Redemokratisierung," in: G. Calcagnotto / B. Fritz (eds), *Inflation und Stabilisierung in Brasilien Probleme einer Gesellschaft im Wandel*, Frankfurt a. M.

Balée, W. / D. Posey (eds) (1989). *Natural Resource Management by Indigenous and Folk Societies of Amazonia* (New York Botanical Garden Advances in Economic Botany Monograph Series), New York

Barbier, E.B. (1989): *Economics, Natural-resource Scarcity and Development. Conventional and Alternative Views*, London

– (1994): The Environmental Effects of Trade in the Forestry Sector, in: OECD (ed.), The Environmental Effects of Trade, Paris

Barbier, E.B. / J.C. Burgess / B. Aylward / J. Bishop (1992): "Timber Trade, Trade Policies and Environmental Degradation," International Institute for Environment and Development (LEEC Paper DP 92-01), London

Barbier, E.B. / J.C. Burgess / J. Bishop / B. Aylward (1994): *The Economics of the Tropical Timber Trade*, London

Bargatzky, T. (1986): *Einführung in die Kulturökologie. Umwelt, Kultur und Gesellschaft*, Berlin

Barnett, H. / C. Morse (1963): *Scarcity and Economic Growth The Economics of Natural Resource Availability*, Baltimore

Barreto, P. (1998): "Exploração de madeira e geração de empregos na Amazônia brasileira," IMAZON, Belém

Barreto, P. / A. Veríssimo / S. Hirakuri (1998): "A exploração de madeira na Amazônia brasileira· situação e perspectivas," IMAZON, Belém (mimeo)

Barreto, P. / P. Amaral / E. Vidal / C. Uhl (1997): "Custos e benefícios do manejo da floresta na Amazônia Oriental," IMAZON (Serie Amazônica No. 10), Belém

Barros, A.C. / A. Veríssimo (eds) (1996)· "A expansão da atividade madeireira na Amazônia: Impactos e perspectivas para o desenvolvimento do setor florestal no Pará," IMAZON, Belém

Beck, U. (1986). *Risikogesellschaft. Auf dem Weg in eine andere Moderne*, Frankfurt a M.

Becker, E. (1992)· "Ökologische Modernisierung der Entwicklungspolitik?," in: *Prokla*, No. 86

Bennett, G. / B. Verhoeve (1994): *Environmental Product Standards in Western Europe, the US and Japan A Guidebook*, Instituut voor Europees Milieubeleid, Arnheim

Berger, J. (1994)· "The Economy and the Environment," in: N.J. Smelser / R. Swedberg (eds), *The Handbook of Economic Sociology*, Russell Sage Foundation, Princeton, New York

Bhaskar, R. (1979): *The Possibility of Naturalism*, Brighton

Binswanger, H.P. (1978)· "Induced Technical Change. Evolution of Thought," in: H P. Binswanger / V.W. Ruttan (eds), *Induced Innovation Technology, Institutions and Development*, Baltimore

Binswanger, M. (1993) "From Microscopic to Macroscopic Theories. Entropic Aspects of Ecological and Economic Processes," in: *Ecological Economics*, Vol. 8, No. 3

Blau, P. (1964): *Exchange and Power in Social Life*, New York

BMELF (Bundesministerium für Ernährung, Landwirtschaft und Forsten) (1997) "5. Tropenwaldbericht der Bundesregierung," Bonn

Bode, W. / M. Hohnhorst (1994): *Waldwende Vom Försterwald zum Naturwald*, Munich

Bonelli, R. (1996): "Produtividade Industrial nos Anos 90. Controvérsias e Quase-Fatos," in: IPEA (ed.), *A Economia Brasileira em Perspectiva 1996*, Vol. 2

Brand, K.-W. (ed.) (1998): *Soziologie und Natur Theoretische Perspektiven*, Opladen

Braz de Oliveira e Silva, A., et al. (1996): "Produto Interno Bruto por Unidade de Federação," IPEA (Texto para discussão No. 424), Brasília

Brockmann, K.L. / J. Hemmelskamp / O. Hohmeyer (1996): *Zertifiziertes Tropenholz und Verbraucherverhalten*, Heidelberg

Browder, J.O. (1986). "Logging the Rainforest. A Political Economy of Timber Extraction and Unequal Exchange in the Brazilian Amazon," Pennsylvania (thesis)

– (1987)· "Brazil's Export Promotion Policy (1980-84): Impacts on the Amazon's Industrial Wood Sector," in. *The Journal of Developing Areas*, Vol. 21, No. 3

– (1988): "Public Policy and Deforestation in the Brazilian Amazon," in: R. Repetto / M. Gillis (eds), *Public Policies and the Misuse of Forest Resources*, WRI, Cambridge, New York

– **(ed.)** (1989) *Fragile Lands of Latin America*, Boulder/Co.

Bruce, R. (1976) "Produção e distribuição da madeira amazônica," IBDF, PRODE-PEF, Rio de Janeiro

Bruckmeier, K. (1994): *Strategien globaler Umweltpolitik*, Münster

Bruenig, E.F. (1996): *Conservation and Management of Tropical Rainforests An Integrated Approach to Sustainability*, CAB International, Wallingford

BUND / Misereor (1996): *Zukunftsfähiges Deutschland Ein Beitrag zu einer global nachhaltigen Entwicklung*, Basel

Bunker, S. (1985): *Underdeveloping the Amazon Extraction, Unequal Exchange, and the Failure of the Modern State*, Urbana, Chicago

Cano, W. (1985)· *Desequilibrios regionais e concentração industrial no Brasil 1930 - 1970*, São Paulo. global editora

Capistrano, A.D. / C.F. Kiker (1995): "Macro-scale Economic Influences on Tropical Forest Depletion," in: *Ecological Economics*, Vol. 14, No. 1

Cardoso, F.H. / G. Müller (1977): *Amazônia - Expansão do Capitalismo*, São Paulo: CEBRAP / Editora Brasiliense

Carlstein, T. (1978): *Making Sense of Time*, London

Carrere, R. (1996). "Pulping the South Brazil's Pulp and Paper Plantations," in: *The Ecologist*, Vol. 26, No. 5

Carvalho, J.O.P. (1987)· "Subsídios para o manejo de florestas naturais na Amazônia brasileira. Resultados de pesquisa da EMBRAPA/IBDF-PNPF," EMBRAPA-CPATU, Belém

CAT (Centro Agro-Ambiental do Tocantins) (ed.) (1992): "Elementos de análise de funcionamento dos estabelecimentos familiares da região de Marabá," CAT, Marabá (mimeo)

Chudnovsky, D. / M. Chidiak (1995): *Competitividad y Medio Ambiente Claros y Oscuros en la Industria Argentina*, CENIT, Buenos Aires

Ciprandi Madeiras Ltda. - CIPRASA (1988): "Projeto Industrial. Colaboração Financeira e Fiscal, Paragominas," SUDAM, Belém (mimeo)

Coase, R. (1960): "The Problem of Social Cost," in: *Journal of Law and Economics*, Vol. 3, No. 1

Coes, D.V. (1995) "Macroeconomic Crises, Policies, and Growth in Brazil, 1964-90," World Bank, Washington

Colby, M.E. (1991)· "Environmental Management in Development. The Evolution of Paradigms," in· *Ecological Economics*, Vol. 3, No. 3

Coleman, J.S. (1990): *Foundations of Social Theory*, Cambridge/Mass., London

– (1994): "A Rational Choice Perspective on Economic Sociology," in: N.J. Smelser / R. Swedberg (eds), *The Handbook of Economic Sociology*, Russell Sage Foundation, Princeton/N.J., New York

Commons, J.R. (1934): *Institutional Economics - Its Place in Political Economy*, New York

Costa, F. (1992): "Ecologismo e questão agrária na Amazônia," NAEA-UFPA, Belém

– (1993): "Grande capital e agricultura na Amazônia. A experiência Ford no Tapajós," UFPA, Belém

– (1995): "Diversidade estrutural e desenvolvimento sustentável: novos supostos de política e planejamento agricola para a Amazônia," Paper do NAEA 44, Belém

Costanza, R. (ed.) (1991): *Ecological Economics The Science and Management of Sustainability*, New York

Coy, M. (1987): "Rondônia. frente pioneira e programa POLONOROESTE. O processo de diferenciação socio-econômica na periferia e os limites do planejamento público," in: G Kohlhepp / A. Schrader (eds), *Homem e natureza na Amazônia*, Geographisches Institut der Universität Tübingen, Tübingen

Cyert, R.M. / J.G. March (1963). *A Behavioral Theory of the Firm*, Englewood Cliffs/N.J.

Daly, H.E. (1990): "Toward Some Operational Principles of Sustainable Development," in *Ecological Economics*, Vol. 2, No. 1

– (1992a): "Allocation, Distribution and Scale. Towards an Economics that is Efficient, Just, and Sustainable," in: *Ecological Economics*, Vol 6, No 3

– (1992b)· *Steady-state Economics*, Second Edition with new Essays, London

– (1992c): "Vom Wirtschaften in einer leeren Welt zum Wirtschaften in einer vollen Welt Wir haben einen historischen Wendepunkt in der Wirtschaftsentwicklung erreicht," in: R. Goodland et al. (eds), *Nach dem Brundtlandbericht. Umweltverträgliche wirtschaftliche Entwicklung*, Bonn

Daly, H.E. / J.B. Cobb (1989): *For the Common Good. Redirecting the Economy towards the Community, the Environment, and a Sustainable Future*, Boston

David, P. (1985): "Clio and the Economics of QWERTY," in: *American Economic Review*, Vol. 75, No. 2

Dean, W. (1987): *Brazil and the Struggle for Rubber*, Cambridge

– (1997): *A ferro e fogo A história e a devastação da Mata Atlântica brasileira*, São Paulo: Companhia das Letras

Deutscher Bundestag (ed.) (1990): "Schutz der Tropenwälder. Eine internationale Schwerpunktaufgabe," Zweiter Bericht der Enquete-Kommission "Vorsorge zum Schutz der Erdatmosphäre" des Deutschen Bundestages, Bonn

– (1998)· "Konzept Nachhaltigkeit. Vom Leitbild zur Umsetzung," Abschlußbericht der Enquete-Kommission "Schutz des Menschen und der Umwelt" des 13. Deutschen Bundestages, Bonn

Dieguez, F. / C.E.L. Silva (1997): "A civilização perdida da Amazônia," in: *SUPER*, June

Dosi, G. (1984). *Technical Change and Industrial Transformation The Theory and an Application to the Semiconductor Industry*, London

– (1997): "Opportunities, Incentives and the Collective Patterns of Technological Change," in: *The Economic Journal*, Vol. 107, No. 444

Dosi, G. / C. Freeman / R. Nelson / G. Silverberg / L. Soete (eds) (1988): *Technical Change and Economic Theory*, London, New York

Dosi, G. / K. Pavitt / L. Soete (1990): *The Economics of Technological Change and International Trade*, Brighton, New York

Dosi, G. / L. Orsenigo (1988): "Coordination and Transformation. An Overview of Structures, Behaviors and Change in Evolutionary Environments," in: G. Dosi et al. (eds), *Technical Change and Economic Theory*, London, New York

Dosi, G. / L. Soete (1988): "Technical Change and International Trade," in: G. Dosi et al. (eds), *Technical Change and Economic Theory*, London, New York

Dosi, G. / R.R. Nelson (1994): "Theorien der Evolution in den Wirtschaftswissenschaften," in. V Braitenberg / I Hosp (eds), *Evolution. Entwicklung und Organisation in der Natur*, Reinbek

Dudley, N. / J.-P. Jeanrenaud / F. Sullivan (1995)· *Bad Harvest? The Timber Trade and the Degradation of the World's Forests*, London

Durkheim, E. (1980)· *Regeln der soziologischen Methode*, Darmstadt

Eder, K. (1988): *Die Vergesellschaftung der Natur*, Frankfurt a.M.

Ekins, P. (1993a): "'Limits to Growth" and 'Sustainable Development'. Grappling with Ecological Realities," in: *Ecological Economics*, Vol. 8, No 3

– (1993b): "Ausverkauf der Zukunft? Umweltschutz vor Freihandel," in: *W&E Informationsbrief-Sonderdienst*, 3.12.1993

EMBRAPA-CPATU / GTZ (1991). "Studies on the Utilization and Conservation of Soil in the Eastern Amazon Region." GTZ, Eschborn

Endres, A. / I. Querner (1993): *Die Ökonomie natürlicher Ressourcen Eine Einführung*, Darmstadt

Ernst & Young (1996) *Pesquisa sobre tendências da indústria paulista na área ambiental*, São Paulo: Ernst & Young

Eßer, K. / W. Hillebrand / D. Messner / J. Meyer-Stamer (1994): *Systemische Wettbewerbsfähigkeit Internationale Wettbewerbsfähigkeit der Unternehmen und Anforderungen an die Politik*, German Development Institute, Berlin

Faillace, S. (no date)· "Uma Leitura de Indústria de Papel e Celulose no Brasil sob a Perspectiva da Sustentabilidade Norte-Sul," FASE, Rio de Janeiro

FAO (1988): "Trade in Forest Products A Study of the Barriers Faced by the Developing Countries." FAO Forestry Paper 83, Rome

– (1995). "Forest Products Prices, 1973 - 1992," FAO Forestry Paper 125, Rome

– (1997). "The State of the World's Forests," Rome

FAO / INCRA (1996): "A agricultura familiar na região norte," Brasília

– / – (1996). "Perfil da agricultura familiar no Brasil dossiê estatístico," Brasília

Fearnside, P.M. (1988) "An Ecological Analysis of Predominant Land Uses in the Brazilian Amazon," in. *The Environmentalist*, Vol 8, No 4

– (1988): "Jari at Age 19 Lessons for Brazil's Silvicultural Plans at Carajás," in: *Interciencia*, Vol. 13, No. 1

– (1988): "O carvão de Carajás," in: *Ciência Hoje*, Vol. 8, No. 48

– (1993) "Deforestation in the Brazilian Amazon. The Effect of Population Growth and Land Tenure," in: *Ambio*, Vol. 22, No. 8

Fearnside, P.M. / J.M. Rankin (1982): "The New Jari· Risks and Prospects of a Major Amazonian Development," in: *Interciencia*, Vol. 7, No 6

– / – (1985): "Jari Revisited: Changes and the Outlook for Sustainability in Amazonia's Largest Silvicultural Estate," in: *Interciencia*, Vol 10, No. 3

FIEPA (Federação das Indústrias do Estado do Pará) (1996) "Proposta para implantação do programa de desenvolvimento do setor de base florestal da Amazônia," 1st version, Belém

Flick, U. (1991): "Stationen des qualitativen Forschungsprozesses," in: U. Flick et al. (eds), *Handbuch Qualitative Sozialforschung*, Munich

FoE / AdT (Friends of the Earth / Amigos da Terra) (1997): "Garimpagem florestal Relatório atualizado sobre extração ilegal de madeira na Amazônia brasileira," São Paulo

Foweraker, J. (1981): *The Struggle for Land A Political Economy of the Pioneer Frontier in Brazil from 1930 to the Present Day*, Cambridge

Franco, G. (1996). "The Real Plan," PUC (Texto para Discussão No 354), Rio de Janeiro

Frankfurter Rundschau (15.9 1998): "Auf dem Tropenholzweg? Schweizer Firma brachte das FSC-Umweltsiegel in Mißkredit," p. 8

Freeman, C. (1982): *The Economics of Industrial Innovation*, London

– (1994): "The Economics of Technical Change," in: *Cambridge Journal of Economics*, Vol 18

Freeman, C. / C. Perez (1988): "Structural Crises of Adjustment, Business Cycles and Investment Behavior," in: G. Dosi et al (eds), *Technical Change and Economic Theory*, London, New York

Fritz, B. (1996): "Das stabile Geld und sein Preis. Ökonomische Transformation in der Folge des Plano Real," in: G. Calcagnotto / B. Fritz (eds), *Inflation und Stabilisierung in Brasilien Probleme einer Gesellschaft im Wandel*, Frankfurt a.M.

– (1997): "O regime de âncora cambial como condição para estabilização e o desenvolvimento? Una contribução à análise do Plano Real," Berlin (mimeo)

FSC Brasil (1998): "Padrões de certificação do FSC - Forest Stewardship Council para manejo florestal em terra firme na Amazônia brasileira," Brasília (mimeo)

Gama e Silva, Z.A.G.P. da / E. Muñoz Braz (1992): "Análise Econômica da Exploração sob Regime de Manejo Para a Produção Florestal Sustentada," in: *Madeira & Cia*

Gazeta Mercantil Latino-americana (28./29.5.1997): "Amazônia perde com exploração predatória," p A-6

– (15.7.1997) "Ibama autoriza a exploração de florestas," p. C-6

– (6 /12.10 1997). "Um mar de florestas Mais da metade dos eucaliptos está plantada no estado," p 19

– (20.10.1997) "Sem política, Brasil terá de importar madeira," p. A-5

– (10 2.1998) "Pará exporta menos madeira de lei," p. C-7

– (7.5.1998): "Madeira é o novo negócio da Klabin. Papel e celulose será o principal alvo na área florestal da companhia e seus novos sócios," p. C-3

– (3 6.1998): "Altamira celebra, mas teme chegada do linhão de Tucuruí, marcada para o próximo dia 15," p. 1 (Supplement for Pará)

Georgescu-Roegen, N. (1975): *The Entropy Law and the Economic Process*, Cambridge/Mass

Giddens, A. (1976): New Rules of Sociological Method, London

– (1984): The Constitution of Society. Outline of the Theory of Structuration, Cambridge

– (1990). The Consequences of Modernity, Cambridge

Gillis, M. (1988a) "Indonesia. Public Policies, Resource Management, and the Tropical Forest," in: R. Repetto / M. Gillis (eds), *Public Policies and the Misuse of Forest Resources*, WRI, Cambridge, New York

– (1988b). "Malaysia. Public Policies and the Tropical Forest," in· R. Repetto / M. Gillis (eds), *Public Policies and the Misuse of Forest Resources*, WRI, Cambridge, New York

– (1988c)· "West Africa Resource Management Policies and the Tropical Forest," in: R Repetto / M. Gillis (eds), *Public Policies and the Misuse of Forest Resources*, WRI, Cambridge, New York

Glaeser, B. / P. Teherani-Krönner (eds) (1992): *Humanökologie und Kulturökologie Grundlagen, Ansätze, Praxis*, Opladen

Glerum, B.B. (1965) "Pesquisa combinada floresta-solo no Pará-Maranhão," SPVEA (Inventários Florestais na Amazônia Vol. 9), Rio de Janeiro

Goodland, R. (1992) "Die These: Die Welt stößt an Grenzen. Das derzeitige Wachstum in der Weltwirtschaft ist nicht mehr verkraftbar," in: R Goodland et al. (eds), *Nach dem Brundtlandbericht Umweltverträgliche wirtschaftliche Entwicklung*, Bonn

Goodland, R. / H. Daly (1993): "Why Northern Income Growth is not the Solution to Southern Poverty," in: *Ecological Economics*, Vol. 8, No. 2

– / – (1996): "If Tropical Log Export Bans are so Perverse, why are there so many?," in. *Ecological Economics*, Vol. 18, No. 3

– / – (1990): "The Missing Tools (for Sustainability)," in: C. Mungall / D.J. McLaren (eds), *Planet under Stress The Challenge of Global Change*, Toronto

Government of Brazil / World Bank / Commission of European Communities (eds) (1991) "Pilot Program for the Conversation of the Brazilian Rainforests" (Preliminary Proposal)

Graaf, N.R. (1982): "Sustained Timber Production in the Rainforest of Suriname," in: J.F Wienk / H.A. de Witt (eds), *Management of Low Fertility Acid Soils of the American Humid Tropics*, San José

Graaf, N.R. / R.L.H. Poels (1990): "The CELOS Management System. A Polycyclic Method for Sustained Timber Production in South American Rain Forest," in: A.B. Anderson (ed), *Alternatives to Deforestation. Steps Toward Sustainable Use of the Amazon Rain Forest*, New York

Griliches, Z. (1957): "Hybrid Corn. An Exploration in the Economics of Technological Change," in: *Econometrica*, Vol. 25

Gross, D. (1975): "Protein Capture and Cultural Development in the Amazon Basin," in· *American Anthropologist*, Vol. 77

GTA / FoE (1996): "Políticas públicas coerentes para uma Amazônia sustentável O Desafio de Inovação e o Programa Piloto," São Paulo

– (1997): "Políticas públicas para a Amazônia. Rumos, Tendências e Propostas" (preliminary version), São Paulo

Guimarães Neto, L. / J.M.B. Rocha (1992): "Projeto de desenvolvimiento da produção florestal-industrial-madeireira na Amazônia," SUDAM, PNUD, Belém

Habermas, J. (1981) *Theorie des kommunikativen Handelns*, 2 Vols, Frankfurt a.M.

– (1993). *Vergangenheit als Zukunft Das alte Deutschland im neuen Europa?*, Munich, Zurich

Hägerstrand, T. (1975) "Space, Time and Human Condition," in: A. Karlqvist (ed.), *Dynamic Allocation of Urban Space*, Farnborough

Hall, A. (1989): *Developing Amazonia Deforestation and Social Conflict in Brazil's Carajás Programme*, Manchester

Harris, M. (1959)· "The Economy has no Surplus?," in: *American Anthropologist*, Vol. 61, No. 2

– (1980): *Culture, People, and Nature*, New York

Hatzfeldt, H. Graf (ed.) (1994) *Ökologische Waldwirtschaft. Grundlagen - Aspekte - Beispiele*, Heidelberg

Hayami, Y. / V. Ruttan (1971/1985): *Agricultural Development. An International Perspective*, Baltimore

Hecht, S. (1982): "Agroforestry Systems in the Amazon Basin: Practice, Theory and Limits to a Promising Land Use," in· S. Hecht (ed.), *Amazonia: Agriculture and Land Use Research*. CIAT, Cali

– (1983) "Cattle Ranching in Eastern Amazonia: Environmental and Social Implications," in. E F. Moran (ed.), *The Dilemma of Amazonian Development*, Boulder/Co.

– (1984): "Cattle Ranching in Amazonia Political and Ecological Considerations," in: M. Schmink / C Wood (eds), *Frontier Expansion in Amazonia*, Gainesville

Hecht, S. / A. Cockburn (1989)· *The Fate of the Forest Developers, Destroyers, and Defenders of the Amazon*, New York, London

Heinsdijk, D. (1966) "Report to the Government of Brazil on Forest Inventory (Part I)," FAO, Report No. 2159, Rome

Heinsdijk, D. / A.M. Bastos (1963): "Inventários Florestais na Amazônia," Ministério de Agricultura/Serviço Florestal (Boletim N° 6), Rio de Janeiro

Hellenbrandt, S. / F. Rubik (eds) (1994): *Produkt und Umwelt Anforderungen, Instrumente und Ziele einer ökologischen Produktpolitik*, Marburg

Henkel, K. (1987): "Agrarräumliche Entwicklungen im östlichen Pará (Amazonien) unter besonderer Berücksichtigung kleinbäuerlicher Landwirtschaft," in· *Tübinger Geographische Studien*, No. 93

Herkendell, J. / J. Pretzsch (eds) (1995): *Die Wälder der Erde Bestandsaufnahme und Perspektiven*, Munich

Herrera, A.O., et al. (1977): *Grenzen des Elends Das Bariloche Modell So kann die Menschheit überleben*, Frankfurt a.M.

Hirsch, F. (1980) *Die sozialen Grenzen des Wachstums*, Reinbek

Hirschman, A. (1981)· "The Rise and Decline of Development Economics," in. A. Hirschman (ed.), *Essays in Trespassing*, New York

Hodgson, G.M. (1993): *Economics and Evolution Bringing Life Back into Economics*, Cambridge, Ann Arbor

– (1994) "The Return of Institutional Economics," in: N.J. Smelser / R. Swedberg (eds), *The Handbook of Economic Sociology*, Russell Sage Foundation, Princeton/N.J., New York

– (1998): "The Approach of Institutional Economics," n *Journal of Economic Literature*, Vol 36, No. 1

Hölscher, D. (1995): "Wasser- und Stoffhaushalt eines Agrarökosystems mit Waldbrache im östlichen Amazonasgebiet," Göttinger Beiträge zur Land- und Forstwissenschaft in den Tropen und Subtropen 106, Göttingen

Homma, A. (1992): "A (ir)racionalidade do extrativismo vegetal como paradigma de desenvolvimento agrícola para a Amazônia," in: J.M.M. da Costa (ed.), *Amazônia, desenvolvimento ou retrocesso*, CEJUP, Belém

Homma, A. / R. Walker (1996): "Land Use and Land Cover Dynamics in the Brazilian Amazon An Overview," in *Ecological Economics*, Vol. 18, No. 1

Horta, R.M. (1994) "O meio ambiente na legislação ordinária e no Direito Constitucional brasileiro." in: *Revista de Informaçao Legislativa*, Vol 31, No. 122

Hotelling, H. (1931) "The Economics of Exhaustible Resources," in: *Journal of Political Economy*, Vol 39

Hurtienne, T. (1986):" Fordismus, Entwicklungstheorie und Dritte Welt," in: *Peripherie*, No. 22/23

– (1988): "Ökologie, Ökonomie und Sozialsysteme Amazoniens: Versuch einer kulturökologischen Bilanz" (Part 1), Berlin (mimeo)

– (1993): "Das Ende eines Mythos? Natur und Kultur in Amazonien," in: Staatliche Kunsthalle Berlin (ed.), *Klima Global - Arte Amazonas*, Berlin

– (1997): "Tropenökologie und kleinbäuerliche Landwirtschaft in Ostamazonien. Ein Vergleich sozioökonomischer Forschungsergebnisse über verschiedene Agrargrenzen mit unterschiedlichen historischen und agrarökologischen Bedingungen," NAEA, Belém (mimeo)

Hurtienne, T. / D. Messner (1994): "Neue Konzepte von Wettbewerbsfähigkeit," in: B Töpper / U. Müller-Plantenberg (eds), *Transformation im südlichen Lateinamerika*, Frankfurt a.M.

IBAMA (1998) "Exportações de madeira do Brasil 1996 e 1997," compilação de dados estatísticos, Brasília

IBAMA / FUNATURA (eds) (1996): "Diagnóstico e avaliação do setor florestal brasileiro. Região Norte," IBAMA, Brasília

Inglehart, R. (1977) *The Silent Revolution Changing Values and Political Styles among Western Publics*, Princeton

– (1990)· *Culture Shift in Advanced Industrial Societies*, Princeton

Inhetvin, T. (1991): "Wo der Pfeffer wächst. Weltmarkt und lokale Produktion im brasilianischen Amazonien," Berlin (mimeo)

IPEA (1996)· "A Economia Brasileira em Perspectiva 1996," IPEA, Rio de Janeiro

Jänicke, M. / H. Weidner (eds) (1995)· *Successful Environmental Policy A Critical Evaluation of 24 Cases*, Berlin

Jentsch, F. (1911)· "Der Urwald Kameruns. Folgerungen aus den auf der Expedition 1908/09 gewonnenen Erfahrungen in bezug auf den Zustand und die Nutzbarmachung des Waldes," in: *Beiheft zum Tropenpflanzer*, Vol. 15, No. 3

Jepma, C.J. (1995). *Tropical Deforestation. A Socio-Economic Approach*, London

Johns, J.S. / P. Barreto / C. Uhl (1996): "Logging Damage during Planned and Unplanned Logging Operations in the Eastern Amazon," in: *Forest Ecology and Management*. No. 89

Johnson, A. (1982): "Reductionism in Cultural Ecology: The Amazon Case," in: *Current Anthropology*, Vol. 23, No 4

Jordan, C.F. (1985a) *Nutrient Cycling in Tropical Forest Ecosystems*, Chichester

– (1985b) "Soils of the Amazon Rainforest," in: G.T. Prance / T.E Lovejoy (eds), *Key Environments Amazonia*, Oxford

– **(ed.)** (1989)· "An Amazonian Rain Forest. The Structure and Function of a Nutrient Stressed Ecosystem and the Impact of Slash-and-Burn Agriculture," UNESCO Man and the Biosphere Series Vol. 2, Paris

Jorge, M.M. (1995)· "Desenvolvimento e competitividade do setor de papel e celulose no Brasil," CEPAL, CIID, Santiago de Chile

Kahn, H. / R. Panero (1965): *New Focus on the Amazon*, Hudson Institute, New York

Kappel, R. (1994): "Von der Ökologie der Mittel zur Ökologie der Ziele? Die Natur in der neoklassischen Ökonomie und ökologischen Ökonomie," in: *Peripherie*, No 54

Karsenty, A. (1997). "Le marché des bois tropicaux en 1996," in: *Marchés Tropicaux*, 19.9 97

Kennedy, C. (1964)· "Induced Bias in Innovation and the Theory of Distribution," in: *Economic Journal*, Vol. 74, No. 295

KfW / GTZ (eds) (1991): "Sektorpapier Tropenwald Brasilien-Amazonas," Frankfurt a.M.

Kitamura, P. (1994)· "A Amazônia e o desenvolvimento sustentável," EMBRAPA-SPI, Brasília

Klinge, H. (1983) "Wälder und Waldökosysteme Amazoniens," in: *Spixiana*, No. 9

Knowles, O.H. (1965). "Estudo da indústria madeireira na Região Amazônica/Brasil 1964," SUDAM, Belém

– (1971): "Perspectiva das oportunidades de investimentos no desenvolvimento da indústria florestal da Amazônia brasileira," SUDAM, Belém

Kohlhepp, G. / A. Schrader (eds) (1987): *Homem e natureza na Amazônia*, Geographisches Institut der Universität Tübingen, Tübingen

Kolk, A. (1996): *Forests in International Environmental Politics. International Organisations, NGOs and the Brazilian Amazon*, Utrecht

– (1998): "From Conflict to Cooperation. International Policies to Protect the Brazilian Amazon," in. *World Development*, Vol. 26, No 8

Krugmann, P. (1979): "A Model of Innovation, Technology Transfer and the World Distribution of Income," in: *Journal of Political Economy*, Vol. 87

– (1982): "A Technology Gap Model of International Trade," International Economic Association Conference on Structural Adjustment in Trade-dependent Advanced Economies, Yxtahohn

Kürzinger, E. (1997a) "Handeln statt verhandeln?! Die drei Umweltkonventionen fünf Jahre nach Rio." in· *Entwicklung und ländlicher Raum*, Vol. 31, No. 4

– (1997b) "Nachhaltige Entwicklung," in: M Schulz (ed.), *Entwicklung. Die Perspektive der Entwicklungssoziologie*, Opladen

Lamprecht, H. (1989): "Silviculture in the Tropics. Tropical Forest Ecosystems and their Tree Species. Possibilities and Methods for their Long-Term Utilization," GTZ, Eschborn

Larcher, W. (1994): *Ökophysiologie der Pflanzen*, Stuttgart

Lauer, W. (1952) "Humide und aride Jahreszeiten in Afrika und Südamerika und ihre Beziehung zu den Vegetationsgürteln," in: *Bonner Geographische Abhandlungen*, No 9

Le Cointe, P. (1945) *O Estado do Pará*. São Paulo Companhia Editora Nacional

Lehmann, S. (ed.) (1993) *Umwelt-Controlling in der Möbelindustrie. Ein Leitfaden*, Institut für ökologische Wirtschaftsforschung, Berlin

Lélé, S.M. (1991): "Sustainable Development. A Critical Review," in: *World Development*, Vol 19, No. 6

Lepenies, W. (ed.) (1981): *Geschichte der Soziologie Studien zur kognitiven, sozialen und historischen Identität einer Disziplin*, Frankfurt a.M.

Leroy, J.-P. / M.C.C. Soares (eds) (1998): "Bancos Multilaterais e Desenvolvimento Participativo no Brasil Dilemas e Desafios," FASE, IBASE, Rio de Janeiro

Levine, A. / E. Sober / E.O. Wright (1987)· "Marxism and Methodological Individualism," in *New Left Review*, No. 162

Levy, P.M. / L.M.D. Hahn (1996). "A Economia Brasileira em Transição. O Período 1993/96." in· IPEA (ed.), *A Economia Brasileira em Perspectiva 1996*, Vol. 1

Lingnau, H. (1996): *Lean Management als Konzept zur Reform öffentlicher Verwaltungen in Afrika südlich der Sahara Schlußfolgerungen aus den Verwaltungen Benins und Ugandas*, Cologne

Loske, R. (1996) *Klimapolitik. Im Spannungsfeld von Kurzzeitinteressen und Langzeiterfordernissen*, Marburg

Loucks, O.L. / A.R. Ek / W.C. Johnson / R.A. Monserud (1981): "Growth, Aging and Succession," in: D.E. Reichle (ed.), *Dynamic Properties of Forest Ecosystems*, Cambridge etc.

Luhmann, N. (1986)· *Ökologische Kommunikation Kann die moderne Gesellschaft sich auf ökologische Gefährdungen einstellen?*, Opladen

Lundvall, B.-Å. (1988)· "Innovation as an Interactive Process. From User-producer Interaction to the National System of Innovation," in: G. Dosi et al. (eds), *Technical Change and Economic Theory*, London, New York

Macedo, R. (1996): "Vom Cruzado zum Real. Die Stabilisierungspläne seit der Redemokratisierung," in B Fritz / G Calcagnotto (eds), *Inflation und Stabilisierung in Brasilien*, Frankfurt a.M.

Madrid, R. / C. Ominami (1989)· *Lineamientos estratégicos para una inserción activa en los mercados internacionales*, Instituto Latinoamericano de Estudios Internacionales, Santiago de Chile

Mahar, D. (1978) "Desenvolvimento econômico da Amazônia. Uma analise das políticas governamentais," IPEA, INPES, Rio de Janeiro

– (1988): "Government Policies and Deforestation in Brazil's Amazon Region," World Bank, Washington

Mahnkopf, B. (ed.) (1988): *Der gewendete Kapitalismus. Kritische Beiträge zur Theorie der Regulation*, Münster

Maia Gomes, G. / J.R. Vergolino (1997) "Trinta e Cinco Anos de Crescimento Econômico na Amazônia (1960/1995)," IPEA, Brasília

Maimon, D. (1995): "Responsabilidade ambiental das empresas brasileiras: realidade ou discurso?," in: C Cavalcanti (ed.), *Desenvolvimento e natureza· Estudos para uma sociedade sustentável*, São Paulo, Recife

Marchés Tropicaux (12 1.1996). "Le Comité du Bois de la FAO examine les marchés forestiers," pp 90 - 94

– (25.10.1996) "Le marché allemand des bois tropicaux en 1995," pp 2305 - 2306

– (1 8.1997): "L'Union europénne et la gestion durable des forêts tropicales," pp. 1726 - 1735

– (19.9.1997) "Le marché des bois tropicaux en 1996. La production, les échanges et les prix," pp. 2070 - 2071

– (16 1.1998) "Le marché européen des bois tropicaux," pp. 133 - 136

Mármora, L. / D. Messner (1992). "Chile im lateinamerikanischen Kontext. Ein Modell für Demokratisierung und Entwicklung der gesamten Region?," in J. Ensignia / D. Nolte (eds), *Modellfall Chile? Ein Jahr nach dem demokratischen Neuanfang*, Münster, Schriftenreihe des Instituts für Iberoamerika-Kunde, Hamburg

Marques, G. (1997): "Complexos industriais integrados para assegurar a sustentabilidade," Paper Presented at the ABIMCI Congress, Nov. 1997, Belém

Martínez Quiroga, R. (ed.) (1994): *El tigre sin selva. Consecuencias ambientales de la transformación económica de Chile, 1974 - 1993*, Santiago de Chile

Martinez-Alier, J. (1995): "The Environment as a Luxury Good or 'too Poor to be Green'?," in. *Ecological Economics*, Vol. 13, No. 1

Mather, A. (1997): "South-North Challenges in Global Forestry," UNU, WIDER, Helsinki

Mathis, A. / R. Rehaag (1993): "Conseqüências da garimpagem no âmbito social e ambiental da Amazônia," FASE, Belém

Mattos, A. / C. Uhl (1994): "Economic and Ecological Perspectives on Ranching in the Eastern Amazon," in: *World Development*, Vol 22, No. 2

Maturana, H. (ed.) (1982): *Erkennen Die Organisation und Verkörperung von Wirklichkeit Ausgewählte Arbeiten zur biologischen Epistemologie*, Wiesbaden

Maturana, H.R. / F. Varela (1980): *Autopoiesis and Cognition. The Realization of the Living*, Dordrecht

McGrath, D.G. (1987)· "The Role of Biomass in Shifting Cultivation," in: *Human Ecology*. Vol 15, No 2

– (1997): "Biosfera ou Biodiversidade. uma avaliação crítica do paradigma da biodiversidade," in T Ximenes (ed), *Perspectivas do desenvolvimento sustentável Uma contribuição para a Amazônia 21*, UFPA, NAEA, Belém

Meadows, D., et al. (1972): *Limits to Growth*, New York

Meggers, B. (1954): Environmental Limitations on the Development of Culture, in: *American Anthropologist*, Vol. 56

– (1971)· *Amazonia*, Chicago

– (1984): "The Indigenous Peoples of Amazonia, their Cultures, Land Use Patterns and Effects on Landscape and Biota," in: H Sioli (ed.), *The Amazon. Limnology and Landscape Ecology of a Mighty Tropical River and its Basin*, Dordrecht

Menzel, U. (1988): *Auswege aus der Abhängigkeit. Die entwicklungspolitische Aktualität Europas.* Frankfurt a.M.

Mercado, R.S. (1980). "Timber Production and Marketing in the Brazilian Amazon," Michigan State University (thesis)

Meyer-Stamer, J. (1997): *Technology, Competitiveness and Radical Policy Change The Case of Brazil*, London

Minsch, J. / Eberle, A. / Meier B. / U. Schneidewind (1996): *Mut zum ökologischen Umbau Innovationsstrategien für Unternehmen, Politik und Akteurnetze*, Basel

MMA (Ministério do Meio Ambiente, dos Recursos Hídricos e da Amazônia Legal) (1995): "Uma Política Nacional Integrada para a Amazônia," Brasília

MMA (Ministério do Meio Ambiente, dos Recursos Hídricos e da Amazônia Legal) / Secretaria de Coordenação da Amazônia (1997): "Programa Piloto para a Proteção das Florestas Tropicais do Brasil," Vol. II, Brasília

Moran, E.F. (1981). *Developing the Amazon*, Bloomington

– (1982). *Human Adaptability· An Introduction to Ecological Anthropology*, Boulder/Co.

– (1990): "Private and Public Colonization Schemes in Amazônia," in: D. Goodman / A. Hall (eds), *The Future of Amazônia. Destruction or Sustainable Development?*, London

– (1993): *Through Amazonian Eyes The Human Ecology of Amazonian Populations*, Iowa

Moran, E.F. / A. Packer / E. Brondizio / J. Tucker (1996): "Restoration of Vegetation Cover in the Eastern Amazon," in· *Ecological Economics*, Vol. 18, No. 1

Müller, H. (1987) *Distribution des Holzes in der Bundesrepublik Deutschland*, 1984, Freiburg

Müller, H.-P. (1992) *Sozialstruktur und Lebensstile. Der neuere theoretische Diskurs über soziale Ungleichheit*, Frankfurt a.M.

Nascimento, J.R. (1985): "Brazilian Amazon Development and the Forest Based Sector," University of Minnesota (thesis)

Nelson, R.R. / S.G. Winter (1982): *An Evolutionary Theory of Economic Change*, Cambridge/Mass., London

Nepstad, D. / C. Uhl / C. Pereira / J. Silva (1996): "A Comparative Study of Tree Establishment in Abandoned Pasture and Mature Forest of Eastern Amazonia," in. *Oikos*, Vol. 75, No. 1

Nepstad, D., et al. (1994): "The Role of Deep Roots in the Hydrological and Carbon Cycles of Amazonian Forests and Pastures," in *Nature*, No. 372

– (1995): "Forest Recovery Following Pasture Abandonment in Amazonia: Canopy Seasonality, Fire Resistance and Ants," in: D Rappaport (ed.), *Evaluating and Monitoring the Health of Large-scale Ecosystems*, New York

– (1996): "The Ecological Importance of Forest Remnants in an Eastern Amazonian Frontier Landscape," in: J Schelhas / R Greenberg (eds), *Forest Patches in Tropical Landscapes*, Washington

Neue Zürcher Zeitung (24.11.1995): "Schonende Waldwirtschaft im Amazonas-Urwald," p 7

– (4.12.1996) "Spanplatten. Holz-Rezyklat aus Holzspänen," p. 39

– (15 /16.3 1997): "Wie ist der Regenwald zu retten?," pp. 61 - 63

Nitsch, M. (1993). "Vom Nutzen des systemtheoretischen Ansatzes für die Analyse von Umweltschutz und Entwicklung - mit Beispielen aus dem brasilianischen Amazonasgebiet," in H. Sautter (ed.), *Umweltschutz und Entwicklungspolitik*, Berlin

– (1994): "Nutzung und Schutz tropischer Regenwälder Zur Problematik der großflächigen Zonierung im brasilianischen Amazonasgebiet," in: M Jänicke / H -J Bolle / A Carius (eds), *Umwelt global Veränderungen, Probleme, Lösungsansätze*, Berlin

Norgaard, R. (1981). "Sociosystem and Ecosystem Coevolution in the Amazon," in: *Journal of Environmental Economics and Management*, No. 8

O Liberal (28 4.1996): "Relatório mostra o caos nos projetos florestais," p. 5

– (1.5.1996): "Devastação malaia entra sem alarde na Amazônia," p 8

– (11 5 1997) "Pará é líder em madeira ilegal," pp. 6 - 7

– (25.5.1997) "Relatório comprova saque florestal," pp. 6 - 7

– (8.6.1997): "Governo vai conceder florestas," p. 6

– (22.6.1997) "Madeireiros questionam relatório," p 12

– (23 10.1997). "Asiáticos vão aumentar exploração florestal," p. 6

– (25.2.1998) "Lei ambiental muda a vida dos brasileiros," p. 4

– (1.3 1998): "Asia desaquece madeira," p. 11

O'Neill, R.V. / D.L. De Angelis (1981). "Comparative Productivity and Biomass Relations of Forest Ecosystems," in: D.E. Reichle (ed), *Dynamic Properties of Forest Ecosystems*, Cambridge etc.

Odum, E.P. (1980): *Grundlagen der Ökologie*, Stuttgart, New York

– (1997) *Ecology A Bridge between Science and Society*, Sunderland/MA

Owens, T. / A. Wood (1997)· "Export-oriented Industrialization through Primary Processing?," in *World Development*, Vol. 25, No 9

Ozorio de Almeida, A.L. / J.S. Campari (1995): *Sustainable Settlement in the Brazilian Amazon*, World Bank, Washington, Oxford

Pandolfo, C. (1969): "A indústria madeireira regional - principais causas de seu primarismo e estagnação," in: *Antologia da cultura amazônica - Ciência em geral*, Vol. 9, Belém

– (1972). "A atuação da SUDAM na preservação do patrimonio florestal da Amazônia," in: *Jornal do Brasil*, 31.3.1972

– (1974): "Estudos básicos para o estabelecimento de uma política de desenvolvimento dos recursos florestais e de uso racional das terras da Amazônia," SUDAM, Belém

– (1978)· "A floresta amazônica brasileira. Enfoque econômico-ecológico," SUDAM, Belém

– (1994) "Amazônia brasileira· Ocupação, desenvolvimento e perspectivas atuais e futuras," Cejup, Belém

Pavitt, K. (1984) "Sectoral Patterns of Technical Change. Towards a Taxonomy and a Theory," in. *Research Policy*, Vol. 13

Pearce, D.W. / R.K. Turner (1990): *Economics of Natural Resources and the Environment*, New York

Penteado, A.R. (1967): "Problemas de colonização e uso da terra na região bragantina do Estado do Pará," 2 Vols, Belém: Universidade Federal do Pará (mimeo)

Pfriem, R. (1995) *Unternehmenspolitik in sozialökologischen Perspektiven*, Marburg

Pigou, A.C. (1932). *The Economics of Welfare*, London

Pinto, L.F. (1986). *Jari Toda a verdade sobre o projeto de Ludwig. As relações entre Estado e multinacional na Amazônia*, São Paulo: Marco Zero

Piore, M.J. (1996): "Review of The Handbook of Economic Sociology," in: *Journal of Economic Literature*, Vol. 34, No. 2

PNUD / IPEA (1996): "Relatório sobre o desenvolvimento humano no Brasil 1996," PNUD, Brasília

Popper, K.R. (1973) *Objektive Erkenntnis Ein evolutionärer Entwurf*, Hamburg

Porst, G. (1996)· "Das Leben der Unternehmen in Zeiten der Hochinflation," in: G. Calcagnotto / B Fritz (eds), *Inflation und Stabilisierung in Brasilien Probleme einer Gesellschaft im Wandel*, Frankfurt a. M.

Prance, G.T. (1989): "Economic Prospects from Tropical Rainforest Ethnobotany," in: J. Browder (ed.), *Fragile Lands of Latin America*, Boulder/Co.

Pressler, M.R. (1858)· *Der rationelle Waldwirth und sein Waldbau des höchsten Ertrags*, Dresden

Prigogine, I. (1973)· "The Statistical Interpretation of Non-equilibrium-entropy," in: *Acta Phys. Austriaca Suppl.*, Vol. 10

Prigogine, I. / I. Stengers (1980): *Dialog mit der Natur, neue Wege naturwissenschaftlichen Denkens*, Munich

Reed, D. (ed.) (1996): *Structural Adjustment, the Environment, and Sustainable Development*, London

Reichholf, J.H. (1990): *Der tropische Regenwald Die Ökobiologie des artenreichsten Naturraums der Erde*, Munich

Reichle, D.E. (ed.) (1981)· *Dynamic Properties of Forest Ecosystems*, International Biological Programme 23, Cambridge

Repetto, R. / M. Gillis (eds) (1988): *Public Policies and the Misuse of Forest Resources*, World Resources Institute, Cambridge, New York

Roosevelt, A. (1980) *Parmana Prehistoric Maize and Maniok Subsistence along the Amazon and Orinoco*, New York

– (1991)· "Determinismo ecológico na interpretação do desenvolvimento social indígena da Amazônia," in· W. Neves (ed), *Origens, adaptações e diversidade biológica do homem nativo da Amazônia*, Belém: Museu Paraense Emilio Goeldi

Ross, E. (1978): "The Evolution of the Amazon Peasantry," in: *Journal of Latin American Studies*, Vol. 10, No. 2

Ros-Tonen, M.A.F. (1993). *Tropical Hardwood from the Brazilian Amazon. A Study of the Timber Industry in Western Pará*, Saarbrücken, Fort Lauderdale

Rudel, T. / J. Roper (1997). "The Paths to Rain Forest Destruction. Crossnational Patterns of Tropical Deforestation, 1975 - 1990," in *World Development*, Vol. 25, No 1

Ruttan, V.W. (1997): "Induced Innovation, Evolutionary Theory and Path Dependence. Sources of Technical Change," in: *The Economic Journal*, Vol. 107, No 444

Sachs, I. (1973). "Population, Technology, Natural Resources and the Environment, Eco-Development: A Contribution to the Development Stiles for Latin America," in: *Economic Bulletin for Latin America*, Vol. 16, No. 1

– (1986)· *Ecodesenvolvimento - crescer sem destruir*, São Paulo: Vértice

Salati, E. (1987)· "Amazônia: um ecossistema ameaçado," in: G. Kohlhepp / A. Schrader (eds), *Homem e natureza na Amazônia*, Geographisches Institut der Universität Tübingen, Tübingen

Salati, E. / A.A. dos Santos (1999): "Amazonien und seine globale Bedeutung," in· M de Lourdes Davies de Freitas (ed.), *Amazonien Himmel der Neuen Welt*, Bonn

Salomão, R. / D. Nepstad / I. Vieira (1996) "Como a biomassa de florestas tropicais influi no efeito estufa?," in: *Ciência hoje*, Vol. 21, No 123

Samuelson, P.A. (1965): "A Theory of Induced Innovation along Kennedy-Weizsäcker Lines," in: *Review of Economics and Statistics*, Vol. 47

Santos, R. (1980)· *História econômica da Amazônia (1800 - 1920)*, São Paulo: T.A. Queiroz

Sapsford, D. / V.N. Balasubramanyam (1994): "The Long-run Behavior of the Relative Price of Primary Commodities Statistical Evidence and Policy Implications," in: *World Develoment*, Vol. 22, No 11

Scatena, E., et al. (1996): "Cropping and Fallowing Sequences of Small Farms in the "terra firme" Landscape of the Brazilian Amazon· A Case Study from Santarém, Pará", in *Ecological Economics*, Vol. 18, No. 1

Schmidt-Bleek, F. (1994): *Wieviel Umwelt braucht der Mensch? MIPS - Das Maß für ökologisches Wirtschaften*, Basel

Schmithüsen, F. (1978) "Contratos de utilização florestal com referência especial à Amazônia brasileira," PRODEPEF, IBDF, PNUD, FAP, Brasília

Schmookler, J. (1966): *Invention and Economic Growth*, Cambridge/Mass.

Schneider, R. (1995) *Government and the Economy on an Amazon Frontier*, World Bank, Washington

Scholz, I. (1993)· *Ökologische Produktauflagen in der Bundesrepublik Deutschland und ihre Auswirkungen auf Entwicklungsländerexporte*, German Development Institute, Berlin

– (1996a) "Effective Donor Action at the Trade and Environment Interface". Study Submitted to the DAC Working Party on Development Assistance and Environment, in OECD (ed.), *Reconciling Trade, Environment and Development Policies The Role of Development*, Paris

– (1996b)· "Foreign Trade and the Environment Experiences in three Chilean Export Sectors," in: *CEPAL Review*, Vol 58

– (1996c). "Nachhaltiger Konsum aus der Nord-Süd-Perspektive. Ökologisierung im Norden - Auswirkungen auf den Süden," in: *Ökologisches Wirtschaften*, No. 3/4

– (1997): "Konzeptionelle Überlegungen für eine zweite Phase des Pilotprogramms der G7 für den Schutz der brasilianischen Tropenwälder (PP-G7)," Gutachten für das BMZ, German Development Institute, Berlin

Scholz, I. / K. Block / K. Feil / M. Krause / K. Nakonz / C. Oberle (1994)· *Ökologische Produktanforderungen und Wettbewerbsfähigkeit. Neue Herausforderungen für chilenische Exporte*, German Development Institute, Berlin

Schönenberg, R. (1993): *Konflikte und Konfliktregulation in Amazonien Ursachen, Formen und Folgen ländlicher Konflikte in Süd-Pará,* Bonn

Schubart, H. (1983) "Ecologia e utilização das florestas," in: E. Salati / H. Schubart / W Junk / A Oliveira (eds), *Amazônia. desenvolvimento, integração e ecologia,* São Paulo: CNPq, editora brasiliense

SCM / CNPq / IPAAM (1996): "Mamirauá Management Plan," IPAAM, Manaus

SERETE (1973): "Mercado internacional: Situação e perspectivas de mercado," SU-DAM, Belém

Serrão, E.A.S. / A. Homma (1993): "Brazil Country Profile," in· National Research Council (ed.), *Sustainable Agriculture and the Environment in the Humid Tropics,* Washington

Sieferle, R.P. (ed.) (1988): *Fortschritte der Naturzerstörung,* Frankfurt a.M.

Silva, J.G.C. (1998) "Participação Fragmentada. O Caso do Projeto de Recuperação das Baixadas da Bacia do Una, em Belém do Pará," in: J -P. Leroy / M.C.C. Soares (eds), *Bancos Multilaterais e Desenvolvimento Participativo no Brasil Dilemas e Desafios,* FASE, IBASE, Rio de Janeiro

Silva, J.N.M. (1993) "Possibilidades Para a Produção Sustentada de Madeira em Floresta Densa de Terra-Firme da Amazônia Brasileira," Ministério da Agricultura & Empresa Brasileira de Pesquisa Agropecuária, Colombo

– (1996): "Manejo florestal," EMBRAPA-CPATU, Brasília

Silva, J.N.M., et al. (1997): "Diagnóstico dos projetos de manejo florestal no Estado do Pará - fase Paragominas," EMBRAPA-CPATU, Belém

Silva, R.A.N. (1994) "Diagnóstico do setor industrial madeireiro no estado do Pará," ITTO, IBAMA, FUNATURA, Belém

– (1995): "Avaliação econômica do uso dos recursos florestais no planalto de Curuá-Una, Amazônia brasileira," Belém (mimeo)

Simula, M. (1997): "Plywood Industry towards the 21st Century," Paper Presented at the III. International Congress on Plywood and Tropical Timber, Belém 4.-9.11.1997, Belém

Sioli, H. (1956): "Über Natur und Mensch im brasilianischen Amazonasgebiet," in: *Erdkunde,* Vol. 10, No 2

– (1983): *Amazonien Grundlagen der Ökologie des größten tropischen Waldlandes,* Stuttgart

Siqueira, J.D.P. (1997)· "Investimentos internacionais na indústria florestal e concentração na produção." Paper Presented at the III. International Congress on Plywood and Tropical Timber, Belém 4.-9.11.1997, Belém

Soete, L. (1985): "International Diffusion of Technology, Industrial Develpment and Technological Leapfrogging," in *World Development*, Vol. 13, No. 3

Sommer, M. / J. Settele / H. Michelsen / B. Unmüssig / P. Sandner (1990): *Countdown für den Dschungel Ökonomie und Ökologie des tropischen Regenwaldes*, Stuttgart

Soto B., F. (1993) "Da indústria do papel ao complexo florestal no Brasil: O caminho do corporatismo tradicional ao neocorporatismo," Instituto de Economia da UNI-CAMP, Campinas

Sperber, G. (1996): "Der Umgang mit Wald - eine ethische Disziplin," in: H. Graf Hatzfeldt (ed.), *Ökologische Waldwirtschaft Grundlagen - Aspekte - Beispiele*, Heidelberg

STCP (1997) "A Indústria de Painéis no Brasil. A Tendência de Mudança no Perfil da Produção Brasileira." in: *Informativo*, No. 1

Steiner, B. / J. Meyerhoff (eds) (1993): *Kommentierte Bibliographie Umwelt und Ökonomie*, IÖW, Berlin

Stephan, G. / M. Ahlheim (1996). *Ökonomische Ökologie*, Berlin etc.

Stevens, W.E. (1968): "The Conservation of Wildlife in West Malaysia," Ministry of Lands and Mines, Seremban

Steward, J. (ed.) (1948) *Handbook of South American Indians*, Bureau of American Ethnology, Washington

Stone, S.W. (1997) "Economic Trends in the Timber Industry of Amazônia. Survey Results from Pará State, 1990 - 1995," in *The Journal of Developing Areas*, Vol 32

− (1998) "Evolution of the Timber Industry along an Aging Frontier. The Case of Paragominas (1990 - 1995)," in *World Development*, Vol. 26, No. 3

Streeten, P. (1984): "Basic Needs Some Unsettled Questions," in: *World Development*, Vol 12, No 9

SUDAM (1967) "Primer Plano Quinquenal de Desenvolvimento 1967 - 1971," Belém

− (1973a). "Considerações sobre o estágio atual do setor madeireiro na Amazônia," Belém

− (1973b): "Levantamentos florestais realizados pela Missão FAO na Amazônia (1956 - 1961)," 2 Vols. Belém

− (1988): "Programa de desenvolvimento florestal," Belém

− (1990). "Avaliação de Técnicas de Manejo Florestal," Belém

− (1995): "Plano Plurianual - 1996/99 Amazônia Legal," Belém

– (1996a) "Distribuição das atividades do setor industrial florestal madeireiro da Amazônia Legal. Projetos aprovados pela SUDAM/FINAM. Período de 1967 à 1995," Belém

– (1996b) "Levantamento das indústrias madeireiras da Amazônia Legal. Projetos incentivados pela SUDAM/FINAM. Período de 1967 a 1995," Belém

SUDAM / PNUD (1988) Relatório do Seminario "Sistemas Integrados da Exploração Racional da Madeira Amazônica," no place

Sunkel, O. (ed.) (1996): *Sustentabilidad ambiental del crecimiento económico chileno*, Santiago de Chile

Takeuchi, K. (1983). "Mechanical Processing of Tropical Hardwood in Developing Countries: Issues and Prospects for the Plywood Industry's Development in the Asia-Pacific Region " Case Studies on Industrial Processing of Primary Products, Vol. 1, World Bank / Commonwealth Secretariat

Terezo, E. (1997) "Plantio em áreas degradadas," Paper Presented at the III. International Congress on Plywood and Tropical Timber, Belém 4 -9 11.1997, Belém

Thiele, R. (1996) *Wirtschaftspolitische Optionen zum Schutz tropischer Wälder. Eine quantitative Analyse für Indonesien*, Tübingen

Thomasius, H. (1996) "Grundlagen eines ökologisch orientierten Waldbaus," in: H. Graf Hatzfeldt (ed.), *Ökologische Waldwirtschaft Grundlagen - Aspekte - Beispiele*, Heidelberg

Toni, A. (1997): "Logging the Planet. An Overview of Asian Companies, in particular Malaysian Companies", Greenpeace International, no place

Trepl, L. (1987) *Geschichte der Ökologie Vom 17. Jahrhundert bis zur Gegenwart*, Frankfurt a M.

Uhl, C., et al. (1990) "Studies of Ecosystem Response to Natural and Anthropogenic Disturbances Provide Guidelines for Designing Sustainable Land-use Systems in Amazonia," in: A.B. Anderson (ed), *Alternatives to Deforestation. Steps toward Sustainable Use of the Amazon Rain Forest*, New York

Uhl, C. / P. Barreto / A. Veríssimo / A.C. Barros / P. Amaral / E. Vidal / C. Jr. Souza (1996) "Uma abordagem integrada de pesquisa sobre o manejo dos recursos naturais na Amazônia," in: A.C. Barros / A. Veríssimo (eds), *A expansão da atividade madeireira na Amazônia Impactos e perspectivas para o desenvolvimento do setor florestal no Pará*, IMAZON, Belém

Uhl, C. / P. Barreto / A. Veríssimo / E. Vidal / P. Amaral / A.C. Barros / C. Jr. Souza / J. John / J. Gerwing (1997): "Natural Resource Management in the Brazilian Amazon," in: *BioScience*, Vol. 47, No 3

UNCTAD (1996) "Implications of the Uruguay Round for Trade in Wood and Wood Products," Geneva

UNEP (1981) "In Defense of the Earth. The Basic Texts on Environment, Founex," Stockholm, Cocoyoc, Nairobi

Valverde, O. (1980) "O problema florestal da Amazônia brasileira," in· O. Valverde / L R Freitas (eds), *Amazônia brasileira*, Petrópolis Vozes

Väth, W. (ed.) (1989)· *Political Regulation in the "Great Crisis,"* Berlin

Velho, O. (1972) *Frentes de expansão e estrutura agrária Estudo do processo de penetração numa área da Transamazônica*, Rio de Janeiro: Zahar

– (1976) *Capitalismo autoritário e campesinato*, São Paulo, Rio de Janeiro: Difel

Veríssimo, A. / E. Lima (1998): "Pólos de exploração madeireira na Amazônia," IMAZON, Belém

Veríssimo, A. / P. Barreto / M. Mattos / R. Tarifa / C. Uhl (1996): "Impactos da atividade madeireira e perspectivas para o manejo sustentável da floresta numa velha fronteira da Amazônia: o caso de Paragominas," in· A.C. Barros / A. Veríssimo (eds) *A expansão da atividade madeireira na Amazônia· Impactos e perspectivas para o desenvolvimento do setor florestal no Pará*, IMAZON, Belém

Veríssimo, A. / P. Barreto / R. Tarifa / C. Uhl (1996): "A exploração de um recurso florestal amazônico de alto valor o caso do mogno," in: A.C. Barros / A. Veríssimo (eds). *A expansão da atividade madeireira na Amazônia: Impactos e perspectivas para o desenvolvimento do setor florestal no Pará*, IMAZON, Belém

Viana, G. (1997)· "Relatório da Comissão de Inquerito Parlamentar sobre as atividades das madereiras asiáticas na Amazônia Legal," Brasília

Vieira, I. / R. Salomão / D. Nepstad / J. Roma (1996): "O renascimento da floresta no rastro da agricultura. Como a floresta amazônica sobrevive ao desmatamento e às queimadas," in *Ciência hoje*, Vol. 20, No. 119

Vincent, J.R. (1990) "Don't Boycott Tropical Timber," in: *Journal of Forestry*, Vol. 88, No. 4

Vitousek, P.M. / P.R. Ehrlich / A.H. Ehrlich / P.A. Matson (1986): "Human Appropriation of the Products of Photosynthesis," in: *BioScience*, Vol. 36, No. 6

Vornholz, G. (1993): *Zur Konzeption einer ökologisch tragfähigen Entwicklung*, Marburg

– (1994)· "The Sustainable Development Approach," in: *Intereconomics*, Vol. 29, No 4

Wagley, C. (1953). *Amazon Town*, New York

Walker, R., et al. (1993): "Sustainable Farm Management in the Amazon Piedmont," in· *Congresso Brasileiro de Economia e Sociologia Rural*, Vol. 31

Walker, R. / A. Homma / A. Conto / R. Carvalho / C. Ferreira / A. Santos / A. Rocha / P. Oliveira / C. Pedraza (1995): "Dinâmica dos sistemas de produção na Transamazônica," EMBRAPA, Belém (mimeo)

Wall, D. (1980): "Industrial Processing of Natural Resources," in: *World Development*, Vol. 8, No 4

Wallace, D. (1995): *Environmental Policy and Industrial Innovation Strategies in Europe, the USA and Japan*, Royal Institute of International Affairs, London

Walter, H. (1973): *Vegetation of the Earth in Relation to Climate and the Ecophysiological Conditions*, New York

Weischet, W. (1980) *Die ökologische Benachteiligung der Tropen*, Stuttgart

– (1985): "Ecological Considerations Concerning the Unsatisfactory Development of the Rural Economy in the Tropics," in: *Applied Geography and Development*, Vol. 26, No 1

Weischet, W. / C. Caviedes (1993): *The Persisting Ecological Constraints of Tropical Agriculture*, Essex, New York

Weizsäcker, E.U. / A.B. Lovins / H.L. Lovins (1995) *Faktor Vier Doppelter Wohlstand - halbierter Naturverbrauch*, Munich

Welford, R. (1995): *Environmental Strategy and Sustainable Development. The Corporate Challenge for the 21st Century*, London, New York

Westoby, J. (1962): 'Forest Industries in the Attack on Economic Underdevelopment," in *Unasylva*, Vol 16, No. 4

Whitmore, T.C. (1975) *Tropical Rainforests of the Far East*, Oxford

– (1993): *Tropische Regenwälder. Eine Einführung*, Heidelberg

Whittaker, R.H. (1965) *Dominance and Diversity in Land Plant Communities*, Washington

Wiebelt, M. (1995) "Stopping Deforestation in the Amazon Trade-off between Ecological and Economic Targets?," in *Weltwirtschafiliches Archiv*, Vol. 131, No. 3

Wiemann, J. (1996) *Rahmenbedingungen und Anforderungen an Handelsförderung in Entwicklungsländern Die Perspektiven nach dem Abschluß der Uruguay-Runde*, German Development Institute, Berlin

Wiemann, J., et al. (1994): *Ecological Product Standards and Requirements as a New Challenge for Developing Countries' Industries and Exports The Case of India's Leather, Textile and Refrigeration Industries*, German Development Institute, Berlin

Williamson, O.E. (1975): *Markets and Hierarchies Analysis and Antitrust Implications*, New York

– (1981): "The Modern Corporation Origins, Evolution, Attributes," in: *Journal of Economic Literature*, Vol. 19, No. 4

– (1994): "Transaction Cost Economics and Organization Theory," in: N J Smelser / R Swedberg (eds), *The Handbook of Economic Sociology*, Russell Sage Foundation, Princeton/N.J., New York

WCED (World Commission on Environment and Development) (1987): "Our Common Future," Oxford, New York

World Bank (1992) "Brazil. An Analysis of Environmental Problems in the Amazon," Report No. 9104-BR, Washington

Die Zeit (20.6.1997) "Sägen für die Umwelt. Ein Projekt am Amazonas zeigt, wie schwierig es ist, den Tropenwald umweltschonend und wirtschaftlich zu nutzen," p 23

– (24.9.1998) "Unbeachteter Absturz," p. 36

APPENDIX

Table A - 1:	Growth of Physical World Timber Output, 1961-97 (%)				
	1961/70	1970/80	1980/90	1990/97	1961/97
Industrial roundwood	2.6	1.3	1.8	-1.9	1.5
Logs	2.0	1.4	1.9	-1.8	1.5
Coniferous	1.6	1.1	2.2	-2.8	1.0
Nonconiferous	3.2	2.3	1.3	0.6	2.6
Sawnwood	2.0	0.9	1.1	-2.2	0.9
Coniferous	1.9	0.6	1.1	-2.5	0.6
Nonconiferous	2.6	1.6	1.3	-1.2	1.7
Wood panels	11.4	3.8	2.2	2.6	6.9
Veneer	12.1	3.3	4.5	-1.8	6.6
Plywood	8.1	1.7	2.0	1.9	4.7
Pulp	5.8	2.4	1.9	0.6	3.8
Paper	5.6	3.0	3.5	2.8	5.2
Source: FAO Forestry Statistics, annual geometrical growth rate in %					

Table A - 2:	Growth of Developing Countries' Physical Timber Output, 1961-97 (%)				
	1961/70	1970/80	1980/90	1990/97	1961/97
Industrial roundwood	4,7	5,0	1,7	1,8	4,7
Logs	5.4	5.0	1.1	1.3	4.5
Coniferous	4.1	6.2	0.6	2.9	4.8
Nonconiferous	5.9	4.5	1.3	0.6	4.4
Sawnwood	4.4	5.3	2.1	0.5	4.5
Coniferous	4.4	4.7	1.7	1.4	4.4
Nonconiferous	4.3	5.7	2.3	0.0	4.6
Wood panels	17.6	8.4	6.4	8.5	14.2
Veneer	20.5	5.5	8.7	-0.8	12.2
Plywood	17.0	7.5	6.5	8.4	13.7
Pulp	9.4	8.3	4.3	7.1	10.1
Paper	5.7	8.5	7.4	7.3	10.2
Source: FAO Forestry Statistics, annual geometrical growth rate in %					

Table A - 3:	Growth of World Physical Timber Exports, 1961-97 (%)				
	1961/70	1970/80	1980/90	1990/97	1961/97
Industrial roundwood	10.4	2.0	-0.3	1.3	4.5
Logs	13.5	1.1			
Coniferous	17.0	1.4			
Nonconiferous	11.7	0.9			
Sawnwood	3.7	3.3	1.1	3.1	3.8
Coniferous	3.4	2.9	1.1	3.4	3.6
Nonconiferous	5.5	5.6	1.5	1.4	5.0
Wood panels	13.6	5.3	6.5	6.2	11.0
Veneer	11.7	5.1	4.1	4.5	8.8
Plywood	13.7	3.4	9.0	3.5	10.4
Pulp	6.3	2.3	1.6	4.7	5.0
Paper	6.9	4.1	4.7	4.8	7.2
Source: FAO Forestry Statistics, annual geometrical growth rate in %					

Table A - 4:	Growth of Developing Countries' Physical Timber Exports, 1961-97 (%)				
	1961/70	1970/80	1980/90	1990/97	1961/97
Industrial roundwood	12.3	1.1	-2.1	-0.2	3.6
Logs	12.2	0.9			
Coniferous	3.8	28.2			
Nonconiferous	12.3	0.6			
Sawnwood	6.3	6.4	0.7	0.4	5.0
Coniferous	2.4	2.9	-1.4	4.6	2.6
Nonconiferous	8.7	7.7	1.3	-0.7	6.2
Wood panels	23.4	5.9	10.7	4.8	15.8
Veneer	15.7	2.7	4.0	7.7	10.1
Plywood	26.1	5.9	11.7	3.3	16.6
Pulp	21.9	16.7	3.4	14.6	19.5
Paper	8.9	10.8	15.3	12.1	16.7
Source: FAO Forestry Statistics, annual geometrical growth rate in %					

Table A - 5:	Timber Exports from Pará, 1987-96 (m³)						
	1990	1991	1992	1993	1994	1995	1996
Logs	0	0	0	0	0	0	0
Sawnwood	311,343	280,189	362,179	395,272	583,055	640,824	544,195
Mahogany	95,495	93,448	104,160	94,588	70,368	62,872	42,070
Tauari	22,749	22,129	30,253	29,022	72,664	69,752	46,006
Virola	40,561	21,331	28,234	14,897	21,635	16,256	13,994
Quaruba	6,137	1,344	9,539	19,468	30,491	31,378	43,763
Angelim vermelho	9,657	9,445	8,328	14,341	17,583	43,310	30,626
Curupixá	590	6,412	22,311	38,327	71,749	50,640	19,909
Others	231,649	219,528	263,514	279,217	368,933	429,488	389,897
Semi-processed goods	8,918	9,435	16,087	19,275	27,017	25,225	19,597
Veneer	24,745	24,351	29,580	22,379	31,345	37,067	32,356
Plywood	119,819	116,338	178,556	228,737	280,939	246,633	224,839
Total	464,825	430,313	526,402	665,663	922,356	949,749	820,987
Source: AIMEX							

Table A - 6: Distribution of Brazilian Timber Exports, 1970-83 (R$ 1000)

	1970	1971	1972	1973	1974	1975	1976	1977	1978	1979	1980	1981	1982	1983
Total	653,856	657,671	660,436	929,377	760,776	547,976	490,611	533,819	605,343	811,207	1,126,420	925,172	626,699	957,887
Logs (coniferous and non-conif.)	18,699	20,924	24,741	66,584	27,311	4,678	6,101	0	0	5,871	0	0	0	0
Sawnwood > 5 mm	460,292	470,114	398,529	442,827	338,759	304,795	166,413	162,775	120,035	151,235	248,606	140,495	108,477	158,566
Brazilian pine	405,196	410,875	327,850	309,092	210,795	218,043	73,117	60,378	72,847	113,293	132,668	67,630	43,477	48,084
Imbuia	10,236	6,781	10,265	24,025	33,875	21,938	13,052	7,511	9,259	5,836	21,922	n.d.	n.d.	n.d.
Jacarandá	8,042	5,449	2,318	1,042	n.d.	n.d.	n.d.	n.d.	n.d.	n.d.	n.d.	n.d.	n.d.	n.d.
Virola	n.d.	13,512	21,841	47,130	52,603	30,600	44,170	46,416	12,322	n.d.	15,233	n.d.	n.d.	18,311
Mahogany	n.d.	11,861	12,475	19,040	41,486	34,214	36,074	48,469	25,607	17,614	43,866	30,491	33,181	63,987
Others	36,817	21,636	23,781	42,497	n.d.	n.d.	n.d.	n.d.	n.d.	14,492	34,918	42,374	31,819	28,184
Semi-processed goods	12,154	12,718	18,261	103,804	165,299	35,432	70,645	80,891	185,912	305,891	373,061	350,031	209,908	343,278
Coniferous (Brazilian pine)	12,154	12,286	15,465	88,020	150,552	26,762	59,656	64,461	69,697	78,252	62,132	54,369	39,210	53,785
Nonconiferous	n.d.	433	2,796	15,783	14,747	8,670	10,989	16,430	116,215	227,639	310,929	295,662	170,698	289,493
Sawnwood < 5 mm, veneers	98,384	106,690	136,983	164,444	29,536	37,872	22,178	16,607	15,580	80,857	100,546	78,940	15,289	92,231
Jacarandá	0	58,066	79,137	78,069	24,926	30,200	16,365	10,180	5,587	4,613	n.d.	n.d.	n.d.	n.d.
Virola	0	12,745	16,150	14,383	n.d.	n.d.	n.d.	n.d.	n.d.	n.d.	n.d.	n.d.	n.d.	n.d.
Mahogany	0	n.d.	n.d.	n.d.	4,610	7,672	5,813	6,427	6,475	8,819	16,176	12,503	n.d.	17,967
Others	0	35,879	41,697	71,992	n.d.	n.d.	n.d.	n.d.	3,518	67,425	84,370	66,436	15,289	74,264

Table A - 6 (continued)

Plywood	144,225	58,855	115,552	117,531	110,881	50,711	36,387	30,253	27,636	32,946	44,135	30,786	24,501	33,877
Fiberboard (hardboard)	125,537	99,529	133,691	143,587	n.d.	n.d.	n.d.	n.d.	n.d.	n.d.	n.d.	n.d.	n.d.	n.d.
Strips	n.d.	n.d.	n.d.	n.d.	10,031	10,565	6,496	4,239	4,686	5,964	n.d.	n.d.	n.d.	n.d.
Doors, windows,etc.	25,891	19,497	44,173	66,746	3,278	4,092	10,613	n.d.	n.d.	n.d.	n.d.	n.d.	n.d.	1,004
Wooden tool handles, brooms	26,983	13,512	18,476	36,676	39,205	26,662	25,359	22,823	16,907	32,716	n.d.	n.d.	n.d.	2,362
Other wood products	41,170	101,629	45,119	40,667	99,317	188,126	191,412	165,314	114,141	126,244	107,495	51,048	22,677	27,084
Charcoal	n.d.	n.d.	n.d.	n.d.	5.757	n.d.	n.d.	n.d.	n.d.	n.d.	n.d.	n.d.	n.d.	n.d.
Pulp and Paper	1,569,683	1,104,304	1,473,711	1,593,405	945,469	489,875	268,721	259,850	296,902	354,393	294,354	195,212	111,126	37,273
Pulp	856,427	687,210	866,278	n.d.	519,982	179,193	66,646	96,688	116,157	154,198	116,079	73,472	26,387	33,826
Paper	636,927	368,911	376,801	n.d.	239,296	115,386	50,383	44,361	11,226	38,925	122,387	64,903	50,013	3,447
Fiberboard	s,o,	s,o,	s,o,	s,o,	105,612	107,115	90,166	71,467	71,408	67,568	n.d.	n.d.	n.d.	n.d.
Others	n.d.	n.d.	230,632	n.d.	80,578	52,650	34,269	14,377	34,204	42,286	49,371	56,837	34,726	0

Source: IBGE - Anuário Estatístico, several issues; prices in R$ as of 1996

Table A - 7:   Comparison of Basic Data of the Timber Industry, 1970-85

Year	Enter-prises	Em-ployees	Employ-ees/en-terprise	Monthly labor costs	GPV/en-terprise	NVA/em-ployee	NVA/em-ployee in produc-tion
Pará				R$	R$	R$	R$
1970	297	4,764	16	193	214,371	7,373	8,666
1975	564	9,200	16	291	502,284	16,988	22,292
1980	1,692	21,432	13	400	413,887	16,871	22,622
1985	1,241	18,050	15	349	495,149	19,549	23,911
Paraná							
1970	2,307	37,325	16	282	445,390	13,111	15,269
1975	2,678	50,068	19	382	880,717	24,688	30,539
1980	2,417	55,701	23	396	1,220,390	26,578	31,157
1985	1,462	41,107	28	330	984,188	20,696	24,420
Brazil							
1970	14,812	135,979	9	284	235,314	12,932	16,055
1975	17,898	203,856	11	384	470,719	21,569	27,861
1980	21,018	263,004	13	413	528,363	22,919	29,283
1985	16,155	218,059	13	360	434,354	18,153	22,635
North							
1970	401	7,494	19	252	311,069	9,590	11,284
1975	811	15,382	19	332	571,891	17,396	22,160
1980	2,431	33,010	14	322	461,750	19,355	24,912
1985	1,946	31,893	16	368	642,090	22,612	27,261
Northeast							
1970	1,782	8,902	5	199	75,842	7,233	10,958
1975	2,015	14,041	7	253	185,750	12,860	18,185
1980	3,835	25,955	7	215	169,144	14,163	20,739
1985	3,286	20,884	6	275	124,833	10,075	13,422

Table A - 7 (continued)							
Southeast							
1970	4,060	33,686	8	353	262,588	15,962	20,600
1975	4,754	48,871	10	460	517,349	24,875	31,630
1980	4,269	52,919	12	449	680,006	29,793	38,013
1985	3,639	47,071	13	493	522,162	21,456	28,884
South							
1970	7,733	80,841	10	272	267,816	12,809	15,344
1975	8,801	114,552	13	383	544,467	22,317	28,393
1980	8,213	132,128	16	349	701,309	23,419	28,714
1985	5,881	103,852	18	323	524,000	17,365	20,874
Midwest							
1970	836	5,056	6	207	105,797	9,689	13,266
1975	1,517	11,010	7	305	221,171	16,060	24,067
1980	2,270	18,992	8	270	295,664	18,447	26,472
1985	1,517	14,359	9	296	247,527	14,867	18,744
Source: IBGE Censo Industrial 1970, 1975, 1980, 1985, values in 1996 R$ prices							

Table A - 8: Brazilian Timber Exports, 1992-97

	1992		1996		Annual growth 1992-96 (%)	
	US $	t	US $	t	US $	t
Sawnwood	161,496	302,357	344,657	858,204	20.9	29.8
Andiroba	1,937	7,438	2,079	7,238	1.8	-0.7
Angelim vermelho	2,144	10,003	3,679	16,688	14.5	13.6
Cedro	10,679	21,472	11,415	15,690	1.7	-7.5
Cedrorana	932	3,137	2,556	6,715	28.7	21.0
Cerejeira	846	2,101	2,163	4,495	26.5	20.9
Dark red	95	96	143	363	10.8	39.4
Freijo	328	978	146	253	-18.3	-28.7
Imbuia	2,545	4,081	4,464	5,339	15.1	6.9
Ipê	1,945	6,104	1,845	12,871	-1.3	20.5
Jacarandá	469	284	310	146	-9.8	-15.3
Jatobá	13,741	46,986	23,609	68,054	14.5	9.7
Mahogany	62,830	n.d.	46,622	52,906	-7.2	n.d.
Pau marfim	310	899	435	1,386	8.8	11.4
Brazilian pine	13,281	20,011	17,705	19,786	7.5	-0 3
Pinus	4,085	14,596	83,600	189,736	112.7	89.9
Quiri	250	391	502	1,433	19.0	38.4
Sucupira	1,802	6,226	n.d.	n.d.	n.d.	n.d.
Tatajuba	1,621	5,867	3,612	9,311	22.2	12.2
Virola	4,236	13,249	2,932	7,659	-8.8	-12.8
Other species	37,420	138,438	136,840	438,135	38.3	33.4
Particle board	4,289	15,637	22,533	43,019	51.4	28.8
Semi-processed goods	108,696	182,566	226,214	238,060	20.1	6.9
Veneer boards	38,355	47,610	74,097	96,096	17.9	19.2
Plywood	150,412	264,606	247,670	359,638	13.3	8.0
Fiberboard	87,817	259,459	83,639	252,602	-1.2	-0.7
Total	551,065	1,072,235	998,810	1,847,619	16.0	14.6

Source: IBAMA, according to data from the foreign-trade department of the economics-affairs ministry

Table A - 9:	Regional Distribution of the GPV of the Furniture Industry, 1959-85 (%)				
	1959	1970	1975	1980	1985
North	0.4	0.7	0.4	1.3	1.4
Pará	*0 3*	*0.4*	*0.2*	*0 5*	*0.4*
Northeast	5.0	5.0	4.9	5.9	6.3
Southeast	80.9	75.4	71.1	60.0	59.1
South	12 9	18.1	22.7	31.1	31.6
Paraná	*3 8*	*6.5*	*7 3*	*9 3*	*9 0*
Midwest	0 7	0.8	0.8	1.6	1.6
Brazil	100.0	100.0	100.0	100.0	100.0
Source: IBGE					

Table A - 10:	Regional Distribution of GPV of the Paper Industry, 1959-85 (%)				
	1959	1970	1975	1980	1985
North	0 1	0.1	0.1	2.2	2.0
Pará	*0 0*	*n d*	*n d.*	*2 1*	*1.9*
Northeast	3 9	2.1	5.3	4.8	4.7
Southeast	83.3	81.4	73.9	72.1	70.0
South	12.8	16.2	20.5	20.7	23.1
Paraná	*4 9*	*7.0*	*8.5*	*9*	*9.8*
Midwest	0 0	0.1	0.2	0.1	0.1
Brazil	100 0	100.0	100.0	100.0	100.0
Source: IBGE					

Table A - 11:   Growth of NVA/Employee in the Timber Industry, 1970-85

	1970	1975	1970-75	1980	1975-80	1985	1980-85	1970-85
	R$ 1000	R$ 1000	%	R$ 1000	%	R$ 1000	%	%
North	9,590	17,396	12 6	19,355	2.2	22,612	3 2	5.9
Pará	*7,373*	*16,994*	*18 2*	*16,871*	*-0 1*	*19,549*	*3,0*	*6 7*
Northeast	7,233	12,860	12.2	14,163	1.9	10,075	-6 6	2.2
Southeast	15,962	24,875	9 3	29,793	3 7	21,456	-6.4	2 0
South	12,809	22,317	11 7	23,419	1 0	17,365	-5.8	2.0
Paraná	*13,111*	*24,684*	*13 5*	*26,578*	*1 5*	*20,696*	*-4 9*	*3 1*
Midwest	9,689	16,060	10 6	18,447	2.8	14,867	-4.2	2.9
Brazil	12,932	21,569	10 8	22,919	1.2	18,153	-4 6	2.3

Source: IBGE, figures in 1996 R$, annual geometric growth rate in %

Table A - 12:   Growth of NVA/Employee in the Furniture Industry by Region, 1970-85

	1970	1975	1970-75	1980	1975-80	1985	1980-85	1970-85
	R$ 1000	R$ 1000	%	R$ 1000	%	R$ 1000	%	%
North	7,827	9,622	4 2	17,942	13.3	14,502	-4.2	4.2
Pará	*7,522*	*8,142*	*1 6*	*11,940*	*8 0*	*9,504*	*-4 5*	*1 6*
Northeast	7,441	12,855	11 6	15,079	3.2	13,688	-1.9	4 1
Southeast	16,079	23,788	8 1	23,807	0.0	20,483	-3.0	1 6
South	10,883	20,017	13 0	24,270	3.9	19,904	-3 9	4 1
Paraná	*11,633*	*19,126*	*10 5*	*21,603*	*2 5*	*16,355*	*-5 4*	*2 3*
Midwest	6,909	11,478	10.7	19,652	11.4	8,520	-15.4	1.4
Brazil	13,873	21,617	9 3	22,914	1 2	19,203	-3.5	2.2

Source: IBGE, figures in 1996 R$, annual geometrical growth rate in %

Table A - 13:	Growth of NVA/Employee in the Paper Industry by Region, 1970-85							
	1970	1975	1970-75	1980	1975-80	1985	1980-85	1970-85
	R$ 1000	R$ 1000	%	R$ 1000	%	R$ 1000	%	%
North	11,293	19,587	11 6	136,474	47.4	23,370	-29 7	5.0
Pará	*n d*	*n d.*	*n d*	*149,222*	*n.d*	*23,495*	*-30.9*	*n d.*
Northeast	14,150	34,735	19.7	49,650	7 4	31,736	-8.6	5.5
Southeast	28,783	44,801	9,3	64,760	7,6	57,711	-2.3	4.7
South	21,636	45,717	16.1	57,491	4.7	55,802	-0.6	6.5
Paraná	*21,643*	*55,740*	*20 8*	*71,490*	*5 1*	*60,323*	*-3 3*	*7 1*
Midwest	17,123	29,276	11.3	26,132	-2.2	37,966	7.8	5 5
Brazil	26,660	44,368	10 7	63,148	7.3	55,151	-2.7	5 0

Source: IBGE, figures in 1996 R$, annual geometrical growth rate in %; data for Pará / North 1980 are not plausible

Table A - 14:	NVA/Employee in the Industrial Sector, 1959-85								
	1959	1970	1975	1970-75	1980	1975-80	1985	1980-85	1970-85
	R$ 1000	R$ 1000	R$ 1000	%	R$ 1000	%	R$ 1000	%	%
North	16,308	17,729	29,470	10.7	45,235	8.9	50,830	2.4	7 3
Pará	−	*11,699*	*22,327*	*13 8*	*29,168*	*5 5*	*32,113*	*1 9*	*7 0*
Northeast	10,663	14,978	25,966	11 6	33,334	5 1	36,503	1.8	6.1
Southeast	20,071	30,312	44,715	8 1	51,134	2.7	50,864	-0.1	3.5
South	15,053	18,707	30,978	10 6	36,866	3.5	37,708	0.5	4.8
Paraná	−	*19,017*	*34,420*	*12 6*	*41,744*	*3 9*	*47,707*	*2 7*	*6 3*
Midwest	14,426	15,650	24,558	9 4	25,734	0.9	30,028	3.1	4.4
Brazil	18,189	26,589	39,784	8.4	45,769	2.8	48,868	1.3	4 1

Source. IBGE, figures in 1996 R$, annual geometrical growth rate in %

Table A - 15:	Investments in the Timber Industry, 1959-80							
	1959	1970	1959-70	1975	1970-75	1980	1975-80	1959-80
	R$ m	R$ m	%	R$ m	%	R$ m	%	%
North	1 8	35 8	31 2	77.3	16 6	212.8	22.4	25.5
Pará	*n d*	*27 1*	*n d*	*19 9*	*-6 0*	*125 3*	*44 5*	
Northeast	2 5	19.4	20.5	34.4	12.1	78.4	17.9	17.8
Southeast	20 1	72.8	12 4	116	9 8	109.8	-1.1	8.4
South	47 0	121.1	9.0	274.9	17 8	355.4	5.3	10.1
Paraná	*n d*	*42.2*	*n d*	*127 8*	*24 8*	*144.5*	*2 5*	
Midwest	3 1	13 8	14.5	59.9	34 1	83.2	6.8	17 0
Brazil	74 6	262.8	12.1	562.8	16 5	839.6	8.3	12.2

Source: IBGE, figures in 1996 R$, annual geometrical growth rate in %

Table A - 16:	Investments in the Furniture Industry, 1959-80							
	1959	1970	1959-70	1975	1970-75	1980	1975-80	1959-80
	R$ m	R$ m	%	R$ m	%	R$ m	%	%
North	0	3.1	n d.	0.7	-25.7	20.7	96.9	
Pará	*0*	*2 8*	*n d*	*0 6*	*-26 5*	*5 2*	*54 0*	
Northeast	1.3	9.4	19.7	13.9	8 1	24.9	12.4	15.1
Southeast	30 1	65 2	7.3	182.5	22 9	143 7	-4.7	7.7
South	3 8	25 1	18.7	68 9	22 4	92.6	6.1	16 4
Paraná	*0*	*7*		*15 2*	*16 8*	*28 3*	*13 2*	
Midwest	0 6	2.5	13.9	2 4	-0 8	6 9	23.5	12 3
Brazil	35 8	105.4	10 3	257.6	19 6	288.8	2 3	10 5

Source: IBGE, figures in 1996 R$, annual geometrical growth rate in %

Table A - 17:	Investments in the Pulp and Paper Industries, 1959-80							
	1959	1970	1959-70	1975	1970-75	1980	1975-80	1959-80
	R$ m	R$ m	%	R$ m	%	R$ m	%	%
North	0	0	n.d.	0 5	n.d.	89.5	182.2	
Pará	*0*	*0*	*n d*	*0*	*n.d*	*89.5*		
Northeast	6 9	2.5	-8 8	39.3	73 5	74 9	13.8	12.0
Southeast	71 5	255 9	12.3	515.1	15 0	533.9	0.7	10 0
South	9 4	68 4	19 8	132.3	14 1	275 5	15.8	17.5
Paraná	*0*	*23 2*		*57 4*	*19 9*	*87*	*8 7*	
Midwest	0	0		1.7		0.6	-18 8	
Brazil	87 8	326.8	12.7	690.5	16 1	974.5	7.1	12.1

Source· IBGE, figures in 1996 R$, annual geometrical growth rate in %

Table A - 18: Number of Enterprises and GPV in the Timber, Furniture, and Pulp/Paper Industries in Pará, 1970-85

	1970			1975			1980		
	Enter-prises	GPV	GPV/en-terprise	Enter-prises	GPV	GPV/en-terprise	Enter-prises	GPV	GPV/en-terprise
Timber industry	222	61,660	278	462	278,222	602	1,863	685,108	368
Sawmills	202	42,440	210	430	205,183	477	1,577	503,317	319
Veneer mills	1	0	0	1	n.d,	n.d.	11	22,964	2,088
Carpenters	10	n.d.	n.d.	16	4,948	309	109	19,977	183
Plywood mills	0	0	0	2	n.d,	n.d.	3	n.d.	n.d.
Furniture in-dustry	28	5,690	203	31	5,007	162	209	21,620	103
Paper industry	2	n.d.	n.d.	1	n.d.	n.d.	6	315,161	52,527
Pulp	0	n.d.	n.d.	0	n.d.	n.d.	1	n.d.	n.d.
Paper	2	n.d.	n.d.	1	n.d.	n.d.	1	n.d.	n.d.
Paper articles	0	0	0	0	0	0	0	0	0

Source: IBGE, Censo Industrial Pará 1970, 1975, and 1980, data for GPV and GPV/enterprise in 1996 R$ 1000

Table A - 19:   Number of Enterprises and GPV in the Timber, Furniture, and Pulp/Paper Industries in Paraná, 1970-85

	1970			1975			1980		
	Enter-prises	GPV	GPV/en-terprise	Enter-prises	GPV	GPV/en-terprise	Enter-prises	GPV	GPV/en-terprise
Timber industry	1,413	1,001,296	709	1,938	2,329,471	1,202	2,417	2,949,684	1,220
Sawmills	991	502,335	507	1,348	1,171,507	869	1,449	1,094,864	756
Veneer mills	97	n.d.	n.d.	140	n.d.	n.d.	158	301,400	1,908
Carpenters	59	23,899	405	125	115,196	922	209	109,670	525
Plywood mills	56	167,501	2,991	56	370,043	6,608	70	661,369	9,448
Furniture in-dustry	248	139,028	561	394	359,119	911	973	627,702	645
Paper industry	75	259,772	3,464	111	n.d.	n.d.	131	1,320,702	10,082
Pulp	44	14,225	323	57	174,301	3,058	60	222,865	3,714
Paper	19	221,817	11,675	31	474,234	15,298	33	770,787	23,357
Paper articles	0	0	0	10	56,819	5,682	28	3,074,412	109,800

Source: IBGE, Censo Industrial Paraná 1970, 1975, 1980, data for GPV and GPV/enterprise in 1996 R$ 1000

Table A - 20:	Physical Roundwood Production in Brazil, 1973-94							
	Plantations		a	b		Primary forest		
	Char-coal	Fuel-wood	Pulp	Other purposes	a + b	Char-coal	Fuel-wood	Logs
	1000 t	1000 m^3	1000 m^3	1000 m^3	1000 m^3	1000 t	1000 m^3	1000 m^3
1973						1,826	132,581	36,665
1974	716	12,441			17,107	2,086	118,399	30,912
1975	510	29,795			17,937	2,396	122,070	31,528
1976	348	27,866			21,661	2,289	128,425	33,194
1977	354	30,239			27,702	2,191	122,453	32,288
1978	369	34,412			33,311	2,344	120,083	32,289
1979	491	35,972			44,706	2,353	120,598	31,550
1980	670	30,961			41,827	2,520	128,116	36,212
1981	927	30,248			45,576	2,638	123,902	35,595
1982	1,158	28,564	25,032	17,334	42,367	2,500	122,730	36,982
1983			25,481	15,923	41,404	2,624	123,345	38,618
1984			23,775	11,547	35,322	3,354	131,929	39,924
1985						3,515	139,730	42,884
1986	2,011	46,404	28,658	11,146	39,804	3,365	126,136	44,670
1987	5,620	45,908	33,419	14,516	47,936	3,582	120,930	45,744
1988	1,867	23,361	33,327	15,132	48,459	3,727	118,013	52,172
1989	1,891	23,623	32,066	13,792	45,857	3,591	115,252	65,850
1990	1,838	22,739	32,953	14,071	47,024	2,793	108,549	97,514
1991	2,089	24,484	35,844	13,861	49,705	2,489	99,763	46,233
1992	1,920	28,316	38,634	13,585	52,218	2,318	95,611	53,068
1993	2,052	27,030	41,737	15,533	57,269	1,938	94,154	66,709
1994	2,383	28,784	51,391	17,983	69,373	1,887	89,748	62,527
Source:	IBGE, Produção da extração vegetal e da silvicultura Vol. 9, years 1973-94 and Anuários Estatísticos do IBGE 1971-73							

Table A - 21:	Physical Roundwood Production in the North, 1973-94							
	Plantations		a	b		Primary forest		
	Char-coal	Fuel-wood	Pulp	Other purposes	a + b	Char-coal	Fuel-wood	Logs
	1000 t	1000 m^3	1000 m^3	1000 m^3	1000 m^3	1000 t	1000 m^3	1000 m^3
1973						32	1,234	8,945
1974						23	1,495	8,358
1975						25	5,795	4,534,
1976						25	5,852	5,948
1977						28	6,273	6,722
1978						30	6,490	7,716
1979					572	30	6,906	8,401
1980					1,391	31	8,308	11,483
1981					946	34	8,620	13,146
1982			969		969	36	8,865	14,652
1983			1,362		1,362	39	9,658	16,094,
1984			1,043		1,043	41	10,667	17,389
1985						42	19,784	19,793
1986			1,077		1,077	49	10,306	32,008
1987	0.253		1,167		1,167	38	10,224	24,606
1988			966	0.710	966	49	10,305	32,008
1989		23,200	1,448		1,448	81	12,686	47,486
1990			1,104		1,104	76	11,149	80,826
1991			1,269	6	1,275	79	10,505	30,755
1992			1,216		1,216	68	10,797	37,799
1993			2,009	402	2,411	72	11,843	51,021
1994	0.004		2,144	463	2,608	96	11,129	47,159
Source:	IBGE, Produção da extração vegetal e da silvicultura Vol. 9, years 1973-94 and Anuários Estatísticos do IBGE 1971-73							

Table A - 22:		Physical Roundwood Production in Pará, 1973-94						
	Plantations		a	b		Primary forest		
	Char-coal	Fuel-wood	Pulp	Other purposes	a + b	Char-coal	Fuel-wood	Logs
	1000 t	1000 m³	1000 m³	1000 m³	1000 m³	1000 t	1000 m³	1000 m³
1973						24	804	3,051
1974						11	805	2,881
1975						12	1,283	3,942
1976						14	1,454	5,144
1977						17	1,636	5,781
1978						18	1,814	6,733
1979					572	19	1,984	7,170
1980			1,391		1,391	20	3,322	10,284
1981			946		946	24	3,908	11,671
1982			969		969	26	4,092	12,353
1983			1,362		1,362	28	4,422	13,785
1984			1,043		1,043	29	5,021	14,072
1985						25	5,965	16,362
1986			1,077		1,077	32	7,405	18,416
1987			1,034		1,037	34	7,341	21,000
1988			743		743	46	7,503	28,428
1989			1,114		1,114	76	7,738	43,139
1990			1,029		1,029	72	6,926	39,866
1991			980		980	75	6,526	28,370
1992			936		936	64	6,256	31,735
1993			1,720	402	2,122	69	7,442	44,178
1994			1,892	463	2,355	92	7,538	44,539

Source. IBGE, Produção da extração vegetal e da silvicultura Vol. 9, years 1973-94 and Anuários Estatísticos do IBGE 1971-73

Table A - 23:   Physical Roundwood Production in the Northeast, 1973-94

	Plantations		a	b		Primary forest		
	Char-coal	Fuel-wood	Pulp	Other purposes	a + b	Char-coal	Fuel-wood	Logs
	1000 t	1000 m^3	1000 m^3	1000 m^3	1000 m^3	1000 t	1000 m^3	1000 m^3
1973						281	39,593	3,974
1974		0.666			1	272	41,677	4,139
1975	0 066	0.720			46	312	43,643	5,210
1976		6			68	329	45,560	5,537
1977		13			116	389	46,912	5,310
1978		68			89	358	46,086	5,398
1979		34			145	374	46,708	5,576
1980	7	367			251	406	52,057	6,600
1981	11	109			249	411	53,660	6,761
1982	0 724	154		313	313	420	53,822	6,894
1983			72	296	368	461	52,892	7,193
1984				201	201	454	55,109	7,710
1985						437	58,749	8,560
1986	5	21,834	157	706	862	422	58,219	8,637
1987	25	326	324	178	502	493	59,206	8,666
1988	12	328	209	328	537	511	54,170	8,189
1989	92	627	145	174	320	504	53,596	7,827
1990	109	922	122	179	300	445	53,065	7,453
1991	55	534	352	500	852	416	50,694	6,985
1992	66	847	1,610	322	1,932	369	50,707	7,049
1993	85	920	1,913	238	2,150	329	48,100	6,323
1994	65	929	2,187	96	2,282	307	45,399	5,756

Source: IBGE, Produção da extração vegetal e da silvicultura Vol. 9, years 1973-94 and Anuários Estatísticos do IBGE 1971-73

Table A - 24: Physical Roundwood Prodction in the Southeast, 1973-94

	Plantations		a	b		Primary forest		
	Char-coal	Fuel-wood	Pulp	Other purposes	a + b	Charcoal	Fuel-wood	Logs
	1000 t	1000 m^3	1000 m^3	1000 m^3	1000 m^3	1000 t	1000 m^3	1000 m^3
1973						1,476,560	37,811	4,160
1974	709	12,441			13,149	1,764,292	30,417	2,185
1975	505	15,945			12,518	2,017,310	29,482	2,211
1976	343	15,630			14,902	1,896,803	34,143	2,045
1977	350	18,965			19,442	1,764,577	27,586	2,015
1978	364	19,588			21,760	1,867,173	26,015	1,540
1979	486	19,984			25,521	1,825,628	25,520	1,239
1980	649	18,421			27,857	1,903,456	27,800	1,224
1981	899	20,863			26,135	1,980,991	26,290	1,562
1982	1,128	17,981	12,995	10,300	23,295	1,814,442	24,326	1,255
1983			10,849	9,354	20,202	1,818,472	25,020	1,682
1984			11,295	7,334	18,629	2,241,388	28,702	2,246
1985						2,323,193	22,971	1,870
1986	1,929	15,074	13,078	3,721	16,799	2,197,959	18,929	1,607
1987	5,457	35,309	17,251	6,742	23,992	2,061,809	17,354	1,278
1988	1,615	12,886	16,493	7,215	23,708	2,045,411	19,828	1,044
1989	1,481	13,554	13,907	6,769	20,675	1,956,231	17,841	987
1990	1,456	12,300	14,730	7,116	21,846	1,557,605	16,438	575
1991	1,680	16,645	15,572	6,005	21,577	1,454,221	14,338	558
1992	1,450	14,273	16,143	5,591	21,734	1,352,212	12,765	391
1993	1,485	11,972	15,220	5,906	21,127	1,005,345	12,049	375
1994	1,969	11,763	17,104	5,465	22,569	1,024,670	11,662	393

Source· IBGE, Produção da extração vegetal e da silvicultura Vol 9, years 1973-94 and Anuários Estatísticos do IBGE 1971-73

Table A - 25: Physical Roundwood Production in the South, 1973-94

	Plantations		a	b		Primary forest		
	Char-coal	Fuel-wood	Pulp	Other purposes	a + b	Char-coal	Fuel-wood	Logs
	1000 t	1000 m³	1000 m³	1000 m³	1000 m³	1000 t	1000 m³	1000 m³
1973						34	40,889	15,880
1974	7	10,517			3,957	22	33,532	13,148
1975	5	13,845			5,373	33	32,612	16,924
1976	5	12,229			6,691	26	32,274	16,841
1977	5	11,231			8,136	44	31,860	15,294
1978	5	14,730			11,455	62	31,513	14,954
1979	5	15,676			18,462	71	30,733	13,366
1980	15	11,830			12,317	83	28,373	13,743
1981	16	9,250			15,243	78	24,629	10,869
1982	29	10,295	11,069	6,721	17,789	72	24,272	10,906
1983			13,199	6,174	19,373	97	23,555	10,212
1984			11,437	4,007	15,443	124	22,701	9,034
1985						137	22,826	8,910
1986	22	9,104	14,346	6,706	21,052	190	23,015	8,486
1987	31	9,218	14,601	7,341	21,942	228	21,944	7,867
1988	30	9,171	15,414	7,456	22,871	226	21,331	7,257
1989	44	8,035	16,248	6,721	22,968	242	20,503	6,906
1990	53	8,383	16,375	6,593	22,968	172	18,877	5,970
1991	54	10,053	18,161	7,430	25,591	93	16,155	4,416
1992	75	11,166	19,234	7,500	26,734	79	14,359	4,726
1993	89	12,483	22,218	8,879	31,097	105	15,155	5,896
1994	95	14,500	29,608	11,841	41,449	87	14,882	4,779

Source· IBGE, Produção da extração vegetal e da silvicultura Vol 9, years 1973-94 and Anuários Estatísticos do IBGE 1971-73

Table A - 26:	Physical Roundwood Production in Paraná, 1973-94							
	Plantations		a	b		Primary forest		
	Char-coal	Fuel-wood	Pulp	Other purposes	a + b	Char-coal	Fuel-wood	Logs
	1000 t	1000 m³	1000 m³	1000 m³	1000 m³	1000 t	1000 m³	1000 m³
1973						14	15,456	7,619
1974	2	5,040			691	11	11,534	6,656
1975	0.135	1,303			1,948	11	10,782	8,627
1976	0.118	1,308			2,181	7	10,455	8,137
1977	0.099	1,360			3,550	7	10,065	6,976
1978	0 189	1,920			4,501	13	9,451	6,300
1979	0 282	1,721			2,861	16	9,129	5,690
1980	0.519	1,957			4,191	23	8,699	5,586
1981	0.428	1,343			5,203	25	7,701	5,189
1982	2	925	5,124	1,323	6,447	30	7,858	5,692
1983			7,393	1,608	9,001	41	7,749	5,388
1984			8,062	1,981	10,043	38	7,473	4,673
1985						52	7,428	4,396
1986	0.257	1,593	9,028,	1,991	11,019	55	7,807	4,259
1987	7	1,565	9,415	2,160	11,575	43	6,853	3,933
1988	8	1,484	10,062	2,007	12,069	44	6,460	3,552
1989	9	1,554	11,784	2,171	13,955	69	6,050	3,397
1990	8	1,805	12,225	2,341	14,566	70	6,205	3,062
1991	8	1,717	12,447	2,828	15,275	63	5,859	2,849
1992	7	1,705	13,122	2,890	16,012	63	5,729	3,619
1993	9	1,941	14,611	3,270	17,881	72	6,732	3,706
1994	13	2,542	14,902	4,613	19,515	58	6,877	3,173

Source· IBGE, Produção da extração vegetal e da silvicultura Vol 9, years 1973-94 and Anuários Estatísticos do IBGE 1971-73

Table A - 27: Physical Roundwood Production in the Midwest, 1973-94

	Plantations		a	b		Primary forest		
	Char-coal	Fuel-wood	Pulp	Other purposes	a + b	Char-coal	Fuel-wood	Logs
	1000 t	1000 m^3	1000 m^3	1000 m^3	1000 m^3	1000 t	1000 m^3	1000 m^3
1973						2	13,053	3,705
1974						6	11,278	3,082
1975		4				8	10,538	2,648
1976		1			0.1	11	10,595	2,823
1977		30			8	16	9,823	2,946
1978		26			7	27	9,979	2,680
1979		278			6	53	10,730	2,968
1980		342			11	97	11,578	3,161
1981		27			3	133	10,704	3,257
1982		134		0 754	0.754	157	11,445	3,275
1983				100	100	207	12,220	3,437
1984				5	5	494	14,749	3,545
1985						575	15,399	3,752
1986	54	392		13	13	512	15,816	3,701
1987	106	1,055	76,620	256	332	762	12,201	3,333
1988	210	977	245,270	132	377	895	12,378	3,675
1989	275	1,383	318,013	129	447	808	10,625	2,644
1990	220	1,134	346,634	184	531	543	9,020	269
1991	300	1,885	489,706	114	604	447	8,071	3,519
1992	330	2,031	431,450	171	602	450	6,983	3,102
1993	392	1,655	376,322	108	484	426	7,007	3,095
1994	254	1,592	347,533	118	465	372	6,676	4,439

Source· IBGE, Produção da extração vegetal e da silvicultura Vol. 9, years 1973-94 and Anuários Estatísticos do IBGE 1971-73

Table A - 28:	Implicit Prices of Timber Production in Brazil, 1973-94							
	Plantations		a	b		Primary forest		
	Char-coal	Fuel-wood	Pulp	Other purposes	a + b	Char-coal	Fuel-wood	Logs
	R$/t	R$/m³	R$/m³	R$/m³	R$/m³	R$/t	R$/m³	R$/m³
1973						213	8	100
1974						175	9	101
1975						194	10	109
1976						172	9	94
1977						163	8	80
1978						190	8	14
1979						191	9	14
1980	253	13			40	210	8	80
1981	235	12			32	153	7	62
1982	175	11	26	38	31	176	7	57
1983			26	29	27	167	6	50
1984			26	20	24	150	6	44
1985						156	6	58
1986	333	1	28	44	32	300	8	95
1987	194	15	29	170	58	212	7	94
1988	172	13	30	81	46	192	7	69
1989	445	22	88	195	121	626	18	153
1990	185	10	22	39	27	163	5	53
1991	119	9	21	23	22	124	5	42
1992	116	9	20	25	21	124	5	37
1993	160	11	32	27	30	198	7	56
1994	171	10	16	28	19	178	6	68

Source· IBGE, Produção da extração vegetal e da silvicultura Vol 9, years 1973-94 and Anuários Estatísticos do IBGE 1971-73; figures in 1996 R$

Table A - 29: Species from Pará Sold in Domestic and Foreign Markets, 1960-96

Commercial species	Exported species	Exported species	Exported species
1962	1972	1978	1990s
	Abiurana		
Acapu	Acapu		
Achuá	Achuá		
Anani			
	Amapá	Amapá	Amapá
Andiroba	**Andiroba**	Andiroba	**Andiroba**
	Andiroba jareua		
	Angelim		
Angelim-rajado		Angelim pedra	**Angelim pedra**
	Angelim vermelho	Angelim vermelho	**Angelim vermelho**
Araracanga	Araracanga		
Assacu	**Assacu**	Assacu	
	Cauxuarana	Cafearana	
		Cascagrossa	
Cedro	**Cedro**	Cedro	**Cedro**
	Cedromogno	Cedrorana	**Cedrorana**
	Cerejeira		
Copaíba	Copaíba	Copaíba	
Cumaru		Cumaru	Cumaru
Cuiarana			**Curupixá**
Cupiúba	Cupiúba	Cupiúba	Cupiúba
	Faveira		Faveira
Freijó	Freijó	Freijó	Freijó
	Gonçalo Alves		Goiabão
Ipê/Pau d'arco	Ipê	Ipê	**Ipê**
Itaúba			
	Jatobá	Jatobá	**Jatobá**
Jacarandá		Jacarandá do Pará	
Jacareúba		Jacareúba	
Jarana			Jarana
Jutaí-açu	Jutaí		
Limaorana	Louro		Louro faia